Adventure Guide to
Southern California

Don & Marjorie Young

HUNTER
PUBLISHING

HUNTER PUBLISHING, INC.
130 Campus Drive
Edison NJ 08818-7816, USA
Tel (908) 225 1900; Fax (908) 417 1744
E-mail: hunterpub@emi.net
Web site: www.hunterpublishing.com

1220 Nicholson Road
Newmarket, Ontario L3Y 7V1, CANADA
Tel (800) 399 6858; Fax (800) 363 2665

ISBN 1-55650-791-7

© 1997 Hunter Publishing, Inc.

Every effort has been made to ensure that the information in this book is correct, but the publisher and authors do not assume, and hereby disclaim, any liability to any party for any loss or damage caused by errors, omissions, misleading information or any potential problem caused by information in this guide, even if these are a result of negligence, accident or any other cause. All opinions expressed in this book stem from the authors' personal experience only or from those of her contributors; consequently, neither they nor the contributors can be held accountable for a reader's personal experience while traveling.

Cover Photo: Sea Otter
Tom & Pat Leeson Nature Wildlife Photography
Maps by Kim André

3   2   1

About The Authors

Don Young

Don Young has written professionally since he was a teenager. Starting first as a reporter for weekly and daily newspapers, he has worked in both radio and television, edited award-winning magazines both nationally and internationally, and served as a public relations executive for two Fortune 500 companies.

His work has appeared in many of the nation's foremost periodicals, and he has authored a dozen books on topics ranging from business management to the treatment of sleep disorders.

Marjorie Young

Marjorie taught elementary school children how to write for 20 years. She is currently practicing what she preached all of those years.

Marjorie's work has appeared in *New Mexico Magazine, Bed & Breakfast Locator, The Appraisers Standard, Global Golfer,* and a number of other publications throughout the country.

Her next effort, also in collaboration with her husband, is another book for Hunter Publishing: *Adventure Guide to the Pacific Northwest.*

We Love To Get Mail!

Hunter Publishing makes every effort to ensure that its travel guides are the most current sources of information available to travelers. If you have any information that you feel should be included in the next edition of this guide, please write to us at 130 Campus Drive, Edison, NJ 08818. Feel free to include your opinion or experiences of the places you've visited, as well as price updates and suggestions for ways in which we could improve this book for future readers.

Contents

MAPS

California, Here We Come...

... and why not?

Ask almost anybody to name his or her favorite vacation spot and, chances are, the answer will be either California or Florida.

There are a number of excellent reasons for that. Year-round good weather, an ample supply of outstanding accommodations and excellent restaurants, and countless attractions entice and entrance visitors of all ages. California has some marvelous beaches, offering swimming, surfing, waterskiing, boating, hiking, biking, camping and horseback riding. It has outstanding saltwater and freshwater fishing. History buffs are also drawn by interesting Indian villages to explore, plus 21 historic Spanish missions that were built while our Colonial forefathers were still battling for their independence from the British crown.

Planet earth supports eight major "ecological communities" or biomes, scientists tell us. Five of them can be found in California.

The North American continent has four separate desert regions. Three – the Sonoran Desert, the Mojave Desert and a small piece of the Great Basin Desert – are in California.

And California encompasses no fewer than eight magnificent national parks: the Channel Islands, Death Valley, Joshua Tree, Kings Canyon, Lassen Volcanic, Redwood, Sequoia and Yosemite.

When you travel to southern California, you can take a daytrip to an exotic foreign country – Mexico.

If you are here in the summer and the heat becomes too oppressive, you can retreat to the cool comfort of the mountains.

In the winter, you can ski those same mountains, go ice skating or snowboarding, or you can stay at the lower elevations where it's warm and explore the California deserts. You can easily do both on the same day!

We *love* southern California. It has an appeal distinctly its own.

Let us show you what we mean...

History

For centuries, the residents of America's West Coast were effectively screened from their Eastern neighbors by the majestic, but almost insurmountable Rocky Mountains. Unique Native American cultures evolved, influenced more by migrating tribes from Alaska and Canada to the north than by the Iroquois, Chippewa, Apache, Comanche and other Indian cultures that flourished along America's East Coast and throughout the vast central plains.

Gabrielino Indians inhabited most of the region which is present-day Los Angeles. The Chumash were found along the Pacific coast between Los Angeles and San Simeon to the north. The Yokuts, Tubaculabah, Kawaisu, Kitanemuk, Tatviam and Serrano occupied California's fertile Central Valley.

Southward from Los Angeles to San Diego, along the Pacific Ocean, could be found the Juaneño and the Luiseño. Around San Diego Bay lived the Ipai and the Tipai. Between San Diego and the Colorado River there were bands of Cahulla, Cupeño and Tipai. Along with the Yuma, the Tipai also inhabited the rich Imperial Valley and the region that parallels what we now recognize as the Mexican border. The Mojave, the Halchidhoma and the Yuma once lived where the Colorado River separates California from its neighboring state of Arizona, while in the pitiless desert to the north and west were the Chemehuevi, the Mojave and the Halchidhoma.

Throughout California, nearly 100 Native American languages once were spoken. Over half of them are now extinct. Only about 30 continue to be spoken as the world approaches the 21st century – and they are spoken almost exclusively by a few of the tribal elders. It is estimated that only two people are still able to speak the Serrano language, for example, and only three Chemehuevis, six Yukis and nine Wintuns can talk in their native tongue.

California's Native Americans lived relatively undisturbed throughout most of the 18th century.

Juan Cabrillo, a Portuguese navigator, became the first European to discover California in 1542. Sir Francis Drake put in for repairs near Point Reyes in 1579. But no effort was made to colonize the area for the next two centuries.

In 1768, aware of its interest in Alaska and alarmed by the possibility that Russia might advance southward into California, King Charles of Spain directed that the region be colonized and that its inhabitants be converted to Christianity.

King Charles' fears were well founded, for the Russians established a fort on the north-central coast of California some 75 miles south of present-day Mendocino. Fort Ross State Park is a popular tourist attraction today.

As a result of King Charles' directive, Father Junipero Serra moved into Alta California (Upper California, as opposed to Baja or Lower California) to establish the first Spanish mission in 1769.

Starting with that mission (San Diego de Alcala), the plan was to build a string of missions and *presidios* (fortresses) northward throughout the state. Each settlement was to be approximately 30 miles from the next – a day's march in the event military reinforcements were required.

Over the next 50 years, 21 such missions were constructed and thousands of Indians were converted to Catholicism. The route leading from mission to mission was known as *El Camino Real* (The Royal Road), and today US Highway 101 closely parallels that historic old byway.

Unfortunately, the Spaniards often used their Indian converts as slave labor. In addition, the Indians were quick to contract diseases brought over with the Europeans – influenza, measles, smallpox, tuberculosis and syphilis.

Whenever conditions became intolerable, the Indians would revolt, sometimes burning down the Spaniards' villages. In self defense, the Spaniards began to protect their buildings under fireproof red tile roofs – a prominent feature in California architecture to this day.

Indian rebellions were not the Spaniards' greatest worry, however. By 1822, Mexico also had grown weary of the Spaniards' oppression. When Mexico proclaimed its independence, it cast out not only the Spanish crown but also the Catholic Church, which was blamed for much of the abuse that had been heaped upon the Mexican people.

California swore allegiance to Mexico, and the church's vast land and cattle holdings were distributed among a number of California's most prominent Mexican settlers in the form of huge land grants.

But Mexico's control over California would continue for less than a quarter of a century. The United States already had announced that it felt its "manifest destiny" was to expand as far west as the Pacific Ocean, and after a short but uneventful war, Mexico was compelled to release California to its northern neighbor on February 2, 1848. That same year, gold was discovered at Sutter's Mill. The California Gold Rush was on.

Two years later, the 31st star on the American flag was assigned to California.

Geography

Since 1962, California has been America's most populous state. More than 32 million people live here today.

Los Angeles is the commercial/industrial hub of the state as well as the state's largest city. San Diego, its near-neighbor to the south, ranks number three.

With an area of 163,707 square miles, California is the nation's third largest state.

The rugged shoreline of the enchantingly beautiful, yet wild and treacherous Pacific Ocean extends 1,264 miles along the state's entire western flank.

Along the eastern border can be found fabulous national forests and parks – Modoc, Lassen, Plumas, Eldorado, Tahoe, Stanislaus, Yosemite, Inyo, Sierra, Kings Canyon, Sequoia, Death Valley, Mojave.

Forests blanket more than 37 million acres of California. Within those forests are the world's largest and oldest living things. The huge California redwood (*Sequoia gigantea*) can be found in the Sierra Nevada, while the bristlecone pine tree, which has been on earth for nearly 5,000 years, can be found in California only at an elevation of 11,000 feet.

The state's thinly populated northern counties shelter vast forests, clear lakes, fast-flowing rivers and high mountain peaks, including three active volcanoes – Mt. Lassen and Mt. Shasta in the Cascade Mountains and Mt. Mammoth in the Sierra Nevada.

California's southern counties are famous throughout the world for their sun-drenched deserts and year-around recreational appeal.

Some 25 million acres of California have been set aside for public use. Over four million acres are within the national parks. State parks account for another 1.3 million acres.

Mt. Whitney, the state's highest point, rises 14,494 feet above sea level. Mt. Whitney is in Sequoia National Park.

Bad Water, the lowest point in the state, sits 282 feet below sea level. Bad Water is located in Death Valley.

How To Use This Book

North of San Simeon, you begin to feel that you've driven out of the Los Angeles/southern California sphere of influence and are heading into the San Francisco Bay/northern California part of the state.

As a result, we opted to trace a line across the state from San Simeon on the west coast to Death Valley Junction on the east and use that as our demarcation point between northern and southern California. All of the territory situated south of the line and north of the Mexican border is covered in this book. (For good measure, we even included a few places south of the Mexican border. It would be a shame to miss them as long as you're in the area.)

Our next step was to "subdivide" southern California into 10 regions, each one unique. Depending on the region, that distinction might have been geographic in nature (coastal cities), ethnic (the Mexican border), cultural (movieland) or climatic (the desert). Perhaps nowhere in America do these things change as dramatically – or as often – as they do throughout southern California. That is one of the area's most endearing charms.

As you begin to read each section, you will find a brief introduction to the area, including some of the local color and some tips on how to get around most efficiently. Following that, we have highlighted specific opportunities for adventure within that region.

We have attempted to be as thorough as our limits allow, but the recommendations we have made in this book are subjective at best. Your experiences may not be the same as ours and your tastes may be different.

We encourage you to keep in mind that nothing remains constant: telephone numbers change, personnel come and go, area and zip codes change, businesses relocate. It is a good idea to call ahead and check that the information we have given here is still correct.

The Nature Of Adventure

Adventure is a difficult thing to define. To most of us, a day of salmon fishing in an isolated mountain stream would be an adventure. To a commercial fisherman, who spends almost every day of his life on the water, it would be a "busman's holiday."

Biting into a hot jalapeño pepper for the first time is an adventure to most of us. To a Mexican, it's just another meal.

Soaring through the sky in a glider, high above the earth, would be considered extremely adventuresome by most people. But to a commercial airline pilot... you get the point.

Often, doing something that you've done a dozen times before, but doing it in a different place, at a different time, or with a different person can make all the difference. Under the right circumstances, even the routine can become an adventure.

Everything in life is an adventure. At least, it is the first time you experience it. Every sight, every sound, every scent, every taste, every sensation is an adventure that once. Why? Because it is a *discovery*. And every new discovery is an *adventure*.

So, we dedicate this book to discovery: to experiencing new places, new people, new activities, new sensations, but above all, to discovering a bunch of new dimensions within ourselves.

The challenge is to try things you've never tried before, to see things from a different perspective, to become more knowledgeable and more understanding than ever before, and to be able to share your adventures with other people.

Greater Los Angeles

On September 4, 1781, 11 families – 44 people, including 26 blacks – walked out of Mission San Gabriel Arcangel to establish a community closer to the harbor. That village, El Pueblo de Nuestra Señora la Reina de los Angeles (*The Town of Our Lady, the Queen of the Angels*), was to become the City of Los Angeles.

Traces of the past still remain here. **Mission San Gabriel Arcangel,** Mission and Junipero Serra Drs., San Gabriel, ☎ 818/457-3035. Founded in 1771, this was the fourth mission along the Spaniards' historic El Camino Real. The lovely old mission, called "The Pride of the California Missions," still hosts an anniversary celebration every September.

Mission San Fernando Rey De España, 15151 San Fernando Mission Blvd., Mission Hills, ☎ 818/361-0186. Founded 26 years after Mission San Gabriel Arcangel and 16 years after the village that would become Los Angeles, San Fernando sits midway between I-5 and I-405. Its restored structures include a church, monastery, the major domo's house, workrooms and living quarters around a quadrangle. The old gardens, now known as **Brand Park**, contain flowers and shrubs brought in from each of the other 20 California missions, and the 35-bell carillon still rings every hour between 9 am and 5 pm. An **Archival Center** preserves and interprets the historic records of the state's Catholic heritage, and the **Museum Theater** regularly presents films depicting the history of the mission, the Archdiocese of Los Angeles, and the life of Father Junipero Serra.

While these and a variety of other attractions reflect the glorious past of this region, others remind us of the state's role in the modern era.

The **Reagan Presidential Library & Museum,** 40 Presidential Dr., Simi Valley, ☎ 805/522-8444. Here, visitors can see a recreation of the President's Oval Office and the Cabinet Room, a 60 x 20-foot scale model of the White House, a piece of the Berlin Wall, and many of the 75,000 gifts received by President Ronald Reagan and his wife.

Richard Nixon Library & Birthplace, 18001 Yorba Linda Blvd., ☎ 714/993-3393 or 993-5075, fax 714/528-0544. This is not far away, in suburban Yorba Linda. It was built and is operated entirely without federal funds. The facility includes 22 galleries, theaters, gardens, a museum, and the small house in which President Nixon was born. President and Mrs. Nixon are both buried on the grounds.

The old and the new blend well in Los Angeles. It is the largest city in the state and the second largest in the nation, and it is California's business and commercial center as well. But overall, the region is most famous perhaps for being the "heartland" of the nation's entertainment industry, a place where fact and fancy blend into one... and every reel has a happy ending.

Getting Around

Los Angeles International Airport (LAX) is the third busiest in the world. Of growing importance is the **Burbank, Glendale, Pasadena Airport**, 2627 N. Hollywood Way, Burbank, ☎ 818/840-8840, which carries an ever-increasing amount of air traffic into and away from the Los Angeles metropolitan area.

Union Station was built in 1939 and is the last grand railroad station in the country. It was designed in a Spanish mission/art deco style and was the background for many old movies, including *Union Station*, starring William Holden, and *The Way We Were*.

Rail travel remains alive and well in California. **Coast Starlight Train**, ☎ 800/USA-RAIL, runs from Los Angeles to Seattle with stops in Santa Barbara, San Luis Obispo, San Francisco/Oakland, Sacramento, Klamath Falls, Eugene and Portland. It is an excellent train, staffed with master chefs and offering an outstanding wine list.

But of course, the mainstay of Los Angeles' transportation system is its freeway infrastructure. Cursed by many and praised by few, it still manages to get hundreds of thousands of people from one place to another, more or less on time, every day of the year.

The East Los Angeles Interchange, where I-5 merges with I-10, State Route 60 and State Route 101, has earned the dubious honor of being labeled one of the nation's 10 worst traffic bottlenecks. Understandably so, since no fewer than 566,000 vehicles a day pass this point.

Wending your way through a concrete cobweb can be confusing, and adding to that confusion is the fact that local residents are never content to bestow a single name on their freeways. If the traffic from downtown Los Angeles is headed northwest, for example, US 101 is called the Hollywood Freeway. If it is headed in the opposite direction, US 101 is called the Santa Ana Freeway. It all depends on where you're going.

For the most part, we have tried to stay with one name (usually the route number) in this book. If you become confused at some point, blame Los Angeles, not us.

Get a good map and refer to it *before* you get in the car to go someplace. It is all but impossible to read a map while driving on the L.A. freeways, and a wrong turn at the wrong time can result in utter disaster.

The freeways are helpful when you have a long way to go. Otherwise, your best bet is to avoid them whenever you can, especially during rush hours. Turn on the radio and listen to the traffic reports; they are an excellent means of learning which streets should be avoided.

By avoiding the freeways, you'll also see and enjoy more of the area you're driving through. Just be sure you know what kind of neighborhood you're in, especially after dark.

Greater Los Angeles

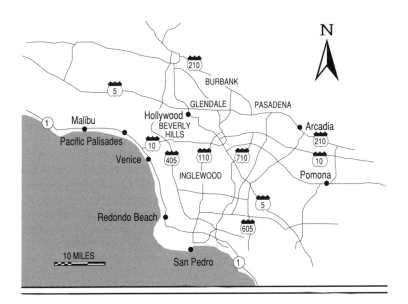

Touring

Los Angeles

Covering 460 square miles, Los Angeles is more a confederation of communities than a single metropolis. Many of the communities that appear to be independent (Hollywood, for example) actually are incorporated into the Los Angeles metropolitan complex.

From a population of just 100,000 at the turn of the century, Los Angeles has grown to more than 3.5 million people – an extremely diverse body of people.

CULTURAL ATTRACTIONS

Mexican

Well represented, of course, are the Mexicans, who were among the earliest inhabitants of the area. This heritage is clearly evident at **El Puebla**

de los Angeles, ☎ 213/628-1274, a group of 27 buildings in "old L.A." Here is the **Avila Adobe,** the city's oldest house, built in 1818, and now a free museum furnished as it was during the Mexican era. Here too is **Old Plaza Catholic Church,** completed in 1822 and still in use, and **Sepulveda House,** a partially restored 1887 boarding house that now serves as a visitor center, with free maps, trail guides and brochures.

Olivera St., ☎ 213/628-4349 or 628-1274, bounded by Main and Los Angeles Sts., is a colorful block-long Mexican marketplace full of quaint shops and restaurants.

Pio Pico State Historic Park, ☎ 310/695-1217, centers around the home of the last governor of Mexican California. Built in 1870, the three-story building once served as the region's finest hotel.

Heritage Square Museum, 3800 Homer St., is in the Highland Park area of Los Angeles on the bank of the Arroyo Seco (dry gully). The museum is located within the four square leagues that constituted the city's original 1781 Spanish land grant. For additional information, contact the museum's business office, 225 S. Lake Ave., Ste. 1125, Pasadena 91101, ☎ 818/796-2898 or 449-0193, fax 818/304-9652.

New to the Los Angeles area is a **Latin American Art Museum,** 621 Alamitos Ave., housed in the historic art deco Hippodrome Skating Rink. The museum is home to the Robert Gumbiner Foundation art collection, and Diego Rivera's nephew, Mexican artist Juan Coronel Rivera, is installing a *Dia de los Muertos* (Day of the Dead) altar in his uncle's honor.

In late April, the **Hispanic Los Angeles Fiesta** is held in the Broadway shopping district, attracting 500,000 participants.

Chinese

Chinatown, ☎ 213/938-7197 or 617-0396, is bordered by Cesar Chavez, Spring, Yale and Bernard Streets. Opened in 1938, this was America's first planned Chinatown. The **Central Plaza** on Gin Lin Way, (Street of the Golden Palace) has a statue of Sun Yat Sen, the "George Washington of China," who led the overthrow of the Chinese Manchu Dynasty in 1911. Notice the lucky animal and fish figures along the rooflines as you move along Gin Lin Way.

In February, Chinatown hosts the annual **Chinese New Year's Parade,** complete with the traditional 100-foot dragons. In July, the **Lotus Festival** is held in Echo Park, ☎ 213/485-1310, which has the largest lotus bed in the United States. During the festival, the shore of the lake is lined with Asian food and crafts booths and there are many forms of entertainment.

Phillipe Restaurant in Chinatown invented the French dip in 1918.

For further information, contact the **Chinese Chamber of Commerce,** 977 N. Broadway, Ste. E, Los Angeles 90012, ☎ 213/617-0396 or 617-2128.

The **Arcadia Chinese School,** 817 First Ave., in nearby Arcadia, ☎ 818/821-0848 or 355-5031, offers classes in Chinese knotting, calligraphy, paper cutting, martial arts, mental arithmetic, folk dance, Chinese painting, flower arranging and Chinese conversation.

Pacific Asia Museum, 46 N. Los Robles Ave., Pasadena 91101, ☎ 818/449-2742, is designed like a Chinese treasure house surrounding a courtyard garden. Founded in 1971, the museum has a 5,000-volume research library and offers exhibits from the Far East and the Pacific. Admission is free on the third Saturday of each month.

Japanese

Little Tokyo, ☎ 213/628-2725 or 689-8822, is bounded by Los Angeles, Temple, 3rd and Alameda Sts. and is one of the largest Japanese communities outside Japan. The community is just southeast of downtown Los Angeles.

Japanese Village Plaza, 327 E. 2nd St., ☎ 213/620-8861, looks like a native Japanese village. Be sure to visit the confectionary shop, which sells rice-paste candy.

Noguchi Plaza, off 2nd St., south of the Village Plaza, has a fan-shaped Japan-America theater that presents live performances. It also has a traditional Japanese garden.

Japanese-American National Museum, 369 E. First St., Los Angeles 90012, ☎ 213/625-0414 or 687-7193, is housed in a restored Buddhist temple. The temple was abandoned in 1969, but has recently undergone a $6 million refurbishment, tripling its original size. On the third Thursday of every month, admission is free.

In early January, **Oshogatsui**, the Japanese New Year, is celebrated.

In early to mid-August, Little Tokyo hosts the annual **Nisei Week**, ☎ 213/734-1164. First organized in 1934, the event includes a parade, dances, rides and craft booths.

The Los Angeles County Museum of Art features a **Pavilion of Japanese Art**.

In Van Nuys, the **Japanese Garden**, 6100 Woodley Ave., ☎ 818/756-8166, fax 818/756-7648, occupies 6½ acres and has paths that wind among small lakes, lawns, bonsai trees, a teahouse, a zigzag bridge and decorative stone lanterns. Self-guided tours may be taken between noon and 4, Monday through Friday, and guided tours are given on the half-hour, 9:30 to 11:30, Monday through Thursday, and 9:30 to 10:30 on Saturdays. Evening tours are offered during the summer.

Vietnamese

"Little Saigon" is in suburban Westminster between Bolsa Ave. and Bishop Pl., with Brookhurst St. on the east and Magnolia St. on the west.

Located southeast of downtown near the city of Anaheim, Westminster is particularly busy on the weekends when the residents of Little Saigon set out to buy traditional "cures," such as ground antler or dried lizard from their Vietnamese vendors.

Many street signs in this area are printed in Vietnamese, and traditional **Tea Festivals** are held during the first weekend in February.

African-American

The **California Afro-American Museum** is in Exposition Park, 600 State Dr., Los Angeles, ☎ 213/744-7432.
Museum of African-American Art, 4005 Crenshaw Blvd., 3rd Floor, ☎ 213/294-7071, presents the work of numerous black artists.

Jewish

The newest Jewish museum in Los Angeles is **Skirball Cultural Center & Museum**, 2701 N. Sepulveda Blvd., ☎ 310/440-4500 or 440-4578, fax 310/440-4500 or 440-4595. It is a 125,000-square-foot, two-story complex on a 15-acre site. The center celebrates the Jewish experience in America.

In the adjacent **Outdoor Archaeology Classroom**, there is a mock-up of an archaeological dig, and docents guide school children through the steps in excavating an ancient site. The students can uncover the simulated remains of an ancient Israeli settlement, including roads, fortification walls, domestic walls, a ritual altar, a wine press and a corral.

An interactive computer game called *Dig It!* lets teams of players, guided by an animated cartoon character, go through the process of choosing a site, excavating it and analyzing the findings.

What Survives Over Time explores how materials decompose over time and the means by which objects can be dated. Aided by computer, visitors can see how an object might have looked thousands of years ago and compare it with the way the object looks today.

History of Writing includes Egyptian hieroglyphics, Mesopotamian cuneiform, and various forms of ancient alphabetic writing. At a rubbings table, visitors can create messages in three different alphabets.

In the **Discovery Center**, there are topographic maps of Israel and the Near East, as well as large color photos of archaeological sites. By moving magnetized icons over the maps, visitors can trace the movement of peoples and natural resources throughout the region. A short program on laser disc explores the different reasons people have been interested in ancient Israel over the centuries.

An affiliate of Hebrew Union College, the facility includes a 350-seat auditorium and a restaurant, Zeidler's.

Museum of Tolerance, 9786 W. Pico Blvd., ☎ 310/553-8403, 553-9036 or 800/900-9036, Web site www.wiesenthal.com, includes the **Simon Wiesenthal Center** and the **Toleran Center**, which features 35 hands-on exhibits and offers continuous tours. The museum has a special section on the Holocaust, some original letters of Anne Frank, artifacts from Auschwitz, artwork from Theresienstadt and bunk beds from the Majdanek death camp.

Martyrs Memorial & Museum of the Holocaust, 6505 Wilshire Blvd., ☎ 213/852-3242, also is dedicated to the Jewish experience during World War II.

Finnish

Finnish? Believe it or not.

The **Finnish Folk Museum**, one of the Pasadena Historical Society Museums, 470 W. Walnut St., Pasadena 91103-3594, ☎ 818/577-1660, is the only one of its kind outside of Finland. Housed in the 18-room 1905 Fenyes Mansion, the museum conducts regular tours.

But Los Angeles has more to celebrate than its ethnic diversity.

OTHER ATTRACTIONS

The 144-acre **Exposition Park**, ☎ 213/744-7400 or 747-7111, includes the **California Museum of Science & Industry**, 700 State Dr., ☎ 213/744-7400 or 744-2014, which has an IMAX Theater, ☎ 213/744-2015. It also includes the **Natural History Museum of Los Angeles County**, 900 Exposition Blvd., ☎ 213/744-3466, which has more than 30 halls and galleries to examine, and the **Ralph M. Parsons Discovery Center** for children. Exposition Park contains a 16,000-seat **sports arena**, the **Los Angeles Swimming Stadium** and the 92,000-seat **Los Angeles Coliseum**, which hosted the 1932 and 1984 Olympics and is the USC football team's home field.

Recently reopened is the **Angels Flight** funicular, 351 S. Hill St., ☎ 213/617-1736 or 935-1914, fax 213/939-7832, which runs for 315 ft. up Bunker Hill, linking the 4th-and-Hill Red Line station to California Plaza. Originally built in 1901, the funicular was closed in May 1969, but reopened in 1996 after 27 years and a $4 million renovation. A one-way ride costs 25¢.

Nearby, see the **Bunker Hill Spanish Steps**, which surround the 73-story First Interstate World Center. Running from Fifth St. to Hope St., the steps connect the downtown hotel district with the Museum of Contemporary Art.

Griffith Park, 4730 Crystal Springs Dr., ☎ 213/665-5188, is one of America's largest city parks. Encompassing 4,107 acres, it is the largest park in America surrounded on all sides by a city. Visitors encounter strolling mariachis, horseback riders, pony riders, golfers and tennis players (there are courts off Riverside Dr. near the merry-go-round). There are four golf courses, an Olympic-size swimming pool, two museums, a zoo, a fern dell and a bird sanctuary with a stream and ponds in a picturesque little canyon. At sunrise and sunset, you can see deer in the canyons. Scenes for such movies as *Jurassic Park, Short Cuts, Rebel Without a Cause, Terminator*, and *Devil in a Blue Dress* were shot there. The caves seen in *Invasion of the Body Snatchers* were the caves in Bronson Canyon. **Travel Town** in Griffith Park has a Victorian railroad station, a free transportation museum and a tiny train with a miniature steam locomotive. It is open from 10 to 5 daily (until 6 on weekends and holidays). ☎ 213/662-5874. The **Greek Theatre**, 2700 N. Vermont Ave., ☎ 213/665-1927, is a natural amphitheater in which musical programs are held from

June through October. **Gene Autry Museum of Western Heritage**, 4700 Western Heritage Way, ☎ 213/667-2000, fax 213/660-5721, e-mail autry@autry-museum.org, has nine galleries, including a Children's Discovery Gallery.

Griffith Park Observatory, 2800 E. Observatory Ave., ☎ 213/664-1191, was prominently featured in James Dean's classic *Rebel Without a Cause*. It has a Hall of Science and a 600-seat planetarium theater. There are daily shows in the planetarium and laserium.

The University of Southern California (USC) at Exposition Blvd. and Figueroa St., ☎ 213/740-2311, is the world's largest independent university.

The University of California, Los Angeles (UCLA), 405 Hilgard Ave., Westwood, opened in 1929 and is the home of Pauley Pavilion, which seats 13,000 fans for basketball games and other events.

The George C. Page La Brea Discoveries Museum at **La Brea Tar Pits**, 5801 Wilshire Blvd., ☎ 213/936-2230, has holograms that give flesh to the bones of a woman and a tiger found there years ago.

INFORMATION SOURCES

Los Angeles Convention & Visitors Bureau, 685 S. Figueroa St., Los Angeles 90017, ☎ 213/689-8822.

Los Angeles Chamber of Commerce, 350 S. Bixel St., Los Angeles 90017, ☎ 213/580-7500 or 580-7511.

Greater Los Angeles Visitors & Convention Bureau, 515 Figueroa St., Los Angeles 90017, ☎ 213/624-7300.

Los Angeles Recreation & Parks Department, City Hall East, 200 N. Main St., Los Angeles 90012, ☎ 213/485-5555.

Pacific Palisades

Excluding the views from the hills to the beaches below, the best sights in this community are **Rustic Canyon Park**, ☎ 310/454-5734, and **Self-Realization Fellowship Lake Shrine**, 17190 Sunset Blvd., ☎ 310/454-4114, a "wall-less temple" housing the Gandhi World Peace Memorial. A pathway around the 10-acre lake affords views of a bird refuge, a sunken garden and various structures representing the five major religions of the world.

For more information, contact the **Pacific Palisades Chamber of Commerce**, 15330 Antioch St., Pacific Palisades 90272, ☎ 310/459-7963.

Redondo Beach

Redondo (round) Beach boasts of an unusual "glass church" designed in 1946 by Lloyd Wright, the son of Frank Lloyd Wright.

Constructed of redwood, glass and local stone, **Wayfarer's Chapel**, 5755 Palos Verdes Dr. South, ☎ 310/377-1650, sits on a knoll overlooking the ocean at Portuguese Bend. The church was built as a memorial to the 18th-century scientist, philosopher and religious reformer Emanual Swedenborg. With the chapel are a visitor center, a library and some beautiful gardens.

For additional information, contact **Redondo Beach Visitors Bureau**, 200 N. Pacific Coast Hwy., PO Box 632, Redondo Beach 90277, ☎ 310/374-2171, 376-6911, 700/CA-BEACH or 800/282-0333.

A self-guiding walking tour brochure is available.

San Pedro

This is the actual Port of Los Angeles, one of the nation's largest deep-water ports.

Fort MacArthur, now inactive, overlooks the harbor. It houses an interesting museum at 3601 S. Gaffey St., ☎ 310/548-7705 or 548-2631. The walls of the old fort measure 16 to 30 feet thick, and there are four batteries, each with a 14-inch seacoast gun capable of firing up to 14 miles.

Point Vicente Lighthouse, 31501 Palos Verdes Dr. West, ☎ 310/541-0334, was erected in 1926 atop a 130-foot high bluff. It is said that the ghost of a woman who hurled herself into the sea after it claimed the life of her sailor sweetheart walks the lighthouse tower each night. The lighthouse is open daily 10 to 5, with extended hours in the summer, and there is an Interpretive Center, ☎ 310/377-5370.

Point Fermin Lighthouse in Point Fermin Park, Gaffey St. and Paseo Del Mar, was built in 1874 of lumber and bricks transported around Cape Horn on a sailing ship. The lighthouse is not open to the public.

The **Los Angeles Maritime Museum**, Berth 84 at the foot of 6th St., ☎ 310/548-7618, occupies the former Municipal Ferry Building. It contains some 300 ship models, including a 21-foot scale model of the *Queen Mary* and an 18-foot scale model of the *Titanic*.

Cabrillo Marine Aquarium, 3720 Stephen White Dr., ☎ 310/548-7562, features 38 seawater aquariums full of southern California marine life. Multimedia shows, seasonal special events, grunion programs and whale-watching tours are offered.

There is a **Marine Mammal Care Center** at 3601 S. Gaffey St., ☎ 310/548-5677.

For further information, contact **San Pedro Peninsula Chamber of Commerce**, 390 W. Seventh St., San Pedro 90731, ☎ 310/832-7272, fax 310/832-0685.

Universal City

Universal Studio on Universal Plaza, ☎ 818/508-9600, is the world's largest movie/TV studio. The entire complex occupies 420 acres. The six-hour extravaganza has been called the Disneyland of movie studio tours. On a narrated tram ride, you see where and how movies are made, visiting sound stages, sets and prop rooms. You will experience special effects, such as an earthquake, a King Kong attack, a bicycle ride with E.T., and becoming trapped in a fiery inferno. Pricey at $33 per person, the studio offers discounts to seniors (over 59), children (3-11) and members of AAA. Open daily at 8 in the morning between Memorial Day and Labor Day, and at 9 the rest of the year. Closed on Thanksgiving and Christmas.

Venice

Once a nude beach (outlawed in the 1970s), this three-mile stretch of coastline is a favorite for swimming and surfing. It was America's original "Muscle Beach."

Actually patterned after the Italian city of Venice, the town was laid out with a one-mile Grand Canal and five quarter-mile side canals. The canals were closed for lack of care in 1942, but reopened in 1993 after a $6 million cleanup.

Wilmington

Drum Barracks Civil War Museum, 1052 Banning Blvd., ☎ 310/548-7509, is the only Civil War-era Army building still standing in southern California. The 16-room structure once stood on 60 acres among 19 similar buildings. Today's museum was the junior officers' quarters.

Greater Hollywood

Stardust and moonbeams! The place where dreams are created! Do you remember *Leave It to Beaver* on TV? You can drive by the Cleavers' home on Buckingham Rd. near Culver City. Were you a fan of *Down and Out in Beverly Hills*? The house occupied by Nick Nolte and Bette Midler is on N. Bedford Dr. in L.A. Other once-famous addresses in Hollywood include:

- ★ Richard Barthelmess, 501 Sunset Blvd.
- ★ Groucho Marx, 710 N. Hillcrest
- ★ Joan Blondell and Dick Powell, 711 N. Maple St.
- ★ George Burns and Gracie Allen, 720 N. Maple St.

★ Wallace Beery, 816 N. Alpine Dr.
★ Edward G. Robinson, 910 N. Rexford Dr.
★ Joe E. Brown, 707 N. Walden Dr.
★ Lionel Barrymore, 802 N. Roxbury Dr.
★ Marion Davies, 1700 Lexington Rd.
★ Charlie Chaplin, 1085 Summit Dr.
★ Harold Lloyd, 1225 Benedict Canyon
★ Robert Montgomery, 144 Monovale Dr.
★ Frederic March & Florence Eldridge, 1026 Ridgdale Dr.
★ Constance Bennett, 280 Carolwood Dr.
★ Ginger Rogers, 1605 Gilcrest Dr.

Some who lived in nearby Brentwood Heights were:

★ Greta Garbo, 350 N. Cliffwood Ave.
★ Joan Crawford, 426 N. Bristol
★ Zasu Pitts, 241 N. Rockingham Ave.
★ Shirley Temple, 227 Rockingham Rd.

... and in Bel Air & Westwood:

★ Claudette Colbert, 615 N. Faring Rd.
★ Joan Bennett, 515 S. Mapleton Dr.
★ Carole Lombard, 609 St. Cloud Rd.
★ Jeanette MacDonald & Gene Raymond, 783 Bel Air Rd.
★ Loretta Young, 10539 Sunset Blvd.
★ W. C. Fields, 655 Funchall Rd.
★ Jane Withers, 10731 Sunset Blvd.
★ Freddie Bartholomew, 226 Tilden Ave.

This is a chance to live your life-long fantasies. This is Hollywood!

Hollywood

Started in 1903 as a religiously-oriented agricultural community, Hollywood is no longer what it once was, the "Tinseltown" of yore. Garden of Allah Hotel, Hollywood and Vine, is now a pair of mini-malls. Hollywood Athletic Club, once the haunt of Chaplin, Valentino and Crabbe, is now an office building, restaurant and billiard parlor.

Safe enough during the day, today's Hollywood is no place to wander about after dark.

Still, this is *Hollywood*, and it's a place everyone who likes the movies should try to visit.

The ever-popular **Walk of Fame**, dotted with bronze stars in recognition of Hollywood's most famous personalities, extends one mile along Hollywood Blvd., between Gower St. and La Brea Ave., including a small portion of Vine St. south of Hollywood Blvd. Here's a list of some of the more popular stars:

★ James Dean's star is at 1717 Vine St.
★ John Lennon's star is in front of 1750 Vine St.
★ Marilyn Monroe's star is at 6774 Hollywood Blvd.
★ Elvis Presley's star is at 6777 Hollywood Blvd., near Marilyn's.

Hollywood Studio Museum, 2100 N. Highland Ave., ☎ 213/874-2276, occupies Hollywood's first movie studio and is the only film history museum devoted to the movies' silent era. It is located on the east side of Highland Ave. at the edge of the Hollywood Bowl parking area, where Cecil B. DeMille made Hollywood's first Western, *The Squaw Man*, in 1913.

New is the **Hollywood Entertainment Museum**, 7021 Hollywood Blvd., ☎ 213/469-9151, fax 213/469-9576, a $5.5 million, 33,000-square-foot exhibition center covered by a giant atrium. It has three sections – a rotunda, an east wing and a west wing – plus underground parking for 1,000 cars. On display are the bar from *Cheers* and a set from the movie *Star Trek*. The Foley Room contains the tools used to create sound effects and permits visitors to watch film on a screen, produce sounds to accompany the film, mix their sounds with the film, and discuss the results with an instructor. Three studios are devoted to the post-production arts of animation, film editing, and sound recording and mixing, while the electronic library contains print archives, pre-recorded historical material, and an electronic job bank.

The **Max Factor Museum** is at 1666 N. Highland Ave., ☎ 213/463-6668, and there is a **Frederick's of Hollywood Lingerie Museum**, 6608 Hollywood Blvd., ☎ 213/466-8506, where the idly curious can see lingerie and bras once worn by such sex symbols as Madonna, Cher, Lana Turner, Elizabeth Taylor, Ava Gardner, Cyd Charisse, Ethel Merman, Shirley MacLaine, Mae West, Bette Davis, Loretta Young, Judy Garland, Marilyn Monroe, Natalie Wood, Joan Crawford, Ingrid Bergman, Joan Collins, Greta Garbo, Doris Day, and – oh, yes – Milton Berle and Tony Curtis.

Hellhouse of Hollywood, 6666 Hollywood Blvd., ☎ 213/465-0550, advertises itself as "Hollywood's haunted history of crime, occult and horror." It presents paraphernalia associated with madman-killer Charles Manson, the Black Dahlia murder case, and mobster Bugsy Siegel, among others, via a tape-guided tour narrated by actor Christopher Lee.

If the theatrical atmosphere entraps you, stop by **Cinema Collectors**, 1507 Wilcox Ave., ☎ 213/461-6516, where you can buy movie posters, photographs, autographs and press kits associated with the stars and films that you most admire.

Another neat stop if you're getting a little homesick is **World Book & News,** Hollywood & Cahuenga, ☎ 213/465-4352, where you probably can pick up a copy of your hometown newspaper. The store is open around the clock and carries over 100 hometown newspapers, plus more than 6,000 foreign and domestic magazines.

INFORMATION SOURCES

For live TV shows, tapings and ticket information, contact:

Audiences Unlimited	☎ 818/753-3483
	or 818/506-0067

Fox TV Center, 5746 Sunset Blvd., open weekdays, 8:30-6.
NBC at 3000 W. Alameda Ave.

Free tickets to various TV shows can be obtained by contacting:

ABC-TV	☎ 818/506-0043
	or 213/557-4143
CBS-TV	☎ 213/852-2458
NBC-TV	☎ 818/840-3537
FOX-TV	☎ 818/506-0067
Paramount	☎ 213/956-5575
Merv Griffin Productions	☎ 213/852-2455
Audience Associates	☎ 213/467-4697

The **Los Angeles Film Office,** 6922 Hollywood Blvd., Ste. 602, ☎ 213/957-1000, can provide you with a free "shoot sheet" that contains information on all of the films currently in production.

Hollywood Memorial Park Cemetery, the final resting place of Cecil B. DeMille, Rudolf Valentino and Tyrone Power, among others, is at 6000 Santa Monica Blvd., ☎ 213/469-1181.

Paramount Pictures Studio, 5555 Melrose Ave., ☎ 213/956-5575, has a visitor center at 860 N. Gower St., ☎ 213/956-1777 or 956-4552, that provides free two-hour guided walking tours each weekday (no weekends or holidays). The tours leave hourly from 9 to 2. Children under 10 are not allowed.

Other studios throughout the area include **Columbia Pictures, Gene Autry/Flying A Studios, Charlie Chaplin/A&M Studios,** and **Stephen J. Cannell Productions,** and more. If you have a particular favorite, check the telephone book.

Arguably the most famous of Hollywood's glamorous old movie theaters is **Mann's** (nee Grauman's) **Chinese Theatre,** 6925 Hollywood Blvd., ☎ 213/464-8111. Since 1927, filmdom's most illustrious stars have left their imprints in cement in the courtyard of this Oriental-looking movie house. Today, there are close to 200 of them. In addition to the traditional hand-

and footprints, other imprints include John Barrymore's profile, Betty Grable's leg, Jimmy Durante's nose and John Wayne's fist.

ORGANIZED TOURS

If you are timid about exploring on your own, many sightseeing tours are available.

Trolleywood Tours, 6715 Hollywood Blvd., #103, ☎ 213/469-8184 or 800/STARBUS, offers Hollywood Fantasy tours, a Hollywood Sign tour, a Beverly Hills trip, as well as a combination Hollywood/Beverly Hills excursion.

Royal Dynasty Tours, ☎ 310/575-3635 or 800/900-TOURS, fax 310/575-0036, provides similar tours, while **Star Limousine**, ☎ 213/874-9969, 310/829-1066 or 818/980-9512, takes you on your tour in a 6- , 8- , 10- , or 12-passenger limousine with a complimentary bar.

California Tour Lines, ☎ 800/989-7234, covers Hollywood, the stars' homes, Beverly Hills, Universal Studios and the beaches. Visitors can even arrange a **Marilyn Monroe Tour**, ☎ 213/MARILYN.

Grave Line Tours, ☎ 213/469-4149, makes the rounds of "75 sites of death, sin and scandal." Visitors, riding in a hearse, spend two hours seeing sites related to Hollywood's most notorious murders, suicides, overdoses and sex scandals. The tours leave the east side of Mann's Chinese Theatre, Hollywood Blvd. and Orchid Ave., at 9:30 am. The company also offers maps to two celebrity-filled cemeteries, pinpointing the burial sites of more than 50 stars.

But Hollywood is not all about TV and movies.

AWAY FROM THE STARS

C.C. Brown's soda and ice cream parlor claims to have produced the world's first hot fudge sundae.

More traditional attractions include the **Hollywood Wax Museum**, 6767 Hollywood Blvd., ☎ 213/462-8860 or 462-5991, which exhibits life-size figures of famous people in TV, the movies, politics and religion.

Guinness World of Records Museum, 6764 Hollywood Blvd., ☎ 213/463-6433, offers both video and hands-on exhibits. A combination ticket that allows admission to both this museum and the Hollywood Wax Museum is available.

Ripley's Believe It or Not! Museum, 6780 Hollywood Blvd., ☎ 213/466-6335, is patterned upon the widely-published newspaper series and showcases oddities from around the world.

Hollywood Bowl, 2301 N. Highland Ave., ☎ 213/850-2000, 480-3232 or 468-2332, is one of the community's major landmarks. Located in the foothills off Highland Ave., just west of Cahuenga Blvd., the natural amphitheater can seat 18,000 people. Built in 1922, it regularly hosts concerts by the Los Angeles Philharmonic and the Hollywood Bowl

Orchestra. Particularly popular are the annual Easter sunrise services held there, the free Sunday concerts, and the jazz concerts which run from late June to mid-September. The **Hollywood Bowl Museum**, located near the entrance, ☎ 213/850-2058, has recently reopened after extensive renovation.

The region holds many of Greater Los Angeles' better and more interesting restaurants (see *Where to Eat*, page 44).

INFORMATION SOURCES

Los Angeles Convention & Visitors Bureau, 8541 Hollywood Blvd., Hollywood 90028, ☎ 213/624-7300 or 800/228-2452, fax 213/264-7066.
Hollywood Chamber of Commerce, 7018 Hollywood Blvd., Hollywood 90028, ☎ 213/469-8311.

West Hollywood

Virtually everyone is aware that gays and lesbians have an affinity for California, but many people are of the belief that they tend to congregate around San Francisco.

The Greater Los Angeles area also has a substantial population of gays and lesbians, and they tend to be found most predominantly in the West Hollywood area. In fact, the community's annual two-day **Christopher Street West Gay & Lesbian Pride Celebration** in West Hollywood is California's third largest parade.

Some of the most popular gay and lesbian haunts in West Hollywood include:

Axis, 652 N. La Peer Dr., ☎ 310/659-0471, the area's largest dance club, where billiards, video games and live entertainment also are featured.

Micky's, 8857 Santa Monica Blvd., ☎ 310/657-1176, is another dance club.

Revolver, 8851 Santa Monica Blvd., ☎ 310/659-8851, is a video cabaret.

The Palms, 8572 Santa Monica Blvd., ☎ 310/652-6188, is the oldest lesbian bar in town.

Gold Coast, 8228 Santa Monica Blvd., ☎ 213/656-4879; **Hunter's**, 7511 Santa Monica Blvd., ☎ 213/850-9428; **Mother Lode**, 8944 Santa Monica Blvd., ☎ 310/659-9700; and **Trunks**, 8809 Santa Monica Blvd., ☎ 310/652-1015, cater to gay men.

Spike, 7746 Santa Monica Blvd., ☎ 213/656-9343, is a levi-and-leather bar.

The Comedy Store, 8433 Sunset Blvd., ☎ 213/656-6225, has special nights for gays and lesbians, as well as for African-Americans, Latinos and female comics.

Buzz Coffee, 8200 Santa Monica Blvd., ☎ 213/650-7742, is a popular gay/lesbian coffeehouse.

San Vicente Inn-Resort, 845 N. San Vicente Blvd., ☎ 310/854-6915 or 854-6915, fax 310/289-5929, also caters to a gay/lesbian clientele.

The Bodhi Tree bookshop on Melrose is visited by Shirley MacLaine.

THEME RESTAURANTS

Understandably, much of the allure derives from the movie industry. **The Globe Playhouse**, 1107 N. Kings Rd., ☎ 213/654-5623, is a half-scale replica of the London original.

8433 Sunset Blvd. formerly was the site of Dino's Lodge, a restaurant owned by Dean Martin, where the once-popular television series *77 Sunset Strip* was filmed.

INFORMATION

For more information, contact **West Hollywood Convention & Visitors Bureau**, 8687 Melrose Ave., Suite M-26, West Hollywood 90069, ☎ 310/289-2525 or 800/368-6020, fax 310/289-2529.

Beverly Hills

This upscale Los Angeles suburb was incorporated in 1914. Will Rogers was the first mayor. It is the birthplace of actress Candice Bergen and actors Richard Chamberlain and Burt Ward. Mary Astor and Douglas Fairbanks Sr. chose to build their magnificent Pickfair estate here.

There is perhaps no shopping street more famous than **Rodeo Dr.** in the area framed by Canon Dr., Wilshire Blvd. and Little Santa Monica Blvd. New to the city are two 90-minute, docent-led trolley tours that focus on Beverly Hills' art and architecture. Included on the tour are the Spanish-style **City Hall**, the **Creative Artists Agency** building designed by I.M. Pei, and two contemporary art galleries. The tours end in front of the **Museum of Television and Radio**, also new.

For more information, contact **Beverly Hills Visitors Bureau**, 239 S. Beverly Dr., Beverly Hills 90212, ☎ 310/271-8174 or 800/345-2210, fax 310/858-8032.

Burbank

In addition to being the birthplace of singer Bonnie Raitt and actors Mark Harmon and John Ritter, Burbank is the home of three of the area's most prominent film studios (no, they're not *all* in Hollywood).

NBC Studios, 3000 W. Alameda Ave., ☎ 818/840-3537 or 840-4444, offers 75-minute tours on the hour, Monday through Friday, from 9 to 3, with extended hours during the summer and on holidays. (They're closed on New Year's, Easter, Thanksgiving and Christmas.) Parking is free, but there is an admission fee. To get free tickets to watch the taping of a show, contact the NBC ticket counter or the NBC ticket kiosk on Universal's CityWalk. To order by mail, write NBC Tickets, 3000 W. Alameda Ave., Burbank 91523.

Warner Bros. Studios, 4000 Warner Blvd., ☎ 818/954-1669 or 954-6000, offers two-hour "VIP tours" leaving Gate 4, Monday through Friday, on the half-hour, between 9 and 4, with extended hours during the summer and on holidays. The tours are preceded by a 15-minute film showing some of the most famous Warner Bros. film excerpts. Groups are limited to 12 people and no children under 10 are permitted.

New is the **Warner Bros. Museum**, the first museum to be erected upon a studio lot. The 7,000-square-foot facility is in a pavilion housing the Steven J. Ross Theater. On display is the piano from *Casablanca*, starring Humphrey Bogart, the mysterious statue of a bird from *Maltese Falcon*, and Guinevere's gown from *Camelot*. Also on display are the studio's four Oscars: one for Technical Achievement (sound) for *The Jazz Singer* and three for Best Picture for *The Life of Emile Zola, Casablanca* and *My Fair Lady*. All of the docents who lead the tours are Warner's retirees.

The Walt Disney Co. is located at 500 S. Buena Vista, ☎ 818/560-1000.

For additional information, contact **Burbank Chamber of Commerce**, 200 W. Magnolia Blvd., Burbank 91502-1724, ☎ 818/846-3111, fax 818/846-0109.

Canoga Park

Known as Owensmouth between 1912 and 1931, Canoga Park has at least one unusual "resident" – **WonderWorks**, which builds many of the models of buildings and towns that are used by the major film studios.

For information, contact **Canoga Park Chamber of Commerce**, 7248 Owensmouth Ave., Canoga Park 91303, ☎ 818/884-4222.

Glendale

This community, at the eastern entrance to the San Fernando Valley, sits on the first land grant in California, issued by King Charles IV of Spain in 1784.

Once called Tropico, the town appears to engender the creative spirit in its residents. It was here, for example, that Burton Baskin, from nearby Pasadena, and his brother-in-law, Irvine Robbins of Glendale, decided to merge in 1946, thereby creating the **Baskin-Robbins** ice cream chain.

It was here, too, that the first franchise for **Bob's Big Boy** opened in 1952.

Of special interest is **Forest Lawn Memorial Park**, 1712 S. Glendale Ave., ☎ 213/254-3131 or 818/241-4151. This park is worth investigating. It is the final resting place of such Hollywood personalities as Walt Disney, Humphrey Bogart, W.C. Fields, Jean Harlow and Buster Keaton. In addition, it is a 300-acre indoor/outdoor "art gallery." **Memorial Terrace** houses a stained glass recreation of Leonardo da Vinci's *The Last Supper*, which is shown daily on the half-hour between 9:30 and 4. In the **Hall of the Crucifixion-Resurrection** is one of the world's largest religious oil paintings, the 45- x 195-foot *Crucifixion* by Jan Styka, and its 51 x 70-foot companion, Styka's *Resurrection*, shown daily on the hour between 10 and 4. The **Wee Kirk o' the Heather** is one of three Old World churches on the grounds.

The **Forest Lawn Museum** has a collection of every coin that is mentioned in the Bible, a gem collection, an assortment of American bronze statuary, a life-size recreation of Michelangelo's *David*, and 520 pieces of cathedral stained glass from the 11th to 15th centuries.

For additional information, contact **Glendale Chamber of Commerce**, 200 S. Louise St., PO Box 112, Glendale 91205, ☎ 818/240-7870, fax 818/240-2872.

Malibu

This 27-mile ribbon between the beach and the Santa Monica Mountains has been a popular getaway for movie personalities for generations. In the 1920s, Clara Bow and John Gilbert lived here. Actors Timothy Hutton and Pierce Brosnan were born here, as was actress Linda Hamilton. Former talk show host Johnny Carson lives here, and actor Martin Sheen was once the honorary mayor.

In 1959, the cult classic *Gidget* was filmed on Malibu (deer) Beach.

For more information, contact **Malibu Chamber of Commerce**, 23805 Stuart Ranch Rd., Suite 100, Malibu 90265, ☎ 310/456-9025, fax 310/456-0195, Web site www.malibu.org.

Manhattan Beach

C'mon in! The water's fine. The Beach Boys, a singing group that was among the first to popularize the California lifestyle in the 1960s, came from Manhattan Beach. Remember their *Good Vibrations, California Girls, Surfer Girl,* and *Wouldn't It Be Nice?*

Contact **Manhattan Beach Chamber of Commerce**, 425 15th St., Manhattan Beach 90266, ☎ 310/545-5313.

Santa Monica

Surrounded on three sides by the city of Los Angeles and on the fourth by the ocean, this upscale community was the birthplace of actresses Shirley Temple, Bonnie Franklin, Shelley Fabares, Geraldine Chaplin, Linda Gray; of actors Robert Redford and Jack Webb (*Dragnet*); and of singer Natalie Cole.

Municipal Pier, with its shops, restaurants, carnival games and fishing, is at the foot of Colorado Ave.

Palisades Park sits atop a cliff overlooking the beach.

For information, contact **Santa Monica Convention & Visitors Bureau**, 2219 Main St., Santa Monica 90405, ☎ 310/392-9631; or **Santa Monica Visitor Information Center**, 1400 Ocean Ave., Santa Monica, ☎ 310/393-7593 or 800/71-BEACH.

Tarzana

This residential community has grown up around the ranch once owned by Edgar Rice Burroughs, creator of *Tarzan*. Burroughs moved to the area in 1919 to be close to the studios that were filming his *Tarzan* movies. In the San Fernando Valley, he bought the 540-acre estate of the late Gen. Harrison Gray Otis, founder of *The Los Angeles Times*, and renamed it Tarzana. Burroughs intended to establish a working ranch on the property, which he stocked with Angora goats, Berkshire hogs and riding horses, but by the mid-1920s, he opted to divide the estate and create a new town. The house and 120 acres of the ranch became El Caballero Country Club. During World War II, Burroughs, then 66, became the oldest war correspondent to cover the South Pacific theatre of action.

Pasadena

Founded in the 1870s as a health refuge, Pasadena (a Chippewa word for "crown of the valley") was incorporated in 1886.

The colorful **Old Town** section is bounded by Union St., Raymond Ave., Green St. and Pasadena Ave.

Pasadena has been the birthplace of an eclectic group of celebrities, including tennis star Stan Smith, humorist Stan Freberg, cooking expert Julia Child, World War II hero Gen. George S. Patton, actor Harry Hamlin and actress Sally Field.

Short-order cook Lionel Steenberger is said to have invented the cheeseburger here in the 1920s.

The faculty and alumni of **California Institute of Technology** (Cal Tech), 1201 E. California Blvd., ☎ 818/395-6327 or 395-6811, have won a remarkable 22 Nobel prizes. Free tours of the campus are conducted Monday through Friday at 2 pm, except on holidays, rainy days or during the winter break, and can be arranged through the Public Relations office, 315 S. Hill Ave.

Cal Tech's **Jet Propulsion Laboratory**, ☎ 818/354-9314, which assembled the Voyager, is at the north end of Oak Grove Dr. in nearby La Cañada Flintridge. Two-hour tours are given occasionally by reservation.

The highlight of Pasadena's year, of course, is the annual **Rose Bowl Parade**, held every New Year's Day.

The **Rose Bowl** itself, located at 1001 Rose Bowl Dr., ☎ 818/577-3100, was built in 1922 and seats 100,184. In addition to being the venue for the annual Rose Bowl game, it is the home field for the UCLA Bruins football team.

Whether or not you are a football fan, Pasadena's **Tournament House** and **Wrigley Gardens** on South Orange Grove Blvd. are worth a visit. The three-story, 22-room, 18,500-square-foot Tournament House was built of concrete and steel in Italian Renaissance style by architect G. Lawrence Stimson, who built the house in 1906 as the family home. Stimson sold the property to chewing gum magnate William Wrigley Jr. in 1914 for $170,000, and the Wrigley family gave the house to the city in 1958 to serve as the permanent base of operations for the Tournament of Roses. The Tournament of Roses Association built new offices attached to the rear of the house, and the house itself was extensively remodeled in 1987.

The home's front door is four-inch-thick Honduras mahogany and is adorned with an ornately-carved lion's head. Inside, there are two staircases, a marble staircase with a cast bronze railing and carved mahogany banisters in the entry hall, and a back staircase for servants. The front staircase houses the 1,500 pipes that were installed with an Aeolian-Skinner player organ in 1915. The back staircase is equipped with a chair-elevator installed to assist Mrs. Wrigley as she grew older.

A formal living room in the house has matched panels of Circassian walnut. The woodwork and door panels were acquired from Romania. The Florentine Italian marble fireplace on the south end of the room was carved in Italy.

There is raised paneling in the library above a black-veined marble fireplace. The wainscot around the base of the walls is monkey pod, a species of acacia found in Hawaii. The chandelier and matching wall sconces are Venetian.

In the sunroom, the wallpaper is silver foil and oil paint on canvas.

The formal dining room is furnished with original pieces, including a table and 12 chairs made of hand-carved wood. The fireplace is veined marble, and there is crotch mahogany paneling from the Philippines. The darker boxed columns also are made of mahogany, and the crystal chandelier is Czechoslovakian.

The second floor of the house originally had a book-lined central hall surrounded by five bedrooms and four baths. The master bedroom, where a portrait of William Wrigley Jr. still hangs over the Victorian carved marble fireplace, is now used for Rose Bowl committee meetings.

The magnificent Wrigley Gardens cover 4½ acres and contain more than 1,500 varieties of roses.

For more information, contact **Pasadena Convention & Visitors Bureau**, 171 S. Los Robles Ave., Pasadena 91101, ☎ 818/795-9311 or 800/307-7977, fax 818/795-9656; **Pasadena Chamber of Commerce & Civic Association**, 117 E. Colorado Blvd., #100, Pasadena 91105-1993, ☎ 818/795-3355.

Arcadia

There aren't many attractions in this town, but it's fun to stop at **Nichols Egg Ranch**, 900 S. Santa Anita, ☎ 818/445-1200, just to watch the egg-grading and loading machine in operation.

The lagoon in **Los Angeles State and County Arborteum** appeared in the film classic *The African Queen*, starring Humphrey Bogart and Katherine Hepburn; the Queen Anne cottage was featured in TV's *Fantasy Island*.

For information, contact **Arcadia Chamber of Commerce**, 388 W. Huntington Dr., Arcadia 91007-3402, ☎ 818/447-2159 or 447/1400, fax 818/445-0273.

Pomona

This is the home of **California State Polytechnic University**, ☎ 714/869-3258, where the seasonal residents are foals, piglets, lambs, calves and ducklings. Self-guided tours allowed during daylight hours and maps are available at the information center, near the campus entrance.

For more information, contact **Pomona Chamber of Commerce**, 485 N. Garey, PO Box 1457, Pomona 91769-1457, ☎ 909/622-1256.

San Gabriel

The **San Gabriel Mission District** includes the **Old Jail**, a small stone milkhouse on the Wilson-Hayes property that was used as a jail on weekends until the wrong-doers could be taken to the County Jail in Los Angeles on Monday. The building also was used as a playhouse by the Hayes' daughter and as a study by Mr. Hayes after his retirement.

Also in the district is the **Mission Playhouse**, now the San Gabriel Civic Auditorium. Starting in 1912, a 4½-hour "Mission Play" was presented in the original playhouse. The play, which had a cast of 150 people, drew audiences from all over the world and ran for 3,500 performances before it was closed due to the Depression in 1933. The new playhouse was built in 1927 with 1,442 seats and an exterior patterned after the Mission San Antonio de Padua. The courtyard on the north side of the building has replicas of all 21 California missions.

A small museum is at 546 W. Broadway, ☎ 818/308-3223, and you will want to pay particular attention to the district's **Historical Walk**, made of tiles created by 600 local 4th-grade students.

Also of interest in San Gabriel is the **Grapevine Room**, built on the site of the old Grapevine Inn, where Helen Hunt Jackson began writing her famous novel *Ramona*. (Ramona, incidentally, was the name of a local resident, Ramona Short, a cousin of World War II Gen. George S. Patton Jr.)

For more information, contact **San Gabriel Chamber of Commerce**, 401 W. Las Tunas Dr., San Gabriel 91776, ☎ 818/576-2525, fax 818/289-2901.

San Marino

El Molino Viego (The Old Mill), 1120 Old Mill Rd., off Oak Knoll Ave., ☎ 818/449-5450, was the grist mill for Mission San Gabriel, operated by the Indians under the supervision of the Spanish padres until 1816. Now the southern California headquarters for the **California Historical Society**, the building houses a working model of the old mill, along with photographs and other exhibits.

Adventures

On Foot

There are few metropolitan areas in the United States that can offer the kind of opportunities for hiking and backpacking that can be found in Greater Los Angeles.

To the northeast are the Santa Monica Mountains. To the north and northwest are the San Gabriel Mountains and Angeles National Forest. To the southwest is Cleveland National Forest.

In the city itself, there are some 50 miles of hiking trails in **Griffith Park** alone. And for those who are *truly* committed to "shank's mare," the **Los Angeles Marathon**, ☎ 310/444-5544, is held each March.

Santa Monica Mountains National Recreation Area

Congress established the Santa Monica Mountains National Recreation Area in 1978, less than a quarter of a century ago, yet it is an area that provides Los Angeles residents with unparalleled recreational opportunities.

There are so many interesting trails and parks to be explored, it is difficult to decide where to start, but it would be hard to find a more fascinating place to begin than the **Paramount Ranch**. ☎ 818/597-9192 or 800/533-7275.

In 1927, Paramount Pictures bought 2,400 acres of the old Rancho Las Virgenes, and used the site for the next 25 years as a backdrop for many of its films. While many of those old movies were Westerns, the ranch was transformed into colonial Massachusetts for *The Maid of Salem*, into ancient China for *The Adventures of Marco Polo*, and into old San Francisco for *Wells Fargo*.

In 1953, a part of the ranch was acquired by William Hertz, who built a permanent Western town on the property. There, a number of the early television series were filmed, including *The Cisco Kid* and *Zane Grey Theatre*.

Hertz sold the ranch in 1955, but his Western town is still used, most recently as the Colorado mining town seen on TV in *Dr. Quinn, Medicine Woman*. Music festivals are often staged on the ranch today.

In addition to exploring the ranch's 300-acre movie set, visitors can hike along a number of challenging trails. There also is an interpretive trail and a 5K running trail.

The **Peter Strauss Ranch** has a history not unlike that of the Paramount Ranch. ☎ 818/597-9192 or 800/533-7275.

In 1926, a stone ranch house, lookout tower and aviary were built on the property. In the mid-1930s, two entrepreneurs turned the place into "Shoson," an early theme park for children and adults. And later, a dam across Triunfo Creek created a small lake, Lake Enchanto, which was closed around 1960.

In 1976, actor Peter Strauss, currently starring in television's *Moloney*, was working on the *Rich Man, Poor Man* mini-series at Malibu Lake when he saw the land and decided to buy it. Strauss lived on the ranch until 1983, when he sold the property to the Santa Monica Mountains Conservancy.

Today, art shows, exhibitions and weddings are frequently scheduled at the ranch, where the free Summer Sunday Concerts in the Park also are held.

The ranch also offers a number of short hiking trails.

Will Rogers State Historic Park, 1501 Will Rogers State Park Rd., Pacific Palisades 90272, ☎ 310/454-8212, was once the actor's private residence. The 186-acre park includes the cowboy philosopher's 31-room home and an information center.

A film about Rogers' life is shown in the house, and an audio tape is available to direct visitors around the grounds. Guided tours also are available.

Picnic facilities are provided, as well as hiking trails, including a two-mile loop that leads to Inspiration Point.

The park is the eastern terminus of the Backbone Trail which, when completed, will parallel the Pacific Ocean coastline for some 55 miles.

Polo matches are held here on Saturdays at 2 and on Sundays at 10.

Rancho Sierra Vista, ☎ 818/597-9192, actually encompasses two distinct areas: **Rancho Sierra Vista,** created in 1937 from part of an 1803 land grant, the 48,672-acre Rancho El Conejo, and **Satwiwa** (bluffs), which was the name of a nearby Chumash Indian village. The Rancho has a number of excellent hiking trails, including one that provides access to **Point Mugu State Park,** a lovely five-mile stretch of beach that, unfortunately, provides only limited lifeguard service. Satwiwa, which is dedicated to the mountains' Chumash inhabitants, includes the interesting Satwiwa Native American Indian Culture Center.

Moderate hikes abound in this region. They include the 1.5-mile **Satwiwa Loop Trail** (no cyclists or horses allowed) and the 1.2-mile **Wendy Trail.** Along **Castro Crest,** there are some trails that trace the inner canyon along a wooded creek, as well as trails that follow the ridgeline, affording outstanding views of the ocean and the nearby offshore islands.

Circle X Ranch sits in a rugged area with many trails. There is a visitor center, ☎ 818/597-9192, and a ranger station, ☎ 310/457-6408. The 1.9-mile **Canyon View Trail** is ideal for hikers of moderate experience, as is the **Mishe Mokwa Trail** to Split Rock, which covers 3.5 miles, round trip. Hikes of intermediate difficulty include the **Grotto Trail,** a 3.5-mile junket that begins at the ranger station and goes downhill, but requires an uphill climb on the way back. More strenuous is the three-mile hike along **Backbone Trail** or the six-mile **Mishe Mokwa Trail** to Sandstone Peak, at 3,111 feet, the highest point in the Santa Monica Mountains.

At **Franklin Canyon Ranch,** the **Discovery Trail** covers 0.3 miles round trip. A 2.3-mile route along the **Hastain Trail** and back follows a fire road to an overlook, then drops down to an old homestead. **Cross Mountain Trail** takes you over the mountains to Colewater Canyon Park and Wilacre Park. Before leaving the ranch, be sure to visit the Sooky Goldman Nature Center.

There are a number of moderate hikes from **Cheeseboro Canyon** and **Palo Comado Canyon:**

The **Modelo/Ridge Trail** drops to the east for 0.7 miles and then joins the **Cheeseboro Canyon Trail.** Watch for raptors and coyotes along here.

The **Ridge Trail** is a mile long and leads to the **Palo Comado Connector Trail,** an old 1.5-mile ranch road on which you can either turn right (east) to Cheeseboro Canyon or turn left (west) to Palo Comado Canyon.

Cheeseboro Canyon Trail/Sulphur Springs Trail winds 4.6 miles along an old ranch road that follows a streambed. After 1.6 miles, you will encounter a picnic area. After 3.3 miles, you will detect the smell of rotten eggs, signifying that you are near Sulphur Springs. The trail ends at an old sheep corral. Keep your eyes open for golden eagles.

The more hardy (and experienced) hiker might prefer:

Ranch Center Trail connects Cheeseboro and Palo Comado Canyons and covers 1.1 miles.

Palo Comado Canyon Trail begins with an easy 1.2-mile walk along a creek, then becomes a bit more difficult. The entire trail covers 4.4 miles.

The winding 0.8-mile **Simi Peak Trail** climbs to the 2,403 feet to Simi Peak, which is the highest point in the immediate area.

For more information about Cheeseboro and Palo Comado Canyons, including maps and trail guides, contact the visitor center, ☎ 818/597-9192.

Off celebrated Mulholland Dr., there are a number of exceptional hiking and backpacking areas.

Stunt Ranch has a nature center and a cool, shaded trail that is especially popular in the summertime. The ranch is another means of gaining access to the Backbone Trail, above (ask for the interpretive trail folder).

A permit is required to use **Cold Creek Preserve**, and you will find no water there, but it is another point of access to the spectacular Backbone Trail.

Malibu Bluffs offer no access to the beach below, but the 8,000-acre **Malibu Creek State Park** has a nature center and a 15-mile network of trails to explore, including one that leads to Century Lake.

Rocky Oaks has an amphitheater and some easy walking trails around a lovely little pond. On the first Sunday of every month, a ranger-led family walk is available.

Charmlee County Regional Park has a nature center, an interpretive trail and a number of additional trails that provide gorgeous views of the nearby coastline. From February through June, wildflowers usually abound here.

From July through October, members of the Sierra Club lead hikes and walks through the Santa Monica Mountains. Contact **Sundays in the Santa Monicas (SITSM)**, 6206 Aura Ave., Reseda 91335. (The group also conducts hikes on days *other* than Sunday.)

Hiking in Los Angeles, ☎ 818/501-1005, will lead hikes virtually anywhere within the region. The guides are fluent in English, French, German, Italian and Japanese.

For more information about the Santa Monica Mountains, contact **U.S. Department of the Interior**, National Park Service, Santa Monica Mountains National Recreation Area, 30401 Agoura Rd., Suite 100, Agoura Hills 91301, ☎ 818/597-9192. The office publishes an interesting quarterly magazine called *Outdoors*. **Santa Monica Mountains Conservancy**, 5750 Ramirez Canyon Rd., Malibu 90265, ☎ 310/589-3200 or 800/533-PARK. Ask for their maps and guides to the hiking trails.

Arcadia

Wilderness Park/Preserve, PO Box 60021, Arcadia 91066-6021, ☎ 818/ 355-5309, has expanded from its original 8.7 acres to 120 acres. Guided nature walks are offered every Sunday at 10 or you can take the self-guided quarter-mile nature hike (ask for a map). From June through September, monthly guided starlight hikes are available, and from March through November, "Evening of Discovery" family-oriented lectures are presented at dusk around the fire circle at the amphitheater. A Junior Ranger Program is offered to children 11 years and older.

Claremont

One of the best ways to reach **Angeles National Forest**, ☎ 714/982-3816, is by taking Mt. Baldy Rd. six miles north out of Claremont. The 1,000-square-mile forest offers a multitude of trails.

Malibu

Malibu Creek State Park, 7.3 miles north of Malibu by way of Malibu Canyon Rd., ☎ 310/880-0367, actually is in the Santa Monica Mountains, but many of its 4,000 acres are closed to the public. None the less, the park provides over 12 miles of hiking trails. From the parking lot, it is just 1½ miles to a lovely little lake, and only 2½ miles to a site where many of the *M*A*S*H* episodes were filmed.

Pasadena

Easton Canyon Nature Center, 1750 N. Altadena, Pasadena, ☎ 818/ 398-5420, offers a number of nature hikes, including one that travels 3½ miles along shaded creek beds from Chantry Flats to Sturtevant Falls and back.

San Dimas

Puddingstone Lake, 1440 Camper View Rd., San Dimas 91773, is in Frank G. Bonelli Regional County Park. In addition to the nature trails, it offers fishing, waterskiing, boating, jetskiing, biking and horseback riding. There also is a golf course and an RV park.

For more information, contact **San Dimas Chamber of Commerce**, 246 E. Bonita Ave., PO Box 175, San Dimas 91773, ☎ 909/592-3818.

San Pedro

Jogging and hiking trails with gorgeous views of the surrounding countryside can be found in 20-acre **Bogdanovich Park**, 1920 Cumbre Dr.

For an interesting urban hike with an unusual twist, take the **Sportswalk**, which begins at the Sheraton Los Angeles Harbor Hotel. Similar to the Hollywood Walk of Fame, the Sportswalk contains plaques honoring various national sports figures. Every October, a public ceremony honors the new inductees.

URBAN HIKING

It isn't necessary, of course, to tramp through the mountains in order to have a pleasant hike. Some of the best hikes are those through a lush garden or arboretum, of which Greater Los Angeles has quite a number.

In the city itself, the **Mildred Mathias Botanical Gardens**, Hilgard and Le Conte, ☎ 310/825-3620, fill an entire eight-acre canyon on the UCLA campus. In **Exposition Park**, there is a sunken rose garden that contains 17,000 plants.

The 127 acres of trees at the **Los Angeles State & County Arboretum**, 301 N. Baldwin Ave., Arcadia 91007-2697, ☎ 818/821-3222, are arranged by their continent of origin. The grounds include tropical and begonia greenhouses, a bird sanctuary and a small lake (Lake Baldwin) fed by underground springs. The park now features a special tram for the disabled. Guided walking tours are offered on Wednesdays at 11.

Rancho Santa Ana Botanic Garden, 1500 N. College Ave., Claremont 91711-3157, ☎ 909/625-8767, fax 909/626-7670, has 86 acres of plants native to California, and is laced with nature trails. Admission is free.

Six miles south of Redondo Beach on the Palos Verdes Peninsula, **South Coast Botanic Gardens**, 26300 Crenshaw Blvd., San Pedro, offers a small stream, a lake and more than 2,000 species of plants and trees from around the world – on an 87-acre site that once was a landfill!

On Horseback

For a large metropolitan area, Greater Los Angeles offers a surprising number of horseback riding opportunities.

Griffith Park in downtown Los Angeles includes 50 miles of horseback riding trails.

In Burbank, there is the **Los Angeles Equestrian Center** at 480 Riverside Dr., ☎ 818/840-9063.

In Hollywood, **Sunset Ranch Hollywood Stables**, 3400 N. Beachwood Dr., ☎ 213/464-9612 or 469-5450, rents horses, provides riding lessons and offers nighttime moonlight rides.

Malibu Equestrian Park, 6225 Merritt Dr., Malibu, ☎ 310/317-1364, rents horses.

In the Santa Monica Mountains, there are equestrian trails at **Paramount Ranch** and at **Rocky Oaks**. Three of the most popular at Paramount Ranch are the Coyote Canyon Trail, the Medea Creek Trail and the

Overlook Trail. **Circle X Ranch** (☎ 310/457-6408) offers horseback riding, **Will Rogers State Park**, ☎ 310/454-8212, has weekend polo matches, and **Rancho Sierra Vista**, ☎ 818/597-9192 or 800/533-7275, has a demonstration horse ranch.

On Wheels

In an area where driving an automobile can definitely be harmful to your health, the popularity of getting around on a bicycle is certainly understandable.

Manhattan Beach has over 20 miles of separated bikeways within the city limits, and you can rent a bike at either **Europa Bicycles**, 1143 Manhattan Ave., ☎ 310/545-8843, or **Fun Bunns Beach Rentals**, 1116 Manhattan Ave., ☎ 310/372-8500.

The **Los Angeles County Bike Path**, also called the **South Bay Bike Path**, ☎ 310/318-0648, runs for 26 miles from the south end of Redondo Beach to Malibu and is shared by bikers, walkers and rollerblade aficionados alike.

In the Santa Monica Mountains, an excellent place for biking is the **Circle X Ranch**. Another route goes along **Santa Monica State Beach**, which has a very picturesque bike path (but be forewarned that there may be upwards of a million people on this beach on a good weekend).

In Redondo Beach, bikes may be rented at **Hermosa Cyclery**, 20 13th St., ☎ 310/374-7816; **Jeffers**, 39 14th St., ☎ 310/372-9492; and **Marina Bike Rental**, 505 N. Harbor Dr., ☎ 310/318-BIKE. In Santa Monica, the places to rent a bike are **Perry's Sport Shop**, 1200 Pacific Hwy., ☎ 310/458-3975, or **Spokes & Stuff**, near Loew's beachfront, ☎ 310/395-4748.

If you prefer a motorcycle, you can rent one at **Eagle-Rider Motorcycle Rental**, 20917 Western Ave., Torrance 90501, ☎ 310/320-3456 or 800/501-8687, fax 310/320-4176. They will provide complimentary airport or hotel shuttle service, offer group and guided tours, and allow one-way rentals between Los Angeles and San Francisco, where they also have an outlet. To sign up, you must be at least 25 and have a valid motorcycle license.

On & In the Water

Californians are absolutely *obsessed* by the water. They like to listen to it, to stretch out next to it, and to hold cook-outs on the beaches beside it. They love to swim, dive and fish in it; kayak, canoe, catamaran, motorboat or go yachting upon it; and hang-glide paraglide, soar or go ballooning above it. They can spend hours simply *watching* it!

Californians will flock to the beaches even in mid-Winter (January through March), the time to watch the annual migration of gray whales as they swim steadfastly southward toward their calving grounds off the coast of Baja California.

In the very shadow of Los Angeles International Airport, Los Angelenos sprawl along the four miles of **Dockweiler State Beach** from the west end of Culver Blvd. north to Marina del Rey.

Outside the city, **Castaic Lake** provides some of the best freshwater bass fishing in the state, if not the nation. The east arm of the lake is the best place for fishing; waterskiers favor the west arm.

Other popular places to enjoy watersports along the Greater Los Angeles coastline include:

Malibu

Malibu Pier is a hotspot for shorebound fishermen, offering good views of popular **Surfrider Beach**, which is famous for its powerful surf breaks. Those who wish to venture upon the briny can arrange half-day and full-day fishing trips here. Food, live bait and fishing tackle are all for sale.

Malibu Lagoon State Beach, on Highway 1 at Cross Creek Rd., ☎ 310/456-8432, is a popular spot for swimming and surfing. The beach flanks the wetlands near the mouth of ocean-bound Malibu Creek.

Leo Carrillo State Beach, along Highway 1, ☎ 800/444-7275, provides a number of interesting sea caves, a tunnel and countless tidepools to be explored. Lifeguards are on hand and the beach is a favorite among swimmers, scuba divers and body- , board- and windsurfers. In the winter, the beach is a good place to do some whale-watching. Surfing is particularly good around **Sequit Point**.

Zuma County Beach/Point Dume State Beach, 8.2 miles west of Malibu on Highway 1, ☎ 310/457-9891, is the longest beach in the Malibu area, extending over four miles. It is popular with swimmers, surfers and bodysurfers, and there are lifeguards to keep an eye on things. Surfing is good around Westwood Beach and off Point Dume. **Pirate's Cove,** near Point Dume, is a notorious nude beach.

The community of Manhattan Beach also has a popular fishing pier, as well as **Manhattan State Beach**, which can be found at the western ends of each street between 1st and 45th. The two-mile beach is widely used for swimming and surfing, and is paralleled by **The Strand**, a popular concrete beachfront pathway. Surfboards can be rented at **Fun Bunns Beach Rentals**, 1116 Manhattan Ave., ☎ 310/372-8500.

Marina Del Rey

In Marina del Rey, you'll find virtually everything associated with the water at **Fisherman's Village**, 13755 Figi Way. **Rent-a-Sail,** ☎ 310/822-1868, will rent you a sailboat, a motorboat, a canoe or a catamaran. **Hornblower Yachts,** ☎ 310/301-6000, will take you on a harbor cruise. **Marina del Rey Sportsfishing,** ☎ 310/822-3625, will provide a charter for your deep-sea fishing adventure.

Redondo Beach

The center of beachfront activity in Redondo Beach, as it is in so many California coastal communities, is **the pier**. Redondo's is at the foot of Torrance Blvd., ☎ 310/374-2171. Expanded in the 1990s, it is lined with seafood restaurants and souvenir shops, and in the winter it is a great place for whale-watching. On a clear day, you can see Catalina Island from here.

King Harbor features restaurants, hotels, an amusement center and the ever-popular International Boardwalk. Bicycling, boating, sportfishing, swimming, snorkeling, sailing, windsurfing, jetskiing and racquetball are all popular around this man-made harbor.

Redondo State Beach, which is 0.3 miles southwest of town along the Esplanade, ☎ 310/372-2166, extends two miles along the coast south of the pier. Here, George Freeth introduced the sport of surfing to America in 1907. Developer Henry Huntington brought Freeth from Hawaii to demonstrate the sport. Under the watchful eye of lifeguards, it is a popular spot for swimming, surfing and skin diving. A bicycle path and jogging trail parallel the beach.

Hermosa Beach, which can be found at the western ends of 3rd through 35th Sts., ☎ 310/376-0951, is just 1½ miles northwest of the downtown area. This two-mile beach is a favorite of both swimmers and surfers.

In March, the Redondo Beach waterfront offers an annual **surf contest** and a **kite festival**. In early August, the city hosts the **International Surfing Festival**, and on the second Thursday of that month, holds its ever-popular **Seaside Lagoon Sand Castle Contest**. In December, there is the traditional **Holiday Harbor Boat Parade**.

If you need some assistance, **Redondo Sport Fishing**, 233 N. Harbor Dr., ☎ 310/372-2111, will rent you a boat and fishing tackle, organize a day or night expedition to an offshore fishing barge, or take you out for a closer look at the gray whale migration.

Bay Surf Rentals, 117 Greenwich Village Dr., ☎ 310/376-2503, or **Jeffers**, 39 14th St., ☎ 310/372-9492, can fix you up with a surfboard.

G'Day Charters, 161 N. Harbor Dr., ☎ 310/798-1310, will take you parasailing, yachting or fishing. It rents kayaks and even teaches you how to use them! It also rents glass-bottom boats, waverunners, pedal boats and gondolas.

In Rancho Palos Verdes, 7½ miles south of town, the **Point Vicente Interpretive Center**, Palos Verdes Dr. South, is another great place to watch the gray whale migration. Be sure to look into the museum while you're there.

Abalone Cove Beach, 1½ miles south of the Point Vicente Interpretive Center, ☎ 310/377-1222, offers another mile of sheltered beach, a favorite of nude bathers. Fishing and tidepooling also are popular here.

San Dimas

Bonelli Regional Park, 120 E. Via Verde, ☎ 909/599-8411, provides a stocked lake, boat rentals, sailing, waterskiing, jetskiing, horseback riding and camping.

San Pedro

San Pedro's **22nd St. Landing**, 141 W. 22nd St., is the home of the largest privately-owned diving and fishing fleet on the West Coast. Sportfishing, scuba diving, snorkeling, charters and whale-watching tours can all be arranged here.

Village Boat House, Berth 78, ☎ 310/831-0996, provides one-hour (daily), 1½-hour (weekends), and two-hour (weekends) harbor cruises. The company also offers whale-watching cruises during the winter migrating season.

Spirit Cruises, in Ports O'Call Village, ☎ 310/548-8080, will take you to sea on your choice of a 65-foot cruise boat, an 85-foot schooner or a 90-foot motor yacht. Both 45- and 90-minute cruises are available daily from May through September and on weekends the rest of year. Luxurious dinner cruises are offeredon Friday and Saturday evenings, and from January through March, the company features 2½-hour whale-watching cruises.

Annie B. Sportfishing Barge, Berth 79, ☎ 310/431-6837, provides off-shore fishing.

Los Angeles Harbor Sportfishing, in Ports O'Call Village, ☎ 310/547-9916, will provide half-day, three-quarter-day or overnight fishing excursions. They also provide gray whale trips between January and April.

Cruises to **Catalina Island** leave a terminal near Vincent Thomas Bridge on a widely-published schedule.

Cabrillo Beach, 3720 Stephen White Dr., ☎ 310/548-7562, features a fishing pier and a mile-long beach, popular with swimmers, surfers, scuba divers and volleyball enthusiasts. **Cabrillo Marine Aquarium** has 35 glass tanks for displaying its exhibits. You can see Catalina Island from here, and windsurfing and jetskiing lessons are available. Following the whale-watching season, the grunion season begins, and twice each month the silvery fish swim onto the beach to lay their eggs under a full or new moon. During part of the season, the delicious little fish may be caught by hand.

Via Cabrillo Marina off 22nd St. is a popular place to walk, bicycle, or rollerblade. **Royal Palms State Beach**, at the south end of Western Ave., is a good place to go tidepooling.

Santa Monica

Santa Monica Pier, ☎ 310/458-8900, at the foot of Colorado Ave., is a city unto itself. Pier fishermen are interspersed with people visiting the restaurants and gift shops and others who are enjoying the carnival games and rides. (Check out the antique carousel with hand-carved wooden horses.)

Santa Monica State Beach has a paved promenade for strollers, skaters and bikers. A number of volleyball courts also can be found there.

A chain of beaches extends westward along the ocean from Santa Monica toward Santa Barbara. Among them:

Nearby **Will Rogers State Beach**, ☎ 310/394-3266, extends 17 miles along the Pacific Coast Highway. It has a wide sandy beach, food concessions and a playground. The beach is popular with swimmers, surfers and sand volleyball players.

From the bluffs above **Topanga State Beach**, which is at the mouth of Topanga Canyon, there is a magnificent view of Santa Monica Bay and the offshore Channel Islands.

Swimming and body surfing are popular at **Las Tunas State Beach**. (Note: Only limited lifeguard service is provided.)

Las Flores State Beach has a rocky shoreline and provides no lifeguard service, but it is a popular place where many of the locals go diving.

The lagoon at **Malibu Lagoon State Beach** is a nursery for fish and a feeding area for shorebirds. Only limited lifeguard service is provided. **Adamson House** (☎ 310/456-8432) presents exhibits that trace the history of Malibu.

Dan Blocker State Beach is popular for swimming. Here, a perennial creek trickles through Solstice Canyon toward the ocean.

Under the right conditions, **Zuma Beach County Park** can have some challenging surf, but it would be wise to check first with locals who are familiar with the area.

Point Dume State Reserve has no lifeguards, but a quarter-mile trail leads to the top of the bluff, which is a good spot for whale-watching in the winter.

It is a moderate eighth-of-a-mile walk to **El Matador State Beach**. There are no lifeguards, but it is a lovely little pocket beach, offering excellent tidepooling at low tide.

A lovely path lined with lemonadeberry and purple sage leads from a bluff to the rocky **La Piedra State Beach** (no lifeguards on duty). Similarly, there is a pleasant downhill pathway to **El Pescador State Beach** (again, no lifeguards). **Nicholas Canyon County Beach** is a secluded spot at the base of some coastal bluffs. Limited lifeguard service is provided and a food concession also can be found there.

Leo Carrillo State Beach has a visitor center, an amphitheater, trails along a creek, as well as some terrific ocean views.

County Line Beach, a popular surfing spot, is on the Los Angeles/Ventura County line. Once more, there are no lifeguards on duty.

For additional information, contact **Santa Monica Mountains Conservancy**, ☎ 310/456-5046; **California Department of Parks & Recreation**, ☎ 818/880-0350; **National Park Service**, 30401 Agoura Rd., Suite 100, Agoura Hills 91301-2085, ☎ 818/597-9192.

On Snow

Snow in southern California? Don't forget that California is a mountainous state, north and south. Some excellent skiing can be enjoyed in the Greater Los Angeles area by visiting **Mt. San Antonio** in the Angeles National Forest, 16 miles northeast of Claremont at the end of Mt. Baldy Rd., or **Mount Waterman** in the San Gabriel Mountains, 40 miles northeast of Pasadena via I-210 and Highway 2.

Mt. San Antonio, also known as Old Baldy Peak, is southern California's largest ski area, providing 400 skiable acres at an elevation of some 10,000 feet. The longest run is 2½ miles, and there are four chairlifts. Skiing season runs from December through mid-April, and there are several restaurants in the skiing area.

Mount Waterman, ☎ 818/790-2002 or 440-1041, at an altitude of 7,000-8,030 feet, has three chairlifts, but no lodgings.

In the Air

There are so many opportunities for airborne adventures in Greater Los Angeles, it would be unfair to single out any of them. Howard Hughes built and flew his Spruce Goose here. Many pioneer aircraft manufacturing companies got started here. A number of the country's greatest military flying aces were born and/or raised here.

There is one place that no aviation enthusiast should miss, however: **Museum of Flying**, 2772 Donald Douglas Loop North, Santa Monica, ☎ 310/392-8822. Located near the south end of 28th St., this museum displays a number of historic aircraft, including a World War I Jenny and the *New Orleans*, which flew around the world in 1924. Of particular interest is "Airventure," an interactive learning center where children can discover the principles of aviation by actually climbing into cockpits and taking the controls of various aircraft.

Eco-Travel/Cultural Excursions

So much to see; so little time. How to squeeze it all in? Every section of Greater Los Angeles has enough points of interest to keep you moving endlessly.

We will present some of our favorites and give you some idea of what they have to offer.

Burbank

The Natural History Museum of Los Angeles County, Third St. and Cypress Ave., ☎ 818/557-3562, is next to the Media City Center and includes a marvelous Children's Discovery Center. Try to go on the first Tuesday of the month, when admission is free.

If music is your fancy, look into the **Burbank Chamber Orchestra,** ☎ 818/848-8841; the **Burbank Civic Light Opera,** 150 S. Glenoaks Blvd., ☎ 818/380-3444; or the **Burbank Symphony Assn.,** ☎ 818/846-5981.

Los Angeles

There are a number of extraordinary cultural institutions in Los Angeles, many of them decidely unique. One such is the **Museum of Neon Art** on the first floor of downtown Renaissance Tower. This museum considers the use of neon to be an art form and conducts nighttime bus tours to examine neon signs, movie marquees and other contemporary neon art throughout the city.

More traditional cultural institutions are the older favorites, such as the **Southwest Museum,** 234 Museum Dr., ☎ 213/221-2163 or 221-2164, the oldest museum in Los Angeles. Founded in 1907, the museum offers artistic performances, classes, films, lectures, festivals and demonstrations, and it is the home of the famous **Braun Research Library**.

The **Los Angeles County Museum of Art,** 5905 Wilshire Blvd., ☎ 213/857-6000, 857-6111 or 937-2590, Web site www.lacma.org, is the largest art museum west of Chicago. The five-building complex is adjacent to La Brea Tar Pits and houses over 150,000 works of art. Over 30 changing exhibitions are presented each year. Don't miss the **Cantor Sculpture Garden** outside.

Among the city's newer attractions are the **Streisand Center for Conservancy Studies,** which occupies the 22½ acres of the actress' former estate. Open to the public are two of four luxury houses, the meadows and the orchards.

Soon to begin construction is the 2,380-seat **Walt Disney Hall,** ☎ 213/626-6222, which will become the new home of the Los Angeles Philharmonic Orchestra. But don't dash out for tickets; the building is not scheduled for completion until late June 2001.

Malibu

The **J. Paul Getty Art Museum,** 17985 Pacific Coast Hwy., ☎ 310/458-2003 or 458-1104 (Spanish), is a mile north of Sunset Blvd. and is difficult to reach. You can get there on MTA bus 434. If you must drive, enter from the south, if possible. Generally speaking, parking reservations must be made at least a week in advance. The museum is currently closed for renovations, so call ahead to check.

This striking museum resembles an ancient Roman villa, the Villa dei Papiri, which stood outside the city of Herculaneum overlooking the Bay of Naples. An information center can be found on the second floor.

Orientation talks are given every 15 minutes between 9:45 and 3:15 at the south end of the Main Peristyle Garden; a slide/tape program is presented in the Orientation Theater near the entrance vestibule; and talks (in Spanish as well as English) are given daily in the galleries and gardens.

Exhibits are constantly changing, and there are demonstrations that are designed to encourage visitor participation.

The Browsing Room on the second floor contains books and audiovisual materials, including an interesting interactive videodisc about illuminated manuscripts. A similar interactive videodisc in the antiquities galleries deals with Greek vases.

Evening lectures are commonly scheduled.

Here, unlike many similar institutions, photography is encouraged, except in the drawings and manuscript and the photographs galleries. No tripods or open flashbulbs may be used, but flashcubes and electronic units are allowed.

Currently under construction on a hilltop in Brentwood just off I-405 is **Getty Center**, an $800-million, 110-acre extension using the J. Paul Getty Museum as its focal point. The new center will include an art museum, a 450-seat auditorium, three restaurants, a bookstore and a research library. The 134,000-square-foot Central Garden is to include a stream, a waterfall and a pool of floating azaleas. To get to the center from the parking lot will require a five-minute ride aboard an electric train.

For more information, write PO Box 2112, Santa Monica, CA 90407.

Pasadena

The **Norton Simon Museum**, 411 W. Colorado Blvd., ☎ 818/449-6840, is to Pasadena what the Getty Museum is to Malibu. Housing one of world's foremost art collections, the museum contains art from the early Renaissance through the mid-20th century, including works by Degas, Monet, Rembrandt, Renoir and Van Gogh. Founded in 1924 as the Pasadena Art Institute, the museum also contains a remarkable display of southeast Asian and Indian sculpture. The present building opened in 1969 and was remodeled and reorganized in 1974.

Pasadena Playhouse, 39 S. El Molino Ave., ☎ 818/356-7529, is justly famous as the training ground for numerous well-known actors. Founded in 1917, the 700-seat theater offers plays throughout the year.

Mount Wilson Observatory, ☎ 818/793-3100, sits atop a 5,710-foot mountain in the San Gabriel range north of town. With its 100-inch reflecting telescope, the staff is credited with discovering that the universe consists of more than one galaxy. Beside the telescope is an interesting museum.

Pasadena Civic Auditorium, 300 E. Green St., ☎ 818/793-2122 or 449-7360, houses the **Pasadena Symphony**, ☎ 818/793-7172. The Auditorium, host to the annual Primetime Emmy Awards, was opened in 1932. The symphony, which was founded in 1928, presents five-yearly Musical Circus programs, free family events that feature a hands-on introduction to various musical instruments, and open rehearsals. A lecture precedes each concert by an hour.

San Marino

The Huntington Library, Art Collection & Botanical Garden, 1151 Oxford Rd., ☎ 818/405-2141 or 405-2100, Web site www.huntington.org, was built by Henry Huntington in the early 1900s. It houses one of the world's great collections of rare books and manuscripts, including a Gutenberg Bible, the Ellesmere Chaucer and Benjamin Franklin's handwritten autobiography.

The art gallery contains 18th-century European paintings, rare tapestries, porcelains, miniatures, sculpture and period furniture. In addition, the Virginia Steele Scott Gallery of American Art displays paintings from the 1730s to the 1930s. Photography and videotaping is allowed, but tripods and flashbulbs are not permitted.

Outside is a 130-acre botanical garden that contains 15,000 kinds of plants, including a palm garden exhibiting 90 different varieties and a rose garden with 2,000 different varieties. Two miles of pathways wend their way throughout the 207-acre grounds.

There is an excellent bookstore and self-guiding tour brochures are available. Formal tours of the gardens depart at 1 Tuesday through Sunday.

Where To Stay

In Greater Los Angeles, there is no shortage of places to stay (barring a special event such as the Olympics or a national political convention) and the rooms come in every price range. Our preference is to stay outside the city, but that's because we like the atmosphere of a smaller, less congested town. Some people prefer to stay where the action is.

B&Bs, Hotels & Inns

Some of the area's more popular stopovers include the following.

The Beverly Hilton, 9876 Wilshire Blvd., Beverly Hills, ☎ 310/274-7777, is owned by show business entrepreneur Merv Griffin and everything is as expensive as Elizabeth Taylor's jewels. Restaurants include

L'Escoffier, Trader Vic's, the Café Beverly coffee shop, and Mr. H, which serves nothing but buffets.

In Malibu, try **The Malibu Beach Inn**, 22878 Pacific Coast Highway, ☎ 310/456-6444 or 800/462-5428, fax 310/456-1499. The 47 rooms provide fireplaces and private balconies with lovely ocean views.

In Pasadena, you might enjoy the 350-room **Doubletree Hotel Pasadena**, 191 N. Los Robles Ave., ☎ 818/792-2727; the 291-room **Pasadena Hilton**, 150 S. Los Robles Ave., ☎ 818/577-1000; or the posh **Ritz-Carlton Huntington Hotel**, 1401 S. Oak Knoll Ave., ☎ 818/568-3700 or 800/241-333, which offers 383 guests rooms, including six cottages and 22 suites. It sits amid 23 acres of gardens and lush courtyards. If you can't afford to stay at the Ritz-Carlton, at least stop by to admire it.

Santa Monica is one of our favorite stopovers and it has three hotels worth considering.

Channel Road Inn, 219 W. Channel Rd., ☎ 310/459-1920 or 454-7577, fax 310/454-9920, has just 14 guest rooms, all decorated differently. It has a small library and a hillside hot tub, and will provide bicycles for exploring the nearby oceanside bike path. Wine and cheese are served every afternoon. Built in 1910, the inn is just one block from the beach at the Santa Monica Canyon.

The Georgian, 1415 Ocean Ave., ☎ 800/538-8147, is across from Palisades Park on a high bluff above the ocean. Some of the scenes from the film *Get Shorty* were shot here. Housed in an eight-story, art-deco building erected in the 1930s and fully restored in 1994, this mini-hotel has only 84 rooms and suites. The wood-paneled breakfast room downstairs once was a speakeasy, often frequented by actors Charlie Chaplin and Fatty Arbuckle.

The **Hotel Shangri-La**, 1301 Ocean Ave., ☎ 310/394-2791, is similar to The Georgian, just down the street. The 1939 art deco, seven-story building has 55 rooms. Hollywood personalities like Diane Keaton, Bill Murray and Nastassja Kinski frequently stop here and stay for weeks. If you decide to stay here, try to get a room on one of the top two floors, which have balconies with stunning ocean views.

Camping

There is a surprising number of camping opportunities within an easy drive from downtown Los Angeles.

Out of Claremont, for example, campers often head for **San Gabriel Canyon**, ☎ 818/969-1012, which provides campsites at Colbrook, Camp Williams, Follows Camp and Glen Camp. In addition, there is good camping on **Mt. Baldy** (visitor center, ☎ 909/982-2829); at **Crystal Lake** (☎ 818/910-1149); and at **Frank G. Bonelli Regional Park**, 120 Puddingstone Dr. (☎ 909/599-8355).

In the **Santa Monica Mountains**, campers like to visit the **Circle X Ranch** (☎ 310/457-6408).

Topanga State Park can accommodate walk-in camping. ☎ 818/706-1310.

Where To Eat

"He was a bold man that first eat an oyster," commented Jonathan Swift in his *Polite Conversation*, certifying beyond a doubt that an act as simple as dining can indeed be a grand adventure.

OK, so maybe you've had it with oysters. How about a turkeyburger? You can get one at **Fatburger**, 7450 Santa Monica Blvd., West Hollywood, ☎ 213/436-0862.

Not exotic enough? Wrap your mouth around a buffaloburger at **Buffalo Inn**, 1814 W. Foothill Blvd., Upland, ☎ 714/981-5515. Perhaps try some "kick ass" chili at **Thunder Roadhouse**, 8371 Sunset Blvd., West Hollywood, ☎ 213/650-6011, a hang-out for motorcycle afficionados that also serves a wicked sweet potato pie.

If you want something more substantial, try an ostrich steak at the **Villa Villekulla**, 8865 Santa Monica Blvd., West Hollywood, ☎ 310/289-9777. Be sure to tell them we sent you.

Cobalt Cantina, 616 N. Robertson Blvd., ☎ 310/659-8691, serves some terrific sweet potato tamales with their cobalt-blue margaritas, the establishment's trademark.

Maybe you'd just like a quaint little tea room, where you can get a quiet cuppa and relax. We think you'll like **La-Tea-Da**, 21 E. Huntington Dr., Arcadia, ☎ 818/446-9988. Once you've been refreshed by their steaming-hot tea, you can wander through the charming little gift shop.

Of course, some restaurants are unusual because of their decor, as well as their cuisine. Try these.

At **Dive!**, 10250 Santa Monica Blvd., Century City, ☎ 310/788-3483, 64 video monitors make you feel as though you're sitting deep beneath the sea as you munch on one of their 22 hot and cold gourmet subs, a burger, or perhaps a salad.

At **Windows**, 1755 N. Highland Ave., Hollywood, ☎ 213/462-7181, you're dining in a revolving rooftop restaurant on the 23rd floor of a Holiday Inn.

The patio of **The Abbey**, 692 N. Robertson Blvd., West Hollywood, ☎ 310/289-8410, is one of the prettiest outdoor dining spots in town. Surrounded by sculpture and a beautiful fountain, you can play pool, listen to live jazz, update yourself on a cyber computer, or have your fortune told with tarot cards while you wait for dinner to be served.

If the roasted double pork chop with cider-pepper glaze isn't tempting enough to lure you to **The Shed**, 8474 Melrose Ave., West Hollywood,

☎ 213/655-6277, then consider that the building in which you're dining was once the carriage house on silent-screen star Harold Lloyd's fabulous estate.

Gourmet food? But of course!

What Paul Prudhomme is to Cajun cookin' in New Orleans, Wolfgang Puck is to the palates of southern California. Puck's first restaurant, **Spago** at 1114 Horn Ave., West Hollywood, ☎ 310/652-4025, is one of authoress Danielle Steel's favorite eating spots. Try the pizza, risotto or roasted lamb.

How does salad of lobster and crispy salmon skin tossed with peppery daikon shoots sound to you? Or perhaps potato pancakes with golden caviar? Amble on over to The Argyle (formerly the St. Jame's Hotel and sometimes referred to as Sunset Tower) at 8358 Sunset Blvd., ☎ 213/848-6677, and have dinner in the art deco **Fenix** restaurant overlooking the hotel swimming pool. The hotel was a favorite haunt of Raymond Chandler's detective, Philip Marlowe, and it has an illustrious assortment of former tenants, including Jean Harlow, Marilyn Monroe and the Gabor sisters.

This is "Tinseltown," isn't it? "Movieville!" Perhaps you would rather go someplace where you might rub elbows with a celebrity at the next table. If so, you should definitely head for West Hollywood.

Pia Zadora and Billy Zane like to drop into **Urth Caffee**, 8565 Melrose Ave., for a cup of their favorite brew, "Manhattan Mud." Faye Dunaway, Angela Davis and Meg Ryan prefer **Euro Coffee** at 8941 W. Santa Monica Blvd.

Brad Pitt, Lisa Bonet and Mel Gibson like the Mediterranean influence at **LunaPark**, 665 N. Robertson Blvd., ☎ 310/652-5952, listed as one of L.A.'s top 10 restaurants. Sample the shrimp ginger wontons and the butterscotch banana tempura.

Christian Slater and k.d. lang enjoy **The Abbey** (mentioned above), while Madonna, Robert Downey Jr. and Lily Tomlin like **Little Frida's** at 8730 Santa Monica Blvd.

Dinner Theater

Sometimes we like to have some entertainment with our dinner, so we head for a dinner theater. The Los Angeles area has several:

Ben Bollinger's **Candlelight Pavilion Dinner Theater**, 555 W. Foothill Blvd., Claremont, ☎ 909/626-1254, offers shows every day, except Monday and Tuesday. From Wednesday through Saturday, the dinner seating is at 6 pm and the show starts at 8:15. The Sunday seating is at 5 pm and the curtain rises at 7:15. There is a Saturday matinee with seating at 11 am and curtain at 12:45.

Bollinger also presents Musical Murder Mystery dinner shows on Friday and Saturday evenings at **Club Musique**, ☎ 909/625-5342, at

Baldwin's Restaurant in The Claremont Inn next door, ☎ 909/626-2411 or 800/854-5733. The Friday seating is at 7 and the Saturday seating is at 6:30.

The newest dinner theater (and magic club) in the Greater Los Angeles area is **Wizardz**, 1000 Universal Center Dr., CityWalk, #217, Universal City, ☎ 818/506-0066, fax 818/506-1616. Wizardz is actually a conglomeration of entertainment, including **Spiritz**, a fortune tellers' bar; **Vizions**, a psychic reading room; the **Magic Potionz Bar**, where magicians perform at your table; and **The Theater of Illuzionz**, which presents magic and laser light shows.

Nightlife

After dinner, why not sample a little nightlife before you turn in? Heck, this is California! And what is California without a little nightlife?

Besides, the Los Angeles area is famous for its comedy clubs, and you really ought to try one.

We suggest **Serendipity Entertainment**, 1100 W. Clark St., Burbank, ☎ 818/557-0505; **Laugh Factory**, 8001 Sunset Blvd., Hollywood, ☎ 213/656-1336; **The Comedy Store**, 8433 Sunset Blvd., West Hollywood, ☎ 213/650-6268; or **The Ice House**, 24 N. Mentor Ave., Pasadena, ☎ 818/577-1894.

North to San Simeon

Everyone knows the feeling of relief associated with watching "the big city" disappear behind you in the rear view mirror... and the anticipation that can grip you as you head for a serene rural countryside.

Nowhere are these sensations more strongly felt than they are as you head north out of Greater Los Angeles on scenic US 101 toward the sandy beaches, golden hills and verdant fields of flowers and vineyards along the coast toward San Simeon.

Concentrating on the highway is increasingly difficult as you are constantly distracted by the sandy, sun-drenched beaches, the surf pounding against the rocky coast, hillsides totally bedecked in flowers of every imaginable color, vineyards stretching for as far as the eye can see, and quaint little communities, lazily watching the time go by while God tends to the crops.

This is a beautiful, peaceful place to be – a lovely stretch of California coast tucked snugly between the mountains and the sea. With slight variations, it is the route followed by the Spanish conquistadors in the 18th century – the glorious *El Camino Real*.

Getting Around

Mountains are never far from the coastline, so travel in this region runs primarily in a north-south direction. The major link between Los Angeles and San Francisco, the state's two major cities, is US 101, which is paralleled in several places by the less frenetic and much more scenic Highway 1.

When speed is not paramount, we recommend using Highway 1, particulary between Malibu and Oxnard, between Gaviota and Arroyo Grande, and from San Luis Obispo northward. The drive along the coast from San Simeon to the Monterey Peninsula is nothing less than spectacular.

Once past Ventura, there is little reason to go inland through the mountains, and there are only five routes to follow should you choose to do so: Route 33 from north of Ventura, Route 166 from Santa Maria, Route 58 from Santa Margarita, Route 41 from Templeton, and Route 48 from Paso Robles.

All but Route 41 head more or less toward Bakersfield. Route 41 goes northward toward Fresno.

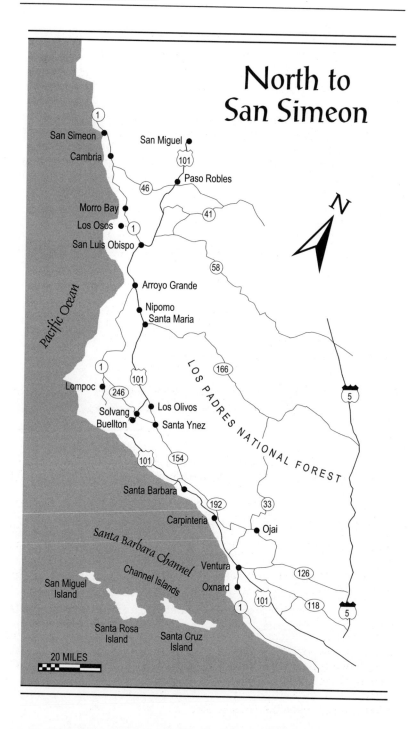

North to
San Simeon

N

Pacific Ocean

San Simeon
Cambria
Morro Bay
Los Osos
San Luis Obispo
Arroyo Grande
Nipomo
Santa Maria
Lompoc
Solvang
Buellton
Los Olivos
Santa Ynez
Santa Barbara
Carpinteria
Ventura
Oxnard
Ojai

San Miguel
Paso Robles

LOS PADRES NATIONAL FOREST

Santa Barbara Channel
Channel Islands
San Miguel Island
Santa Rosa Island
Santa Cruz Island

20 MILES

Juan Bautista de Anza National Historic Trail

This stretch of road is a part of the projected **Juan Bautista de Anza National Historic Trail**, authorized by Congress in 1990. When completed, it will start in Culiacan, Mexico; travel north through Tubac, Arizona (the oldest community in the American Southwest); turn west to Los Angeles; and then follow El Camino Real north to San Francisco.

Juan Bautista de Anza was captain of the Spanish Royal Presidio at Tubac when the Viceroy of New Spain authorized him to lead an expedition to San Francisco in 1775. De Anza left Tubac with a force of 240 men on October 23 of that year and reached Mission San Gabriel Arcangle on January 4, 1776. He then passed through Mission San Luis Obispo de Toloso and Mission San Antonio de Padua, arriving at Mission San Carlos Borromeo de Carmelo near Monterey, California on March 10, 1776.

The de Anza Trail will be administered by the National Park Service. For more information, contact the **National Park Service**, 600 Harrison St., Suite 600, San Francisco 94107-1372, ☎ 415/744-3968, fax 415/744-3932; or the **Heritage Trails Fund**, Amigos de Anza, 1350 Castle Rock Rd., Walnut Creek 94598, ☎ 510/926-1081, fax 510/937-7661, e-mail htrails@earthlink.net.

Touring

Ventura

The stone-and-adobe **Mission San Buenaventura**, 211 E. Main St., ☎ 805/643-4318, was founded by Father Junipero Serra in 1782 and completed in 1809. Its walls are six feet thick, and it has a picturesque bell tower, a beautiful little cloister garden with a fountain, and a small museum.

Olivas Adobe Historical Park, 4200 Olivas Park Dr., ☎ 805/644-4346, surrounds a two-story hacienda built in 1847. The former home of Don Raimundo Olivas, owner of Rancho San Miguel, is said to be haunted by the ghost of a lady in black.

Another historic home, filled with the original furnishings, is the **Ortega Adobe**, 100 W. Main St., ☎ 805/648-4726, which was built in 1857.

A delightful way of touring the town is with **Classic Horse-Drawn Carriage Rides**, ☎ 805/386-3586.

Historic tours also are conducted by the city's **Office of Cultural Affairs**, ☎ 805/658-4728. They include:

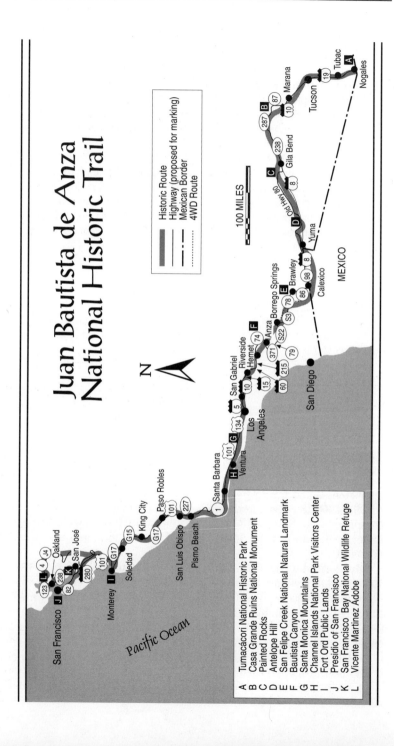

Juan Bautista de Anza National Historic Trail

Historic Route
Highway (proposed for marking)
Mexican Border
4WD Route

N

100 MILES

A   Tumacácori National Historic Park
B   Casa Grande Ruins National Monument
C   Painted Rocks
D   Antelope Hill
E   San Felipe Creek National Natural Landmark
F   Bautista Canyon
G   Santa Monica Mountains
H   Channel Islands National Park Visitors Center
I   Fort Ord Public Lands
J   Presidio of San Francisco
K   San Francisco Bay National Wildlife Refuge
L   Vicente Martinez Adobe

Pacific Ocean

MEXICO

Nogales
Tubac
Tucson
Marana
Gila Bend
Yuma
Calexico
Brawley
Borrego Springs
Anza
Hemet
Riverside
San Gabriel
Los Angeles
San Diego
Ventura
Santa Barbara
Pismo Beach
San Luis Obispo
Paso Robles
King City
Soledad
Monterey
San José
Oakland
San Francisco

★ A one-hour tour of the Olivas Adobe.

★ A one-hour tour of City Hall.

★ A two-hour tour of Perry Mason's Ventura (Erle Stanley Gardner once lived and worked in Ventura).

★ A two-hour tour devoted to "The Mysteries of Main St.," which covers the Albinger Museum, the "mystery of the wooden bells" at the Spanish mission, the former site of Chinatown, the mystery of the lost Taoist Temple, and little-known courts, coffeehouses, bookstores and art galleries.

★ A two-hour "Legends & Lore of Old Ventura" tour that delves into ghosts and poltergeists, Ventura's headless horseman, the phantom lady who cries out in the night, ghosts in the old courthouse, the ghosts at Bella Maggiore Inn, and Cemetery Park.

★ A "Phantoms and Folklore" bus tour.

★ A "Ghosts and Ghouls" tour.

★ The "Chilling Tale of Old Ventura" tour.

Ventura is one of the most popular places to arrange a trip to the **Channel Islands**. Contact the **Ventura Visitors & Convention Bureau**, 89-C S. California St., Ventura 93001, ☎ 805/648-2075 or 800/333-2989, fax 805/648-2150.

Channel Islands

Actually a group of eight islands, the Channel Islands once were occupied by the Chumash (island people) Indians, who had several villages on the northern islands and traded with the mainland Indian tribes. The southern island of Santa Barbara was inhabited by the Gabrielino Indians.

Explorer Juan Rodriguez Cabrillo, who discovered the islands for Spain, wintered here (probably on San Miguel or Santa Rosa, although he called it San Luis) in 1542 and died here. He is believed to have been buried on one of the islands.

As civilization expanded throughout the area, sea otters were hunted almost to extinction for their fur. When that happened, the hunters turned to the seals and sea lions, both for their fur and their oil. During the 1800s, the islands were successfully farmed and ranched. Santa Cruz Island produced sheep, cattle, honey, olives and a fine early California wine. Santa Rosa Island produced wool. In the early 1900s, the Coast Guard (then known as the U.S. Lighthouse Service) settled on Anacapa Island. With the arrival of World War II, the Navy occupied San Miguel Island.

In 1938, President Franklin D. Roosevelt made Santa Barbara and Anacapa a National Monument. In 1976, San Miguel was added, and in

1978, Santa Cruz. Finally, in 1980 Congress designated the four northern islands, Santa Barbara Island, and an area of one nautical mile (125,000 acres) surrounding the islands America's 40th National Park. Later that same year, the ocean for six miles around each island was designated a National Marine Sanctuary.

Anacapa Island is actually three small islands - East, Middle and West Anacapa. Almost five miles long, they are the most accessible of the Channel Islands, generally brown throughout the year, except for the winter, when rains bring out some green. East Anacapa is about a mile long and a quarter-mile wide. There is a ranger there, but no telephone. Arch Rock, a popular landmark, is off the eastern point.

San Miguel Island, eight miles long and four wide, is the group's westernmost island. It is distinguished by two 800-foot rounded hills and a plateau at 500 feet.

Santa Barbara Island is small, just one square mile (640 acres) in size. Triangular in shape, it has two peaks, the highest of which is 635-foot Signal Peak. Indians did not live on this island because it has no fresh water.

Santa Cruz Island, on the other hand, was inhabited by Chumash Indians for more than 6,000 years (as many as 2,000 lived there when Jaun Cabrillo arrived in 1542). It is the group's largest and most diverse island, 24 miles long and providing 77 miles of coastline. The island encompasses 96 square miles (62,000 acres) and has the group's highest mountain (2,400 feet).

Santa Rosa Island, the group's second largest island, is 15 miles long and 10 miles wide, encompassing 84 square miles (53,000 acres).

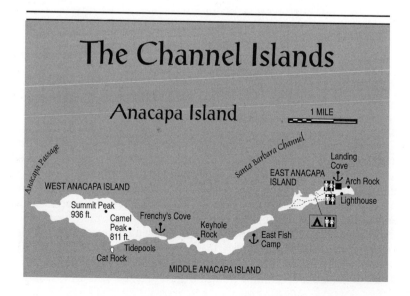

The Channel Islands

Anacapa Island

1 MILE

Anacapa Passage

Santa Barbara Channel

WEST ANACAPA ISLAND

EAST ANACAPA ISLAND

Landing Cove

Arch Rock

Lighthouse

Summit Peak
936 ft.

Camel Peak
811 ft.

Frenchy's Cove

Keyhole Rock

East Fish Camp

Tidepools

Cat Rock

MIDDLE ANACAPA ISLAND

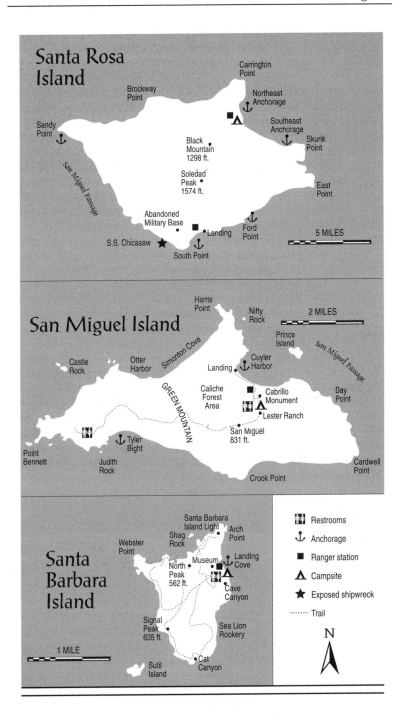

Santa Rosa Island

Carrington Point
Brockway Point
Northeast Anchorage
Southeast Anchorage
Skunk Point
Sandy Point
Black Mountain 1298 ft.
Soledad Peak 1574 ft.
East Point
Abandoned Military Base
S.S. Chicasaw
Landing
Ford Point
South Point
5 MILES
San Miguel Passage

San Miguel Island

Harris Point
Nifty Rock
2 MILES
Prince Island
Castle Rock
Otter Harbor
Simonton Cove
Cuyler Harbor
Landing
Bay Point
San Miguel Passage
GREEN MOUNTAIN
Caliche Forest Area
Cabrillo Monument
Lester Ranch
San Miguel 831 ft.
Point Bennett
Tyler Bight
Judith Rock
Crook Point
Cardwell Point

Santa Barbara Island

Santa Barbara Island Light
Arch Point
Webster Point
Shag Rock
Museum
Landing Cove
North Peak 562 ft.
Cave Canyon
Signal Peak 635 ft.
Sea Lion Rookery
Sutil Island
Cat Canyon
1 MILE

Legend

- 🚻 Restrooms
- ⚓ Anchorage
- ■ Ranger station
- ⛺ Campsite
- ★ Exposed shipwreck
- ----- Trail

N

Experienced kayakers can cross to the islands, but they should exercise extreme caution. Crossing to Anacapa Island can be tricky, and strong currents (the strongest are often encountered near the island), shifting swells and strong winds can turn a three- to four-hour trip into a six-hour struggle. Crossing to the Channel Islands from Oxnard or Ventura takes the kayaker across some of the busiest shipping lanes in California, and the threat of ships speeding along at 25-35 knots and the ever-present possibility of dense fog present a special hazard.

Kayaking Across to the Islands

★ Obtain a Channel Islands National Park map, the Channel Islands National Park *Sea Kayaking* brochure, and the Channel Islands National Marine Sanctuary Synopsis of Regulations map.

★ You must get the required permits. Back country permits are needed for access beyond the beach areas on San Miguel and Santa Rosa Islands. The permits are available free of charge at the park headquarters in Ventura, ☎ 805/658-5700.

★ File a float plan with a responsible party and/or the local harbor master's office.

★ Go properly equipped, which means carrying a compass, air horn/whistle, signal mirror, flares, a portable marine weather radio in a waterproof pouch, a bilge pump or bailing device, a spare paddle or paddle float, a personal flotation device (lifejacket), and a helmet.

If you opt to go in your own boat, refer to National Ocean Survey Charts 18720, 18727, 18728, 18729 and 18756. All rock islets within the park are closed to access above the mean high tide.

Aircraft are not allowed to land on any of the Channel Islands, and fly-overs below 1,000 feet are also illegal.

NOAA weather broadcasts are transmitted out of San Luis Obispo – KIH-31 162.55 MHz – and out of Santa Barbara – KIH-34 162.40 MHz.

Understandably, most people prefer to visit the islands by way of a chartered service. **Island Packers**, 1867 Spinnaker Dr., Ventura 93001, ☎ 805/642-1393, conducts boat trips to the islands, and **Channel Islands Aviation**, 305 Durley Ave., Camarillo 93010, ☎ 805/987-1301, will take you out by air.

For more information, contact **Channel Islands National Park**, 1901 Spinnaker Dr., Ventura 93001-4354, ☎ 805/658-5730.

Ojai

In 1874, Ojai (pronounced OH-hi) was named Nordhoff in honor of author Charles Nordhoff, who was a resident. A high school and a cemetery in town still bear his name. Ojai, a Chumash Indian word, means "moon."

Bart's Corner, 302 W. Matilija St., ☎ 805/646-3755, is at the corner of Matilija and Cañada. Covering half a city block, the place is essentially an outdoor bookstore featuring over 100,000 used books. The books are shelved in a maze of rooms and courtyards under an enormous oak tree. After hours, customers pay for the books they take by dropping coins into a slot in the gate.

The **Ojai Community Yellow Bike Program** fights traffic congestion by inviting visitors to park their car and hop on a bright yellow municipally-provided bicycle to explore the town. **Pink Moment Jeep Tours**, ☎ 805/646-3227, and **Ojai Valley Trolley**, which runs Monday through Friday 7:15 to 5:40 and on Saturday and Sunday 9 to 5, provide other sightseeing opportunities.

For more information, contact **Ojai Valley Chamber of Commerce**, 338 E. Ojai Ave., PO Box 1134, Ojai 93024, ☎ 805/646-8126, fax 805/646-9762.

Oxnard

Oxnard is another popular point from which to reach the **Channel Islands**. An aggressive public arts program has garnished the city with numerous sculptures. Contact the **Greater Oxnard & Harbor Tourism Bureau**, 200 W. Seventh St., Oxnard 93030, ☎ 805/385-7545 or 800/269-6273, fax 805/385-7452; or the **Channel Islands Harbor Visitor Center**, 3810 W. Channel Islands Blvd., Suite G, Oxnard 93035, ☎ 805/985-4852 or 800/994-4852, fax 805/985-7952.

Santa Barbara

History dominates the beautiful city of Santa Barbara in the form of **Old Mission Santa Barbara**, located at the upper end of Laguna St., ☎ 805/682-4713. Founded in 1786 as the tenth in a string of Spanish missions connected by El Camino Real, it is often referred to as the "Queen of the Missions" for its lovely facade and its unusual bell towers. It is the only mission to have *two* towers. Inside the church is an interesting little museum.

El Presidio State Historic Park, 122 E. Canon Perdido St., ☎ 805/969-9719, preserves the last *presidio* (garrison) built by Spain. One of four constructed along the California coast, the *presidio* was founded in 1782.

Presidio Days are celebrated each April, and a traditional shepherds' play, *Una Pastorela*, is presented each December.

At one time, Santa Barbara was the world's film capital. Before the industry settled in Hollywood, the American Film Co. opened the Flying A Studios at the corner of State and Mission Sts. here. For many years, it was the largest studio in the world.

Mary Pickford once owned some property in the Santa Barbara hills, and in 1928 Charlie Chaplin built the Montecito (little mountain) Inn to cater to the movie crowd. Actor Ronald Coleman bought the San Ysidro Ranch resort to entertain such guests as William Powell and Jean Harlow.

The beachfront Miramar Hotel originally was the home of Josiah Doulton, a member of the British family that manufactures Royal Doulton porcelain china.

Nexxus, Big Dogs, Carrows, Lockheed and Motel 6 all got their start in Santa Barbara, now the home of mystery novelist Sue Grafton.

The city takes pride in the **Santa Barbara County Courthouse**, Anacapa and Anapamu Sts., a Spanish-Moorish architecture that rose from the rubble of a 1925 earthquake. The courthouse has hand-painted ceilings, imported carved tiles, a magnificent 80-foot-tall clocktower, and some adjacent sunken gardens.

Santa Barbara Botanic Garden, 1212 Mission Canyon Rd., ☎ 805/682-4726, showcases over 1,000 species of indigenous California plants. There are 5½ miles of trails and an historic dam that was built by the Indians in 1806.

From Santa Barbara northward, wineries and vineyards begin to dot the landscape. Countywide, nearly 10,000 acres are planted in wine grapes.

INFORMATION SOURCES

Visitors Information Center, Cabrillo Blvd., ☎ 805/965-3021.

Santa Barbara Chamber of Commerce, 504 State St., ☎ 805/965-3023.

Santa Barbara Convention & Visitors Bureau, 12 E. Cabrillo St., Santa Barbara 93101, ☎ 805/966-9222, fax 805/966-1728.

Santa Barbara County Vintners' Assn., PO Box 1558, Santa Ynez 93460-1558, ☎ 805/688-0881 or 800/218-0881, fax 805/686-5881.

Buellton

The former Buell Ranch between Lompoc and Solvang was once served by a post office officially listed as Child's Station. It didn't become a city until 1992.

Tucked away amid the area's numerous wineries is **Ostrich Land,** 610 E. Highway 246, ☎ 805/686-9696, which raises ostriches for their meat (it tastes like lean beef but is lower in fat and cholesterol). The average bird produces 100 pounds of meat. The farm also uses the birds' hides (ostrich leather is supple but very durable); their feathers (each bird produces about 1½ lbs per season); their eggs, which weigh between three and four pounds apiece (equal to 25 chicken eggs); and their chicks (a pair of ostriches will produce about 50 offspring each year).

For more information, contact **visitors information center,** 376 Avenue of the Flags, PO Box 231, Buellton 93427, ☎ 805/688-7829 or 800/324-3800, fax 805/688-5399.

Carpinteria

It was in the home of Judge Clinton P. Moore at 919 Maple Ave. that actor Charlie Chaplin married Oona O'Neill, the daughter of playwright Eugene O'Neill, in a secret ceremony in 1943.

It also was in Carpinteria that a seaman returning from South America in the late 1860s showed his brother, Robert McAlister, some flat white beans that the ship's cook had served at dinner and told him that the beans were named for the capital of Peru, where they were a common crop. McAlister distributed a 10-lb bag of the beans among his friends... and Carpinteria became the first place in the United States to grow lima beans commercially.

It is a fitting story, because agriculture is a mainstay of the economy in Carpinteria. From US 101, row upon row of greenhouses can be seen. There are enough in the county to cover 933 football fields.

But lima beans, wine grapes and flowers are not Carpinteria's sole crop. People who visit during the first weekend in October can attend the annual **California Avocado Festival,** ☎ 805/684-0038. Held along Linden Ave., this event celebrates virtually *anything* that can be made from avocados. There is the world's largest bowl of guacamole dip and even avocado ice cream. There are over 100 arts and crafts booths, many of them featuring products hand-carved from avocado pits. And there are prizes for the biggest avocado and for the best avocado recipes.

Some 5,300 Chumash Indians currently live between Carpinteria and Santa Ynez.

For additional information, contact **Carpinteria Valley Chamber of Commerce,** 5320 Carpinteria Ave., Suite J, PO Box 956, Carpinteria 93014, ☎ 805/684-5479, fax 805/684-3477.

Los Olivos

If this place looks familiar, it may be because Los Olivos was the setting for the movie *Return to Mayberry*.

Among the area's wineries is the **Fess Parker Winery & Vineyard**, 6200 Foxen Canyon Rd., ☎ 805/688-1545 or 800/841-1104, fax 805/686-1130. Parker is the actor who portrayed Davy Crockett in the early television series.

Santa Ynez

Route 154, which crosses the Santa Ynez River between US 101 and Santa Ynez, has been designated a state scenic route.

Residents of the valley include Michael Jackson, Fess Parker, Jimmy Connors, James Garner, John Forsythe, Rona Barrett, Efrem Zimbalist Jr., John and Bo Derek, Cheryl Ladd, Steven Segal, Bob Eubanks and Doc Severinsen.

Nearby is the **Santa Ynez Indian Reservation**.

Harms Ostrich Farm, ☎ 805/688-6262, fax 805/688-6262, and **Ostrich World**, 43229 Baseline Ave., ☎ 805/686-1788, produce ostriches that grow to 8½ feet tall and weigh as much as 350 lbs. Ostriches can run faster than any two-legged animal on earth – up to 45 mph.

While there are vineyards and wineries here, the area also has numerous apple orchards which produce bountiful harvests of royal galas, red delicious, golden delicious, Fuji, granny smith, empire, jonagold, crispin (Mutsu) and winesap apples. To get the flavor of the orchards (pun intended), take Highway 246 west from Santa Ynez to Alamo Pintado Rd. and turn right. There, you will find **Apple Lane**, 1200 Alamo Pintado Rd., Solvang, ☎ 805/688-5481. Continue north to Baseline Ave. and turn right (east) to **Ballard Apple Farm**, 2599 Baseline Ave., Solvang, ☎ 805/688-2968, then return to Alamo Pintado Rd. and turn right to find **Greenhaven Orchard**, 2275 Alamo Pintado Rd., Solvang, ☎ 805/688-3141. Continue north on Alamo Pintado Rd. to Roblar Rd. and turn right (east). Cross Highway 154 and turn left (north) on Calzada Ave. **Golden Hills Orchards** are at 2610 Calzada Ave., ☎ 805/688-5928. Return to Roblar Rd., take a left (east), and watch for Long Canyon Rd. on the left. Turn up Long Canyon Rd., then make a left into Stag Canyon to reach **Country Harvest Apple Orchard**, 2425 Stag Canyon Rd., ☎ 805/688-9377. Return to Roblar Rd. and make a left. At Mora Ave., turn right (south) and go to Baseline Ave. Turn right onto Baseline for **Loyal's Family Farm**, 4235 Baseline Ave., ☎ 805/688-7092. Now continue west to Edison and turn left (south). At Olive St., turn left (east), and go to Meadowvale. Turn left again. **Mueller's Apple Farm** is at 1420 Meadowvale Rd., ☎ 805/688-7092.

For more information, contact **Santa Ynez Valley Apple Growers Assn.**, PO Box 562, Santa Ynez 93460.

Solvang

Looking like a typical Danish community, Solvang (Danish for "sunny field") is one of the most colorful towns in southern California. Founded in 1911, the village has a population of less than 5,000, yet it plays host to more than two million visitors each year.

There are storks atop the chimneys (a symbol of good luck) and *Nissermen* (Danish Christmas elves) on the rooftops. The gas streetlights came from Copenhagen.

Many of the town's buildings have half-timbered walls (*bindingsvaerk*). Some have simulated thatch roofs and others feature copper roofs; many have stained glass windows. A few of the sidewalks are made of cobblestone.

The citizens of Solvang still engage in *Rejsegilde*, a celebration held when the highest rafter of a new building is raised.

Denmark's most recognizable feature, the windmill.
Credit: Solvang Tourist Bureau

Visitors can eat *aebleskiver*, ball-shaped pancakes about three inches in diameter that are sprinkled with powdered sugar and drizzled with raspberry jam. The dish is served at the **Greenhouse Café**, 487 Atterdag Rd. in Petersen Village, ☎ 805/688-8408, and at **Little Mermaid**, 1546 Mission Dr., ☎ 805/688-6141.

You also can eat *medisterpolse*, a Danish sausage, and *frika-dellers*, Danish meatballs, washing them down with Danse-Skjold, Solvang's first original microbrewed beer.

Bethania Lutheran Church, built in 1928, is a Danish-styled place of worship. Its interior is adorned with a hand-carved altar, altar rail and pulpit. The scale model of a Danish sailing ship hangs from the ceiling. Nearby is a chiming windharp.

Hans Christian Andersen is well represented here. **Hans Christian Andersen Park**, on Atterdag Dr., ☎ 805/688-PLAY, has tennis courts, a fitness track and a playground. And at **Hans Christian Andersen Square**, you can rent a remote-controlled boat to sail on the pond. There also is a **Hans Christian Andersen Museum** at 1680 Mission Dr., ☎ 805/688-2052, above the Book Loft.

Danish folk-dancing in the streets.
Credit: Solvang Tourist Bureau

Solvang residents enjoy their holidays. In February, storytellers from around the world compete in the **Flying Leap Storytelling Festival**, ☎ 805/688-9533. In April, the **Gourmet Century Bike Ride**, ☎ 805/688-6385, is a 100K bike ride through Santa Ynez Valley with stops to sample gourmet food along the way. **Danish Days**, ☎ 805/686-9386, is a weekend celebration held in August. The festival includes colorful street dances in Danish costumes while street artists engage in *Gade Maling*, a Danish form of chalk art.

Nearby **Santa Ynes Mission**, 1760 Mission Dr., ☎ 805/688-4815 or 688-7889, was dedicated in 1804. It was the 19th of California's 21 Spanish missions, and the mission cemetery contains 1,700 unmarked Indian graves. Partially destroyed by an earthquake in 1812, the mission has remained in continuous use since 1817.

Inside, there is possibly the finest collection of paintings in any California mission, as well as a show of 16th-century vestments, including one actually worn by Father Junipero Serra. A half-hour tape talks you through a self-guided tour of the premises.

Mission Santa Ynez.
Credit: Solvang Tourist Bureau

For more information, contact the **visitor center**, 1511 A Mission Dr., Solvang, ☎ 800/468-6765. Be sure to pick up a free postcard and mail it home to all your friends and family.

You can also get information at the **Solvang Conference & Visitors Bureau**, PO Box 70, Solvang 93464, ☎ 805/ 688-6144, 686-1991 or 800/ 468-6765, fax 805/688-8620.

Summerland

This interesting little community was founded by a religious group called The Spiritualists in the 1840s. The group had a strong belief in the presence and power of ghosts.

That belief might well have seemed reasonable in the 1890s, when youngsters playing baseball along Lillie Ave. discovered that they could pound pipes into the ground, touch a match to the escaping gas, and continue playing their games long after dark. Predictably, this led to the discovery of oil in Summerland in 1895, and by the early 1900s, wooden derricks covered most of the nearby beach. The area gained the dubious distinction of having the world's first offshore oil wells.

Blue Sky Tours, ☎ 805/564-1811, conducts mini-bus tours to the wineries around Solvang, Santa Barbara and Santa Ynez.

Santa Maria

Known as Central City until 1882 when the narrow-gauge Pacific Coast Railroad arrived from San Luis Obispo, Santa Maria is a busy town. The **Santa Barbara County Vintners Festival**, ☎ 805/688-0881, and the **Strawberry Festival**, ☎ 805/925-8824, are celebrated in April, and the **Santa Barbara County Fair**, ☎ 805/925-8824, in June. In October, the city hosts the annual **Grapes & Grains Festival**, ☎ 805/925-2403, and in December, **La Purisima Mission Founding Day**.

The magnificent **Gamboa Flower Fields** line US 101 at Betteravia Rd., and are ablaze with the color of giant ranunculus from April through May.

Santa Maria Valley Historical Society Museum, 616 S. Broadway, ☎ 805/922-3130, boasts a **Barbecue Hall of Fame**.

For information, contact **Santa Maria Chamber of Commerce**, 614 S. Broadway, Santa Maria 93454-5111, ☎ 805/925-2403 or 800/331-3779, fax 805/928-7559, e-mail smvcc@santamaria.com, Web site www.santamaria.com. Ask for a Wine Trail Map to guide you through the local vineyards.

Lompoc

Lompoc (pronounced LOM-poke) is the Flower Seed Capital of the World. It sits in a valley 12 miles long and three miles wide and offers a number of wineries – something of a heresy for a community that began as a temperance colony.

Of California's 21 historic Spanish missions, just three are protected within the state park system. **La Purisima Mission State Historic Park**, 2295 Purisima Rd., ☎ 805/733-1303 or 733-3713, is one of the three. The

11th mission to be built, Mission La Purisima Concepcion de Maria Santisima was dedicated in 1787, but in 1812, El Año de los Temlores (The Year of the Earthquakes), the original mission was destroyed. In 1813, four miles north of the original site, construction was begun on a replacement, and the new mission was completed in 1818. Abandoned in 1834, the mission sat idle for an entire century, but in 1934 restoration was begun by the Civilian Conservation Corps (CCC), which made the adobe bricks and the roof and floor tiles by hand. Nine of the original buildings and more than 37 rooms have been completely restored and furnished. Trained docents lead nature walks on the second Sunday of each month and demonstrate pioneer methods of weaving and candlemaking.

Today, flower seeds are Lompoc's primary claim to fame. More flower seeds come from here than any other place – over one-third of the world's supply. Lompoc's flower fields cover 1,600 acres. Lompoc growers sell almost $7 million worth of seeds a year, and develop at least half of the 25-50 new varieties that are introduced each year.

Throughout town are a number of colorful murals, part of a project that began in 1988. The Chamber of Commerce has a free map that will lead you on a self-guided tour past 23 of them.

- ★ *The Lighthouse* at 400 W. Ocean Ave.
- ★ *Lost Mission* at South H St. and Cypress Ave.
- ★ *Main Street 1900-1930* at 100 South E St.
- ★ *La Purisima Mission* at 206 E. Ocean Ave.
- ★ *Chumash Indians* at 126 E. Ocean Ave.
- ★ *Steelhead Fishing* at 123 W. Ocean Ave.
- ★ *Domingos Blacksmith Shop* at 126 W. Walnut Ave.
- ★ *The Old West* at 832 E. Ocean Ave.
- ★ *Salute to Aerospace* at State Hwys. 1 & 246.

In mid-February, a **Chocoholic Festival** (our kinda thing!), ☎ 805/733-4567, is held in the Grange Hall.

For additional information, contact **Lompoc Valley Chamber of Commerce**, 111 South I St., PO Box 626, Lompoc 93438-0626, ☎ 805/736-4567, fax 805/737-0453, Web site www.lompoc.com.

Nipomo

From the Chumash Indian word *nipomah*, meaning "at the foot of the hills," Nipomo's most interesting attraction is the 13-room **Casa de Dana** adobe at 671 Oakglen, built by mission Indians in 1839. The house became the home of William Goodwin Dana, a sea captain who founded the town. Dana was a cousin of author Richard Henry Dana, who wrote *Two Years Before the Mast*.

For more information, contact **Nipomo Chamber of Commerce**, PO Box 386, Nipomo 93444, ☎ 805/929-1583, fax 805/929-1583.

San Luis Obispo

Mission **San Luis Obispo de Tolosa**, 782 Monterey St., ☎ 805/543-6850 or 543-2034, was named after a 13th-century French saint, the Bishop of Toulouse. It was founded by Father Junipero Serra in 1772 and was the fifth in the string of 21 California missions.

The town is the home of **California State Polytechnic University** (Cal Poly), ☎ 805/756-1111.

In late May, the city hosts an annual **Festival of Beers**, which it cleverly balances off with a **Central California Wine Festival** in late August.

Central Coast Touring Co., 1039 Chorro St., ☎ 805/773-3100 or 781-3090, provides tours of the city, the North County wine country, the South County wine country, and Hearst Castle.

INFORMATION SOURCES

San Luis Obispo Visitors & Conference Bureau, 1037 Mill St., San Luis Obispo 93401, ☎ 805/541-8000 or 800/634-1414, fax 805/543-9498.

San Luis Obispo Chamber of Commerce, 1039 Chorro St., San Luis Obispo 93401, ☎ 805/781-2777 or 543-1323.

Central Coast Tourism Council, PO Box 14011, San Luis Obispo 93406-4011, ☎ 805/544-0241, fax 805/544-0241.

Arroyo Grande

Arroyo Grande (big ditch) offers an interesting walk through the old downtown area, where the buildings date back to the late 1800s.

A self-guided wine tour stops at **Talley Vineyards**, 3031 Lopez Dr., ☎ 805/489-0446, which occupies the historic El Rincon adobe; **Edna Valley Vineyard**, 2585 Biddle Ranch Rd., in nearby San Luis Obispo, ☎ 805/544-9495, which offers tours of its underground cellars and has a lovely herb garden; and **Alban Vineyards**, 8575 Orcutt Rd., ☎ 805/546-0305, the first American winery established exclusively for the production of Rhone varietals.

INFORMATION SOURCES

Edna Valley Arroyo Grande Vintners Assn., 2195 Corbett Canyon Rd., Arroyo Grande 93420, ☎ 805/541-5868, Web site www.thegrid.com/vintners.
Arroyo Grande Chamber of Commerce, 800 W. Branch St., Arroyo Grande 93420, ☎ 805/489-1488.
Arroyo Grande Village Improvement Assn., PO Box 1526, Arroyo Grande 93421, ☎ 805/473-2250.

Atascadero

Atascadero (pronounced Ah-task-ah-dare-oh) was originally the home of the Salinan Indians. Nestled in the oak-studded Santa Lucia Mountains, it is the second largest city in San Luis Obispo County.

Tom Mix once filmed a movie here. Sally Rand once danced in the local theater.

The nearby Salinas River is one of the few northward-flowing streams in the Northern Hemisphere. It also is one of the world's largest underground rivers.

➡ *NOTE: A caution for motorists: Sometimes early morning and late evening coastal fog comes over the Santa Lucia range, making visibility difficult.*

For added information, contact **Atascadero Chamber of Commerce**, 6550 El Camino Real, Atascadero 93422, ☎ 805/466-2044, fax 805/466-9218.

Cayucos

Once a part of the 8,845-acre Rancho Moro y Cayucos Spanish land grant, Cayucos is the name of a kayak or canoe once used by the Aleut Indians for hunting sea otters along this coast.

The town was a stagecoach stop, a cattle town and a thriving seaport. The old **Cayucos Tavern** once was the meeting place for gamblers and seafarers.

Colorful wall murals are scattered throughout the town. For more information, contact **Cayucos Chamber of Commerce**, 241 S. Ocean Ave., PO Box 141, Cayucos 93430, ☎ 805/995-1200, 995-2133 or 800/563-1878.

Los Osos

In 1769, Father Crespi named this region La Cañada de Los Osos (The Valley of the Bears).

Much of the movie *Pete's Dragon* was shot in a cave in nearby **Spooner's Cove**.

For more information, contact **Los Osos/Baywood Park Chamber of Commerce**, 1188-A Los Osos Valley Rd., PO Box 6282, Los Osos 93412-6282, ☎ 805/528-4884.

Morro Bay

Morro Bay's signature landmark is 576-foot **Morro Rock**, "The Gibraltar of the Pacific," the last in a chain of extinct volcanoes that includes **Black Hill**; 911-foot **Cabrillo Peak** that stands in Morro Bay State Park; 1,404-foot **Hollister Peak** (of deep religious significance to the Chumash Indians); 1,306-foot **Cerro Romauldo**, which was named for an Indian; 1,257-foot **Chumash Peak**, source of the rock used to build nearby Cuesta College; 1,559-foot **Bishop Peak**, whose quarries provided the rock for the foundations, curbing and buildings in San Luis Obispo; 1,292-foot **Cerro San Luis**; and 777-foot **Islay Hill**, which is situated near the county airport.

Otters often raft in the channel at Morro Bay.

At **Centennial Park** on the Embarcadero, ☎ 805/772-6278, is a giant chess board, 16 feet square, one of only 12 in the world. Each redwood chess piece weighs 18 to 20 pounds. If you need some competition, contact the Parks & Recreation **Chess Club**, ☎ 805/772-6278. It holds meetings here every Saturday between noon and 5 pm.

For more information, contact **Morro Bay Chamber of Commerce**, 880 Main St., PO Box 876, Morro Bay 93443, ☎ 805/772-4467 or 800/231-0592, fax 805/772-6038.

Pismo Beach

Noted throughout the country for its locally grown clams, the Pismo Beach **Clam Festival**, ☎ 805/773-4382, is held every October. A weekend event, the festival celebrates the wedding of Sam and Pam, the clams, and is highlighted by a parade, an arts and crafts fair, a sand sculpture contest, a queen pageant, a kids' carnival and – of course – a clam chowder cook-off.

In July, the city hosts the **World's Worst Poetry** competition.

For additional information, contact **Pismo Beach Conference & Visitors Bureau**, 581-585 Dolliver St., Pismo Beach 93449, ☎ 805/773-4382 or 800/443-7778.

Paso Robles

The popular misconception is that California's magnificent wine industry is limited to Napa, Sonoma and Mendocino Counties north of San Francisco. In reality, several other regions of the state also produce enormous amounts of excellent wine. The coastal region between Los Angeles and San Simeon is one of them. The wine-making history of this area began in 1797 at the Mission San Miguel Arcangel. By 1997, the county was producing $40.7 million worth of wine grapes per year.

Those who have never experienced a trip through the wine country, admiring seemingly endless fields of grapevines, watching the grapes being harvested, touring a winery, and sampling different varieties of wine produced by California's sun and soil, can easily do so here.

From US 101 in Paso Robles, start your self-guided tour of the vineyards by heading west on Adelaida Rd. At 5805, you will encounter **Adelaida Cellars**, ☎ 805/239-8980 or 800/676-1232, fax 805/239-4671, situated on a lovely ranch. Continue west on Adelaida, then turn right at Vineyard Dr. and go to Chimney Rock Rd. At 11240 is **Silver Canyon Estate Wines**, ☎ 805/238-9392 or 800/282-0730.

Next, travel east on Chimney Rock Rd. to Nacimiento Lake Rd. and take a right to **Twin Hills Winery**, 2025 Nacimiento Lake Rd., ☎ 805/238-9148. From there, continue on to **Jardine Ranch's Country Nut House**, 910 Nacimiento Lake Rd., ☎ 805/238-2365, where you can purchase nuts, dried fruits, honey, olives, candles, jams and jellies.

Continue south on Nacimiento Lake Rd. and you will return to Adelaida Rd. Turn left and cross US 101, where the road becomes Highway 46. One mile east of US 101 is **Martin Brothers Winery**, 2610 Buena Vista Dr., ☎ 805/238-2520, which specializes in Italian varietals such as Sangiovese, Gemelli, Vin santo, Primitivo appassito, and Grappa di nebbiolo. You can buy cheeses and other snacks in the winery deli, and seasonal concerts are held in the amphitheater.

About three miles farther east on Highway 46, you will find **Eberle Winery**, ☎ 805/238-9607, where they will take you on a tour of their new wine caves, and another 1.7 miles brings you to **Arciero Winery**, ☎ 805/239-2562. Self-guided tours through the winery's 700 acres of vineyards are available. There is a lovely rose garden, a deli and a gift shop. Another half-mile takes you to **Laura's Vineyard**, 5620 Highway 46 East, ☎ 805/238-6300, and three miles beyond that, **Meridian Vineyards**, 7000 Highway 46 East, ☎ 805/237-6000.

To return to town, either backtrack or, for variety, go east on Highway 46 until you come to Union Rd., take a right, and follow it until it rejoins Highway 46.

Sylvester Winery, 5115 Buena Vista Dr., ☎ 805/227-4000, fax 805/227-6128, operates **Il Treno**, an Italian restaurant in a 1948 Santa Fe Budd dining car, which is a good place to get lunch. The winery also has some Haflinger horses, a rare Austrian breed.

White Rose, ☎ 805/239-8938, will take you on a tour of the wine country in a limousine.

Understandably, wine permeates the Paso Robles community calendar. In mid-March, there is the annual **Zinfandel Weekend**; in May, the **Wine Festival Weekend**; and in mid-October, the **Harvest Wine Fair**.

Of course, there is a good deal more to Paso Robles than wine. Almond orchards are numerous.

Linn's at the Granary, 12th and Riverside, ☎ 805/237-4001, produces preserves, tea, syrup, vinegar, muffins and pies containing olallieberry, an unusual fruit that was developed at Oregon State University in 1949 by crossing a loganberry with a youngberry. The name is an Indian word meaning "blackberry," which is what the fruit looks like. Genetically it's blackberry and European red raspberry.

INFORMATION SOURCES

For more information, contact the **Paso Robles Visitors & Conference Bureau**, 1225 Park St., Paso Robles 93446, ☎ 805/238-0506 or 800/406-4040; or the **Paso Robles Vintners & Growers**, 1940 Spring St., PO Box 324, Paso Robles 93447, ☎ 805/239-8463, fax 805/237-6439, e-mail prcga@aol.com.

Cambria

Cambria is a good place to spend the night when you're visiting the Hearst Castle, but the town has a lot of fascinating tidbits all its own.

The community once was an active seaport and a whaling station. Known at various times as Slabtown, Rosaville, San Simeon and Santa Rosa, the town finally became Cambria in 1869. Today, the village is an artists' colony and a haven for pick-your-own fruit farms.

Shamel Park, adjacent to Moonstone Beach on Windsor, is a good place for shell- and rock-collecting. It also is popular for hiking, kite-flying and soccer, and has a playground, a horseshoe pit and a swimming pool.

Sharon Lovejoy's **Heart's Ease Herb Shop & Gardens**, 4101 Burton Dr., ☎ 805/927-5224 or 800/266-4372, carries botanicals, fresh herbs, everlastings and rare books and prints. Lovejoy writes the "Heart's Ease" column in *Country Living Gardener*, a Hearst publication.

For more about Cambria, contact **Cambria Chamber of Commerce**, 767 Main St., Cambria 93428, ☎ 805/927-3624 or 800/444-4445.

San Miguel

Mission San Miguel Arcangel was the 16th of California's 21 Spanish missions. The local wine industry traces its roots to this mission.

Silver Horse Vineyards, 2995 Pleasant Rd., ☎ 805/467-WINE or 467-9309, raises thoroughbred horses as well as grapes.

San Simeon

William Randolph Hearst's **Hearst Castle** on State Highway 1, ☎ 619/452-1950 or 800/952-5580, is the closest thing America has to a castle. It stands on a rocky knoll (La Cuesta Encantada or "The Enchanted Hill") in the Santa Lucia Mountains, five miles inland and 1,600 feet above San Simeon Bay. Publisher Hearst called his 275,000-acre estate The Ranch.

Now a state park set on 127 acres, the opulent complex contains 165 rooms, 41 fireplaces, 61 bathrooms, two pools, tennis courts, a private zoo and stables.

The Neptune Pool at Hearst Castle.
Credit: Robert Holmes, CA Div. of Tourism

Excavation for the mansion began in 1922 and the house was ready for occupancy in 1927, although additions continued until 1947.

The first buildings completed were the guest cottages: the six-bedroom La Casa del Mar (House of the Sea); the four-bedroom La Casa del Monte (House of the Mountain); and the eight-bedroom La Casa del Sol (House of the Sun).

Done in an Italian Renaissance style, La Casa Grande (The Grand House) covers 60,645 square feet. It has 41 bathrooms and 38 bedrooms. Outside is an 18,665-square-foot Roman pool with golden tiles. It measures 81 feet long.

Tours leave at least hourly between 8:20 am and 3 pm in the winter, and more frequently during the summer and on holidays. Recently, a series of two-hour **Evening Tours**,

☎ 805/927-2020, 619/452-8787 or 800/444-4445, was introduced on Fridays and Saturdays from March through May and from September through December. Docents don 1930s attire and portray Mr. Hearst's guests and staff as they may have appeared during the castle's heyday.

Also new is a 420-seat IMAX theater with a five-story, 70 x 52-foot screen and seven-channel SurroundSound. Next to the park's main entrance, **Hearst Castle Theatre**, ☎ 805/927-6811, fax 805/927-6701, portrays Hearst's life and the construction of his castle in a 40-minute film entitled *Enchanted Castle*.

For more information, contact **San Simeon Chamber of Commerce**, 9511 Hearst Dr., PO Box 1, San Simeon 93452, ☎ 805/927-3500 or 800/342-5613.

Adventures

On Foot

Arroyo Grande

A **Swinging Bridge**, the only one of its kind in California, measures 171 feet long and hangs 40 feet above a creek. Originally built in 1875, the bridge was damaged in 1995 after a storm-struck tree fell on it. The bridge was immediately reconstructed and reopened just four months later.

Buellton

Nojoqui Fall County Park, a few miles south of town on Highway 101, is an 88-acre park with a breathtaking, 160-foot waterfall.

Cambria

Shamel Park has deer, raccoons, bobcats, wild turkeys and mountain lions (careful!). The surrounding hills also hold several abandoned quicksilver (mercury) mines.

Carpinteria

Toro Canyon Park has some excellent hiking trails. It is between Carpinteria and Summerland. Take the Santa Claus exit off US 101 to the frontage road and turn right onto Toro Canyon Rd.

Monte Vista Park, at the end of Ballard Ave., has a nice jogging course with 20 fitness games, a horseshoe pit and a playground.

The early Indians used tar found in **Tar Pits Park** to caulk their plank canoes (*tomols*). In time, cities as far away as San Francisco were paving their streets with Carpinteria asphalt. Between the 1880s and 1915, Alcatraz Asphalt Mines operated on the site. To reach the park, take Concha Loma to Calle Ocho, park, and cross the railroad tracks to the lookout point.

Carpinteria Salt Marsh, ☎ 805/893-4127, covers 230 acres along the coast just west of the city. Historically, the site was known as El Estero (the estuary). **Sandyland**, on the edge of the marsh, was a Bohemian artists' colony in the 1920s.

Carpinteria State Beach Park offers some excellent birdwatching. Look for brown pelicans, gulls, marbled godwits, ravens, banded pigeons, avocets, stilts, curlews and herons.

Channel Islands

Visitors may not proceed beyond the beach areas of West Anacapa Island and Middle Anacapa Island, but on **East Anacapa Island** there is a small visitors center and a 1½-mile self-guided nature trail. The trail loops from the landing to the visitor center, then to Cathedral Cove and back to the landing. There is a lighthouse on the east side of the island that was built in 1932, but visitors are cautioned to stay away from it to avoid serious damage to their hearing should the lighthouse horns become activated. Guided walks and evening programs can be arranged, as can access to Middle Anacapa with a ranger escort.

On **San Miguel Island**, many undisturbed archaeological sites have been discovered. Juan Cabrillo is believed to have died on Cuyler Beach in 1543. San Miguel has a three-mile trail from the Cuyler Harbor to the Cabrillo Monument, Lester Ranch, San Miguel Hill and Caliche Forest, then over Green Mountain and past a dry lakebed to the Adams Cove overlook. A 15-mile hike across the island will take you to Point Bennett where, from an overlook a mile from the beach, thousands of seals, sea lions, elephant seals and northern fur seals can be observed through binoculars.

➡ *NOTE: With two exceptions, you must always hike with a ranger when you are on the island. From the mid-1940s to the mid-1950s, the island was used as a bombing range, and live ordnance still can be found. STAY ON THE TRAILS.*

Stands of giant coreopsis 10 feet tall can be seen on **Santa Barbara Island**, and their tiny, bright-yellow flowers blanket the hillsides in the spring. A permit is not required to land on the island, and there are numerous trails to follow. The self-guided **Canyon View Nature Trail** begins near the ranger station and campground (a trail booklet is available). In the spring, California sea lions breed and pup on the beaches; in the winter, it is the elephant seals. Hiking might afford you a glimpse of the island deer mouse or the threatened island night lizard.

Santa Cruz Island boasts some 600 plant species, nine of which occur *only* on this island. The east end of the island is jointly owned by the National Park Service and private land-owners, but 90% of the island is owned by The Nature Conservancy, which will arrange a day trip. Contact the **Santa Cruz Island Project**, Nature Conservancy, 213 Stearns Wharf, Santa Barbara 933101, ☎ 805/962-9111.

Santa Rosa Island was a cattle ranch from the 1840s to the 1850s, and a sheep ranch from the 1860s to the early 1900s, when cattle were reintroduced. The island is populated by morning glory, mallow, tree poppy, island monkey flower, island manzanita, dudleya and endemic sage. Island oaks can be seen on the slopes and there are two groves of Torrey pines near Beechers Bay. The eastern tip of the island has large freshwater marshes.

➡ *NOTE: Permits are not required to land on the beaches for daytime use, but a back country permit and a ranger escort are required to travel beyond the beach areas.*

Trails include:

★ **Lobo Canyon Trail**, which goes from the mouth of Lobo Canyon, once a Chumash village site, to the mouth of Cow Canyon, which offers some excellent tidepooling (a five-mile round trip).

★ **East Point Trail**, a one-mile round trip into the Torrey pines.

★ **Cherry Canyon Trail**, which offers a view of the interior and Beechers Bay en route to a ranch complex (a four-mile round trip).

Animal life on the island includes Roosevelt elk, island fox, tree frogs, Pacific slender salamanders, gopher snakes, deer mice and the endemic spotted skunk, which is found only on Santa Rosa and Santa Cruz Islands. Visitors should be careful to avoid the seals and sea lions on the beaches, particularly during pupping season (March to July).

More than 500 largely undisturbed archaeological sites have been mapped on Santa Rosa Island, and in 1994 the nearly complete skeleton of a pygmy mammoth was excavated from an eroding sand dune.

Birdwatchers will be delighted at the opportunities to see the California brown pelican, cormorant, Xantus murrelet, western gull and black oystercatcher. The numerous sea caves contain nesting sites for pigeon guillemots and pelagic cormorants from March through July. The snowy plover, proposed for designation as a threatened species, nests on the beaches of San Miguel and Santa Rosa Islands from mid-March to mid-September.

Santa Rosa Island is favored by 195 different species; Santa Cruz Island, 140 land species. The slopes of West Anacapa Island are the nesting place of the California brown pelican, while Western gulls, xantus murrelets, American kestrels, brown pelicans, barn owls, horned larks and meadowlarks can all be seen on Santa Barbara Island.

Guadalupe

The Guadalupe Nipomo Dunes Preserve is located five miles west of town on Main St. (Highway 166), ☎ 805/545-9925. These 3,500 acres of dunes and beach are an excellent place to hike or do some whale-watching.

Two miles farther south is Mussel Rock, a local landmark. To reach Mussel Rock, use the parking lot at the end of West Main St. in Nipomo and walk south along the beach. The round trip will take more than half a day.

Lompoc

Jalama Beach County Park is another good spot for whale-watching. The park harbors such plants as sand verbena, saltbush, sea rocket and beach buckwheat, and such animals as rodents, deer, fox, bobcat and various reptiles.

Nearby Morro Bay State Park, ☎ 800/444-7275, offers a variety of nature walks covering the whale migration (January and February), the great blue heron breeding season (January through June), and the monarch butterfly migration (December to March).

The butterfly migration is spectacular and brings to mind the Chumash Indian myth about the origin of the butterfly:

The Great Spirit created the mountains, the streams, the valleys,
and the plains so that there would be a suitable
place for people to live after he created them.

He created a huge pile of pebbles, painted with marvelous
colors that he borrowed from the rainbow, and scattered
them in the beds of the streams.

So moved was the Great Spirit by the great beauty of
the pebbles that he asked South Wind to breathe life into them.

The pebbles that South Wind touched slowly rose and flew away on
beautiful, rainbow wings, to be called butterflies and moths.

Morro Bay State Park also contains Black Hill, the second in a string of ancient volcanoes known as The Nine Sisters, and the Morro Bay State Park Museum of Natural History, ☎ 805/772-2694, which provides exhibits, lectures, nature walks, videos, puppet shows and tours for school groups.

Del Mar Park, Ironwood and Island Sts., has numerous hiking trails.

Jalama Beach County Park near Lompoc contains travertine, agate, chert, jade, marcasite, fossils and petrified whale bone.

Jalama Beach County Park offers some exciting birdwatching. Contact the La Purisima Chapter of the **Audubon Society,** ☎ 805/733-2499, for suggestions.

Ojai

Ojai Valley Trail follows the route of a century-old rail line that once was used to haul oranges. It links Ojai to Foster Park in Ventura, nine miles south, and is equally popular with walkers, joggers, cyclists and equestrians. The Chamber of Commerce has a map.

Los Padres National Forest is interlaced with 211 miles of scenic hiking trails. Wildlife includes black bear, coyote, mountain lion, bobcat, rattlesnake, red-tailed hawk, golden eagle and Nelson bighorn sheep. Wildflowers include lupine, monkey flower, Matilija poppy, larkspur, Indian paintbrush, purple nightshade, wooly blue curls and prickly phlox.

Matilija Canyon Trail in the 29,600-acre Matilija Wilderness portion of Los Padres National Forest can be reached by driving north of Ojai on Highway 33 for 6.4 miles then turning left into Matilija Canyon Rd. Drive until you reach a locked gate. Hike down the road across private property. About 100 yards after you cross the second stream, the trail will be on your right, entering the wilderness and following a perennial creek. After two miles, you will reach Middle Matilija; after another 3.7 miles, Maple Camp. The trail connects with a dirt road that leads 2.7 miles down Cherry Canyon to Highway 33. The eight-mile hike makes a good overnighter.

Upper Sespe Creek and **Matilija Creek** in Los Padres National Forest have been designated Wild and Scenic Study Rivers. The **San Rafael Wilderness** northwest of Ojai is southern California's largest.

Sespe Condor Sanctuary is in the Sespe Wilderness, a part of Los Padres National Forest northeast of town.

Santa Barbara

Travel Pals, 315 Mellifont Ave., ☎ 805/963-8339, fax 805/966-3811, has Saturday "surprise" outings, which may include mountain picnics, sunset beach walks, winetastings or visits to local artists' studios.

Santa Barbara Native Sun, ☎ 805/898-6745, takes you out for half a day or a full day. You can go hiking, on beach walks, visit historic landmarks, tour the local restaurants or simply sightsee. And they provide door-to-door service.

Santa Barbara Day Hike Excursions, ☎ 805/965-8349, conducts hikes along coastal canyon trails. The hikes usually last about two hours.

Santa Barbara Adventures, 1417 Mountain Ave., ☎ 805/963-8852, offers two- and four-hour hikes.

The region's best rock climbing is in **Rocky Nook Park** behind the mission in Santa Barbara.

The **Andree Clark Bird Refuge**, 1400 E. Cabrillo Blvd., has lovely gardens and a lagoon that are attractive to birds. There is a footpath and bikeway beside the lagoon.

Solvang

Nojoqui Falls County Park on Alisal Rd. offers a pleasant hike up a short canyon trail.

Paso Robles

There are some excellent spots for rockhounds around Paso Robles. For suggestions, contact **Rockhounds**, 940 Park St., Paso Robles, ☎ 805/238-7873.

From early January to early March, there is an annual eagle watch at **Lake San Antonio**.

Atascadero

Atascadero Lake Park, ☎ 805/461-5000, has a marvelous two-mile walkway. To learn what birds are about, contact the local **Audubon Club**, ☎ 805/466-6222.

Goleta

Goleta Slough is famous for its birdwatching opportunities.

Los Osos

Montaña de Oro (Mountain Of Gold) **State Park** offers good birding, as does **Sweet Springs Nature Preserve** in the 600 block of Ramona Ave., a 25-acre freshwater marsh and sanctuary at the edge of the bay.

Morro Bay

There is a Heron Rookery in **Morro Bay State Park** where great blue herons bask among the eucalyptus trees and the monarch butterflies nest between October and March. Unfortunately, people are not allowed to enter the rookery.

Some excellent birding is available, however, at the boat basin in Morro Bay State Park. The best spots are along both sides of the causeway leading to Morro Rock, in the eucalyptus groves north of the museum, at the turnouts overlooking the tidal flats and at the bridge along South Bay Blvd., at **Turri Creek** and the delta along Turri Rd., on **Sunset Terrace** north of the golf course. Also try the beaches, bluffs and creeks of **Montaña de Oro State Park**.

Morro Rock is a nesting place for peregrine falcons, the fastest bird in the world, and you also might catch a glimpse of a kite, a gull-like bird that feeds on rodents.

The **Morro Coast Audubon Society**, PO Box 160, Morro Bay 93442, ☎ 805/528-7182 or 544-1777, can be helpful.

Pismo Beach

Unless you're a bird purist, the monarch butterfly migration can be an interesting corollary. On January and February weekends, butterfly tours are offered in Pismo Beach, and the Morro Bay State Park Museum of Natural History maintains an interpretive trailer at **Pismo State Beach** during the butterfly season.

To view the butterflies, exit US 101 at Grand Ave., turn left and drive to Highway 1, then turn right and look for a trailer with a butterfly sign on it about a mile down the road on your left.

On Horseback

Atascadero

Cerro Alto Recreation Site in Los Padres National Forest, ☎ 805/925-9538, has a steep, well-maintained trail that climbs 1,600 feet through the oak and bay trees.

Pozo Summit, an area that includes some undisturbed Indian sites and the remnants of some old mining camps, offers good riding in the spring and the fall.

Rinconada Trail can be found by taking Highway 58 east, then going right on Pozo Rd. to Rinconada Mine in the town of Pozo. Rides along the **Salinas River** bed around 11665 Viejo Camino are nice in the summer and fall when the bed is dry, but avoid it if it's raining or the bed is wet.

Santa Margarita Lake Regional Park, ☎ 805/438-5485 or 781-5219, has five equestrian trails (ask for a map at the front gate). **Trout Creek Trail** in the Garcia Wilderness near Pozo, is an easy, well-defined, 2½-mile trail that's also good for overnight backpackers.

For indoor sport, there is an equestrian center at **Paloma Park**, 11665 Viego Camino, ☎ 805/461-5000.

Sometimes it's fun to just sit around and *talk* about horses with a friendly group of people. Atascadero abounds with such types. Depending on your special area(s) of interest, you can contact **Wranglerettes Horse Drill Team**, 7785 Aragon Rd., Atascadero, ☎ 805/466-9557; **Cattlewomen of San Luis Obispo County**, ☎ 805/543-2197; **Arabian Horse Assn.**, ☎ 805/238-0576 or 239-7366; the San Luis Obispo Chapter of the

A horseback ride along the beach.
*Credit: San Luis Obispo County
Visitors & Conference Bureau*

California Dressage Soc., ☎ 805/238-3767; **Paint Horse Assn.,** ☎ 805/238-1929; **Quarter Horse Assn.,** ☎ 805/434-1594; **Horsemen's Assn.,** ☎ 805/461-5813 or 466-6521; **Hunter-Jumper Assn.,** ☎ 805/239-2322 or 239-4887; the **Riding Club** at the Paloma Creek Equestrian Center, ☎ 805/227-4536; or **Trail Riders,** ☎ 805/927-5572.

The Atascadero High School has a **Rodeo Team,** ☎ 805/462-0765.

Carpinteria

Santa Barbara Polo & Racquet Club, 3375 Foothill Rd., ☎ 805/684-6683, fax 805/684-8667, holds matches on Sundays at 1 and 3 between April and October. In July and August, the club's "High Goal season" draws top players from around the world.

Goleta

Circle Bar B Stables, 1800 Refugio Rd., ☎ 805/968-3901, gives lessons and rents horses. Sunrise, morning, afternoon and sunset rides are offered, as are half-day lunch rides. Overnight accommodations, ☎ 805/968-1113, provide cabins with fireplaces, a swimming pool, a spa and three meals a day.

Nipomo

Nipomo County Regional Park, a 132-acre park less than a mile west of US 101 (West Tefft St. at Pomeroy Rd.) has an equestrian ring and riding trails.

Ojai

Wachter's, 114 S. Montgomery, ☎ 805/646-4581; **Andria Kidd Training Center,** ☎ 805/525-9220; **Ojai Valley Farms,** 10901 N. Creek Rd., Oak View, ☎ 805/649-5884; **Rancho Royale,** 10480 Creek Rd., Oak View, ☎ 805/649-2755; and **Riverview Ranch,** El Roblar; and Rice Rd., Meiners Oaks, ☎ 805/646-8816, all rent horses.

Rancho Dos Rios, ☎ 805/646-5511, ext. 456, is a stable associated with the Ojai Valley Inn that offers scenic trail rides into the Ojai Mountains, carriage rides, lessons, pony rides and a children's farm for youngsters under eight.

Ojai Valley Arabian Horse Assn. holds a horse show on the first Sunday of each month in Soule County Park, and Ventura County Saddle Club holds a horse show there on the third Sunday of each month.

Paso Robles

The Paint-O-Rama Horse Show in April is followed by the San Luis Obispo Country Quarter Horse Show in mid-May and the Memorial Day Cattle Drive. In early June, there's a Moonlight Trail Drive, and in September, the Arabian Horse Show.

The Rodeo and Cattle Drive comes in April and the annual California Mid-State Fair off Riverside Ave., ☎ 805/238-3565 or 800/909-FAIR, arrives between late July and early August. If you go to the Mid-State Fair, don't miss the pig races!

Just opened is The Stockyard, a Western theme town with a blacksmith shop, gunfighters, draft horses and other Western attractions.

Santa Barbara

Rancho Oso Riding Stables, Star Route Paradise Rd., ☎ 805/683-5110, provides breakfast and lunch rides in Los Padres National Forest.

Solvang

Quicksilver Miniature Horse Ranch, ☎ 805/686-4002, conducts tours.

Buellton

"Souper" 101 Days features a rodeo in mid-October. The celebration also includes a parade, arts and crafts, a Wild West show, a car show and more.

Pismo Beach

The annual Rodeo and Parade is in June.

Santa Maria

The annual Elks Rodeo and Parade, ☎ 805/922-6006, comes in June.

On Wheels

Arroyo Grande

The ride to Pozo requires navigating a difficult mountain road with no shoulders, but a stop at the 1858 **Pozo Saloon** makes it worthwhile. Order a "Pozo martini" – a beer, served in a pint jar and garnished with an olive.

Cayucos

For a nice mountain biking trail, look for a sign indicating the start of Old Creek Rd. The road climbs toward Whale Rock Reservoir and ends at Highway 46. **Santa Rosa Creek Rd.**, which can be dirty and narrow in places, begins there and leads west to Cambria.

Lompoc

The Chamber of Commerce can supply you with a map that will guide you along a 19-mile flower field tour that is ideal for either biking or motoring. Giant delphinium grow five feet tall here and the fields are a virtual rainbow of color during most of the year. Other nice local biking trips include:

★ A 20-mile ride west on Hwyy 246 to the former town of Surf.
★ A 40-mile trip to Buellton on Highway 246 and a return trip on Santa Rosa Rd.
★ A 50-mile, five-hour trail bike ride to Point Sal Beach over the 1,300-foot Casmalia Hills on a dirt road. There are some terrific views, but the walking trail from the parking area to the beach is precipitous.

Particularly enjoyable is Lompoc's annual **Poker Bike Rally**. Instead of a race, participants ride at a leisurely pace to five points throughout the valley. At each place, they pick up a playing card, and at the end of the rally, they see what kind of a poker hand they can come up with. Combinations of poker hands win prizes.

Los Olivos

Pathfinder Tours, ☎ 805/686-1991 or 800/555-4260, fax 805/688-9709, conducts a 19-mile all-downhill bicycle adventure starting at the top of Figueroa Mountain and descending through Los Padres National Forest into town. The fee includes a ride to top of the mountain, the bicycle rental, a helmet, a guide and the services of a support vehicle. "Gourmet" picnics also are available.

Ojai

Scenic mountain, lake and ocean views can be found by cycling Highway 150 past Lake Casitas to US 101 on the coast and then returning by way of Highway 33.

Another nice ride starts at the south end of Ventura St., turns down **Creek Road**, a picturesque country lane that follows a stream shaded by giant oaks and sycamores, and then meets Highway 33 in Oak View.

The **Grand Ave. Loop** heads east on Ojai Ave. (Hwy 150) to Boccali's Restaurant, turns left on Reeves Rd., and goes one mile to McAndrew Rd., where you turn left (north) to Thacher School and then head back to town on Thacher Rd. (Notice the stone walls that surround the citrus groves. They were built by Chinese laborers before the turn of the century.)

A ride up **Meditation Mountain**, 10340 Reeves Rd., provides excellent views of the valley, as does the ride along **Shelf Road** from the end of North Signal St. to Gridley Rd. – a three-mile round trip.

Sisar Canyon Trail, from the end of Sisar Rd. in Upper Ojai Valley along an oak-shaded stream and over the Topa Topa Ridge to Sespe, covers 20 miles.

Breathtaking views of the valley on one side and the ocean and Channel Islands on the other can be enjoyed by beginning at the end of **Sulphur Mountain Rd.** in Upper Ojai and following the ridge road.

Bicycles can be rented at **Bicycles of Ojai**, 108 Canada St., ☎ 805/646-7736; **Bicycle Doctor**, 212 Fox St., ☎ 805/ 646-7554; **Bicycles &**, 108 Canada St., ☎ 805/646-7736; and **Bicycle Coalition**, ☎ 805/640-8732, Web site: www.fishnet.net/_reese3/tcalm.html, e-mail Ojaibikes@aol.com.

The **Ojai Ranger Station**, 1190 E. Ojai Ave., ☎ 805/646-4348, can answer questions and provide you with a free map of the mountain bike trails in Los Padres National Forest.

Pismo Beach

Beach Cycle Rentals, 150 Hinds Ave. next to Pismo Pier, ☎ 805/773-5518, not only rents regular bikes by the hour, day or week, but also rents banana bikes, surreys, wetsuits, boogie boards, surf boards and a variety of other gear.

The newest extreme sport in the area is mountain boarding, a cross between surfing, snowboarding and skateboarding. A mountain board, which looks like a tricycle skate-

ATV riding on Pismo Beach.
Credit: San Luis Obispo County Visitors & Conference Bureau

board on eight-inch tires, maneuvers like a skateboard but is capable of handling rough terrain.

San Luis Obispo

Rinconada Trail is a hiking, mountain biking or horseback trail. Take US 101 north over the Cuesta Grade to the Santa Margarita exit at Highway 58. Go east on Highway 58 until it forks. Take the left fork and continue straight on Pozo Rd. for about 10 miles. Look for a sign that says "Rinconada Trailhead ¼ mile," turn right and go up a short dirt drive to the parking lot.

The well-marked trail begins with a series of steep climbs. Stay left. After a mile, you will be on a narrow, rocky dirt road heading uphill. A single track will appear on the left. Take it to the top for a beautiful view of Lopez Canyon.

At the summit, a trail sign will direct you down a steep, rocky decline. *Be careful!* The trail leads to Hi Mountain Rd., where you have several choices. Downhill to the right will take hikers to the Little Falls and Big Falls trails, both of which are nice. Bikers should turn uphill to the left and climb Hi Mountain Rd. for about a mile, then turn left at the first opportunity, going up a short hill.

The next part of the trail goes downhill with a last short climb, taking you back to the summit. An exit to the right of the small single-track trail that you climbed in the beginning will send you down 1½-miles of twisting single track that will test all of your biking skills. Be careful of hikers and horses!

Alamo Bicycle Touring Co., 1108 Vista del Lago, ☎ 805/781-3830 or 800/540-2453, fax 805/543-2269, conducts two-hour bike tours on the weekends. They provide the bicycle and the gear, arrange for motel/hotel accommodations on long trips, and send a mechanic along in case of breakdowns.

Santa Barbara

Beach Rentals, 22 State St., ☎ 805/966-6733, rents regular, mountain, tandem bikes, and four-wheel cycle surreys. **Downtown Hazards Cycle Sport,** 735 Chapala, ☎ 805/966-3787, also rents bikes. **Cycles 4 Rent,** ☎ 805/966-3804, rents bikes at three locations – 101 State St., 633 E. Cabrillo Blvd., and 1111 E. Cabrillo Blvd. **Open Air Bicycles,** 224 Chapala St., %% 805/963-3717, and **Traffic Solutions,** rent bikes and provide bike path maps. **Pacific Traveller's Supply,** 529 State St., ☎ 805/963-4438, doesn't provide a two-wheel friend, but it can supply you with the map.

Adventure Outdoor Excursion, ☎ 805/963-2248, and **Pedal & Paddle of Santa Barbara,** ☎ 805/687-2912, will sign you up for a cycling tour.

Santa Margarita

Four mountain bike trails ranging from one to nine miles in length begin in **Santa Margarita Lake Park**.

This is also a great town for meeting new friends with similar interests. Contact **Concerned Mountain Bikers**, ☎ 805/438-4361; **North County Bicycle Club**, ☎ 805/434-2298; **Real Riders Mountain Bike Club**, ☎ 805/238-4343; **Rockriders**, ☎ 805/534-9431; or **San Luis Obispo County Bicycle Club**, ☎ 805/438-5837.

Ventura

Surrey Cycle Rentals at the Holiday Inn on Harbor Blvd., ☎ 805/643-1233, rents mountain bikes and four-speed pedal carriages. **Cycles 4 Rent**, 239 W. Main St., ☎ 805/652-0462, rents bicycles, quadricycles, mountain bikes, tandems and three-wheelers.

During the summer, bikes also can be rented at **San Buenaventura State Beach**, ☎ 805/654-4610.

On & In the Water

Arroyo Grande

Lopez Lake offers fishing, boating, camping, hiking and "California's best inland windsurfing."

Trade Winds Dive & Travel, 1355 Grand Ave., ☎ 800/887-2822, and **Scuba Adventures**, 1039 Grand Ave., ☎ 805/473-1111, both offer scuba and snorkeling instruction and rentals.

Atascadero

Lake Nacimiento, ☎ 800/323-3839, and **Lake San Antonio**, ☎ 800/310-2313, both provide swimming, boating, camping and boat rentals, including ski boats and jetskis. Both also offer lodging. Lake Nacimiento is over 17 miles long, covers 5,000 acres, and has 165 miles of shoreline. Lake San Antonio is over 12½ miles long and covers 3,200 acres.

Atascadero Lake Park, 9305 Pismo St., has a mile-long trail that encircles the lake amid the cottonwoods and willows; a pier from which to fish for catfish, bass and trout; and a place to rent paddleboats. It also has volleyball courts, horseshoe pits, a wading pool and a playground.

Avila Beach

At Avila Beach, you can launch your sailboat, kayak or jetski, or you can visit **Avila Beach Sport Fishing**, on Pier 3, Port San Luis, PO Box 899,

☎ 800/714-FISH, where they'll take you out for a half-day or a full day of deep-sea fishing for rock cod, ling and cabazon. The salmon season runs from March to September, and the halibut season from June to August. The company also offers harbor, coastline and lighthouse cruises.

Buellton

Apart from the ocean pier fishing, this area is blessed with some superb freshwater fishing as well. The famous **Lake Casitas** is in nearby Lake County, as is the **Lake Cachuma Recreation Area**, Star Route, Highway 154, Santa Barbara 93105, ☎ 805/688-8780 or 688-4658. While the former is noted nationwide for its bass fishing, the latter offers fishing, boating, eagle-watching, camping and biking.

Stocked with trout from October to May, Lake Cachuma also contains bass, catfish, bluegill, crappie and red-ear perch. It provides equestrian trails and six sites in which to camp horses overnight. There is an interpretive nature center and naturalists conduct tours, including a two-hour trip on the 48-foot *Osprey*, ☎ 805/568-2460 or 688-4515, to watch eagles from November through February and other wildlife from March through October.

Cambria

In Cambria, you can go tidepooling, diving, swimming, windsurfing, kayaking and fishing, as well as birdwatching, hiking, biking and jogging. From late December to early February, the best whale-watching is at **Leffingwell Landing** and at the public parks along **Moonstone Beach Dr.** Leffingwell Landing, at the north end of Moonstone Beach Dr., affords both beach access and great coastline views.

Rock and surf fishing are available along Moonstone Beach and at the wide sandy beach in **William Randolph Hearst State Beach**, seven miles north of town. There also is a fishing pier at the latter, and you can arrange half-day or all-day fishing trips (or whale-watching excursions during the winter) aboard a party boat.

Carpinteria

Its gently-sloping shelf and mild waves make **Carpinteria City Beach**, from the foot of Linden Ave. to Ash St., "the world's safest beach." (Don't worry, they still have lifeguards on duty from 10 am to 6 pm daily.)

Small vessels can be launched off Ash Ave.; there are volleyball courts at Linden Ave.; and bikes, kayaks and beach equipment are available for rent (☎ 805/684-5847).

Day-use parking off Linden St. gives access to **Carpinteria State Beach Park**, 5361 Sixth St., ☎ 805/684-2811 or 800/444-7275. The 48-acre park provides 4,000 feet of ocean frontage noted for saltwater fishing, surfing, swimming, cycling, camping and nature programs. Fishermen surf-cast right off the beach, and there is excellent tidepooling off the east end of the park. The visitor center contains a tidepool aquarium and other exhibits.

Cayucos

Cayucos Beach at the end of Cayucos Dr. is marvelous for beachcombing, hang gliding, skin diving, swimming, surfing, windsurfing, kayaking and fishing. A lifeguard is on duty during the summer.

Particularly good for surf fishing and surfing is **Estero Bay**. **Cass' Wharf** is a free pier for rock fishing.

Channel Islands

Jacques Cousteau once said that the Channel Islands "offer the best diving conditions in the world." It is inconceivable that anyone would argue. There is a wide variety of marine life, including spiny lobster, abalone, hermit crab and mussels. It also includes gray whales, Pacific white-sided dolphins, harbor seals, Steller sea lions, northern elephant seals, California sea lions, northern fur seals and Guadalupe fur seals.

Spiny lobster (*Panulirus interruptus*), locally known as "bugs" in southern California, are abundant around the Channel Islands, on Cortes Bank, on Tanner Bank, and around San Nicholas and San Clemente – the islands slightly farther out. The delicious crustaceans are quick and therefore hard to catch. The technique is to spot the lobster, aim for the back of its carapace (body) or the base of the antennae, pin it firmly to the bottom, and then yank it out of its hole before it can react – all easier said than done. The hunt is more easily accomplished at night when the creatures leave their caves and crevices to forage. Take some sturdy gloves, a "bug" bag, a night light and a backup light. You'll also need a California license. Although the lobster season runs from October to March, the best hunting usually comes between October and December.

January through March is the best season to watch the gray whales near the Channel Islands.

For those operating their own boats, good anchorages include East Fish Camp and, in good weather, Frenchy's Cove.

Fishing in the Channel Islands requires a California license. The landing dock at East Anacapa Island is for loading and unloading only. Boats are not to be moored to the dock, and kayaks must be lifted 10-12 feet onto the dock (a davit is provided). A permit is not required to land at the Landing Cove dock on East Anacapa Island or at French's Cove beach, a popular spot for snorkeling and tidepooling, on West Anacapa.

From January 1 to October 31, the waters approximately a third of a mile from the cliffs facing northeast on **West Anacapa Island** are closed to entry by any craft in order to protect the cliff-side nests of the California brown pelican. There is good diving on the south side of West Anacapa, where there is a rocky bottom, depths of 40-60 feet, and clear water whenever there is a calm southern swell. **Middle Anacapa Island** has two interesting shipwrecks to explore. The steamer *S.S. Winfield Scott*, a 225-foot side paddle-wheeler built in 1851, rammed into the island and sank during a dense midnight fog on December 1, 1853, while attempting to set a San Francisco-to-Panama speed record. The wreck can still be seen. The wreck of the *Equator* lies on the opposite (south) side of the island.

Sea conditions often rough at **San Miguel Island**. There is safe anchorage at Cuyler Harbor on the north side of the island in normal weather and this is the only landing area on the island. On the south side of the island, the best anchorage is at Tyler Bight. Seals and sea lions populate the beaches of San Miguel. For much of the year, watercraft may not approach within 100 yards of the shore from Judith Rock on the south to Castle Rock on the north. Off the island's eastern tip lies the wreck of the *Tortuga*. Off the western tip lies the 307-foot *S.S. Cuba*, a Pacific Mail steamer built in 1879 that sank September 8, 1923 en route from Panama to San Francisco. Off the northwest coast lies the 145-foot *Comet*, a three-masted coast lumber schooner built in 1886 that was sailing from Aberdeen, Washington to San Pedro, California when it hit Wilson Rock on August 30, 1911, drifted through the surf and beached.

Access to **Santa Barbara Island** is permitted only at the landing cove, and anchoring usually is confined to the east side of the island due to the prevailing winds and waves.

There are numerous harbors along the north coast of **Santa Cruz Island** – Potato, Chinese, Prisoner's, Pelican Bay, Twin Harbors, Platts, Fry's, Diablo, Baby's, Lady's, Cueva Valdez and Hazards, progressing from east to west; and along the east end of the island – Scorpion, Little Scorpion, Hungrymans, Smuggler's, Yellowbanks, and Middle, from north to south. Painted Cave is the world's largest underwater cave. The wreck of the *Peacock (Spirit of America)* is off the northeastern point of the island. For permission to land at Smugglers Cove or Scorpion Beach, voice or radio (VHF Channel 16) contact must be made with the National Park Service ranger at Smugglers Cove. A landing permit may be obtained for a fee from **Santa Cruz Island Preserve**, PO Box 23259, Santa Barbara 93121, ☎ 805/962-9111.

Sea conditions around **Santa Rosa Island** are often rough, but the sandy beaches abound with harbor seals. Depending on weather conditions, anchorage is possible in Bechers Bay or at Johnsons Lee. Landing permits are required for travel beyond the beaches at Bechers Bay, Officers Beach and La Jolla Canyon Beach. Shipwrecks found here include the *Goldenhorn*, which sank in 1892; *Crown of England*, which sank in 1894 off Ford Point on the southeast coast; *Aggi*, which sank in 1915 at Talcott Shoal off the northwest coast; *Dora Bluhm* and *S.S. Chickasaw*, 439-foot class C-2 freighters built in 1942 that ran into the south shore of the island during heavy fog while en route from Japan to Los Angeles, then sank between Sandy Point and South Point on the southwest coast on February 7, 1962; and *Jane L. Stanford*, a 215-foot, four-masted barkentine built in 1892 and later converted into a fishing barge that was rammed by the Mail Steamer *Humboldt* on August 30, 1929. The damaged hull of the *Stanford* was set afire, then drifted onto the island near Skunk Point on the northeast point.

To reach the islands from Oxnard, contact **Island Packers**, 3600 S. Harbor Blvd., ☎ 805/642-1393; **Oaars**, ☎ 805/642-2912; or **Pacific Scuba**, 3600 S. Harbor Blvd., ☎ 805/984-2566. The latter runs charter boats for small groups (up to six) and rents scuba equipment.

In Santa Barbara, contact **Paddle Sports**, 100 State St., ☎ 805/899-4925, located just a block from the pier.

From Ventura, contact **Island Packers**, 1867 Spinnaker Dr., Ventura 93001, ☎ 805/642-1393, for either landing or non-landing trips of half-day, full day or multiple-day duration.

For further information, contact **Channel Islands Harbor Visitor Center**, 3810 W. Channel Islands Blvd., Suite G, Oxnard 93035, ☎ 805/644-8262, 658-5730 or 800/994-4852. There are telescopes atop a third-floor tower deck plus free slide, lecture (Saturday and Sunday at 3), movie (*Treasures of the Sea*, a 25-minute color film), and exploratory (tidepool) programs. **Channel Islands National Park**, 1901 Spinnaker Dr., Ventura 93001-4354, ☎ 805/644-8262, 658-5730 or 658-5711, fax 805/658-5799, Web site www.nps.gov/chis/.

For more information about the Nature Conservancy's portion of Santa Cruz Island, contact **Nature Conservancy**, Santa Cruz Island Preserve, PO Box 23259, Santa Barbara 93121, ☎ 805/962-9111.

Grover Beach

Sand sculpting, scuba diving, beach volleyball and fishing for perch, halibut and salmon are all popular in this little community.

Nipomo Dunes State Preserve is nearby (see Nipomo, page 87). For more information, contact **Grover Beach Chamber of Commerce**, 177 S. 8th St., Grover Beach 93433, ☎ 805/489-9091.

Guadalupe

Oso Flaco Lake is one of a dozen freshwater lakes in the dunes northwest of town. It has an 18-mile shoreline and covers 18,000 acres. There also is a marine beach and marshland. Off Highway 1, turn west on Oso Flaco Rd.

To get to the **Nipomo Dunes** from the lake, drive to the end of Oso Flaco Lake Rd., park, and pick up a map at The Nature Conservancy kiosk. Follow the short signed walk to the lake, and from there, take the boardwalk 1.3 miles across the dunes to the beach. From the end of the boardwalk, walk toward the ocean, cross Oso Flaco Creek, then turn inland across the dunes toward the distant green hills (in the summer covered with yellow coreopsis blossoms). The round-trip back to your car will cover five miles.

As an alternate, go south along the beach for about a mile to the state park boundary sign and turn inland into the deep dune hollows.

Guided all-day seven-mile hikes are available to **Hidden Willow Valley**, a secluded spot with willow woodlands tucked between steep dunes, ☎ 805/545-9925. **Bill Denneen**, ☎ 805/929-3647, a local naturalist, also leads hikes into the area.

Lompoc

Jalama Beach County Park, ☎ 805/736-6316 or 736-3504, is 20 miles southwest of town off SR 1 on Jalama Rd. Camping, windsurfing, tidepooling and photography are all popular. Surf fishing produces surf perch, while cabezon, kelp bass and halibut can be caught off the nearby rocks.

Tarantula Point is a good spot for surfing, particularly between April and July when the winds are best. A little store provides a snack bar, bait and tackle.

Morro Bay

Boats can be launched in **Tidelands Park** at the south end of the Embarcadero.

➡ *Morning and evening fog is common, and a calm morning often is followed by afternoon winds. As a rule of thumb, if spray can be seen along the top wall of the western breakwater from inside the harbor, one should be careful about leaving the harbor. And one should never try to beach a boat outside the breakwaters.*

There are over 10 miles of protected shoreline inside the bay. Weather is broadcast over **KUHL** (144 kHz) every hour on the half-hour; over **KSMA** (1240 kHz) at 6:30, 7:30, and 8:30 am; and over **VHF Channel WX1** (162.55 MHz). For other weather information, contact **National Weather Service**, ☎ 805/925-0246 (direct), 925-0909 (recording); **KBAI** radio 1150, ☎ 805/772-4141; or **KSBY-TV**, ☎ 805/541-6666, ext. 25.

Tiger's Folly, 1205 Embarcadero, ☎ 805/772-2257 or 772-2255, is an old sternwheeler that is available for daily one-hour bay cruises, dinner cruises, or cruises with a Sunday champagne brunch.

Sub-Sea Tours, 699 Embarcadero, #9, ☎ 805/772-9463, provides half-hour and 90-minute bay cruises aboard a semisubmersible "submarine," containing two seven-foot glass windows below the waterline. In addition to getting the underwater view, passengers also can walk out on top of the sub.

Lingcod, red snapper, red rockcod, rockcod, cabezon, albacore, shark and salmon can be caught off one of two T-piers.

The marina at **Morro Bay State Park**, ☎ 805/772-8796, located behind the Bayside Café on State Park Rd., will equip a fisherman with a rowboat or a canoe.

Bob's Sport Fishing, 845 Embarcadero, ☎ 805/772-3340, and **Virg's Fish'n**, 1215 Embarcadero, ☎ 805/772-1222 or 800/762-5263, will take you on a fishing excursion. Virg's also operates off the pier in San Simeon, ☎ 805/927-4676.

For something different, you might try fishing from a kayak. **Kayaks of Morro Bay**, 699 Embarcadero, #9, ☎ 805/772-1119, rents kayaks and canoes (including a 25-foot war canoe!). **Barrons Motor-boat Rentals**, 1215 Embarcadero, ☎ 805/772-1368; **Morro Rock Marina**, Embarcadero and Pacific Sts., ☎ 805/772-8085; and **Kayak Horizons**, 551 Embarcadero, ☎ 805/772-6444, also rent kayaks.

To learn how to dive, contact **Depth Perceptions Diving Services**, 3280 Main St., ☎ 805/772-3128. The following all offer access to fishing waters:

Mariner Park at the Embarcadero and **Anchor Memorial Park**. **Tidelands Park** has a boat launch and a children's play area. **Bayshore Bluffs Park**, Main St. and Bayshore Dr., offers hiking trails. **Morro Rock & Beach Area** provides some excellent surfing opportunities. **Morro Strand State Beach**, Yerba Buena St., ☎ 800/444-7275, has swimming and surfing. **Morro Bay State Park** offers canoe rentals, boat and hand launch, campsites, a golf course and driving range, a natural history museum, and nature and walking trails.

Nipomo

Nipomo Dunes, the largest remaining dune system in the nation, stretch from Pismo Beach in the north to Vandenburg Air Force Base in the south, 18 miles of 200-to 500-foot sand hills, seashore, wetlands and tidal marshes.

The best place to access the dunes is from the parking lot at the end of Pier Ave. in Oceano. Walk south half a mile past the mouth of Arroyo Grande Creek and start climbing. This is a good spot to wander among the tall dunes and it is close to Highway 1.

Ojai

Lake Casitas, 11311 Santa Ana Rd. near Oak View, ☎ 805/649-2043 or 649-2232, has a bait and tackle shop and offers boat rentals. The 2,700-acre lake was the site of the 1984 Olympic canoeing and rowing events, and offers good swimming and waterskiing opportunities. The state record largemouth bass was caught here and catfish, crappie and trout also can be taken.

Oxnard

One of the most popular departure points for the **Channel Islands**, ☎ 800/269-6272, this area is also known for its fishing. Blue shark, halibut, marlin, sea bass, swordfish, cod, mackerel, sailfish, smelt, yellowtail, crab, mako, salmon, snapper and yellowfin are all taken here. Annual fishing tournaments include the **Halibut Derby**, the **Firecracker 500 Shark Tournament**, the **Channel Islands Shark Tournament** and the **Billfish Tournament**.

Divers find abalone, mussels, clams, urchins, crab and lobster in these waters, while dolphin, otter, seal, flying fish, porpoises, whales, grunion and sea lions are seen along the coast.

CHARTERS & RENTALS

C.I. Landing Sail & Electric Boats
3821 S. Victoria Ave.   ☎ 805/985-6059
Cisco's Sportfishing
4151 S. Victoria Ave.   ☎ 805/985-8511
Duffield Electric
2950 S. Harbor Blvd.   ☎ 805/984-3366
Easy Cruisin' Electric Boats
2810 S. Harbor Blvd.   ☎ 805/984-4379
Gold Coast Sportfishing
3600 S. Harbor Blvd.   ☎ 805/382-0402
Harbor Hopper
Harborwide Stops   ☎ 805/985-HOPP
Marina Sailing
3600 S. Harbor Blvd.   ☎ 805/985-5219
Offshore Island Sailing
3150 S. Harbor Blvd.   ☎ 805/985-3600

Paso Robles

Lake Nacimiento is 18.6 miles long, has a 165-mile shoreline, and covers 5,379 acres. It contains white bass, largemouth bass, smallmouth bass, catfish, crappie and bluegill.

Lake Nacimiento Resort, Star Rt. 2770, Bradley 93426, ☎ 805/238-1056, has a marina and rental boats – fishing boats, ski boats, pleasure boats, pontoon boats, watersports toys, paddleboats, kayaks and canoes.

Piru

Pyramid Lake Recreation Area in the hills north of Santa Clarita Valley off I-5 is in Angeles National Forest. A snack bar and a marina that offers boat rentals provide outdoor opportunities for fishing and swimming.

Trout, small- and largemouth bass, catfish, striped bass, crappie and bluegill inhabit the lake.

Pismo Beach

Famous as the "Clam Capital of the World," this area produces the succulent Pismo clam, a crustacean that burrows only six inches into the sand and is found at low tide in just one to three feet of water. To enjoy some of these tasty little fellers, get a spade or a special clamming rake (one with 10-inch tines) and dig up some of your own. Mark a 4½" length on the handle of your spade or rake so you can check the size of your catch. Smaller clams must be returned to the sand and reburied *on their edge* with the points of their shell toward the ocean and the tiny dark buttons near the hinges pointing upward.

Some Additional Tips On Clamming

★ Face toward the incoming surf in order to anticipate any big surges.
★ Never dig in water deeper than waist-high.
★ Be sure your clam bags are easily detachable so they don't become an anchor if you should slip.

Clamming is allowed year-round, but there are some protected areas that don't allow it. Ask for local information. The limit is 10 clams per day.

Fishermen can try the pier for red snapper and ling, and tidepooling, kite-flying, horseback riding and sandcastle building are all popular here.

San Luis Obispo

Central Coast Surfboarding, 736 Higuera (pronounced Hi-GARE-ah) St., ☎ 805/541-1129, rents surfboards and snowboards (yes, it's true!).

Ocean Currents, 3121 S. Higuera, Ste. B, ☎ 805/544-7227, is the place to go if you're looking for scuba lessons.

San Simeon

William Randolph Hearst Memorial State Beach on Highway 1 opposite the Hearst Castle has a beach for strolling and a pier for fishing and boating. There is no lifeguard on duty.

Piedras Blancas Lighthouse is four miles north of the castle. It is not open to the public, but is a popular spot for whale-watching from late December to early February, when the whales are heading south, and during March and April, when they are heading north.

Central Coast Adventures, 250 San Simeon Ave., Suite 5-B, ☎ 805/927-4386, located on the Plaza del Cavalier, rents kayaks and mountain bikes and conducts guided tours.

Virg's Landing at William Randolph Hearst State Beach on Highway 1, ☎ 805/927-1777 or 800/ROCKCOD, rents fishing tackle and escorts sportfishing excursions after rockcod, lingcod and red snapper.

Santa Barbara

Surfing in this area centers around Rincon Point, Carpinteria, Leadbetter, Arroyo Burro, Summerland and the University of California Santa Barbara beaches.

Stearns Wharf in the Santa Barbara harbor was built 1872, making it California's oldest working wooden wharf. Plaques explain the wharf's colorful history.

Fishing is excellent both at the wharf and on the breakwater.

Anacapa Dive Center, 22 Anacapa St., ☎ 805/963-8917, provides diving lessons in a heated indoor pool.

Captain Don's Charters and Cruises, 219 Stearns Wharf, ☎ 805/969-5217, conducts 40-minute cruises between 11 am and 5 pm, May through October.

Sunset Kidd Sailing Charters at the breakwater, ☎ 805/962-8222, offers one-hour harbor cruises, two-hour coastline cruises, cocktail and dinner cruises, whale-watching cruises, and sunset and twilight cruises.

Sea Landing Sportfishing, also at the breakwater, ☎ 805/963-3564, fax 805/564-6754, conducts sportfishing, scuba diving, whale-watching, coastal and island excursions.

Santa Barbara Sailing Center & Boat Rentals, at the breakwater, ☎ 805/962-2826, will rent 13- to 53-foot skippered, sail or power boats. They also conduct classes and offer cruises.

Santa Barbara Jet Boats, ☎ 805/962-0887, at the Sailing Center next to the boat-launch ramp, rents boats by the hour and provides the fuel, life vests, wetsuits, safety orientation and lessons. **Jetski Rentals,** also at the Sailing Center near the launch ramp, ☎ 805/962-2826, rents... jetskis, of course.

Captain McCrea's Santa Barbara Sportfishing, at Sea Landing on the breakwater, ☎ 805/569-5866, arranges fishing excursions.

WaveWalker Charters, Gate 3 at the Harbor Marina, ☎ 805/964-2046 or 895-3273, has a 31-foot boat captained by Capt. WaveWalker (aka David Bacon). The boat can be chartered by four to six passengers for fishing, whale-watching, surfing and diving. The captain provides tackle and bait.

Kayak Adventures, ☎ 805/568-9589, is on West Beach behind Sea Landing. The owners rent ocean kayaks equipped with a life vest, a paddle, and a backrest by the hour or day.

Santa Margarita

Santa Margarita Lake Regional Park, ☎ 805/438-5485 or 781-5219, can provide fishing, swimming, boating, hiking, biking, equestrian trails, camping and paintball games.

The **marina**, ☎ 805/438-3886, rents boats, allowing anglers to fish the 22 miles of shoreline for striped bass, trout, catfish, crappie, black bass and bluegill.

A swimming pool is open from Memorial Day weekend to Labor Day weekend.

Shell Beach

The foot of Vista Del Mar St. is a good place to launch a kayak.

San Simeon Cove and the backwaters of **Morro Bay** offer easy kayaking, while more advanced kayakers might prefer the ocean between Cambria and Cayucos or between Montaña de Oro and Port San Luis.

Central Coast Kayaks, 1879 Shell Beach Rd., ☎ 805/773-3500, fax 805/773-9767, Web site www.webmill.com/pismo/kayaks, rents kayaks and provides instruction. They also offer tours (☎ 805/489-7052) from Friday to Sunday, to Refugio, Big Sur, Elkhorn Slough and San Simeon.

Solvang

Zaca Lake, ☎ 805/688-4891, is one of the two natural lakes in southern California. Tucked away into a 320-acre recreational preserve in Los Padres National Forest, the lake offers camping, hiking and rowboating.

Ventura

At 1,200 feet, **Ventura Pier** is the longest wooden pier in California. It was built in 1872 and fully renovated in 1994.

McGrath State Beach, 2211 Harbor Blvd., ☎ 805/654-4744, is 4½ miles southeast of town. Lifeguards protect the two-mile sandy beach and there is a campground, ☎ 800/444-PARK, although it has no hookups.

Surfer's Point is a favorite spot for longboard surfing.

Bay Queen, Slip 14, Ventura Harbor Village, ☎ 805/642-7753, provides 40-minute harbor cruises and dinner cruises, too. The ship once was used to take passengers off the Santa Monica coast to gamble.

Liberty, 1567 Spinnaker Dr., Ste. 203-59, Ventura Harbor, ☎ 805/642-6655 or 818/352-8855, is 84 feet long and 24 feet wide, with 40 single and six double bunks. It is available for three-quarter-day, full-day or multi-day trips, including diving excursions. Available on a similar basis are *Peace*, ☎ 805/658-8286, and *Spectre*, ☎ 805/483-6612.

Duchess III, ☎ 805/642-5402, was built as a prison boat in 1925, used as a hospital boat in Alaska, and ran guns in the Philippines. She also is said to have been operated by Al Capone and his family, and is reputed to be haunted. None the less, the vessel is available for charter – for breakfast, lunch or dinner; for business functions; for tours; or for private parties.

FISHING CHARTERS

Harbor Village Sportfishing	☎ 805/658-1060
Ventura Dive & Sport	☎ 805/650-6500
Ventura Sportfishing Landing	☎ 805/650-1255

Nearby **Lake Casitas Recreation Area**, 11311 Santa Ana Rd., can be reached from US 101 by taking the Highway 33 turnoff to Highway 150 and then turning left to the entrance gate, which is four miles down the road. The 6,200-acre lake has a large island in the middle and is well stocked with trout, bass, channel catfish, red-ear sunfish, crappie and bluegill. In fact, four state records have been set here: Largemouth bass (21 lbs., 3¼ oz.), channel catfish (41 lbs.), red-ear sunfish (3 lbs., 7 oz.), and rainbow trout (9 lbs., 4 oz.)

There is a store, open daily between April 15 and September 15; a snack bar, ☎ 805/649-2514, that is open all year; and a bait and tackle shop, ☎ 805/649-2043, which rents boats.

No swimming or wading is allowed in Lake Casitas. No canoes, kayaks, rafts, inflatables or collapsibles, and no boats with toilets or drains are allowed. Boats between 11 and 24 feet are permitted, but must be at least 48 inches in width, and no boat may travel faster than 40 mph on the lake.

In the Air

Goleta

Petroleum Helicopters, 302 Moffett Pl., ☎ 805/964-0684, takes tours to the Channel Islands and into wine country.

Santa Barbara Airbus, 5755 Thornwood Dr., ☎ 805/964-7759 or 800/733-6354, provides a shuttle to Los Angeles International Airport, as well as flights of a more recreational nature.

Lompoc

The annual **West Coast Piper Cub Fly-In**, ☎ 805/733-1914, is held at Lompoc Airport in mid-July.

Newbury Park

Hot Air Balloon Adventure, 144 Montenegro Circle, ☎ 805/499-4444, arranges balloon trips.

Oceano

Warren E. Crain, ☎ 805/466-5537 or 546-2660, offers flight instruction out of airports in Paso Robles, San Luis Obispo or Santa Maria.

Oxnard

Aspen Helicopter, 2899 W. 5th St., ☎ 805/985-5416, furnishes flights to the Channel Islands.

Paso Robles

Paso Robles Airport, which hosts the annual **Warbirds Air Show,** covers 900 acres, has clear skies 95% of the time, and offers flat terrain for easy approaches.

Estrella Warbird Museum houses 10 acres of vintage aircraft and has just announced plans to add a 4,000-square-foot building to house the Confederate Air Force Estrella Squadron.

At **Antique Aero,** Chuck Wentworth rebuilds and maintains antique aircraft from World Wars I and II in three hangars located off Dry Creek Rd.

Blue Sky Adventures, 4990 Wing Way #B2, ☎ 805/239-3483, offers skydiving. You must be 18 years old or older and weigh less than 220 lbs., and you can't skydive within 48 hours of scuba diving or within 24 hours of giving blood.

San Luis Obispo

Surf the Sky, 1256 Galleon Way, #3, ☎ 805/544-8190, operates paragliding outings.

Santa Barbara

Blue Edge Parasailing, on Stearns Wharf across from the Moby Dick restaurant, ☎ 805/684-0022 or 966-5206, will take you soaring 300-500 feet above the blue Pacific.

SEA Santa Barbara at the breakwater, ☎ 805/963-3564 or 800/932-6556, will take you parasailing, whale-watching or cruising on a yacht. Packages include a motel stay (at the Best Western Beachside Inn) and dinner (at Andria's Harborside Restaurant Oyster & Piano Bar).

Seventh Heaven, 133 Vista de la Cumbre, ☎ 805/687-8459, offers balloon flights.

Heli-Tours, Santa Barbara Airport, ☎ 805/964-0684, will provide tours of the city and harbor or take you to Santa Cruz Island for a picnic. **Channel Islands Adventures,** ☎ 805/987-1301; **Mercury Aviation,** ☎ 805/964-6733; and **Santa Barbara Aviation,** ☎ 805/967-5608, offer similar charters.

Santa Ynez

Windhaven Glider Rides, Santa Ynez Airport, ☎ 805/688-2517, charters flights in a piloted, two-seater sailplane from June through August and from September through May.

Solvang

Helinet Aviation Services, Atterdag and Copenhagen, ☎ 805/686-8313, provides helicopter sightseeing services.

Ventura

Channel Islands Aviation, 305 Durley Ave., Camarillo 93010, ☎ 805/987-1301, fax 805/987-8301, Web site www.flycia.com, makes 25-minute flights from Camarillo Airport to Santa Rosa Island in the Channel Islands group. Daytrips and camping trips also can be arranged.

Eco-Travel/Cultural Excursions

Cambria

Pewter Plough Playhouse, 828 Main St., West Village, Cambria 93428, ☎ 805/927-3877, offers a program of community theater.

Carpinteria

Carpinteria Valley Museum of History, 956 Maple Ave., ☎ 805/684-3112, houses a "Pictorial History Quilt" that includes 19 scenes depicting local history.
   Seaside Theatre Co., ☎ 805/684-6380, provides community theater.

Lompoc

Lompoc Civic Theatre, Flower Valley Plaza, Suite D, 1137 N. H St., ☎ 805/735-ACT 1, presents a murder mystery each month in the century-old Belluz House.
   Vandenberg Air Force Base, home of the 30th Space Wing and the only place in America that tests ICBMs, is seven miles northeast of town. Tours of the 98,000-acre facility can be arranged at **Western Spaceport Museum & Science Center**, 2999 Lompoc-Casmalia Rd., ☎ 805/736-6381.
   Lompoc Museum, 200 S. H St., ☎ 805/736-3888, occupies a former 1910 Carnegie Library, one of 1,679 funded by the philanthropist. The museum is the home of **Monster Bug Store**, which specializes in bug books, T-shirts, toys and a "swarm" of other bug stuff. The museum also contains

a collection of Chumash Indian artifacts and exhibits that depict the area's Mission Period, its Rancho Period and early Lompoc. Behind the museum is a 12- x 48-foot mural portraying the old mission.

Ojai

Biblical Garden, Presbyterian Church, 304 Foothill Rd., ☎ 805/646-1437, is an ecumenical garden that contains 50 plants, all mentioned in the Bible.

Ojai Center for the Arts, 113 S. Montgomery St., ☎ 805/646-0117, provides art, dancing and live theater.

Gallery of Historical Figures, McNell Rd. at Reeves Rd., ☎ 805/646-6574, contains life-size figures from the pages of history.

Oxnard

Heritage Square has a summer concert every Friday evening between 6 and 8 pm from late June through August.

Ventura County Maritime Museum, 2731 Victoria Ave. at Fisherman's Wharf, ☎ 805/984-6260, exhibits model ships and shipwreck artifacts. There are educational videos and docent-guided tours.

For the current offerings of **Channel Islands Ballet Co.**, contact ☎ 805/981-1434; **New West Symphony Orchestra**, 3451 Foothill Rd., #202, ☎ 805/643-8646; **Carnegie Art Museum**, 424 S. C St., ☎ 805/385-8157; **Ventura County Master Chorale**, ☎ 805/653-7282; and **Performing Arts Center**, Oxnard Community Center, 800 Hobson Way, ☎ 805/486-2424

San Luis Obispo

San Luis Obispo Little Theatre, 888 Morro St., City Playhouse, ☎ 805/543-3737, performs Thursday through Saturday at 8 pm and has Sunday matinees at 2 pm.

San Luis Obispo, 1010 Broad St., ☎ 805/543-8562, presents lectures, workshops and lessons.

Apple Farm Mill House, 2015 Monterey St., ☎ 805/544-2040, is a recreation of a working mill that produces stone-ground grains and creamy homemade ice cream. Ask for a free sample of the locally pressed apple cider.

For the current offerings of **San Luis Obispo Film Festival**, contact ☎ 805/546-FILM, Web site www.slonet.org/vv/sloiff; **Cuesta Master Chorale**, ☎ 805/756-2787 or 546-1124; and **San Luis Obispo County Symphony**, 1160 Marsh St., ☎ 805/543-3533.

Santa Barbara

Santa Barbara Museum of Art, 1130 State St., ☎ 805/963-4364, presents films, lectures and performances in the lower-level Mary Craig Auditorium. Bilingual tours are offered, as are tours for the hearing- and sight-impaired. Docent-led tours are available at 1 pm daily, except Mondays. A fee is charged except on Thursdays and the first Sunday of the month.

Santa Barbara Museum of Natural History, 2559 Puesta del Sol Rd., ☎ 805/682-4711 or 966-1601, fax 805/966-1603, Web site www.rain.org/_inverts/ is the city's oldest museum. It covers 11 acres along Mission Creek and contains nine exhibit halls. Included are a planetarium, an insect zoo, a space lab and the skeleton of a great blue whale.

Sea Center, 211 Stearns Wharf, ☎ 805/962-0885, has a touch tank, aquariums, life-size models of dolphins and whales, shipwreck artifacts, an art gallery and interactive computers to help explain the ecology of the Santa Barbara Channel.

At **Santa Barbara Historical Museum**, 136 E. de la Guerra St., ☎ 805/966-1601, fax 805/966-1603, the Gledhill Library stores a collection of 30,000 historic photographs.

For the current offerings of **Granada Theatre**, home of the **Santa Barbara Civic Light Opera** and **State Street Ballet of Santa Barbara**, contact 1216 State St., ☎ 805/966-2324 or 800/366-6064; **Alhecama Theatre**, home of the Ensemble Theatre Co. productions, 914 Santa Barbara St., ☎ 805/962-8606; and **Santa Barbara Grand Opera**, ☎ 805/898-3890, fax 805/898-3892.

Santa Maria

Pacific Conservatory of the Performing Arts, Allan Hancock College, ☎ 805/922-8313 or 800/549-7272, tours the Central Coast performing musicals and plays.

Allan Hancock College, 800 College Dr., hosts a **Theaterfest**, ☎ 805/922-8313, 928-7731 or 800/549-7272, in the 448-seat Marian Theatre and the 185-seat Severson Theatre.

Santa Maria Civic Theatre, 1660 N. McClelland St., ☎ 805/922-4442, has just 100 seats, so reservations are a must. The curtain goes up at 8 pm.

Santa Maria Symphony, ☎ 805/922-7748, performs at the First Assembly of God Church, Santa Maria Way and Bradley Rd. in the Orcutt area. It presents five concerts a year.

Ventura

Ventura County Museum of History and Art, 100 E. Main St., ☎ 805/653-0323, has over 300 historical figures representing 17 separate periods from Martin Luther in the Renaissance to Abraham Lincoln during the Civil War, all hand-made by George Stuart.

Where To Stay

B&Bs, Hotels & Inns

Arroyo Grande

Crystal Rose Inn, 789 Valley Rd., ☎ 805/481-1854 or 800/ROSE-INN, fax 805/481-9541, occupies an 1890 Victorian home set on 1½-acres. There are nine rooms, all with private baths, and an outstanding restaurant – **The Hunt Club.** Try the steamed mussels and cockles, the rabbit, the steak-and-ale pie, the angels on horseback (oysters wrapped in bacon), the eggs à vila (two poached eggs over smoked salmon and English muffins with hollandaise) or the sweet apple sausage.

To be sure their guests don't go away hungry, the inn provides afternoon high tea and evening hors d'oeuvres with wine.

Buellton

Pea Soup Andersen's Best Western Inn, 51 E. Highway 246, ☎ 805/688-3216 or 800/528-1234, fax 805/688-9767, was Andersen's first restaurant/inn. Now an institution throughout California, Andersen's is noted for its mouth-watering soup.

Cambria

What a great place to stay in a B&B! And there are several outstanding ones.

Exquisitely located on the beachfront are **The Sand Pebbles Inn,** 6252 Moonstone Beach Dr., ☎ 805/927-5600; **Blue Dolphin Inn,** 6470 Moonstone Beach Dr., ☎ 805/927-3300; and **The Blue Whale Inn,** 6736 Moonstone Beach Dr., ☎ 805/927-4647.

The Pickford House, 2555 MacLeod Way, ☎ 805/927-8619, has eight rooms, all named for movie stars of the William Randolph Hearst era: Mary Pickford, Douglas Fairbanks, Rudolph Valentino, Clara Bow, Norma Talmadge, Lillian Gish, Harold Lloyd and the three Barrymores – John, Lionel and Ethel. Three rooms have fireplaces; all have private bathrooms and TV. Fruit bread is served at 5 pm; wine in the evening; and such regional treats as aebleskiver, ball-shaped pancakes served with raspberry jam and powdered sugar, and bran muffins at breakfast.

The J. Patrick House, 2990 Burton Dr., ☎ 805/927-3812 or 800/341-5258, is in an authentic log cabin. There are eight rooms, one in the main house and seven in the carriage house, and all have wood-burning fireplaces and private baths. All bear Irish names: Limerick, Donegal, Kilkenny, Kerry, Galway, Tipperary, Dublin and Clare (the room in the main house). The rooms have no phone, no radio, and no TV. Stop in between noon and 3 pm to get a "killer" chocolate chip cookie... free!

Carpinteria

Carpinteria Shores, 4975 Sandyland Rd., ☎ 805/684-3570, fax 805/566-3361, offers vacation rentals on the shore of "the world's safest beach." Each unit has a balcony or a patio.

Cayucos

Beachwalker Inn, 501 S. Ocean Ave., ☎ 805/995-2133, is like staying at Grandma's house. The rooms are decorated in a comfy, old-fashioned, feel-at-home style, right down to the fireplaces in every room. The inn is just a block from the beach.

Ojai

Ojai Valley Inn, Country Club Rd., ☎ 805/646-5511 or 800/422-6524, Web site www.ojairesort.com, has 207 rooms, an 18-hole golf course, a driving range, a putting green, horseback riding, guided trail rides, riding lessons, a children's petting farm, tennis, two heated pools, a fitness facility, steam rooms, saunas, walking/jogging trails. Did we leave anything out? Check out the Native American Chumash foods served in the **Shangri-La Restaurant.**

Paso Robles

Justin Vineyards & Winery, 11680 Chimney Rock Rd., ☎ 805/238-6932 or 800-726-0049, fax 805/238-7382, has a B&B, **Just Inn**, along with some beautiful English gardens, right on the vineyard grounds.

Hope Farms, 2175 Arbor Rd., ☎ 805/238-6979, fax 805/238-4063, also has a lovely little B&B on the property. **The Arbor Inn B&B**, 2130 Arbor Rd., ☎ 805/227-4673, has eight rooms and a "penthouse suite," replete with fireplaces and balconies in a gorgeous Victorian house. Appropriately, the rooms are named for various wines, such as Bordeaux, Syrah and Cabernet.

San Simeon

There are several motels along the highway just south of the Hearst Castle, but our favorite is **Best Western Cavalier Inn**, 9415 Hearst Dr., ☎ 805/927-4688, which sits on a bluff high above the ocean and offers the warming comfort of a wood-burning fireplace in every room.

Santa Barbara

Fess Parker's Doubletree Resort, 633 E. Cabrillo Blvd., ☎ 805/564-4333 or 800/879-2929, fax 805/962-8198, will be a favorite among those old enough to remember Parker for his early television series. There are 360 rooms and suites, tennis courts and a putting green.

   Simpson House Inn, 121 E. Arrellaga St., ☎ 805/963-7067, is one of two historical inns in California. It is a small hotel sitting within an acre of English gardens. Most rooms have fireplaces.

Solvang

Alisal Guest Ranch and Resort, 1054 Alisal Rd., ☎ 805/688-6411, claims to be California's only full-service guest ranch. It sits on 10,000 acres and offers horseback riding, 36 holes of golf, tennis, boating and fishing.

   Storybook Inn B&B, 409 First St., ☎ 805/688-1703 or 800/786-7925, fax 805/688-0953, has three floors and offers nine rooms, all named for classic Hans Christian Andersen stories, such as *The Ugly Duckling*, *The Emperor's New Clothes*, *The Little Mermaid*, *The Princess and the Pea*, or *Thumbelina*. All rooms but one have a fireplace.

Camping

Buellton

Gaviota Beach on US 101 12 miles south of town has RV and camping facilities.

   Nearby **Lake Cachuma Recreation Area**, ☎ 805/688-8780, has 500 regular campsites, 90 with full EWS (electric, water and sewer) hookups and 38 with partial hookups. There is a general store, laundromat, snack bar, boat and bike rentals, full-service marina, and a bait and tackle shop. The lake enjoys a gorgeous setting, and the region is well populated with birds. Visitors also may see deer, bobcat or an occasional mountain lion.

Cambria

San Simeon State Beach has sites for overnight camping.

Carpinteria

Carpinteria Beach State Park has 262 camping sites, ☎ 800/444- 7275, including 86 RV sites with full hookups and 34 with partial hookups. There are nice views of the Santa Ynez Mountains and of the Channel Islands, 30 miles offshore, including some outstanding sunsets and an occasional glimpse of dolphins, seals and whales. Rangers give campfire programs several nights a week during the summer, and there is a special Junior Ranger program for children between seven and 12.

Channel Islands

There are campgrounds on Anacapa, Santa Cruz, Santa Rosa and San Miguel Islands.

On **Anacapa Island**, overnight camping is restricted to the primitive campground on East Anacapa. Frenchy's Cove on West Anacapa is for day use only.

Free camping on **San Miguel Island** is limited to seven days. Strong winds, rain and fog are constant. Landing is allowed only at Cuyler Harbor. Daytime use of the beach and the short hike to the ranger station do not require a permit, but access farther inland or beyond the beach at Cuyler Harbor requires a back country permit. Campground facilities are available at the Lester Ranch area near Cuyler Harbor, where stays are limited to three days.

On **Santa Cruz Island**, overnight sporting packages, a fee campground and B&B facilities are available at Smugglers' Cove on the privately owned east end, between Chinese Harbor and Sandstone Point. Contact **Island Adventures**, ☎ 805/646-2513.

At Bechers Bay on **Santa Rosa Island**, camping is allowed only at the Water Canyon campground.

Morro Bay

Montaña de Oro State Park, ☎ 800/444-7275, south of Morro Bay and Los Osos, has 50 campsites. There is a visitor center in the historic Spooner Ranch house, ☎ 805/772-2694.

Ojai

Rose Balley/Lion's Camp, 25 miles from town on Highway 33, provides camping, hiking, backpacking, swimming, fishing and a posted shooting area.

Wheeler Gorge, on Highway 33 eight miles north of town, ☎ 805/646-3428, has 70 campsites along Matilija Creek and a one-mile nature trail loop that begins at the north end of the campground. In **Los Padres National Forest**, 1190 E. Ojai Ave., ☎ 805/646-4348, 15.4 miles north of town on Highway 33, are Lion and Middle Lion campgrounds, plus many trails that lead into the Sespe Wilderness.

Gridley Trail starts at the north end of Gridley Rd. and ends 4.3 miles later on top of Nordhoff Ridge. **Gridley Springs Camp**, at 2.2 miles, is the only campsite along the trail. It is primitive, but it does have a water trough for horses.

Horn Canyon Trail begins at Thacher School and ends just east of Chief Peak and west of Topa Topa Bluffs. Pines Campground is 1.7 miles along the trail.

Camp Comfort, 11969 N. Creek Rd., ☎ 805/646-2314, sits in a valley astride San Antonio Creek. RV and tent camping are available. The Sioux Tepee will sleep 10.

Paso Robles

Heritage Ranch, ☎ 805/238-5800, is on the south shore of Lake Nacimiento. There are RV sites, swimming pools, tennis courts, shuffleboard courts, playground, equestrian area, riding and hiking trails, a club house and a boat launch on the 9,250 acres.

Piru

Los Alamos Campground in the Pyramid Lake Recreation Area has 93 campsites.

Where To Eat

Avila Beach

Olde Port Inn, ☎ 805/595-2515, sits at the end of Pier 3 amid a clutter of wooden sheds and fishing nets. The owner, himself a former fisherman, not only provides outstanding food and fine wines, but also a unique form of entertainment. Through glass-topped tables, diners can peer straight through the table – and the pier – into the water below, where fish, seals and various types of waterfowl put on a special "floorshow." The result is somewhat like dining in a glass-bottom boat, but without the seasickness. Much of the inn's wine comes from the restaurant's own winery, Four Corners Cellars in nearby Santa Maria.

Buellton

Pea Soup Andersen's, 376 Avenue of the Flags, ☎ 805/688-5581, has turned pea soup into a statewide institution. This was the first in a string of Andersen's restaurants and inns that blanket southern California. At the Highway 246 exit off US 101.

Cambria

The Sow's Ear Café, 2248 Main St., ☎ 805/927-4865, incorporates its home-grown herbs in fresh-baked breads, desserts, ginger apricot butter, mango-tangerine salsa, sausages, baby pork ribs, salmon in parchment, peppercorn pasta and beer-spiced shrimp. Sample the honey pinenut crust on their halibut and sea bass.

Fillmore

Fillmore & Western Railway, on Highway 126 in Central Park, ☎ 805/524-2546, is dinner-theater (murder mysteries and vaudeville) aboard a 1940-era passenger train. The shows are offered every Sunday at 11 and at 1:15, and on some Friday and Saturday evenings.

Goleta

Circle Bar B Dinner Theatre, 1800 Refugio Rd., ☎ 805/965-9652, offers shows on Fridays, Saturdays and Sundays. On Fridays and Saturdays, dinner is served at 7 pm and the play goes on at 8. On Sundays, a 1 pm brunch is served, followed by a 2 o'clock curtain.

Los Alamos

Union Hotel & Victorian Mansion, 362 Bell St., ☎ 805/344-2744 or 800/230-2744, occupies an 1880 building with a lovely patio garden. Try their Wild West buffalo burger or their buffalo stew.

Oceano

Great American Melodrama & Vaudeville, 1863 Pacific Blvd., ☎ 805/489-2499, invites total audience participation. Located on Highway 1 three miles south of Pismo Beach, the troupe presents old-fashioned melodrama while the audience cheers the hero and hisses the villain. The floor is covered with sawdust, and the patrons dine on pretzels, candy bars, jerky, hot dogs, BBQ beef, Polish sausage, potato salad, baked potatoes and soup.

Ojai

Garden Terrace, 1002 E. Ojai Ave., ☎ 805/646-1133, serves a sinful chocolate hazelnut flourless cake with raspberry sauce and cream.

L'Auberge, 314 El Paseo, ☎ 805/646-2288, occupies a 1910 mansion and combines a French country menu on a charming terrace with a splendid view of the Topa Topa Mountains.

Bodacious Grill, 11400 N. Ventura Ave., ☎ 805/649-1575, serves BBQ that is among the best in the country.

Oxnard

Theatre-By-the-Sea, Fisherman's Wharf, ☎ 805/645-5624, provides dinner-theater, as the name implies.

San Luis Obispo

Old Country Deli, ☎ 805/541-2968, was singled out by *American Way* magazine for its terrific BBQ.

Santa Barbara

CyberState Café, 1224 State St., ☎ 805/899-3723, provides its customers with gourmet coffee and access to the Internet. You can rent a computer, a printer, a fax and even open an e-mail account over a steaming cup of decaf.

Santa Barbara Brewing Co., 501 State St., ☎ 805/730-1040, serves "armadillo eggs," deep-fried jalapeños, as a starter.

Madhouse, ☎ 805/962-5516, calls itself "the most decadent cocktail lounge in town."

Be Bop Burgers, 111 State St., ☎ 805/966-1956, offers the atmosphere of the 1950s and 60s. Check out their Buddy Holly BBQ sandwich, chili potato skins, mozzarella cheese sticks and old-fashioned chocolate shakes.

Andersen's, 1106 State St., ☎ 805/962-5085, provides Danish cuisine served on a sidewalk patio.

Santa Maria

Residents of this upscale community have developed their own style of BBQ, which *Sunset* magazine has called "the best in the world." It is cooked over a red oak fire, served on a skewer and should be eaten immediately. Most locals like their beef rare (cooked for two hours), rather than well done. Some prefer a "tri-tip" (a triangular piece of bottom sirloin), while others, claiming that the tri-tip is too stringy, prefer the "top block" (a top sirloin cut). There is even a special local side dish: pinquitos (small, pink, pinto-like beans grown only in the Santa Barbara Valley).

Solvang

Mollekroen, 435 Alisal Rd., ☎ 805/688-4555, is located across from the town post office. It serves a daily smorgasbord (appropriate for this tiny Danish community) and offers entertainment on Friday and Saturday evenings.

    River Grill, Alisal Guest Ranch, 1054 Alisal Rd., ☎ 805/688-7784, has been called "the valley's most picturesque dining spot."

Ventura

Andria's Seafood, 1449 Spinnaker Dr., ☎ 805/654-0546, has been voted the town's best seafood restaurant for more than 10 years in a row.

The Central Valley

Everyone leaves the surf, the beaches, and the colorful little communities of the coastal region with a great deal of reluctance. In spite of that, the drive across California's gentle, golden hills into the Central Valley is an enjoyable, peaceful experience.

State Route 48 takes us eastward out of Paso Robles through Cholame, scene of the tragic automobile accident that claimed the life of acting idol James Dean so many years ago.

Along the way, we are surrounded by rolling hills and vast ranchlands. Occasionally, a vineyard or a farm will appear, but for the most part these are the wide open spaces common to Western folklore.

The towns are small and far between. Billboards and other signs of civilization are seldom encountered. Even the occasional highway route marker seems inappropriate and out of place.

Just past Cholame, we turn onto State Route 41 headed toward Kettleman City, Lemoore, Hanford and Visalia, where the road intersects State Route 99 about two-thirds of the way between Bakersfield and Fresno.

Getting Around

Interstate 5 is the high-speed link between Los Angeles and San Francisco through the Central Valley. Some 20 miles south of Bakersfield, however, Route 99 branches off I-5 to serve all of the major cities in the region – Bakersfield, Visalia and beyond.

In short: If you're in a hurry to get through the Central Valley, take I-5. If you want to see something, Route 99 is a better choice.

Out of Corona, I-15 passes through Ontario and San Bernardino on its way to Barstow and, eventually, Las Vegas, Nevada, a popular vacation destination for many residents of southern California.

Interstate 215 skirts San Bernardino and Riverside on its way south to San Diego. Interstate 10 is the major east-west corridor running through the southern part of the region.

The Central Valley

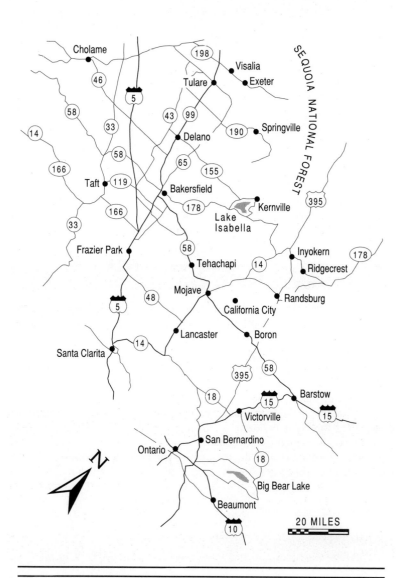

Touring

Visalia

Visalia was the first town to be settled in the San Joaquin Valley and was named for a town in Kentucky. An extremely fertile region, there are over 225 different crops grown throughout the valley.

Visalia's other claim to fame is its proximity to two national parks, Sequoia and Kings Canyon, ☎ 209/561-3314, and the Sequoia National Forest, ☎ 209/784-1500, which makes the town a wonderful place to spend the night or to stock up on supplies.

INFORMATION SOURCES

Visalia Chamber of Commerce, 720 W. Mineral King, Visalia 93291, ☎ 209/734-5876, fax 209/734-7479.
Visalia Convention & Visitors Bureau, 301 E. Acequia St., Visalia 93291, ☎ 800/524-0303.
Sequoia Regional Visitors Council, 4125 W. Mineral King, Ste. 104, Visalia 93277.

Exeter

This town of 8,000 population is known throughout the region for its murals depicting the area's agriculture. For information, contact **Exeter Chamber of Commerce**, 101 W. Pine St., ☎ 209/592-2919.

Lindsay

This small town is the home of **Lindsay Olive Growers**, 650 W. Tulare Rd., ☎ 209/562-5121. The tasting room is open Monday through Friday from 10 to 4. For more information, contact **Lindsay Chamber of Commerce**, 147 N. Gale Hill, Lindsay 93247, ☎ 209/562-4929.

Sequoia National Park

Established in 1890, this is California's first and the nation's second oldest national park. Sequoias are the world's largest living objects, growing to over 250 feet in height and ranging from 15 to 35 feet in diameter.

Big Tree, which is a five-minute walk from the highway, is nearly 3,000 yrs old and is claimed to be the largest living thing in the world. The **General Sherman Tree**, two miles northeast of **Giant Forest Village**, weighs 2.7 million pounds and is believed to be between 2,300 and 2,700 years old. The tree stands 274.9 feet tall, and has a 102.6-foot ground-level circumference. The growth each year is enough to create a tree 60 feet tall.

General Grant Sequoia, at **Grant Grove** near the entrance to Kings Canyon, is the third largest tree on earth. From the parking area, take a gently graded, half-mile, self-guided trail past historic Gamlin Cabin and Fallen Monarch Tree, in which the cavalry guarding the park in the 1890s stabled their horses, to the General Grant.

INFORMATION SOURCES

Visitor centers
Foothills	☎ 209/565-3134
Lodgepole	☎ 209/565-3782

Other sources
General information	☎ 209/565-3134
Road and weather	☎ 209/565-3351
Lodging reservations	☎ 209/561-3314
Campground reservations	☎ 800/365-2267

Springville

Almost everything in Springville involves apples! During the annual **Apple Festival** on the first weekend in October, it is possible to find burritos, apple butter, jelly, jam, preserves, cider, syrup, crisp, dumplings, strudel, juice, pancakes, pie, cobbler and turnovers... *all made of apples*. You also can buy caramel apples, hot caramel-drizzled apples, candied apples and baked apples. Popular events at the festival include the Big Apple 5K run, 10K run and two-mile walk, and a contest to select Miss Apple Blossom and Johnny Appleseed. The Lions Club holds an Apple Pancake Breakfast, and there are pie-eating and pie-baking contests.

Tulare

Bob Mathias, a two-time Olympic decathlon champion who was dubbed "the world's greatest athlete," came from Tulare. When he won his first gold medal in 1948, he was just 17, the youngest person ever to win the event. Mathias later served in Congress.

Adm. Elmo R. Zumwalt Jr., once the U.S. Chief of Naval Operations and America's highest-ranking naval officer, also came from here.

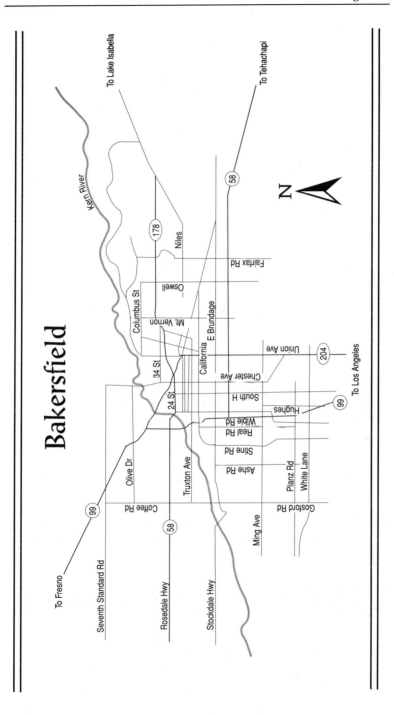

Bakersfield

Bakersfield

Bakersfield is the seat of Kern County, the third largest county in California. Kern is the nation's largest oil-producing county and the nation's fourth-largest producer of agriculture products.

Bakersfield is the home of the world's largest ice cream plant (Nestlé).

Lawrence Tibbett, America's greatest baritone, was born in Bakersfield in 1896. His father, a sheriff's deputy, was shot and killed in a frontier-style shoot-out. His career accomplishments include a performance in the first complete Technicolor musical with a full soundtrack (*Rogue Song*, 1930); an appearance in the first film ever released by 20th Century Fox (*Metropolitan*, 1935); and a starring role in the first movie directed by Otto Preminger (*Under Your Spell*, 1936).

Country music star Merle Haggard also was born in Bakersfield.

Cal State Bakersfield, 9001 Stockdale, ☎ 805/644-2397, fax 805/664-3156, is the home of the Roadrunners. Memorial Stadium at **Bakersfield College**, 1801 Panorama Dr., ☎ 805/395-4518, fax 805/395-4241, is where Jim Ryan ran the world record mile in 1978.

Many people of Basque extraction live in Bakersfield. Originally from Eskualherria, a small country in the Pyrenees, Basques are known for their skills as shepherds and as the originators of jai alai. Their language, Eskuara, is a blend of Latin, French and Castilian.

INFORMATION SOURCES

Greater Bakersfield Convention & Visitors Bureau
1033 Truxtun Ave., Bakersfield 93301
☎ 805/325-5051 or 800/325-6001, fax 805/325-7074

Bakersfield Chamber of Commerce
☎ 805/327-4421

Kern County Board of Trade
2101 Oak St., PO Bin 1312, Bakersfield 93302
☎ 805/861-2367 or 500-KERN, fax 805/861-2367

North of the River Chamber of Commerce
☎ 805/393-4556

Delano

During the depression and economic panic of 1873, the finances of the railroad, which had spurred the growth of the Central Valley, began to dry up. Where the tracks ended, the town of Delano (pronounced Dee-LANE-oh) began to develop. With time, the region grew into a major agricultural area where grapes, kiwi, oranges, almonds and vegetables are grown.

Delano has a substantial Philippine population and hosts an annual **Philippine Weekend Festival,** ☎ 805/725-3246. There also is a Filipino American Culture Education Assn., Filipino Athletic League, Filipino Community of Delano, and Filipino Women's Club in the town. The Bayan Filipino radio program on KCHJ (AM 1010) every Sunday between 6 and 9 am is billed as "Your hometown connection to the islands."

A 1,350,000-watt **Voice of America** relay station is based in Delano. Programs are received directly from Washington via telephone and then rebroadcast worldwide in 12 languages.

For additional information, contact **Delano Chamber of Commerce,** 931 High St., Delano 93215, ☎ 805/725-2518.

Kernville

Once known as Whiskey Flat, Kernville developed during the mining era. **Kern Valley Historical Society Museum,** Big Blue Rd., ☎ 619/379-2087, next to the post office, conducts tours of the original mining town and of the Big Blue mine site.

For more information, contact **Kernville Chamber of Commerce**, PO Box 397, Kernville 93238-0397, ☎ 619/376-2629.

Taft

What mining was to Kernville, oil was to Taft.

Originally called Moron (now *why* would you want to change a name like that?), the town had three men to every woman in the 1930s – and 20 all-night bars!

West Kern Oil Museum, 1186 Wood St., ☎ 805/765-6664 or 765-7371, exhibits a tent house, a blacksmith shop, a firehouse with a 1937 fire truck and an original 1917 wooden derrick over the original well, drilled just weeks after the United States entered World War I. There also is a museum building with three acres of native plants.

For more information, contact **Taft District Chamber of Commerce,** 314 4th St., Taft, ☎ 619/765-2165.

Frazier Park

Located 40 miles south of Bakersfield along I-5, Frazier Park sits on the edge of Los Padres National Forest. It is a scenic area, and many movies and TV shows have been filmed here over the years. In the late 1960s, TV's *The FBI* was shot here. An episode of TV's *America's Most Wanted* was filmed in Brit's Mountain Inn. In the mid-1970s, the town appeared as Gideon, Colorado in the TV *Doc Elliot* series, starring James Franciscus.

In **Lockwood Valley**, southwest of town, Paramount TV shot the *Star Trek: Voyager* series. Walt Disney shot racing scenes for the *The Love Bug* there, and Dennis Hopper and Peter Fonda did *Easy Rider* in 1969. *Thelma and Louise* traveled through there in 1991 on their way to Lake of the Woods, where they hid out at The Stumble Inn.

Some of the scenes for the *Doc Elliot* series were shot in **Cuddy Valley**, as was some of the original *Planet of the Apes*. *Daniel Boone* and *The Virginian* were also filmed in Cuddy Valley, as were Robert Redford's *The Milagro Beanfield War* and Michael Jackson's fantasy music video *Childhood*. Lorimar TV shot *The Homecoming – A Christmas Tale* in the valley and, by turning **Mount Piños** into Walton's Mountain, launched *The Waltons* television series. Mount Piños also was Ben Cartwright's Ponderosa Ranch in the *Bonanza* television series.

Mil Potrero Park appeared in *Alf*, Robin Williams' *Toys*, and Janet Jackson's debut film *Poetic Justice.*

The Chamber of Commerce maintains a list of all current film locations, extras, Screen Actors Guild actors and crews.

S. L. Ranch, 2700 Johnson Rd., is southern California's largest llama ranch.

For more information, contact **Mountain Communities Chamber of Commerce**, PO Box 763, Frazier Park 93225, ☎ 805/245-1212 or 242-2500, e-mail fmguide@frazmtn.com.

Lebec

Lebec Hotel (now gone) was a popular hangout for Hollywood celebrities during the 1920s and 30s. Built in 1921, it was frequented by such stars as Clara Bow, Carole Lombard, Clark Gable, Jerry Colona and Bing Crosby. Roscoe "Fatty" Arbuckle and his wife hid away here while returning from one of his three San Francisco murder trials. Today, only the foundation of the coffeeshop can be seen.

Interstate 5 was once one of the world's most dangerous highways, a three-lane road called "The Road to Kingdom Come," because of the numerous head-on collisions that occurred there.

North of town, actor James Dean got a speeding ticket at the Grapevine section of I-5 just two hours before he was killed in a car crash.

Nearby **Tejon Lake** was originally known as Castac Lake, but was renamed to avoid confusion with Castaic Lake. The Katanamuk village of Kashtiq once occupied the north shore.

For further information, contact **Hungry Valley SVRA**, PO Box 1360, Lebec 93243, ☎ 805/248-7007.

Santa Clarita

William S. Hart Park and Museum occupies the grounds of the silent-screen cowboy's 265-acre Newhall estate. The museum was Hart's 1927 mansion. There are hiking trails, barnyard animals and buffalo on the grounds.

For more information, contact **Santa Clarita Valley Tourism Bureau**, ☎ 800/718-TOUR.

Tehachapi

The drive to Tehachapi from Bakersfield along Highway 68 is magnificent. Nearing town, hundreds of metallic "windmills" appear, seemingly out of nowhere. This is the **Tehachapi Wind Farm**, a system used to generate electric power. For a self-guided tour of the scenic wind farm, take Oak Creek Rd. to Willow Springs Rd., then take Willow Springs Rd. over Willow Springs Pass to Tehachapi Blvd. Turn right (east) and continue on to the Sand Canyon interchange. Take Highway 58 to the Cameron Rd. exit and follow Cameron Rd. until it meets Tehachapi Willow Springs Rd.

Special vantage points from which to view the Wind Farm include:

★ Sand Canyon interchange: views of Cameron Ridge, Pajuela Peak and Zond Systems' "Wind Wall."

★ SeaWest Gate/Oak Creek Rd.: a view of the Japanese and Danish wind turbines. The Japanese turbines are among the largest in the world.

★ Mountain Valley Airport: a view of 1,200 wind turbines.

★ Pacific Coast Trail trailhead: take the trail north towards Cameron Ridge, which is three miles away.

The historic **Tehachapi Loop** was an engineering miracle when it was completed in 1876. Railroad tracks circle a hill in such a way as to enable the train to gain a strenuous 77 feet in elevation. At times, the front of the train actually passes over the rear of the train during the ascent.

Speaking of which, the **Tehachapi Loop Railroad Club** gives its officers some distinctive titles. The president is called the superintendent; the vice president, the dispatcher; the secretary, the stationmaster; and the treasurer, the paymaster.

Indian Point Ostrich Ranch, Giraudo and Sasia Rds., ☎ 805/822-9131, occupies 80 acres.

Tehachapi Ostrich Ranch, 18518 Pellisier, ☎ 805/823-1440 or 822-3557, is operated by three men from South Africa and provides daily tours. It also has an interesting gift shop where you can buy such things as carved and painted ostrich eggs, ostrich feather dusters and ostrich shell jewelry.

Mourning Cloak Ranch and Botanical Gardens, 22101 Old Town Rd., ☎ 805/822-1661 or 822-5062, is named for a local butterfly.

The Rodeo Grounds on Dennison Rd. are the site of the **Tehachapi Mountain Festival** held every August. One of the highlights of the festival is the Flossie Flop Contest. A small pen housing "Flossie," a cow, is marked off in numbered squares; each square corresponds to a number on the $5 chance that players can purchase from the local Rotary Club. If Flossie "flops" on a participant's square, that player wins. A $300 first prize, a $200 second prize and a $100 third prize are awarded during the contest. Visitors can buy "Flossie Flops" T-shirts and hats. As a fund-raiser, the Rotary Club sells chocolate fudge "cow chips."

Other points of interest include a state prison, apple orchards and Brite Lake.

For more information, contact **Tehachapi Chamber of Commerce**, 209 E. Tehachapi Blvd., PO Box 401, Tehachapi 93581, ☎ 805/822-4180.

Inyokern

Originally "Siding 16" on the Southern Pacific Railroad, this town took the name of Magnolia when the first post office opened in 1913. Eventually, the name Inyokern was formulated by combining the names of two counties, Inyo and Kern.

The region abounds in strange-sounding names. Robber's Roost, Last Chance Canyon, Burro Schmidt's Tunnel, Jawbone Canyon, Dirty Socks Pool and Fossil Falls are but a few.

For added information, contact **Inyokern Chamber of Commerce**, 1249 Broadway, PO Box 232, Inyokern 93527, ☎ 619/377-4712.

Mojave

Mojave Airport, ☎ 805/824-2433, a former Navy/Marine air station, has America's only civilian test pilot school, founded in 1981. Some 150 students enroll each year.

Burt Rutan, the aircraft designer who developed the Voyager, which went around the world without refueling in 1986, has an unusual dome-shaped house here. Voyager was flown on its round-the-world journey by Jeana Yeager and Rutan's brother Dick.

Some of Kevin Costner's movie *Waterworld* was filmed at the Mojave airport.

For more information, contact **Mojave Chamber of Commerce**, 15836 Sierra Hwy., Mojave 93501, ☎ 805/824-2481.

Randsburg

This high-desert community, which began with the discovery of gold at the base of Rand Mountain in 1895, is a living ghost town. At its peak, it had a population of 14,000, and giant stamping mills processed the gold ore taken from the local mines. A few of the region's gold mines are still active.

Ridgecrest

A town of 35,000 people, Ridgecrest supports the nearby **Naval Air Weapons Center** at China Lake.

China Lake Exhibit Center, Inyokern Rd. and China Lake Blvd., ☎ 619/939-3105 or 939-8645, has exhibits that deal with the space program and the development of 50 years of weaponry.

Woman Undone starring Randy Quaid, Sam Elliott and Mary McDonnell was filmed at **Rocky Top Ranch** south of town.

For more information, contact the **Ridgecrest Chamber of Commerce**, 400 N. China Lake Blvd., Ridgecrest 93555, ☎ 619/375-8331, fax 619/375-0365, e-mail chambers@ridgecrest.ca.us; or the **Ridgecrest Area Convention & Visitors Bureau**, 100 W. California Ave., Ridgecrest, ☎ 800/847-4830.

Lancaster

Lancaster is the business center of Antelope Valley, which covers 2,500 square miles, including parts of Kern, Los Angeles and San Bernardino counties.

Located in the high desert, it is 15 miles west of **Edwards Air Force Base**, Edwards 93523, the site of **Rogers Dry Lake** and "Birthplace of Supersonic Flight." In 1946, Capt. Charles E. "Chuck" Yeager, flew from here in the X-1 to become the first person ever to break the sound barrier.

In 1979, Stan Barrett drove the Budweiser Rocket across the desert here to become the first person to break the sound barrier *on land.*

Air Force Flight Test Center Museum, 1100 Kincheloe, Edwards AFB 93524, ☎ 805/277-8050, fax 805/277-8051, occupies Building 7211 near the main entrance to the base as a new facility is being completed. Get a pass and a museum map at one of base's three entry gates. An annex at USAF Plant 42, **Blackbird Airpark** in nearby Palmdale is the only place where you can see the SR-71 Blackbird, its predecessor, the A-12, and the ultra-secret D-21 drone.

Hugh L. Dryden Flight Research Center, PO Box 273, Edwards 93523-0273, ☎ 805/258-3311, 258-3446 or 258-3460, is operated by NASA and conducts two free 90-minute tours daily, Monday through Friday (except holidays) at 10:15 am and 1:15 pm.

Aerospace Walk of Honor, Lancaster Blvd. from 10th St. West to Sierra Hwy., encompasses 10 blocks. Six-foot-tall granite monuments along the way commemorate the achievements of America's greatest test pilots.

For more information, contact **Lancaster Chamber of Commerce**, 554 W. Lancaster Blvd., Lancaster 93534, ☎ 805/948-4518, fax 805/949-1212.

Boron

Home of the world's largest open pit mine, this tiny community is a major source of borax.

Twenty Mule Team Museum, 26962 Twenty Mule Team Rd., ☎ 619/762-5810, features both indoor and outdoor exhibits, including an old Santa Fe depot and an early miner's cabin.

For additional information, contact **Boron Chamber of Commerce**, 26962 Twenty Mule Team Rd., Boron 93516, ☎ 619/762-5810.

California City

Desert Tortoise Natural Area, a part of the California Desert Conservation Area, sits here between Desert City and Randsburg. Committed to preserving the official state reptile, the facility encompasses 25,000 acres, jointly administered by the Bureau of Land Management (BLM), the California Department of Fish & Game, and several supporting conservation organizations.

Rosamond

Exotic Feline Breeding Compound, Mojave-Tropico Rd. and Ryolite, ☎ 805/256-3332, fax 805/256-6867, has an interesting motto: "Support Your Local Cat House."

For more information, contact **Rosamond Chamber of Commerce**, 2861 Diamond, PO Box 365, Rosamond 93560, ☎ 805/256-3248.

Victorville

Roy Rogers and Dale Evans have lived in this high-desert community for 30 years.

Southern California International Airport, 18374 Readiness St., ☎ 619/246-6115, fax 619/246-3108, formerly George Air Force Base, covers 5,300 acres.

The community is the home of the **San Bernardino County Fair** and the largest regional shopping center between San Bernardino and Las Vegas.

OK Corral Ostrich Farms, 14989 Chamber Lane in nearby Apple Valley, ☎ 619/242-0997, conducts tours.

In the process of construction is a new 76-acre, $45 million theme park and retail center called **RogersDale**, which broke ground in 1996. The park will employ "Edutainment" to tell the story of the West from 1860 to 1960 and to portray the lives of Roy Rogers and Dale Evans. It will have a 300-seat amphitheater, a Western music dinner-theater, a Western Music Hall of Fame, a radio station and broadcast studio, and the California Route 66 Museum (16849 Route 66 D St., ☎ 619/261-US66 or 951-0436). All of the employees will dress in Western attire.

After the first phase of the complex has been completed, a second stage is planned to include a hotel, an "opry hall," a convention center and an RV park.

For more information, contact **Victorville Chamber of Commerce**, 14174 Green Tree Blvd., PO Box 997, Victorville 92393-0997, ☎ 619/245-6506, fax 619/245-6505.

San Bernardino

This severely depressed city seems to be waiting for something to happen, good or bad. It looks like a city that has lost the will to survive, and a substantial part of the population acts accordingly.

San Bernardino International Airport, the former Norton Air Force Base, provides convenient shuttle transportation and short-haul, interstate flights. The airport was the setting for *Desperate Measures*, a movie starring Michael Keaton.

Movie buffs might be interested to know that actor Gene Hackman was born in San Bernardino.

The city's greatest draw, perhaps, is its function as the gateway to **Big Bear Lake** and **Lake Arrowhead**, two of southern California's most popular summer vacation destinations for generations.

For more information, contact **San Bernardino Area Chamber of Commerce**, 546 W. Sixth St., San Bernardino 92410, ☎ 909/885-7515; or **San Bernardino Convention & Visitors Bureau**, 201 N. E St., San Bernardino 92410, ☎ 909/889-3980.

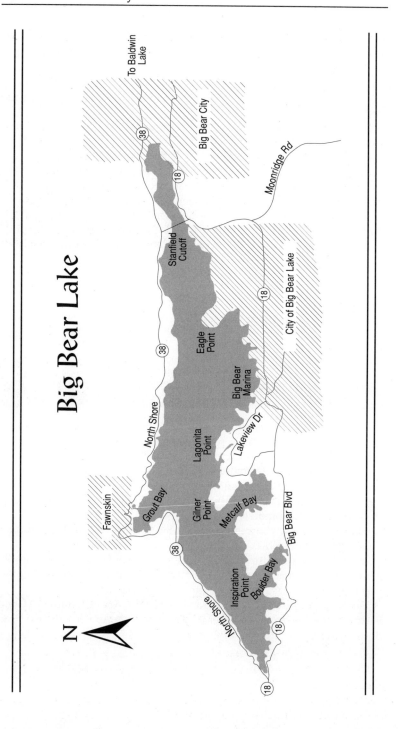

Big Bear Lake

At an elevation of almost 7,000 feet, this has been a popular place to escape the summer heat since the dam that formed the lake was built in 1912.

Pontoon boats on Big Bear Lake.
Credit: Robert Holmes, CA Div. of Tourism

The lake is six miles long. It sits within the 200,000-acre **San Bernardino National Forest,** ☎ 909/866-3437, and is serviced by **Rim of the World Drive**, which connects Crestline and Big Bear Lake along Route 18, and by **MARTA**, ☎ 909/584-1111, a metropolitan bus service which takes visitors from the Radisson Hotel in San Bernardino to the lake and provides transportation throughout Big Bear Valley.

Big Bear Jeep Tours, 40687 Village Dr., Big Bear, ☎ 909/878-5337, provides two- to four-hour tours to **Holcomb Valley**, where Bill Holcomb first struck gold. The tour visits a gold mine (**Rose Mine**); a silver mine (**Tip Top Mine**); **Santa Ana River**; **Jacoby Canyon**, where gold is still being panned; and **White Mountain.**

INFORMATION SOURCES

Big Bear Chamber of Commerce, 630 Barlett, Big Bear Lake, ☎ 909/866-4607.
Big Bear Lake Resort Assn., ☎ 909/866-6190, 866-7000 or 800/4 BIG BEAR, Web site www.bigbearinfo.com.
Big Bear Lake Visitors Authority, 630 Bartlett Rd., Box 2860, Big Bear Lake 92315, ☎ 909/866-7000.
Big Bear Ranger Station, ☎ 909/866-3437.

Lake Arrowhead

At 5,150 feet, Arrowhead isn't as high as Big Bear, but it's still high enough to provide plenty of relief from the mid-summer heat.

The 740-acre reservoir is private, the product of a dam that was completed during the 1920s.

For additional information, contact **Lake Arrowhead Communities Chamber of Commerce**, Lake Arrowhead Village, Building F-280, Box

155, Lake Arrowhead 92352, ☎ 909/337-3715 or 800/550-5253, Web site www.lakearrowhead.com, e-mail lachamber@js-net.com. There also is a 24-hour info line: ☎ 909/336-3274.

Riverside

March Field Museum, 16222 Interstate 215 at the Van Buren off ramp, ☎ 909/655-3715, 655-2138 or 697-6600, commemorates two World War II fighter units: the P-38 National Assn. and the 475th Fighter Group, the war's leading unit with 596 victories to its credit.

Victoria Avenue, 6475 Victoria Ave., ☎ 909/684-0596, is a linear drive-through park and arboretum containing over 4,000 trees representing 95 species. There are pepper trees from Peru and eucalyptus trees from Australia, some nearly 200 feet tall and 10 feet in diameter. The avenue is lined with thousands of ragged robin trees. The Roosevelt palm at Victoria Ave. and Myrtle St. was planted by President Theodore Roosevelt in 1903. Citizens can contribute a Commemorative Tree in memory of a loved one or to mark a special occasion. The park has 7½ miles of bike lanes and separate walking/jogging paths.

Mission Inn Hotel, 3649 Seventh St., ☎ 909/781-8241, 784-0300 or 788-9556, was built in stages between 1902 and 1932. Features include a Court of the Birds, the Presidential Lounge, Spanish Patio, Famous Fliers' Wall, Music Room, Rotunda, Oriental Ho-O-Kan Room and St. Francis Chapel.

Baseball star Barry Bonds and basketball player Cheryl Miller were born in Riverside.

Horse-drawn carriage tours of the town are available. For more information, contact Greater Riverside Chamber of Commerce, 3685 Main St., Ste. 350, Riverside 92501, ☎ 909/683-7100, fax 909/683-2670, Web site www.riverside-chamber.com.

Beaumont

Meaning "beautiful mountain," Beaumont was a stop on the road to the gold fields near Yuma, Arizona in 1860. In the early 1880s, it was known as Summit, and in 1884, as San Gorgonio.

"Mad" King Ludwig's Bavarian Oktoberfest is held on the last two weekends in September. Traditional entertainment includes men's team log sawing and pretzel eating contests.

For additional information, contact Beaumont Chamber of Commerce, 450 E. 4th St., Beaumont 92223, ☎ 909/845-9541, fax 909/769-9080.

Ontario

Don't think a trip to the mall can be an adventure? Then be sure to see the new **Ontario Mills** center, 1 Mills Circle, ☎ 305/846-2300 or 909/481-5883, located between Inland Empire Blvd. and 4th St. and between Rochester Ave. and Milliken Ave., north of I-10 and west of I-15. The $150 million, 1.7-million-square-foot center includes 15 anchors and 200 specialty shops. Noteworthy are the unusual visual effects:

★ **The Magical Grapevine** shows a man in the moon telling a story while a vibrant gold-and-red caterpillar attempts to pull juicy purple grapes off a leafy vine.

★ **City Beautiful Rotunda** depicts a magic urn that travels from flower to flower watering the lush foliage. As the flowers grow, a bear, a hummingbird and a butterfly sing and celebrate.

★ **The American Wilderness Experience** allows visitors to stroll through the environments of five distinct Califor- nia regions that feature the live animals, plants, scents and climates indigenous to each.

The facility also has 20 giant video screens and seven video walls that entertain visitors as they stroll through the mall.

Ontario International Airport, ☎ 909/988-2720, already one of the busiest airports in the area, is in the process of completing two new terminals and 10,000 new parking spaces. The terminals will cover 550,000 square feet and provide 28 new gates.

A new 225,000-square-foot **Convention Center** has been built on 17½ acres at Holt Blvd. and D St., north of the airport.

For more information, contact the **Ontario Chamber of Commerce**, 121 W. B St., Ste. F, Ontario 91762, ☎ 909/984-2458; or **Ontario Convention & Visitors Bureau**, 421 N. Euclid Ave., Ontario 91762, ☎ 909/984-2450 or 800/455-5755, fax 909/984-7895, Web site www.ontariocvb.org.

Ghost Towns

Southern California has a few ghost towns for those who fancy visiting old souls.

Although still shown on many maps, **Bodfish**, south of Lake Isabella, is a virtual ghost town. A few miles north of Inyokern is **Brown**, now largely a ghost town. An old cemetery south of Kernville is called **Gunmen's Row**. Two ghost towns near Ridgecrest are **Ballarat** and **Garlock**.

Adventures

On Foot

Lake Arrowhead

There are many trails throughout the area. Check with the local ranger for a trail map and current hiking conditions.

Big Bear Lake

North American Hiking & Packing Co., ☎ 909/585-1226, offers day hikes ranging from 30 minutes to two hours with lunch included. They also provide romantic sunset dinners for two and three-day expeditions in groups of five or less. Llamas carry the load.

Delano

Kern National Wildlife Refuge, ☎ 805/725-2767, 17 miles west of town, is a great place for upland bird hunting (dove, pheasant, quail).

Exeter

Lake Kaweah has an interesting nature trail (**Horse Creek**) and a pleasant hiking trail (**Cobble Knoll**).

At **Mineral King**, the **Eagle Lake Trail** to the southeast covers 3½ miles one way and utilizes the Eagle Crest trailhead. The lake sits at 10,000 feet elevation. Also to the southeast is the **Farwell Gap Trail**, while to the southwest the **Tar Gap Trail** leads to Hockett Meadow.

Hiking from the **Eagle Crest** parking lot to **White Chief Meadows** covers four miles, one way. At the top are some interesting marble caves. As you pass over the grassy meadow, keep an eye out for wildflowers and marmots. At the end of the trail are White Chief Lake and White Chief Peak.

The **Atwell-Hockett Trail** near Silver City is less strenuous.

Frazier Park

Cuchupate Ranger Station, 34580 Lockwood Valley Rd., ☎ 805/245-3731, has topographic maps available.

Earth Skills, 1113 Cougar Court, ☎ 805/245-0318, offers classes in tracking, nature and other outdoor skills.

McGill Trail (21W02 on USGS Topographic Map Quadrangle) is a four-mile hike one way. It begins at McGill Campground on Mt. Piños. Look for the trail sign at the top of the road across from the kiosk near the campground entrance. To keep this a downhill hike, park a second car at the well-marked site about three-quarters of a mile up from the intersection of Mt. Piños Road and Mill Potrero Highway. Follow the signs carefully because you will encounter a junction of several roads along the way. This is a good spot for birdwatching and for viewing meteor showers, particularly the Perseid meteor shower between late July and late August. Keep an eye on the weather because the summit of Mt. Piños gets as many as 800 lightning strikes each summer. If you plan to be out after dark, be sure to wear warm clothing.

Kernville

California Department of Fish & Game **Kern River Fish Hatchery** has a number of nature trails.

Dam Tough Run is a 10K, 50K, and relay on- and off-road race around Isabella Lake on the third Sunday in October.

Kern River Preserve, PO Box 1662, Weldon 93283, ☎ 619/378-2531, where five of California's six ecosystems converge, covers 1,127 acres. Over 240 species of birds frequent the area, including California yellow-billed cuckoos, willow flycatchers, red-shouldered hawks, brown-crested flycatchers and summer tanagers. Southwestern pond turtles can be found in the backwaters and ponds. There is a one-mile nature trail with numbered stops (pick up a brochure at the visitor center).

Tule Elk State Reserve, Kern National Wildlife Refuge, a wintering spot for migratory birds, and the 2,000-acre **South Fork Wildlife Area**, which is currently considering the construction of a series of nature trails, are all close to town.

Carrizo Plain Natural Area has tule elk and antelope, spectacular wildflower displays after the spring rains, and sandhill

Tule Elk Reserve
Credit: Bakersfield Convention & Visitors Bureau

cranes that winter around Soda Lake from October to late February. The preserve, which has exceptional views of the San Andreas Fault, occupies 180,000 acres west of town.

Trail of 100 Giants is half a mile off Route 190 (Great Western Divide Highway) in **Sequoia National Forest**.

If pools and slides in icy creeks and a look at **Peppermint Falls** sound inviting, drive north on Lloyd Meadows Rd. about half a mile west of Johnsondale. Park six miles past the intersection and hike a mile to the confluence of Alder and Dry Meadow Creeks.

For a nice combination of hiking and driving, take Highway 99 along the river for 22 miles until you reach Johnsondale Bridge, then hike the **Bridge Trail**. After the hike, return to your car and proceed about a mile past the bridge, where the road veers west, providing a view of 150-foot **South Creek Falls**.

Whiskey Flat Trail begins just north of Kernville and runs parallel to the Kern River for 14 miles. It makes a good backpack trip, during which you will cross Bull Run, Ant Canyon and Tobias Creeks. There are great views of Stormy Canyon, Yellow Jacket Peak and Baker Point, a fire lookout. The hike ends after it forms a junction with **Fairview Mine Trail**, where it crosses a suspension bridge over the river.

From **Lion Ridge to Frog Meadow** is a 15-mile loop just southeast of California Hot Springs that is accessible from dirt road 23S04. From the parking lot, **Deer Creek Trail** leads to **Frog Meadow Motorcycle Path** and joins another road that eventually leads to Frog Meadow Campground, an old cabin at the end of an adjacent meadow.

Golden Trout Wilderness has a 27-mile loop trail that begins at junction of Parker Pass Dr. and Lloyd Meadows Rd. Follow **Lewis Camp Trail** (33E01) to see Little Kern River Canyon and the waterfalls.

Kern Slab is across from Camp 3 north of Kernville and offers rock climbing. **Sierra South Mountain Sports**, ☎ 619/376-3745, arranges climbs for people 14 years old or older.

Lancaster

California Poppy Reserve, 15101 Lancaster Rd., ☎ 805/942-0662 or 724-1180, occupies 1,800 acres 15 miles west of town. Swathed in California's state flower plus a number of other flowers, such as the multicolored davy gilia, daisy-white tidy-tips and deep purple lupine, the reserve is open daily between 9 and 4 around mid-March when the flowers are in bloom. There is an annual **California Poppy Festival**, ☎ 805/723-6250. Accessible from Highway 138 via 70th St. West is the **Jane S. Pineiro Interpretive Center** and seven miles of trails. **Poppy Loop Trail** explores the lower east side of the reserve, while **Antelope Loop Trail** begins to the left of the visitor center and climbs to Kitanemuk Vista Point, three-quarters of a mile away. You can continue on to Antelope Butte Vista Point, the highest point in the park, and from there join the south loop of the trail to return to the center.

Porterville

Success Lake permits shotgun hunting in the 1,400-acre wildlife area (essentially, the region around Kincade Cove). Pheasant, dove, chukar and waterfowl can be taken. There also is an information center and a nature trail.

Balch Park in **Mountain Home State Forest** has a hunting season for mule deer, black bear, squirrels, quail and grouse. It may be late April or May before the snow leaves this region, but several interesting hikes can be found. A self-guided, one-mile nature trail with an easy grade begins in the park. **Loop Trail**, a two-mile hike with a moderate grade, begins and ends at Shake Camp and passes Adam Tree, Eve Tree and two intriguing "Indian bathtubs" (ask for a map and brochure at the park entrance). **Adam Tree** is 27 feet in diameter and 240 feet tall – the largest tree in the forest. Naturalist John Muir once said that the huge redwoods in this area are the finest in the Sierras.

Redwood Crossing Trail starts at Shake Camp. It is an easy two-mile hike to Redwood Crossing on Rule River, a hard seven-mile hike to Summit Lake, and a strenuous 10-mile hike to Hockett Lakes or Maggie Lakes. A wilderness permit is required. Contact the nearest Ranger Station.

At **Moses Gulch Camp**, look for a sign indicating **Griswold Trail**, which crosses Galena and Silver Creeks on a strenuous seven-mile hike to Maggie Lake. **Moses Gulch Trail,** connecting Moses Gulch and Shake Camp, is much shorter (two miles) and easier (a moderate grade).

Randsburg

To reach **Short Canyon** in Indian Wells Valley, look for a road just south of Brady's Café and turn west. At the fork 1.3 miles beyond, turn left. The road terminates at a trail. Over a hill along the trail, you will encounter a stream where you can turn upstream to find a 20-foot waterfall during the spring.

Butterbredt Spring and Wildlife Sanctuary in Butterbredt Canyon offers good birding (230 species) and a chance to see bighorn, bobcat, coyote, mule deer and mountain lion.

The **El Paso Mountains** provide good rockhounding for petrified wood, jasper-agate, gold and fossils.

Rock climbers should head to **Fossil Falls**. To get there, begin at the junction of US 395 and California 14. Take US 395 north for 20 miles, then turn east on Cinder Cone Rd. After a half-mile, turn right (south) on a dirt pole-line road and go another 0.3 miles to a road heading left (east). After about half a mile, there is a parking area. Follow the trail to the falls about a quarter-mile away. There are two sets of falls, the second a few hundred yards south of the first.

➡ *CAUTION: This is a high, steep and potentially treacherous cliff.*

Redlands

Carolina Park has hiking trails and a nature study area with a demonstration garden, wildflower meadows and wildlife areas.

Prospect Park, Highland and Cajon, occupies 35.4 acres and offers trails as well as a lovely outdoor amphitheater.

Ridgecrest

Red Rock Canyon State Park, where *Jurassic Park* was filmed, covers 4,000 acres and has numerous hiking trails. The area is shown on the "Saltdale" USGA topo map, but you can get a free map at the visitor center that is adequate for most purposes. The picturesque park is layered in an ever-changing blend of colors, but it can be very hot in the summer and most of the roads are dirt.

Trona Pinnacles National Natural Landmark, ☎ 619/375-7125 or 800/847-4830, is 22 miles east of town off Highway 178 at the end of a six-mile dirt road. Here there are 500 strange tufa towers that rise as much as 140 feet from the bottom of Searles Dry Lake basin. *Star Trek V – The Final Frontier, Lost in Space,* and *Cyborg 3,* which featured an unknown Kato Kaelin, were all filmed here. Fall through spring is the best time to visit.

Nearby **Searles Valley** is the long-dry bed of a glacial-age lake. Ninety percent of the earth's 104 natural elements can be found here.

Running Springs

Guided hikes from **Arrowhead Ranger Station,** ☎ 909/337-2444, begin at Deerlick Fire Station, a half-mile east of town.

Santa Clarita

Placerita Canyon Nature Center and Park was the site of California's first gold discovery in 1842. It contains 350 acres of hiking trails and there are guided nature walks, animal shows and family activities, as well as the Nature Center Museum.

Castaic Lake, best known for its freshwater fishing, is also an excellent spot for hiking. In May, a triathlon is held here; in September, a duathlon; and in October, a 10K dam run.

Vasquez Rocks Natural Area Park is a good place for rock climbing.

Sequoia National Park

Congress Trail begins at General Sherman Tree and loops two miles through a sequoia grove.

Marble Falls Trail is a 3½-mile dead-end trail from the upper end of Potwisha Campground (located four miles below the park). Follow the dirt road from the back of the campground until it crosses a concrete ditch.

A short distance beyond, a sign marks the start of the trail as it climbs a steep bank on the right. The trail ends at the base of the falls.

➡ *CAUTION: Watch for poison oak, ticks and rattlesnakes.*

Tehachapi

Tehachapi Mountain Park contains several good hiking trails. At the park entrance, ask for a map to **Nuooah Nature Trail**, where there are signs that identify the trees, lichens, bushes, a spring, marble, limestone, a spot hit by lightning and a spot where acorn woodpeckers store their nuts in a tree stump. Nuooah (the people) were the earliest Indian inhabitants of the area.

Tehachapi Gem & Mineral Society, ☎ 805/822-5154 or 821-1082, hosts field trips to such places as Castle Butte in Mojave Valley for jasper, agate and petrified wood.

Visalia

Kaweah (*raven*) **Oaks Preserve**, Road 182 and Highway 198, ☎ 209/627-4328 or 738-0211, is a 324-acre preserve owned by The Nature Conservancy. It's seven miles east of town on the Kaweah River and east of the Visalia Wildlife Preserve. Over 100 species of birds, 11 species of reptiles and amphibians and 14 species of mammals can be found there.

Two areas will be of interest to the rock climber: **Dome Rock**, in Sequoia National Forest; and **The Needles**, northeast of Dome Rock.

Bakersfield

Sawtooth Hill is the most fossil-rich Miocene marine bone bed in the world. Its 110 square miles contain the fossilized remains of all the major marine groups of animals.

Kern County Mineral Society, PO Box 3004, Bakersfield 93385, ☎ 805/837-8456, hosts field trips and stages the annual **Gem-A-Rama** show on the first weekend in May at Kern County Fairgrounds.

Lebec

Mount Piños is a place for attempting to see the California condor, North America's largest land bird, which recently has been reintroduced to the area. From the southwest end of the parking lot, take the marked dirt road to the summit, a distance of two miles.

➡ *CAUTION: The area is subject to lightning strikes in the summer.*

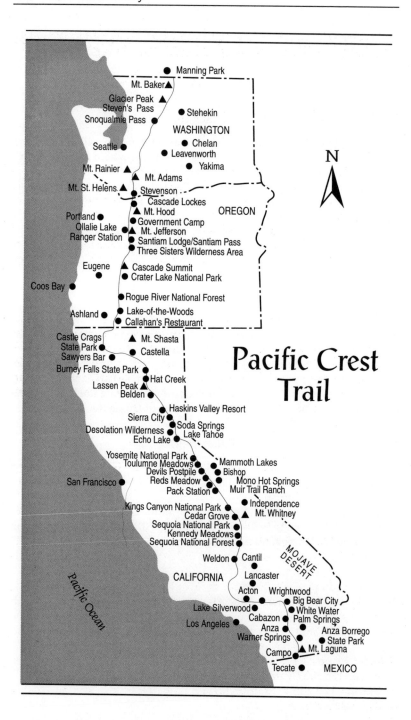

On Horseback

Bakersfield

Rio Brave Ranch Riding Club, ☎ 805/872-9331, rents horses.

Big Bear Lake

Magic Mountain Stables, 40355 Big Bear Blvd., ☎ 909/878-4677 or 585-6482, rents horses and conducts quarter-hour, sunset and pony rides. There is also a fun park with two waterslides and two toboggan slides.

Baldwin Lake Stables at the east end of the valley, ☎ 909/585-6482, offers quarter-and half-hour rides with a view of Erwin Lake, plus three-to four-hour rides along the Pacific Crest Trail, which runs from Canada to Mexico. Also available are sunset rides and pony rides for children six and under.

Exeter

Mineral King is 25 winding miles from Highway 198 north of Three Rivers. In that distance, the road climbs from 1,200 feet in Three Rivers to 7,800 feet at Mineral King Valley. There are many small lakes that offer good trout fishing, and the pack station, ☎ 209/561-4142, which outfits pack trains and trail rides. The summers are short, and heavy rainstorms are common in the afternoons.

Redlands

Carolina Park, Sunset Dr. and Mariposa, covers 16.8 acres and has a number of horse trails.

Ridgecrest

Wild Horse & Burro Corrals, three miles east of town on Highway 178, ☎ 619/446-6064, is where the Bureau of Land Management (BLM) holds animals for adoption.

Desert Empire Fairground & RV Park, 520 S. Richmond Rd., ☎ 619/375-8000, provides full hookups and horse stalls.

Riverside

Rancho Jurupa Park, 4800 Crestmore, ☎ 909/684-7032, has equestrian trails and provides fishing, hiking and camping.

Martha McLean Park, 5900 Jurupa Ave., ☎ 909/682-3031, has hiking and equestrian trails.

Hidden Valley Wildlife Area, 11700 Arlington Ave., ☎ 909/275-4310, is a good spot for riding, hiking and wildlife.

Rosamond

J.G. Stallion Station - Pony Time, 9201 W. Ave. A, ☎ 805/256-0221, rents horses.

Sequoia National Park

Horseback riding can be arranged at the **Wolverton** and **Mineral King** pack stations. ☎ 209/565-3341.

Tehachapi

Tehachapi Mountain Park, eight miles southwest of town, has a number of good horse trails. The park covers 570 acres and resides at an elevation of 6-7,000 feet.

Tulare

Circle N Stables, 12742 Ave. 240, Tulare 93274, ☎ 209/686-4476, rents horses.

Victorville

Mojave Narrows Regional Park on the eastern edge of town has horseback riding, camping, fishing and paddleboats.

Visalia

Whitendale Equestrian Center, 14899 Ave. 295, ☎ 209/733-7878, and **Grant Grove Stables**, 1716 Meadow Lane, ☎ 209/561-4621, both rent horses.

RODEOS

Banning

Stagecoach Days, ☎ 909/849-4695, are held in Smith Creek Regional Park on the last weekend in September or the first weekend in October. They feature a rodeo, parade, carnival and beard-growing contest.

Bakersfield

Stampede Days Rodeo, Kern County Fairgrounds, ☎ 805/391-7627, is held in May.

Glennville Round-Up, 196 Pascoe Rd., in neighboring Glennville, ☎ 805/871-7858, takes place in June.

Frazier Park

Frazier Mountain Lions Club Rodeo also takes place in June.

Kernville

In February, the four-day **Whiskey Flat Days** include a rodeo and a parade. In October, the two-day **Kernville Wild West Daze Rodeo** is held in the John E. McNalley Arena, ☎ 619/378-3157.

Lancaster

A carnival and rodeo are part of the annual **Antelope Valley Fair**, 155 E. Ave. I, ☎ 805/948-6060.

Ridgecrest

Every October, a **High School Rodeo** is part of the Desert Empire Fair, 520 S. Richmond Rd., ☎ 619/375-8000.

Porterville

Annual events include the rodeo, Stagecoach Stampede, Jack-ass Mail Run, Veteran's Day Parade, Indian Pow Wow, and Pumpkin Festival, plus "California's Finest Barrel-Racing Futurity," ☎ 209/784-7502, held at Dunn Ranch.

Springville

Every April, this old mountain logging town holds the **Jackass Mail Run & Rodeo**.

Tehachapi

The **Tehachapi Mountain Festival**, held every August, includes a rodeo.

On Wheels

CYCLING

Bakersfield

Keyesville Classic Mountain Bike Race, held in late March, is one of the largest races in the western United States. Six races are run over a weekend.

Fat Tire Festival, which is held on the last weekend in October each year, features guided rides.

Kern Canyon Road outside of Bodfish is a good route for beginners, while **Cannell Trail**, beginning near Sherman Peak, is an excellent choice for experienced bikers.

Big Bear Lake

Mountain bikes can be rented at **Big Bear Bikes**, 41810 Big Bear Blvd., ☎ 909/866-2224; at **Skyline Ski & Sport**, 653 Pine Knot Ave., ☎ 909/866-3500; and at **Team Big Bear**, 800 Summit Blvd., ☎ 909/866-4565.

Ridgecrest

College Heights trails include the seven-mile **High Sierra** loop, the 10-mile **Lathrop Canyon** loop, and the 15-mile **Wagon Wheel Trail**.

El Paso Mountains trails include the 10-mile **Powerline** loop, the 10-mile **Sheep Springs to Goler Gulch Trail**, the 10-mile **Sheep Springs to Mesquite Canyon Trail**, and the 15-mile **Sheep Springs to Last Chance Canyon Trail**.

Sierra Canyon trails include the five-mile **Indian Wells Canyon Eastern Sierra Climb** and the five-mile **Short Canyon Trail**.

Riverside

For a biking map of the area, contact ☎ 909/683-7100.

Santa Clarita

Vasquez Rocks Natural Area Park contains 745 acres and is a local favorite for biking and horseback riding.

In April, there are **Tour de Canyons**, 20-, 50-, and 100-mile bike races.

Near **Castaic Lake**, there are mountain bike races in April, May, June and October.

Silverwood

Silverwood Lake Recreation Area has miles of biking trails.

Visalia

The annual **Visalia Criterium** cycling classic makes a 0.7-mile loop of the city streets, including five left turns and one right turn (most criteriums are square, with all left turns).

MOTORING

Gorman

Hungry Valley State Vehicular Recreation Area has a visitor center just outside the entrance. It contains 115 miles of trails running from one to nine miles each. There also are 2,000 acres of open riding areas. Each spring weekend, there are wildflower tours. The **Quail Canyon** area contains one of the finest natural terrain motocross racing tracks in the country. Races are scheduled there on weekends throughout the year. Classes are given (contact **California Assn. of 4-Wheel Drive Clubs**, ☎ 800/494-3966), and there is a fenced mini-track for the kids.

For an easy two-hour drive, take Gold Hill Rd. 1½ miles into the SVRA and turn left (east) onto Powerline Rd. Climb to the top of Gorman Ridge – a good place to see wildlife – and look down into Gorman Canyon 1,000 feet below. At the pass atop the ridge, look down at Tejon Pass. On a clear day, you'll be able to look past Quail Lake to Antelope Valley and the Mojave Desert to the east. For the next two miles, descend from the ridge to a trailhead sign that will direct you to Freeman Canyon Trail. Turn right at the sign and follow the trail along a sandy wash through the woodlands (a good place to see wildlife). At the mouth of the canyon, turn left (east) on Pipeline Rd. for an easy 1½-mile drive to Lower Hungry Valley Rd. Turn left (east) to access I-5 at Smokey Bear Rd. , or turn right (west) and stay on Lower Hungry Valley Rd. to Gold Hill Rd., where a right turn (north) will take you back to the SVRA entrance near Gorman.

Mojave

Jawbone Canyon off Highway 14 north of town is good for off-highway driving. Check at the visitor center.

Porterville

Off Highway Vehicle Park, 701 W. Scranton Ave., ☎ 209/782-4010, has a motocross track and a kid's track.

On & In the Water

Lake Arrowhead

South Shore Marina permits swimming for a fee. **Lake Arrowhead Marina**, 870 Highway 173, ☎ 909/337-2553, rents boats.

Arrowhead Queen, waterfront at Lower Village, ☎ 909/336-6992, is a 60-passenger paddlewheeler that leaves for a 50-minute narrated cruise on the hour each afternoon during the summer and on weekends during the winter (weather permitting).

Bakersfield

The city is proposing a **Kern River Parkway** that will front the river as it flows through town. The parkway is to include an equestrian staging area and trail, a marsh area, a bird habitat, an environmental studies area, a bicycle path, a sand volleyball area, four picnic areas and a wildflower display area.

Although Bakersfield is an inland city, the ocean is but an hour or two away. **Outdoor Adventures**, 6602 Wofford Heights Blvd., ☎ 800/323-4234, will arrange canoeing or ocean (sit-on-top) kayaking excursions lasting from one hour to three days between April and September.

Captain Frog, 1609 S. H St., ☎ 805/833-3781, will provide scuba diving lessons and trips, as will **Innerspace Divers**, 1305 N. Chester, ☎ 805/399-1425, and **Sea Fox Scuba**, 1801 Chester Ave., ☎ 805/631-9842.

Buena Vista Aquatic Recreation Area, Golf Course Rd. off Highway 119, is located between Bakersfield and Taft and includes two lakes, 86-acre **Lake Evans**, which is used for fishing, sailing and boating (5 mph speed limit), and 748-acre **Lake Webb**, which is used for boating, water-skiing and fishing (125 acres are set aside for watercycles). The park also has two swimming lagoons and a bike path. For more information, contact **Kern County Parks & Recreation Dept.**, 1110 Golden State Ave., Bakersfield 93301, ☎ 805/861-2063.

Lake Ming, on the outskirts of town, is a half-mile-long, half-mile-wide impoundment used for sailing, skiing and power-boating. The lake is the venue for annual National and International Drag Boat Assn. boat drags. No jetskiing is allowed.

Big Bear Lake

Meadow Park Swim Beach, Park Ave. and Mountainaire Lane, ☎ 909/866-0135, is the only swimming beach on the lake. During the summer, visitors may swim for a fee. Lifeguards are on duty.

Alpine Trout Lakes provide trout fishing.

BOAT RENTALS

Big Bear Marina
Paine Rd. & Lakeview Dr.   ☎ 909/866-3218
Holloway's Marina
398 Edgemoor Rd.   ☎ 909/866-5706
Pine Knot Landing
439 Pine Knot Ave.   ☎ 909/866-2628
(also operates 75-0minute narrated lake cruises)
Pleasure Point Landing
Big Bear Blvd.,   ☎ 909/866-2455

Crestline

Lake Gregory Regional Park, 24171 Lake Dr., in nearby Gregory, ☎ 805/338-2233, is an 86-acre, mile-long reservoir with a beach containing two 300-foot waterslides, boat rentals and fishing. For more information, contact **Crestline Chamber of Commerce**, ☎ 805/338-2706.

Delano

Lake Woollomes provides swimming and boating, as well as fishing for largemouth bass, crappie, bluegill, catfish and rainbow trout.

Frazier Park

Quail Lake offers striped bass, rainbow trout, catfish and bluegill.
    Where the **California Aquaduct** parallels Highway 138, locals fish for striped bass and catfish.
    Another local fishing secret near the town of Grapevine is **Edmonton Pumping Plant**, which has striped bass and catfish.
    In **Los Padres National Forest**, trout are stocked at **Reyes Creek Campground, Camp Shiedeck, Pyramid Lake, Frenchman's Flat** and below **Pyramid Dam**. Pyramid Lake also provides striped bass, largemouth bass, crappie, bluegill and catfish.
    Halfmoon Campground, Sunset Campground, Mutau Creek, Buck Creek, and the area of **Piru Creek** below Hardluck Campground are stocked with trout.
    The pond in **Frazier Kern County Park** contains trout and striped bass.

Kaweah Lake

Thirty miles from Porterville, and also near Exeter and Visalia, **Kaweah Lake** was formed in 1962 by damming the Kaweah River. The lake is popular for houseboating, boating, camping, fishing (largemouth bass, crappie, bluegill, perch, catfish, rainbow trout) and watersports.

Fishing access is available at **Lemon Hill, Kaweah, Horse Creek, Slick Rock** and **Cobble Knoll.**

Boat-launch ramps can be found at **Lemon Hill** and **Kaweah Marina,** 35597 Sierra Dr., Lemon Cove 93244, ☎ 209/597-2526. The marina also rents boats, jetskis and houseboats. **Kaweah River** tributaries near Three Rivers are stocked with trout in late April and early May.

For additional information, contact **Corps of Engineers**, PO Box 346, Lemon Cove 93244, ☎ 209/597-2301.

Kernville

Kern River begins near 14,494-foot Mount Whitney, the highest point in the 48 contiguous United States, and flows 170 miles, dropping at a rate of 60 feet per mile. In some places, the rate of descent is 75 feet per mile, the steepest of any river west of the Mississippi. Over the last 25 years, 176 people have drowned in the Kern.

The Kern River is classified according to difficulty in three sections, the Upper Kern, the Lower Kern, and the Forks of the Kern.

KERN RIVER

Upper Kern actually is the middle section of the three Kerns – short, fast, and filled with foam.

★ The top section (Limestone Run) begins just below the Limestone Bridge and continues downriver to above the Fairview Diversion Dam. The rapids are big and powerful, and kayakers can make several runs in one day.

★ The middle section (Thunder Run) is Class III-V whitewater, and can be done in one day.

★ The lower section is almost all Class III water. Boaters put in at Camp 3, Riverkern or Powerhouse. Trips usually last only one or two hours.

Lower Kern is used primarily for one- and two-day trips. The first day is scenic; the second day more exciting. The rapids are classed I-IV. The prime season is from June through September.

Forks of the Kern is the uppermost part of the river adjacent to Golden Trout Wilderness Area. It is virtually inaccessible, except on foot or with a mule, and generally involves a three-day trip. The season is limited (May through early July). Too much water and the stretch is too dangerous; too little water and the boats can't float. This area, listed as Class III-V, is one of the most demanding and intense whitewater experiences in North America.

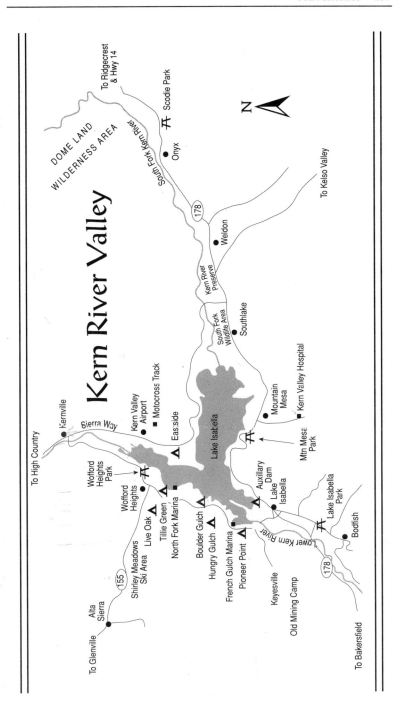

Tackling whitewater on the Kern.
Credit: Bakersfield Convention & Visitors Bureau

Rafting on the "killer" Kern has become a business as well as a sport.

Whitewater Voyages, 5225 San Pablo Dam Rd., PO Box 20400, El Sobrante 94820-0400, ☎ 800/488-7238, fax 510/758-7238, e-mail raft@wwvoyages.com, arranges half-day to week-long runs on all three branches of the Kern. "California's largest, most experienced" whitewater firm also provides schools, summer camps and workshops. The company operates throughout California and southern Oregon, leading groups on the Rogue, Klamath, Salmon, Yuba, American and Stanislaus Rivers, among others.

Sierra South Mountain Sports, ☎ 619/376-3745 or 800/457-2082, fax 619/376-1706, offers one-hour to all-day trips on the Kern from April through September for everyone over the age of six.

Mountain & River Adventures, 11113 Kernville Rd., ☎ 619/376-6553 or 800/861-6553, arranges trips on the Kern as well as renting mountain bikes. They will set up a bike tour, a climbing trip or a two-day bike-and-raft combination. In the winter, they offer snow cat cruises, snow-boarding, snowshoe treks and cross-country skiing. Nearby, the firm operates **Boulder Creek Adventure Campground**, which has an amphitheater, a climbing wall, facilities for golf and campsites (tents only, no RVs or trailers), and a High Adventure Camp for kids.

The annual **Kern River Races**, ☎ 619/376-2629, begin in Limestone Campground, 18 miles north of town, and end in Riverside Park. The races, which include a downriver race, a whitewater rodeo and a slalom kayak race, are the oldest kayak races in California.

Downstream from Riverside Park in Kernville, the Kern River has some lazy sections suitable for innertubing.

Fishing is good in the Kern from Fairview Dam upstream to Johnsondale Bridge. Rainbow trout are stocked in the Upper and Lower river weekly during the summer months and semi-weekly the rest of the year. Brown trout also are caught in the river.

California Dept. of Fish & Game operates the **Kern River Fish Hatchery**, 14400 Sierra Way (Highway 99), Kernville 93238, ☎ 619/376-2846, 379-5895 or 379-1981, a mile north of town adjacent to the river. There is a visitor center and a museum, as well as llamas to look at. The center is open daily, and the second Saturday in June is a free Kids' Fishing Day. Coming is a natural history museum, a number of nature walks and a new, expanded visitor center. The 33-acre hatchery annually distributes

117,000 pounds of rainbow trout throughout the local waterways. Pellet fish food can be purchased and fed to the fish.

Lake Hughes

Forest Lakes Resort, 17000 Elizabeth Lake Rd., ☎ 805/724-1412, provides camping, a swimming pool and fishing. For more information, contact **Lake Hughes Chamber of Commerce**, PO Box 100, Lake Hughes 93532, ☎ 805/724-2025.

Lake Isabella

Lake Isabella is a town. **Isabella Lake** is a 7,000-acre impoundment popular for fishing, swimming, waterskiing, jetskiing, sailing, windsurfing and birdwatching.

Created by the Corps of Engineers for flood control and agricultural purposes, the lake has four arms. There are 31 recreation areas and three marinas.

The old town of Isabella is underwater, as is the old town of Kernville (originally called Whiskey Flat), but during dry years, the water level drops sufficiently to reveal the foundations.

Red's Kern Valley Marina, ☎ 619/379-1634 or 800/553-7337, rents jetskis, pontoon boats, fishing boats, party barges, paddleboats and runabouts. For 24-hour reports on wind conditions, ☎ 619/379-JIBE.

Dean's North Fork Marina, ☎ 619/376-1812, rents boats.

French Gulch Marina, ☎ 619/379-8774, is on the west shore of the lake near the main dam about a mile from town.

Chuck Richards' Whitewater, ☎ 619/379-4444 or 800/624-5950, arranges one- and two-day rafting trips from May through September.

Kern River Tours, ☎ 619/379-4616 or 800/844-7238, fax 619/379-2103, e-mail krt@kernvalley.com, provides one-, two- and three-day Kern River trips and takes photos or videos to take home as souvenirs. Also available are two- and four-hour ATV (All-terrain Vehicle) tours at Mammoth Lakes, ☎ 619/934-0606. In addition, the company operates a school for prospective guides and a kayak school.

INFORMATION SOURCES

Corps of Engineers, PO Box 997, Lake Isabella 93240, ☎ 619/379-2742.

Lake Isabella Chamber of Commerce, PO Box 567, Lake Isabella 93240-0567, ☎ 619/379-5236.

The Kern River Valley Visitors Council, PO Box O, Lake Isabella 93240, ☎ 619/379-3867.

Lancaster

Apollo County Park, 4555 W. Ave. G, ☎ 805/940-7701 or 259-1750, is stocked with fish every two weeks.

Antelope Valley Scuba/Valley Swim School, 1430 W. Ave. I, ☎ 805/949-2555, fax 805/940-9189, is a good place to tune up before heading for the coast.

Littlerock

Littlerock Reservoir southeast of Palmdale is a good spot for fishing. For more information, contact **Littlerock Chamber of Commerce**, PO Box 326, Littlerock 93543, ☎ 805/944-6421, or **Sun Village Chamber of Commerce**, 10164 E. Palmdale Blvd., PO Box 151, Littlerock 93543, ☎ 805/944-2341.

Piru

Pyramid Lake Recreation Area is in Angeles National Forest north of Santa Clarita Valley off I-5. Swimming is permitted. There is a snack bar and a marina that rents boats. Fishing is excellent for trout, small- and largemouth bass, catfish, striped bass, crappie and bluegill. The area is open year-round.

Porterville

Success Lake provides for houseboating, waterskiing, sailing, jetskiing, windsurfing and birdwatching. There are two launch ramps in the Tule Recreation Area and another in the Rocky Hill Recreation Area. **Success Marina** is in the Tule Recreation Area. Shoreline fishing for black bass, striped bass, white crappie, bluegill and channel catfish is good in the spring and summer. In the fall, the lake is stocked with several thousand rainbow trout. Fish attractors located in the area of the north Tule launch ramp and in Kincade Cove make those areas particularly productive.

Balch Park in Mountain Home State Forest has three ponds stocked with rainbow trout that can be reached by foot or on horseback.

Fishing for rainbow, brown and brook trout is also good along miles of the North Fork or the Middle Fork of the **Tule River** and its tributaries.

Santa Clarita

This community is well situated for fishermen. Nearby are **Pyramid, Piru** and **Castaic Lakes**. Of the three, Castaic Lake is the largest and busiest.

In February, there are jetski races and a bass tournament on Castaic Lake, followed by two more bass tournaments in March and April. May brings another jetski race and a bass tournament, while June provides a boat race and yet another bass tournament. The bass tournament in July concludes that activity for the season, but another round of drag boat races and jetski races takes place in August.

Sequoia National Park

There is excellent year-round fishing for rainbow, eastern brook, German brown and golden trout throughout the park.

Silverwood

Silverwood Lake Recreation Area, ☎ 909/389-2303, is a 1,000-acre reservoir reached by taking Highway 189 out of San Bernardino to Highway 138. The lake is popular for swimming, boating, sailing, waterskiing, camping and fishinf for trout and panfish. Recently, 640 "fish spheres" were placed in the Cleghorn and Miller Canyon areas to attract fish. Each 6½-foot sphere was placed in water 10-40 feet below maximum lake level (usually 3,353 feet). Rock reefs were placed in key areas as well.

Silverwood Lake Marina, Cleghorn Rd., ☎ 909/389-2320, rents boats.

Taft

An annual Trout Derby is held at **Lake Evans.**

Victorville

Horseshoe Lake is stocked with trout until late April, then stocked with catfish beginning in May. The lake also contains largemouth bass.

Pelican Lake contains the same fish as Horseshoe Lake and is stocked on approximately the same schedule.

On Snow

Bakersfield

Nordic skiing is available at **Frazier Mountain** in the Los Padres National Forest and in the **Greenhorn District** of Sequoia National Forest. **Greenhorn Summit,** eight miles west of Wofford Heights on Highway 155, has numerous trails for cross-country skiers and snowshoe enthusiasts. Sledding also is good in this area, while **Portuguese Pass Rd.** heading north from Summit provides snowmobilers with access to roads and trails that extend for many miles. The road just past Johnsondale is not plowed after a snow and opens miles of roads and trails to cross-country skiers and snowshoers. The **Piute Mountains** south and east of Lake Isabella are the least developed, and high-country access is

Experienced skiers choose Bakersfield.
Credit: Bakersfield Convention & Visitors Bureau

limited. **Ponderosa Lodge,** Highway 190 (Great Western Divide) rents skis and snowshoes. It also offers limited overnight accommodations.

Alpine skiing is available at **Shirley Meadows Ski Resort,** PO Box Q, Wofford Heights 93285, ☎ 619/376-4186. The 7,000-foot facility is on Greenhorn Summit off Rancheria Rd. It offers two double chairlifts. Skis and snowboards are for rent, and lessons can be scheduled. The resort is open from Friday through Sunday and on holidays.

Big Bear Lake

Bear Mountain Ski Resort, Club View Dr., ☎ 909/585-2519, is 3.6 miles southeast of the village. It provides 11 chairlifts and a half-mile trail for snowboarders with its own chairlift. The season begins before Thanksgiving and runs into April. There is a restaurant and lounge.

Snow Summit, at the end of Summit Blvd., ☎ 909/866-5766, is 1.8 miles southeast of the village and also has 11 chairlifts. The longest run is 1¼ miles, and there is a permanent "half-pipe" (a banked, U-shaped course) that is a favorite of snowboarders. **Westridge Freestyle Park,** containing over a mile of spines, tabletops, volcanoes, and other types of terrain, also is popular with snowboarders, although skiers are welcome. The slopes are lighted most nights, there is a rental shop, and lessons can be scheduled. If it's your birthday, you get to ski free. Restaurants, lounges and lodgings are available. On New Year's Eve there is a torchlight parade, and in January, the California Cup race series is held. A Scenic Sky Chair takes hikers, bikers and sightseers to the top during the summer.

Big Air Green Valley, ☎ 909/867-2338, is a small (40-acre) alpine skiing area with two surface lifts and one chairlift.

Snow Valley, Highway 18 near Running Springs, ☎ 909/867-2751 or 800/680-SNOW, is a 235-acre ski area with eight double chairlifts, five triple chairlifts and one tow. The longest run is 1.2 miles, and there is lighted skiing from Wednesday through Sunday at night. Food is available, but there are no lodgings. A new snowboard park has been installed.

Snowdrift Tube-boggins, Highway 18, ☎ 909/867-2640, provides rubber inner tubes with belly straps and handles for sliding down the hills.

For more information, contact **Running Springs Chamber of Commerce,** ☎ 909/867-2411.

Palmdale

Ski Sunrise, ☎ 818/249-6150, provides three surface lifts and one quad chairlift on a 100-acre slope.

Snowcrest at Kratka Ridge, ☎ 818/440-9747, covers only 58 acres, but it provides two chairlifts and one rope tow.

In the Air

BALLOONING

To go hot-air ballooning in Bakersfield, contact **Sunset Balloon Flight**, 1528 White Lane, ☎ 805/397-1757.

In Lancaster, contact **The Ultimate Adventure Ballooning Co.**, 43625 60th St. West, ☎ 805/722-2924.

Ridgecrest is the home of the **U.S. Navy Hot Air Balloon Team**, at China Lake Naval Air Weapons Station. Established in Albuquerque, New Mexico in 1977, the team moved to China Lake in 1994.

GLIDING

For a glider ride around California City, contact **Caracole Soaring**, California City Airport, 6301 Lindberg Blvd., ☎ 619/373-1019.

In Llano, contact **Crystal Soaring**, 32810 165th St. East, ☎ 805/944-3341, 944-0305 or 800/801-GLIDE, for flight instruction or for rides in a one-or two-person glider. They'll provide either smooth sailing or, for a touch of the wild life, aerobatics.

Mountain Valley Airport, ☎ 805/822-5267, in Tehachapi also books sailplane rides.

AIRPLANES & HELICOPTERS

Aero Haven, ☎ 909/585-9663, at the airport 4½-miles northeast of the village at Big Bear Lake, offers flight lessons as well as 30- and 50-minute scenic flights. **Mountain Hawk Aviation**, 222 N. Hayes St., Tehachapi, ☎ 805/822-8153, provides similar services out of Tehachapi Municipal Airport, ☎ 805/822-2220.

Antelope Valley Aviation, 4555 W. Ave. G, Ste. 2, Lancaster 93536, ☎ 805/723-7366, and **Barnes Aviation**, PO Box 1959, Lancaster 93539, ☎ 805/948-4048, provide flight instruction.

PARASAILING & PARACHUTING

In Riverside, **Jim Wallace Skydiving School,** ☎ 800/795-3483; **Perris Valley Skydiving,** ☎ 800/832-8818; and **Skydiving Adventures Parachute School,** ☎ 909/925-8197, will all take you skydiving.

Eco-Travel/Cultural Excursions

Bakersfield

Kern County Museum, 3801 Chester Ave., ☎ 805/861-2132, includes the main museum building and over 50 other structures covering 14 acres of space. Located two miles north of downtown, this eclectic collection of structures includes:

★ The Moorish, five-level **Beale Memorial Clock Tower,** built in 1904 by Truxtun Beale, former ambassador to Spain, in memory of his mother.

★ Barnes Log Cabin, built in 1868 and wallpapered with copies of *The Bakersfield Californian* and *San Francisco Chronicle* newspapers. Barnes was the first in the valley to grow peach trees and one of the first to grow alfalfa.

★ **Howell House,** an 1891 Queen Anne built by John Singleton for $7,000. Singleton went broke and finished the building by working at carpenter's wages ($2-$3 a day), then headed into the deserts of east Kern, where he and two partners struck it rich on gold.

★ **Pinkney House,** home of one of first black families in the area.

★ **Quinn Sheepherder's Cabin,** built in 1906 to house the sheepherder who followed Quinn's flock. Designed for mobility, the cabin was equipped with skids and it could be pulled from place to place by horses.

Melodrama Musical Theatre, 206 China Grade Loop, ☎ 805/393-7886, contains seating for 300.

Bakersfield Community Theatre, 2400 S. Chester Ave., ☎ 805/831-8114, was established in 1927 and is the oldest continuously operating community theater in California.

California Living Museum, 14000 Alfred Harrell Hwy., ☎ 805/872-2256, is an intriguing combination zoo, natural history museum and botanical garden.

Kern County Fairgrounds, 1142 S. P St., ☎ 805/833-4900, which occupies 166 acres, hosts the county fair in late September each year.

Banning

Malki Festival is celebrated each May on the Morongo Indian Reservation, ☎ 909/849-7289.

Malki Museum, 11795 Fields Rd., also on the Morongo Indian Reservation, ☎ 909/849-7289, contains an assortment of Indian artifacts.

Banning Playhouse Bowl, ☎ 909/849-4695, hosts outdoor concerts on Thurday evenings throughout August.

Delano

Delano City Heritage Park, 330 Lexington St., ☎ 805/725-6370 or 725-9657, displays the 1876 Jail House, the 1888 Victorian Weaver House, the 1890 Wong House, an 1890 Homesteader's Cabin, the 1916 Jasmine School and a large display of old farm equipment.

Lancaster

Antelope Valley Indian Museum, 15701 E. Ave. M, ☎ 805/942-0662, is closed from mid-June to mid-September.

Antelope Valley African American Museum, 43437 N. Gadsden, B-5, ☎ 805/723-0811, traces Black history in the West.

Lancaster Performing Arts Center, 750 W. Lancaster Blvd., ☎ 805/723-5950, provides theater in a 758-seat auditorium.

Western Hotel Museum, ☎ 805/723-6250, is housed in Lancaster's oldest structure.

Lebec

Fort Tejon State Historic Park, I-5 at the Fort Tejon exit, Lebec, ☎ 805/248-6692, offers educational tours and Civil War reenactments. During the summer, 1,000 volunteer candlemakers, physicians, laundry workers and kitchen personnel demonstrate "the old ways." In 1853, Gen. Edward F. Beale, a hero of the Mexican-American War then serving as Superintendent of Indian Affairs for California and Nevada, moved the local Indians to the Sebastian Indian Reserve east of Grapevine Canyon. The following year, Beale suggested the site for a new Army fort, Fort Tejon, which became headquarters for the Dragoons.

Tejon Ranch, ☎ 805/248-6774 or 327-8481, was created by Edward Beale after the Civil War closed Fort Tejon. Beale bought and united four Mexican land grants, and he left a ranch consisting of 269,215 acres when he died in 1893. The holdings, nearly the size of Los Angeles, begin below Gorman and extend to Bakersfield. Beale's son Truxtun (see *Bakersfield*, page 144) sold the ranch in 1912 to a group of investors that included newspaper publisher Harry Chandler and his father-in-law, Harrison Gray Otis of *The Los Angeles Times*. It is now owned by a publicly traded corporation that advertises "Farming, Livestock, Land Management,

Filming Locations, Oil & Minerals, Hunting & Fishing, Horseman's Club." *Wild Bill*, a movie starring Jeff Bridges, and *Star Trek Generations*, a picture with William Shatner, were filmed on the ranch.

Porterville

Native American Heritage Celebration, ☎ 209/784-7502, is held at Porterville Fairgrounds every September.

Redlands

Asistencia Mission de San Gabriel, 26930 Barton Rd., ☎ 909/793-5402, was built between 1830 and 1834 by the Franciscan Fathers of the Mission San Gabriel. It was the last of the California's 21 Spanish missions to be built and is now a museum and wedding chapel.

Lincoln Memorial Shrine, 125 W. Vine St., ☎ 909/798-7632, is an unusual octagonal building housing letters, manuscripts and memorabilia relating to the Civil War and Abraham Lincoln. The collection includes 2,000 books and 1,800 rare pamphlets.

During the winter, **Redlands Symphony Orchestra** performs at University of Redlands, 1200 E. Colton Ave., ☎ 909/793-2121.

Ridgecrest

Maturango Museum of the Indian Wells Valley, 100 E. Las Flores, ☎ 619/375-6900, fax 619/375-0479, preserves the culture and natural history of the northern Mojave Desert and Death Valley National Park. The multipurpose facility includes a Death Valley Tourist Center, a Northern Mojave Tourist Center, a museum store, a children's discovery area and an art gallery. Tours are arranged to Big and Little Petroglyph Canyons in the Coso Mountains, where the desert's largest concentration of rock art is found, and onto China Lake National Weapons Center land, normally off-limits to visitors.

Riverside

To obtain the current programs featured by **Inland Cities Opera Assn.**, write to 3900 Market St., ☎ 909/686-2234. For **Riverside County Philharmonic**, contact 4091 10th St., ☎ 909/787-0251. The **Riverside Ballet Theater** is at 3840 Lemon St., ☎ 909/787-7850. For the **Louis Rubidoux Nature Center,** ☎ 909/683-4880. For the **California Museum of Photography,** ☎ 909/787-4787.

Sherman High School, ☎ 909/376-6719 or 340-1408, contains an **Indian Museum**.

Tehachapi

Tomo-Kahni (Kawaiisu for "winter home") **State Park,** ☎ 805/942-0662 or 822-8152, is on the site of a Kawaiisu Indian village. Entry is by guided tour only. Tours are offered in the spring and in the fall.

Where To Stay

B&Bs, Hotels & Inns

Lake Arrowhead

Lake Arrowhead Resort, 27984 Highway 189, ☎ 909/336-1511 or 800/800-6792, fax 909/336-1378, has 261 rooms and suites with lake or alpine views, a spa, heated pool, private beach, two restaurants, and a lounge, but it is expensive, especially during the summer (July 1 through September 2). The **Kid's Club** offers adventures such as nature walks, face-painting, duck-feeding and sandcastle-building for children four through 12.

 Antlers Inn, 26125 Highway 189, Twin Peaks, ☎ 909/337-4020, is 4.6 miles from Lake Arrowhead Village. A large turn-of-century log lodge with a big stone fireplace, the inn closed for a time but reopened in 1993. Try their buffalo burgers.

Bakersfield

Residence Inn by Marriott, 4241 Chester Ln., ☎ 805/321-9800 or 800/331-3131, fax 805/321-0721, provides a free breakfast, hospitality hour between Monday and Friday, and (seasonally) a complimentary Thursday-night dinner. **Ramada Inn,** 3535 Rosedale Highway, ☎ 805/327-0681 or 800/228-2828, is located on the north side of town. The inn has 200 rooms and a pool.

 Rio Bravo Tennis & Fitness Resort, 11200 Lake Ming Rd., ☎ 805/872-5000 or 800/282-5000, fax 805/872-6546, is well away from town. It can provide tennis on 18 lighted courts, golf, swimming, a fitness center, basketball, volleyball, cycling, jogging, whitewater rafting, windsurfing and waterskiing. It also has a magnificent restaurant for fine dining.

Big Bear Lake

Alpine Village Suites Lodge, 546 Pine Knot Ave., ☎ 909/866-5460, fax 909/866-0031, provides 700-square-foot suites with fireplaces, full kitchens, king-size beds and cable TV.

Big Bear Inn, ☎ 909/866-3471 or 800/BEAR INN, located a mile from Bear Mountain and Snow Summit, has gas fireplaces, marble bathrooms with heated towel racks, a restaurant, a lounge, a sports bar and an outdoor jacuzzi.

Apples B&B, ☎ 909/866-0903, has 12 rooms with king-size beds, private baths, gas fireplaces, TV and VCR. It also has an outdoor hot tub, a game court, a movie library and a bridal garden. A country gourmet breakfast is served, as well as cider and herb cheese in the afternoon and dessert in the evening. If you're still hungry, there's an all-day snack and beverage bar.

Switzerland Haus B&B, 41829 Switzerland Dr., ☎ 909/866-3729, is near the Snow Summit ski area. It has five guest rooms, including one with a stone fireplace and a private deck.

California City

Silver Saddle Ranch & Club, 20751 Aristotle Dr., ☎ 619/373-8617, includes a hotel, a restaurant, a saloon, a pool, spas, horseback riding, archery range, camping and tennis.

Lancaster

Essex House, 44916 N. 10th St. West, ☎ 805/948-0961 or 800/524-2924 in-state, 800/84-ESSEX out-of-state, fax 805/945-3821, offers racquetball, three weight rooms, an indoor pool, an outdoor pool, a spa and a sauna. There is a hospitality suite on weekday evenings.

Ontario

There's lots of "country" in this town: **Country Side Suites,** 204 N. Vineyard Ave., with 107 units; **Country Suites by Ayres,** 1945 E. Holt Blvd., with 167 units; and **Country Inn & Suites by Carlson,** 231 N. Vineyard Ave., with 120 units.

There's also a couple of **Doubletrees** (339 rooms & 170 rooms), ☎ 909/391-6411 or 909/983-0909, a **Marriott** (299 units), ☎ 909/391-6151, and a **Hilton** (309 rooms), ☎ 909/948-9309.

Randsburg

White House Saloon & Floozy House, 168 Butte Ave., ☎ 619/374-2464, is a one-room B&B with a restaurant nearby.

Visalia

Radisson Hotel, 300 S. Court, ☎ 209/732-5611, 636-1111 or 800/333-3333, has 201 rooms and 12 suites and is adjacent to the convention center. The hotel is owned by the city.

   LampLiter Inn, 3300 W. Mineral King, ☎ 209/732-4511, offers either bungalows or suites.

Camping

Camping in and around **Lake Arrowhead** and **Big Bear Lake** is abundant. For maps and guides, contact the ranger station.

Bakersfield

Buena Vista Aquatic Recreation Area, Golf Course Rd. off Highway 119 between Bakersfield and Taft, has 112 campsites.

Calico

Calico Ghost Town, PO Box 638, Yermo 92398, ☎ 619/254-2122 or 800/TO-CALICO, has 110 camping units available.

Lake Haweah

Lake Haweah, PO Box 44270, Lemon Cove 93244, ☎ 209/597-2301, was formed by the construction of Terminus Dam, completed in 1962. There are developed campsites at **Horse Creek** and undeveloped sites at **Limekiln Hill**. There also are three information centers: **Park office, Kaweah** and **Horse Creek**.

Lake Isabella

Near the town and the lake are 12 campgrounds with 800 campsites, ☎ 619/379-5646. Most of the campgrounds are open from Memorial Day weekend through the Labor Day weekend.

Mojave

Red Rock Canyon State Park, north of Jawbone Canyon on Highway 14, has campsites and miles of trails. Numerous movies have been filmed there.

Piru

Pyramid Lake Recreation Area has 93 campsites in the **Los Alamos Campground.**

Porterville

Balch Park in Mountain Home State Forest offers campsites.

Success Lake, 10 miles east of Highway 190 at Frazier Valley Rd., has 250 surface acres and a 30-mile shoreline, but no swimming beaches (however, the south Tule area and the northern portion of Rocky Hill in this area are popular for swimming). There are 110 primitive camping sites at **Rocky Hill Recreation Area** and 104 improved sites in **Tule Recreation Area**.

For more information, contact **Corps of Engineers**, PO Box 1072, Porterville 93258, ☎ 209/784-0215.

San Bernardino

Silverwood Lake Recreation Area has a campground.

Sequoia National Park

With **Kings Canyon National Park** to the north, there are 1,200 campsites in this magnificent region. Trailers are permitted in the **Potwisha, Dorst, Grant Grove** and **Cedar Grove** areas and in portions of the **Lodgepole** campgrounds, but there are no trailer hookups and trailers may not exceed 35 feet. RVs and single vehicles may not exceed 40 feet.

Tehachapi

Tehachapi Mountain Park eight miles southwest of town has 61 family campsites.

Where To Eat

Bakersfield

Not surprisingly, considering the large Basque population in this region, Basque restaurants are extremely popular here. Traditional meals, sometimes served family-style at long tables, include soup, salad, bread, salsa and beans. This is followed by an entrée (or sometimes, more than one) of steak, seafood, lamb or poultry, accompanied by a variety of vegetables. Wine is served throughout the meal.

Noriega Hotel, 525 Sumner St., ☎ 805/322-8419, operated by the Elizalde family, dates from 1893 and is the oldest Basque restaurant in town. Breakfast ($7 plus tip) is served Tuesday through Sunday between 7 and 9 am and includes wine or coffee. Lunch ($8 plus tip) and dinner ($15 plus tip) are served daily, except Monday. The cost of a child's plate is calculated according to a simple formula: Lunch costs $1 for each year of the child's age up to the age of 8 and dinner costs $1 for each year of the child's age up to the age of 12. Typical dinner offerings include meatballs and steak, lamb stew and prime rib, beef stew and spare ribs, oxtail stew and fried chicken, beef stew and baked chicken.

Other excellent Basque restaurants include **Benji's French Basque Restaurant**, 4001 Rosedale Hwy., ☎ 805/328-0400; **Chalet Basque**, 200 Oak St., ☎ 805/327-2915; **Chateau Basque**, 101 Union Ave., ☎ 805/325-1316; **Maitia's Basque Restaurant**, 3535 Union Ave., ☎ 805/324-4711; **Pyrenees**, 601 Sumner St., ☎ 805/323-0053; and **Wool Growers Restaurant**, 620 E. 19th St., ☎ 805/327-9584.

Goose Loonies, 1623 19th St., ☎ 805/631-1242, offers some exciting Greek food. Try their gyros (pronounced YEE-ro); spanakopita, a spinach pie made of spiced spinach and feta cheese wrapped in phyllo pastry; tzatziki, a spread containing yogurt, cucumber and fresh garlic, served with homemade pita; keftethes, Greek meatballs with feta cheese and tzatziki; and hummus, a tangy garlic chickpea pâté, served with pita bread and a Greek salad.

Guild House, 1905 18th St., ☎ 805/325-5478, was founded in 1958 and is operated entirely by volunteers, who cook, serve, clean, wash dishes... and then donate the proceeds to the Henrietta Weill Child Guidance Clinic. The operation has succeeded in raising over a million dollars to date. The Barlow House, built in the early 1900s and still adorned with authentic period chandeliers, leaded glass cabinets and windows, and hardwood floors, provides an excellent setting for the restaurant. Only lunch is served, Monday through Friday between 11:30 and 1:30, and only from mid-September through mid-June. A meal ($8 plus tax and gratuity) includes soup, entrée, salad and/or vegetable, rolls, a beverage and dessert. Entrées sometimes include game hens Italiano, garlic lime marinated beef, sesame chicken with apricot sauce or salmon with mango salsa. Dessert may be strawberry parfait pie, Norwegian apple pudding or raspberry swirl pie. Beer and wine are available. A fashion show is held every Thursday.

For those addicted to dinner-theater, **Bakersfield Civic Light Opera**, 324 Bernard St., ☎ 805/325-6100, has presented dinner-theater for a quarter of a century. The shows change every few weeks.

New to Bakersfield is **Buck Owens' Crystal Palace Museum and Theater** on Sillect Ave. The restaurant sports a 50-foot bar. Buck Owens and the Buckaroos provide the entertainment.

Lancaster

West & Co./Buffalo Club, 44275 N. Division, ☎ 805/942-3200 or 948-6585, provides the flavor of the Old West, right down to the pool tables. Both indoor and outdoor dining are available.

Randsburg

Randsburg Dinner Theater, ☎ 619/375-9589, provides entertaining theater along with a sumptuous dinner.

Rosamond

Villa Basque, 4417 Rosamond Blvd., ☎ 805/256-4182, serves delicious Basque food.

San Bernardino

Le Rendez-Vous French Restaurant, 4775 N. Sierra Way, ☎ 909/883-1231, may be the best eating establishment in town. Located on the outskirts, it serves excellent French cuisine (including a personal favorite, vichyssoise) in an intimate country atmosphere. The restaurant is closed on Mondays.

Tehachapi

The Summit Dining Hall & Saloon, 480 Steuber Rd., serves wild game specials on Friday and Saturday nights. Typical offerings include venison flank steak, rabbit fajitas, alligator brochette, sauteed rattlesnake, elk steak with walnut roquefort sauce, smoked pheasant, marinated quail, antelope steak, smoked wild turkey, ostrich, buffalo steak ($14.95) or buffalo burgers ($6.50).

Victorville

Mojave Mike's Grub Stop & Waterin' Hole, 12249 Hesperia Rd., ☎ 619/241-7759, merits a stop on the basis of its name alone.

South to Oceanside

To travel south along the coast from Greater Los Angeles is a totally different experience than the travel north from there.

Certainly, the coastline is beautiful in both directions, but where the northern reaches are given to older, more self-contained communities, rapidly giving way to a totally rural environment, the southern coast is a mecca for yuppies. This is where the large shopping malls can be found, the nouvelle cuisine, the jam-packed yacht harbors, the trendy art colonies, the all-glass churches, the manicured golf courses.

From Los Angeles to San Diego, very little open space remains, save for the state beaches, the wildlife sanctuaries, and the enormous Marine Corps base (Camp Pendleton) that commands the waterfront from San Juan Capistrano to Oceanside.

This, perhaps, is the stereotypical southern California, a place where young men and women wear a perpetual tan, where surfboards and swim fins are two of the most common household appliances, and where every day affords the opporunity for new adventures.

Getting Around

Just south of L.A., Highway 1 (often called the Pacific Coast Highway) continues to dominate the coast from Long Beach to San Clemente, while I-5 gradually works its way toward the sea from Santa Ana. But once the interstate reaches the beach, it becomes the "Main Street" for this part of California.

Like capillaries leading to a major artery, side streets link the many little seaside communities to the interstate and hence to the outside world.

Rail transportation is making something of a resurgence here. San Clemente, for example, can now be reached from Fullerton, Anaheim and Santa Ana to the north; and from San Diego and Oceanside to the south by way of Amtrak. The **MetroLink Beach Train** connects San Clemente Pier with Rialto, San Bernardino, Riverside, La Sierra, West Corona and San Juan Capistrano, providing seven arrivals and departures daily. MetroLink is the only suburban-to-suburban rail service remaining in the United States.

Those who would rather have someone else do the driving will have no difficulty arranging a tour with one of the local companies.

Odyssey Tours International, ☎ 800/304-1001, use mini-buses for more intimate trips. **Pacific Coast Sightseeing Tours/Gray Line**, ☎ 800/828-6699, provides guided tours throughout Los Angeles, Hollywood, Beverly Hills, San Diego and Tijuana to see such attractions as Sea

World, Magic Mountain, Knott's Berry Farm and others. **Tour Connection**, ☎ 714/517-6655 or 800/678-9590, takes tours to such places and events as Tijuana, the Rose Parade and Sea World.

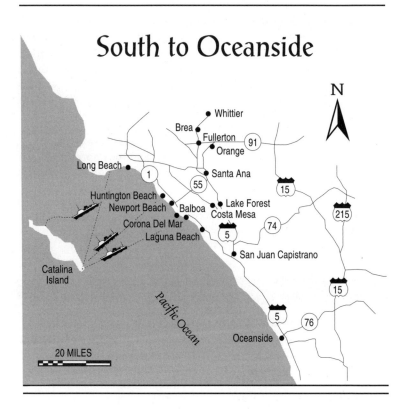

South to Oceanside

N

Whittier

Brea
Fullerton   91
Orange

Long Beach   1   Santa Ana
55
Huntington Beach   15
Newport Beach   Balboa   Lake Forest
Corona Del Mar   Costa Mesa
Laguna Beach   74   215
5

San Juan Capistrano

Catalina
Island

15

Pacific Ocean

5   76

20 MILES   Oceanside

Touring

Anaheim

Founded in 1857 by German immigrants, Anaheim was the wine capital of California until the late 19th century. After a blight destroyed the vines in 1885, the farmers turned to growing Valencia oranges. Anaheim is now the second largest city in Orange County.

Today's primary attraction, of course, is **Disneyland**, a favorite for young and old alike. No trip to Anaheim would be complete without making a pilgrimage to Walt Disney's most endearing achievement. And by the year 2001, there will be a newer, larger Disneyland resort, already on the drawing boards.

For more information, contact **Anaheim/Orange County Visitor & Convention Bureau**, 800 W. Katella Ave., PO Box 4270, Anaheim 92802, ☎ 714/999-8999 or 635-8900, fax 714/999-8913.

Brea

The Indians used brea (tar) for medicinal purposes as well as pitch for waterproofing their boats. The early Spanish and Mexican settlers used it to waterproof their roofs.

Then, in 1898, the first oil well came in. In 1917, Brea became Orange County's eighth city. A few oil pumps can still be seen working in the area.

Concerts are performed in **City Hall Park** between 6:30 and 7:30 pm each Wednesday evening during July and August.

An "Art in Public Places" program has put more than 100 sculptures throughout town. To take a self-guided tour, ask for a brochure at the Civic Center. Narrated bus tours, ☎ 714/990-7735, also can be arranged.

A new 52,000-square-foot **Community Center**, ☎ 714/990-7643, has recently opened. It contains a sports complex (fitness center and gymnasium), banquet facilities, meeting rooms, ballroom and art garden.

A video and a commemorative 75th anniversary book are available by contacting the Historical Society, ☎ 714/990-7735.

For more information, contact **Brea Chamber of Commerce**, Number One Civic Center Circle (Randolph and Birch Sts.), Brea 92621, ☎ 714/529-4938, fax 714/529-6103.

Buena Park

Only Disneyland draws more visitors than the cluster of attractions lining Beach Boulevard in Buena Park.

Strangely, **Knott's Berry Farm**, 8039 Beach Blvd., ☎ 714/220-5143 or 220-5200, did not start out to become a tourist attraction. In 1920, Walter and Cordelia Knott rented 20 acres on which to open a roadside stand and a chicken restaurant. In 1932, Walter Knott and a neighbor, Rudolph Boysen, crossed the blackberry, red raspberry, and loganberry to produce the first boysenberry. Knott built his first theme park, a Wild West attraction with staged gun fights that he called **Ghost Town**, to entertain the people who were waiting to be seated in his restaurant. Today, there are five additional theme areas on the premises: Indian Trails; Fiesta

Village; Roaring "20s; Wild Water Wilderness; and Camp Snoopy, designed especially for kids.

Knott's latest addition is **The Boardwalk**, a tribute to the California beaches. The attraction includes the Windjammer roller coaster (the park's fourth).

Not far from Knott's is a full-size reproduction of **Independence Hall**, 8039 Beach Blvd., ☎ 714/827-1776, built by the Knotts.

Ripley's Believe It or Not! Museum, 7850 Beach Blvd., ☎ 714/522-7045, opened in 1990. Robert L. Ripley, cartoonist and creator of the concept, was born in California. The 100,000-square-foot "odditorium" contains interesting, humorous and bizarre exhibits from around the world.

Movieland Wax Museum, 7711 Beach Blvd., ☎ 714/522-1154, contains more than 300 figures of movie and TV stars shown in realistic settings.

Discount coupons for most of these attractions are readily available.

The **International Printing Museum**, 8469 Kass Dr., ☎ 714/523-2070 or 523-2080, is somewhat unusual in that it is *not* on Beach Blvd. It can be reached from either Highway 91 or I-5, by taking the Magnolia exit and going north to Orangethorpe, then turning left and going a half-mile to Kass Ave. (the first street on the left after you go across the I-5 overpass). Make a sharp left on Kass and you are at the 25,000-square-foot museum, the second largest of its type in the world. In addition to its exhibits of printing equipment dating from the 15th century, the museum contains the 85-seat Victorian-style **Heritage Theatre,** which presents actors imitating historic figures – Mark Twain, Benjamin Franklin, Johannes Gutenberg, William Randolph Hearst, Jimmy Walker, Eleanor Roosevelt – explaining the influence that printing had on their lives. The performances are given each Saturday at 7:30 pm.

For additional information, contact the **Buena Park Convention & Visitors Office**, 6280 Manchester Blvd., Suite 103, Buena Park 90621, ☎ 714/562-3560 or 800/541-3953, fax 714/562-3569; or the **Buena Park Chamber of Commerce**, 6280 Manchester Blvd., #102, Buena Park 90621, ☎ 714/521-0261 or 800/541-3953.

Fullerton

Fullerton Municipal Airport, Dale and Gilbert Sts., once a hog farm, is the oldest (1927) and largest general aviation field in Orange County.

Fullerton Arboretum, 1900 Associated Rd. at Yorba Linda Blvd., ☎ 714/773-3579 or 773-3250, is centered around the 1834 Victorian Heritage House, which is open for tours on Sundays between 2 and 4 pm. The 26-acre botanical garden has meandering paths that pass lakes, streams and a waterfall. The California Native Plant Society offers field trips.

For more information, contact **Fullerton Chamber of Commerce**, 219 E. Commonwealth Ave., Fullerton 92832, ☎ 714/871-3100.

Garden Grove

Crystal Cathedral, 12141 Lewis St., ☎ 714/971-4069, 971-4000 or 971-4013, harbors an all-glass sanctuary that *Newsweek* once called "the most spectacular religious edifice in the world." Built in 1980, the structure resembles a four-pointed star and is made of 10,000 panes of glass connected by a web of steel trusses. The building has a stainless steel 52-bell carillon tower and a 236-foot mirrored steeple. It houses the world's largest church organ, a 16,000-pipe instrument that is demonstrated every weekday at noon. Sunday services are accompanied by a 110-voice choir and a 20-piece orchestra. Morning services are held at 9:30 and 11, Spanish services at 12:45, and evening services at 6 pm (7 in the summer). Free guided tours are offered. the 32-acre grounds contain massive gardens and an impressive collection of statuary.

Two annual pageants, ☎ 714/54-GLORY, are held in the Crystal Cathedral: *The Glory of Easter* and *The Glory of Christmas*, both unique productions featuring live camels, goats, sheep and "angels" flying overhead.

Each Sunday, the *Hour of Power* television show with Rev. Robert Schuller is taped in the Crystal Cathedral. Schuller began his preaching career from the roof of a snack bar at a nearby drive-in movie theater.

The annual **Strawberry Festival** on the Village Green, Main St. and Acacia Pkwy., ☎ 714/638-0981, is a four-day event held on Memorial Day weekend. In addition to the usual parade, carnival games, and arts and crafts, the festival boasts of having the world's largest strawberry shortcake.

Heritage Park/Stanley House, 12174 Euclid St., ☎ 714/530-8871, is a two-story 1891 house-turned-museum. It is colored blue and yellow and is surrounded by a white picket fence. Walt Disney's original studio, a garage dating from 1923, is on the grounds. The house is open on Sundays from 1:30 to 4 pm.

Long Beach

Southern California's third largest city, Long Beach sprang from the oil boom of the 1920s, but turned into a blight by the 1960s. In 1975, the city began to redevelop its waterfront, initiating a gradual turnaround.

Long Beach Airport, 4100 E. Donald Douglas Dr., ☎ 310/570-2600, is a popular alternate to Los Angeles International, particularly for shorter flights.

The fabled *Queen Mary*, 1126 Queens Hwy., ☎ 310/435-3511, Web site www.queenmary.com, is one of the largest passenger liners afloat. Sitting on the waterfront, the ship is now a 50,000-ton shopping mall containing a hotel, restaurants, lounges, convention facilities and specialty shops.

Naples Island, four miles east on 2nd St. via Ocean Blvd. and Livingston Dr., is a tiny community that sits on an island (actually, three small islands) that were dredged from Alamitos Bay in the early 1900s. Accessed by a bridge at either end of 2nd St., a walkway overlooks the bay and marina. Footbridges span narrow, pleasant, well-maintained canals. The quaint streets have Italian names, and gondolas ply the canals (contact **Gondola Getaway**, 5437 E. Ocean Blvd., Naples, ☎ 213/433-9595, about one-hour rides).

For added information, contact **Long Beach Area Convention & Visitors Council**, One World Trade Center, Suite 300, Long Beach 90831-0300, ☎ 310/436-3645 or 800/4-LB-STAY.

Long Beach

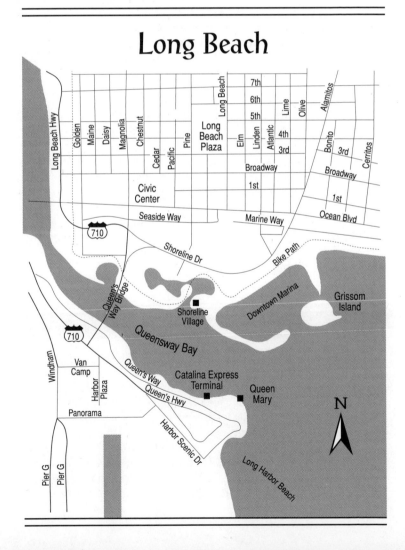

Orange

In 1869, lawyers Alfred Chapman and Andrew Glassell accepted 1,385 acres of land from the Rancho Santiago de Santa Ana in lieu of their legal fees. They laid out a town and named it Richland, but when they learned that there was another city of that name, they changed the name to Orange.

Placentia

In the late 1800s, George Hinde formed a spiritual colony here called the Societas Fraterna. The members were vegetarians.

Placentia Trolley, ☎ 714/993-8245, operates Monday through Friday from 9 to 5 and on Saturday from 10 to 2. The trolley makes 30 stops in a 75-minute run. It's free.

Whittier

Pio Pico State Historic Park, 6003 Pioneer Blvd., ☎ 310/695-1217, contains an 1850s adobe mansion, the home of Pio Pico, who was the first governor of California under Mexican rule. The house is open Saturdays and Sundays 1 to 4 pm. A seven-minute video on Pico's life is shown on request.

Rose Hill Memorial Park, 3900 S. Workman Mill Rd., ☎ 310/699-0921, is one of the world's largest memorial parks. There are lakes and arched bridges, and the west park has a meditation house in a Japanese garden. A 3½-acre Pageant of Roses Garden has more than 7,000 bushes in 600 varieties.

Catalina Island

Discovered by the Spanish in 1542, the "Island of Romance" has a permanent population of just over 2,000 people. Measuring just 20 x 8 miles, it is California's only island resort, a part of Channel Islands National Park. The island's only town, Avalon, can easily be toured in a day. Summer temperatures rarely go above the mid-70s and winters seldom get below the 50s.

In 1864, a group of Union soldiers visited the island to survey it as a site for a possible Indian reservation. Their barracks still stand at Two Harbors.

In 1919, chewing gum magnate William Wrigley Jr. bought the island and used it to lavishly entertain his friends.

Visitors are not allowed to drive on the island. Along the narrow streets of Avalon, people drive golf carts. The 42,000-acre interior is a nature preserve for deer, fox and buffalo (left over from a movie made in the 1920s).

Twin-engine air service from Long Beach to Catalina Island is available through **Allied Air Charter**, ☎ 310/510-1163 or 510-2412. Helicopter connections from San Pedro's Catalina Terminal, Los Angeles International Airport, Long Beach Airport, Burbank or Orange County can be arranged through **Helitrans**, ☎ 310/548-1314, 510-0384 or 800/262-1472; or from Long Beach and San Pedro, through **Island Express Helicopter Service**, 900 Queensway Dr., Long Beach, just north of the *Queen Mary*, ☎ 310/491-5550, 510-2525 or 800/228-2566. From Ventura County, contact **Flightline Flying Service**, ☎ 805/987-9842; from Newport Beach, **Pacific Coast Airlines**, 4600 Campus Dr., #103, Newport Beach 92660, ☎ 714/261-

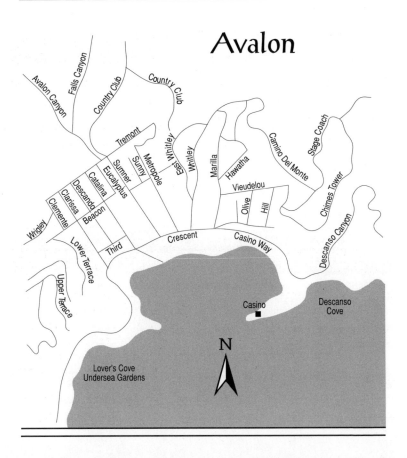

1600 or 800/426-5400; and from San Diego, **Island Hopper/Catalina Airlines,** ☎ 619/279-4595, has three departures daily, seven days a week.

Island tours are available by contacting **Island Tram Tours,** ☎ 310/510-1600, or **Santa Catalina Island Co.,** PO Box 737, Avalon 90704, ☎ 310/510-2000 or 800/4-AVALON.

INFORMATION SOURCES

Chamber of Commerce & Visitors Bureau, Box 217, Avalon 90704, ☎ 310/510-1520. (Get it? Five-ten-fifteen-twenty.) The office is located on Green Pleasure Pier in downtown Avalon.

Visitors Information Center, PO Box 1150, Avalon 90704, ☎ 310/510-2000 or 800/4-AVALON.

Catalina Visitors & Activities Center, ☎ 310/510-2888 or 510-2078.

Catalina Island Convention Bureau, PO Box 2040, Avalon 90704, ☎ 310/510-2848.

Irvine

When it was incorporated in 1971, this was the largest master-planned community in the United States.

Divided into many little villages, the area was developed by The Irvine Co., named for James Irvine (1827-86), a Scotch-Irish settler who bought many of the old ranchos until he controlled a total of 93,000 acres.

Fightertown, 8 Hammond, Suite 100, ☎ 714/855-8802, has life-size flight simulators. For a fee, you can "fly" by the half-hour. An "air traffic controller" provides basic flight information when needed.

At **Woodbridge Lake,** you can see tai chi (one of the martial arts) performed nearly every morning.

Costa Mesa

In the late 1800s, there three tiny towns were scattered among the farms and orchards in this region: Fairview, Paularino and Harper.

During World War II, the Santa Ana Army Air Base stood where the Orange County Fairgrounds and Orange Coast College are today.

Orange County Fair, Fair Dr. and Fairview Rd., ☎ 714/751-3247, is held on these fairgrounds during the second and third weeks in July. Among the more unusual features: ostrich races, dog acts and speedway racing. When the fair isn't on, **Centennial Farm,** ☎ 714/751-3247, has one-hour tours where children can pet the animals and learn about farming.

For more information, contact **Costa Mesa Chamber of Commerce**, 1835 Newport Blvd., E-270, Costa Mesa 92627, ☎ 714/574-8780, Web site www.focusoc.com/cities/costamesa/chamber.

Laguna Beach

This area was once inhabited by the Ute-Azteca and later by the Shoshone Indians, who named it Lagonas (lakes). The body of Laguna Woman found here is estimated to be at least 17,000 years old.

The Spanish called the area Cañada de las Lagunas (Canyon of the Lakes).

This is a very arboreal area due to the Timber Cultures Act of 1871, which gave 160 acres of land to each person who would plant 10 acres of trees. Primarily, the settlers planted Australian eucalyptus.

For generations, this community has been noted as the home of "The Greeter," a man who would walk up and down the main streets of the town, loudly hailing everyone within shouting distance. The original Greeter was Joe Lucas, who appeared in the 1880s. When Lucas passed away, the second (and best known) "Greeter" was Eiler Larsen. Larsen died in 1975, but is commemorated by two statues in town, one in front of the Pottery Shack and the other in front of Greeter's Corner Restaurant on the Coast Highway. The present "Greeter" is known only as "Number One Archer" and has handled his duties as the town's ex officio ambassador since 1981.

Former residents of the community include Mary Pickford, Douglas Fairbanks, Judy Garland, Bette Davis, Rudolph Valentino, Barbara Britton, Polly Moran, Mary Miles Minter, Charlie Chaplin, Mickey Rooney and Victor Mature. John Steinbeck wrote *Tortilla Flats* while living at 504 Park Ave. here. Current residents of the town include Bette Midler and former astronaut Buzz Aldrin.

If you take Broadway inland for two miles (during which, it will become Laguna Canyon Rd.), you will see a small park behind a chain link fence on your right. This is **Dog Park**, two grassy acres where dog-owners can take their pets and let them run free to get some exercise. Litter bags and receptacles are provided at the entrance gate so that pet owners can remove their dog's messes.

INFORMATION SOURCES

Visitor Information Center, 252 Broadway, PO Box 221, Laguna Beach 92651, ☎ 714/497-9229 or 800/877-1115, fax 714/376-0558.
Laguna Beach Chamber of Commerce, 357 Glenneyre, Laguna Beach 92651, ☎ 714/494-1018 .
Laguna Beach Visitors Bureau, PO Box 221, Laguna Beach 92651, ☎ 800/877-1115.

Lake Forest

Previously known as El Toro, this is the home of **El Toro Marine Corps Air Station**, Trabuco and Sand Canyon, ☎ 714/726-2932. Three-hour tours are provided free on the third Wednesday and Saturday of every month. Tours include a demonstration by the Canine Corps, a simulated crash fire and rescue drill, and a tour of the Command Museum.

Newport Beach

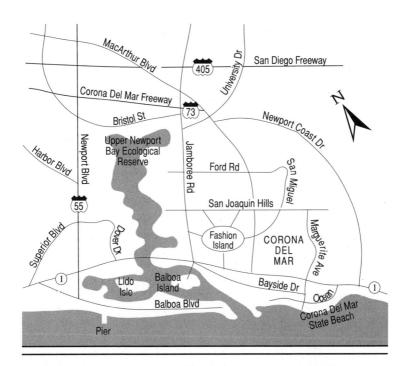

Newport Beach

This town's landlocked harbor was a serene lagoon until 1870. Dredging began at the harbor entrance in 1876, but the jetties were not built until 1936, when the present channels and turning basins were created. Today, the town boasts an area of 37½ square miles – 15½ square miles of land, 1.9 square miles of bay, and 20.1 square miles of ocean.

A long peninsula cradles Balboa and Lido Islands within the bay. Balboa Island, the largest, has narrow streets and 1,500 beach cottages. A ferry takes three cars at a time across Newport Harbor to Balboa Island.

Former residents of the community include John Wayne and Shirley Temple.

The Dory Fishing Fleet, started in 1891, can be found beside Newport Pier. The last beachside fishing cooperative of its kind in America, the fishermen who constitute this fleet unload their catch into large bins along the pier at 9 each morning. Professional buyers, chefs and private citizens come from miles around to purchase the fresh fish.

INFORMATION SOURCES

Newport Harbor Area Chamber of Commerce, 1470 Jamboree Rd., Newport Beach 92660, ☎ 714/729-4400 or 644-8211, fax 714/729-4417, e-mail info@newportbeach.com.
Newport Beach Conference & Visitors Bureau, 3300 W. Coast Hwy., Newport Beach 92663, ☎ 714/722-1611 or 800/94-COAST, fax 714/722-1612, Web site www.city. newport_beach.ca.us.

Balboa

On May 10, 1912, Glenn Martin flew a primitive hydroplane biplane that he had built in Santa Ana from Balboa to Avalon on Catalina Island and back. The flight took 37 minutes and was the longest, fastest over-water flight ever recorded at that time. The event is marked by a plaque at the foot of Balboa Pier.

Balboa Pavilion, 400 Main St., ☎ 714/673-5245, was built in 1906 as a Victorian bathhouse. In the 1930s and 1940s, it was used by the big bands. Later, it was a bingo parlor, amusement arcade and the first home of the Newport Harbor Art Museum.

To get added information, contact **Balboa Island Business Assn.**, PO Box 64, Balboa Island 92662.

Corona del Mar

Situated on a bluff at the south end of Newport Beach, Corona del Mar (Crown of the Sea) was once the home of Chuck Jones, creator of Bugs Bunny, Wile E. Coyote, Roadrunner, Daffy Duck and other cartoon characters. It also was the home of Ferd Johnson, who created the Moon Mullins comic strip. Residents here often have a nice view of Catalina Island.

For additional information, contact **Corona del Mar Chamber of Commerce**, 3135 E. Coast Hwy., PO Box 72, Corona del Mar 92625, ☎ 714/673-4050.

Huntington Beach

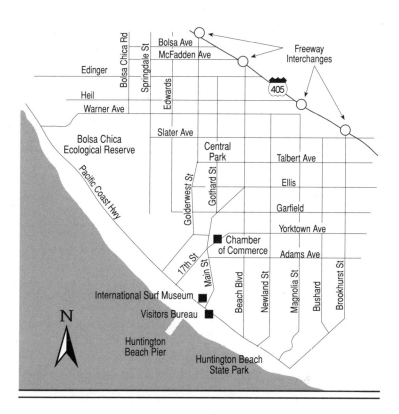

Huntington Beach

In 1889, it was known as Shell Beach. In 1901, it changed its name to Pacific City.

During the 1920s oil boom, every major oil company began to tap the rich oil field on which Huntington Beach sits. After Bolsa Chica #1 blew in with a roar that was heard 15 miles away in 1920, the town grew from 1,500 people to more than 5,000 people in less than a month. By the 1940s, wooden oil derricks covered virtually all of the mesa and much of the eastern portion of the coastal marsh. The region became the second largest oil producer in California and the seventh largest in the nation.

Most of the town's growth, much of it due to annexation, came between 1957 and 1960. Now it is the tenth largest city in California.

Huntington Pier was constructed of wood in 1904. The wooden one was replaced with a concrete pier in 1914, the first of its kind in America – and the longest (1,300 feet) and highest. Damaged and restored several times, the pier received nearly $11 million worth of damage in 1988, requiring the construction of a new pier, completed in 1992. The present pier is 1,853 feet long and 35 feet wide.

Popular actors who once lived between here and neighboring Laguna Beach include Errol Flynn, James Cagney, Bette Davis and Rudolph Valentino.

In 1995, the city was chosen as the "Safest City in America" among the nation's 100 largest cities. Their Fourth of July parade, ☎ 714/536-5486, is the largest in the West.

Visitors and residents alike enjoy hiking, jogging, swimming, frisbee, frisbee golf, equestrian events, kite-flying, basketball, sailing, boating and inline skating.

During September's **Hoop-It-Up Basketball Tournament**, ☎ 310/314-1777, over 800 three-person teams play half-court basketball in the beach parking lot off Huntington St.

In December, there is a week-long **Cruise of Lights**, ☎ 714/840-7542, to benefit the Huntington Harbor Philharmonic Committee, which supports local school music programs. The cruises take place at 5:30, 6:30, 7:30 and 8:30 pm daily, making a narrated tour of the waterways to view the seasonally lighted and decorated homes and boats.

For more information, contact **Huntington Beach Conference & Visitors Bureau**, 101 Main St., Suite A, Huntington Beach 92648-8118, ☎ 714/969-3492 or 800/SAY-OCEAN, fax 714/969-5592.

San Clemente

Virtually unknown until President Richard Nixon selected it for his winter White House, San Clemente stetches along a five-mile stretch of wide, sandy beach.

It is the home of volleyball star Karch Kiraly, a three-time All-American at UCLA and winner of two Olympic gold medals. In 1992, Kiraly won 13 consecutive tournaments, and in 1994, 16 out of 22 open tournaments. He has won more than 115 open titles on the Pro Beach Volleyball Tour, has won the "King of the Beach" title four times, and makes about $2 million a year playing the sport.

San Clemente also is the home of volleyball coach and Hall-of-Famer Burt DeGroot.

Be sure to stroll along the lovely **San Clemente Pier**.

For additional information, contact **San Clemente Chamber of Commerce**, 1100 N. El Camino Real, Box 338, San Clemente 92672, ☎ 714/492-

1131; or **All About San Clemente**, Web site www.sancle-mente.com/city/.

Dana Point

Like San Clemente, Dana Point owes its fame to notoriety, in this case, the O.J. Simpson murder case. It is here that Nicole Brown Simpson's parents live and where Simpson's children were cared for during the long, lurid trial.

Festival of the Whale is celebrated over two weekends in February with parades, a street fair, a 5K run and whale-watching.

For more information, contact **Dana Point Chamber of Commerce**, 24681 La Plaza, #2, Dana Point 92629, ☎ 714/496-1555 or 800/290-DANA.

San Juan Capistrano

Located three miles inland from Dana Point, **Mision San Juan Capistrano**, 31882 Camino Capistrano, #218, ☎ 714/248-2049 or 248-2026, fax 714/240-8091, is best known, perhaps, as the place where the swallows come each spring after their winter migration.

Cliff swallows have returned here on St. Joseph's Day, March 19, for over 200 years, having completed a 6,000-mile journey to Argentina and back. An old legend says the birds fly to Jerusalem for the winter, carrying twigs in their beaks to use in making a "raft" on which to rest when they cross the open ocean.

The return of the swallows is celebrated on the third Saturday in March with the **Fiesta de las Golondrinas.**

The most romantic of the California chain of missions – and the best preserved– Capistrano is often called the "Jewel of the missions."

The mission was founded in 1776, the year of the American Revolution, by Father Junipero Serra, who established over eight missions and has been called the "Father of California." Serra named the mission for Saint John of Capistrano.

The early Indian inhabitants called themselves Acagchemem (pronounced As-ha-SHAY-mem). The Spaniards called them Juaneños, and taught them how to make such practical items as cloth, olive oil, candles, soap and wine, as well as teaching them how to tan hides and make metal objects like keys, locks, wrought iron and knives. Previously, the Indians knew only stone tools.

The mission complex includes three churches:

★ **Great Stone Church** was built by the Indians between 1797 and 1806. It was nearly destroyed by an earthquake in 1812 that killed 40 Indians during its collapse. Today, it is a ruin surrounded by gardens.

★ **Serra Chapel** is the oldest building still in use in which Father Serra actually said Mass. A restored adobe decorated with primitive designs and art, the chapel is built in 1777 and is the oldest building in California. The Baroque altar, 22 feet high and 18 feet wide, was made of Spanish cherry wood, covered with gold leaf, and decorated with 52 carved, gold-leaf angels. The altar was given to the mission in 1922 and is over 350 years old.

★ **Young Parish Church**, with its multiple domes and lovely belltower, occupies a 10-acre site laced with walkways, fountains and gardens.

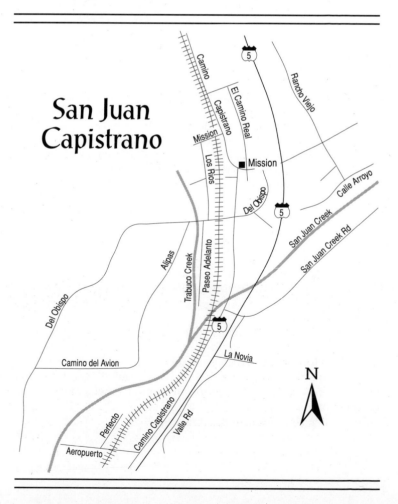

Self-guided tours include the padres' living quarters, the soldiers' barracks, a cemetery and a museum.

Los Rios Historic District, next to the old Capistrano Depot, depicts a small California town at the turn of the century. It includes 31 adobe homes, the earliest built in 1794.

Capistrano is the seventh oldest community in California.

For more information, contact **San Juan Historical Walking Tours,** ☎ 714/493-8444.

Santa Ana

John Wayne Airport, 18741 Airport Way, ☎ 714/252-5200, is rapidly becoming the most popular alternate to Los Angeles International. Amtrak service is available to Los Angeles and San Diego.

Tustin

Tall blimp hangars used in World War II are still standing and are visible for miles. The hangars are located on the recently phased out **Tustin Marine Corps Air Station,** Red Hill and Barranca, ☎ 714/726-7303, where they were used to house helicopters.

Trinity Broadcasting Networks, 2442 Michele, ☎ 714/832-2950, is the Christian broadcasting cable network where the television program *Praise the Lord* is taped. One-hour tours are available.

Adventures

On Foot

Anaheim

Oak Canyon Nature Center, 6700 E. Walnut Canyon Rd., Anaheim Hills, ☎ 714/998-8380, is at the end of Walnut Canyon Rd. off Nohl Ranch Rd. The 58-acre park has six miles of well-maintained hiking trails, a stream that flows year-round and a small visitor center with nature displays. Guided tours are conducted in the evening one night a week during the summer. Cycling is not allowed. Birdwatching is good.

Brea

Carbon Canyon Regional Park was once the site of an oil-drilling operation and a small town named Olinda. Both failed after the turn of century. The park has equestrian, hiking and biking trails, and a grove of 200 coastal redwoods planted in 1975. There is a small lake stocked with catfish at the back of the park, two miles from the entrance, and there are tennis courts. 4422 Carbon Canyon Road, ☎ 714/996-5252.

Golfers might enjoy playing a round at **Birch Hills Golf Course**, 2250 E. Birch St., ☎ 714/990-3900. The course has some unusual hazards: a former industrial site, train tracks and an old oil well.

Buena Park

Ralph B. Clark Regional Park, 8800 Rosecrans Ave., ☎ 714/670-8045, is reminiscent of La Brea Tar Pits. It contains rich fossil pits and a museum, along with playgrounds and picnic areas. **Ralph B. Clark Paleontological Museum** has 6,000 square feet of exhibits, including seven full skeletons of such prehistoric creatures as the saber-toothed cat, the mammoth and the ground sloth. There is a free fossil program every Sunday afternoon at 1, and a free nature walks on the second and fourth Saturday of every month. Groups can arrange to work in the fossil beds, but must give all of their finds to the museum. A three-acre lake stocked with bass and catfish is on the grounds.

Cleveland National Forest

Blue Jay Campground, ☎ 800/283-CAMP, can be reached by taking Highway 74 (Ortega Highway) to Forest Service Road 6S05, 12 miles west of Lake Elsinore, and following the signs from there. The campground is open year-round and provides nice back country hiking through the Santa Ana Mountains. The campground also is near the San Juan Trail and Chiquito Trail trailheads.

Upper San Juan Campground, ☎ 619/673-6180, is 21 miles northeast of San Juan Capistrano off Highway 74 (Ortega Highway). The campground, which is close to trailheads for San Mateo Canyon and the Santa Ana Mountains, is open from April to October and is popular with hikers.

Laguna Mountain Recreation Area also has a number of excellent hiking trails:

★ **Wooded Hill Nature Trail** covers 1½-miles and goes to one of highest points in the area, 6,223 feet, but it is a difficult hike. A shorter half-mile loop does not go to the peak. No horses or vehicles are allowed. A trail brochure is available.

★ **Big Laguna Trail** begins opposite the Laguna Campground parking lot near the amphitheater. After a mile, you enter a meadow, where the trail turns west then bends around another portion of the meadow containing Big Laguna Lake. Wildflowers abound by the lake in April and May. The trail is open to equestrians as well as hikers.

★ **Indian Creek Trail** is the first riding/hiking trail to connect Cuyamaca Rancho State Park with the Laguna Mountain Recreation Area. Take Sunrise Highway to Penny Pines Trailhead, about five miles north of Mt. Laguna. Park there and take Noble Canyon Trail two miles west to the junction with the Indian Creek Trail. From there, it is four miles to Cuyamaca.

★ **Lightning Ridge Trail** is a fairly strenuous 1.3-mile climb with many switchbacks beginning near the Laguna Campground amphitheater. No horses or vehicles are allowed.

★ **Desert View Nature Trail** is a 1.2-mile loop that begins in Burnt Rancheria Campground and follows the mountain rim. On a clear day, it is possible to see the Salton Sea. In places, the trail joins the Pacific Crest Trail. No horses or vehicles are allowed.

★ **Kwaaymii Cultural Trail** starts near the Visitor Infor- mation Office and climbs half a mile to Pinyon Point. Signs indicate the Indian uses of native plants. No horses or vehicles are allowed.

★ **Sunset Trail** begins across the road from the Meadows Infor- mation Kiosk at the 19.1-mile marker on Sunrise Highway and leads to Water-of-the-Woods Lake (look around for animal tracks). There are Kwaaymii Indian grinding holes in some of the granite rocks.

Look for the Laguna aster in this area. It is a rare plant with stems reaching 15-30 inches tall, and has large, showy flowers that bloom from August to September. The flowers are mostly deep lavender, but are sometimes white.

Pine Creek Wilderness is a 13,000-acre park containing several trails. Not even bicycles are allowed, and a (free) visitor permit is required. Pine Creek holds rainbow trout and bass. The wilderness is within the Cleveland National Forest, ☎ 619/445-6235.

Corona del Mar

Crystal Cove State Park has 23 miles of hiking trails and a tiny village of 45 shacks (soon to be removed) that were held over from the early 1920s when several movies were filmed there. The park encompasses **El Moro Canyon**, which has 18 miles of trails for hiking or horseback riding. The canyon contains tall sage, with patches of bright yellow dry mustard.

Dana Point

Hide Trail begins at the end of Amber Lantern St. and follows the edge of the bluffs for a quarter-mile. At Violet Lantern St. is the "hide drogher statue," which illustrates how cowhides were once thrown over the bluffs to sailors waiting below. The sailors would gather them up and load them aboard their vessels for shipment to market.

Fountain Valley

Mile Square Park, 16801 Euclid, ☎ 714/962-5549 or 839-8611, is honeycombed with asphalt paths for hikers and bikers. There are two lakes stocked with bass, bluegill, carp and catfish, plus two golf courses.

Snail's Pace Running Shop, ☎ 714/842-2337, holds training classes for those interested in running marathons.

Fullerton

Hillcrest Park (1155 North lemon Street, no phone), **Laguna Lake Park** (3120 Lakeview Drive, ☎ 714/871-3419) and **Trail Rest Park** (Brea Boulevard, just south of Bastonchury, no phone) all have hiking trails.

Huntington Beach

Huntington Central Park has six miles of cycling and hiking trails, two lakes and a public shooting range, 18221 Gothard St., ☎ 714/847-0607, maintained by the Huntington Beach Police Officers Assn. **Shipley Nature Center**, ☎ 714/960-8867, is an 18-acre preserve in the middle of the park with a mile of self-guided nature trails, a park naturalist who leads group tours and a visitors center with a small museum containing live rattlesnakes, turtles and other local species. The park also contains an 18-hole Frisbee golf course (in Frisbee golf, a basket represents a golf "hole") and a 1¼-mile jogging course with 18 exercise stations.

Bolsa Chica (Little Pocket) **Ecological Reserve**, Pacific Coast Highway at Warner Ave., ☎ 714/897-7003 or 379-6488, covers 300 acres and has a 1½-mile loop trail. Indians lived on the bluffs during the Milling Stone Period 4,000 years ago and cogstones – stone discs an inch thick and three to five inches in diameter – are found. The edges of the stones are notched, and some of them have holes in the middle, but their use is uncertain and they are presumed ceremonial. Once a gun club, then an oil field, the reserve is divided into two bays, Inner and Outer, and faces Bolsa Chica State Beach. Tours are given on the first Saturday of each month, and a trail guide to 1½ miles of hiking trails through the wetlands is available from **Bolsa Chica Conservancy**, 3842 Warner Ave., ☎ 714/846-1114. There is an interpretive center at Pacific Coast Highway and Warner Ave.

Irvine

Turtle Creek Nature Center, 1 Sunnyhill, ☎ 714/854-8151, has displays of snakes, raccoons and turtles.

William R. Mason Regional Park offers nature trails and provides interpretive programs. 18712 University Drive, ☎ 714/984-2491.

Laguna Beach

Jim Dilley Greenbelt Reserve, Laguna Heights Park off Alta Laguna Blvd., ☎ 714/854-7108, is open the third Saturday of each month from October through June.

Laguna Niguel

Aliso/Wood Canyons Regional Park, 28373 Alicia Pkwy, ☎ 714/831-2791, offers day hikes in the San Joaquin Hills. Archaeological finds have been made there. Take the La Paz Rd. exit off I-5 and go west. Turn right at Aliso Creek Rd. and left onto Alicia Pkwy. The park entrance is two-tenths of a mile on the right. Look for unpaved Awma Rd. The park has rugged terrain and contains mountain lions, rattlesnakes and poison oak.

Mission Viejo

Lake Mission Viejo, Marguerite Pkwy., between Alicia Pkwy. and Vista del Lago, iss a man-made lake surrounded by a 2½-mile jogging path.

Newport Beach

Windy afternoons are good for kite-flying and beach volleyball in this upscale community with 37 parks that span 154 acres and contain 73 miles of trails.

Upper Newport Bay Ecological Reserve and Regional Park, Backbay Dr., ☎ 714/640-6746, covers 752 acres and is southern California's largest estuary. It has a 10-mile trail for hikers, inline skaters and bikers. Free two-hour adult walking tours are offered by park representatives every Saturday and Sunday to study plants and wildlife, including the 200 rare and endangered birds found there.

Orange

Santiago Oaks Regional Park, 2145 N. Windes Dr., ☎ 714/538-4400, covering 350 acres, was once a part of Rancho Santiago de Santa Ana. The area around Santiago Creek, a main tributary of the Santa Ana River, was once inhabited by Gabrieleno Indians. The Butterfield Stage used to go through this canyon, and bandits once hid in the foothills, providing the name for a spot called Robber's Roost. Mule deer, coyote, bobcat and over

130 species of birds inhabit the area. The park's nature center, with wildlife exhibits and an audio-visual room, is in a 1938 ranch house. Self-guided nature trails lead from the nature center to high bluffs, such as Rattlesnake Ridge. Trails connect with the Anaheim Hills trail system.

Irvine Regional Park, 21501 Chapman Ave., ☎ 714/633-8074, is in Santiago Canyon, six miles east of town. The oldest regional park in California, this 477-acre area was opened in 1898. There is a nature center/museum, and the William Harding Nature Area lies along a hiking trail. The surrounding hills are full of wildlife, and there are numerous walking trails.

Pacific Wilderness Institute, 1132 E. Katella Ave., ☎ 714/997-5506 or 998-4596, offers classes in hiking, backpacking, mountaineering, rock climbing, ski touring and ski mountaineering. They also rent diving gear and provide diving instruction.

Santa Ana Mountains

Ronald W. Caspers Wilderness Park, ☎ 714/831-2174, is on Highway 74 (Ortega Highway) near San Juan Capistrano. It is the county's largest park (7,600 acres) and extends nearly five miles along the highway. The park has a campground, a nature center, miles of trails and excellent equestrian facilities. It also is a good place to see wildlife.

O'Neill Regional Park is a 3,100-acre area with miles of trails and excellent equestrian facilities.

San Juan Loop Trail begins across from the Ortega Country Cottage general store 19½ miles up Ortega Highway from I-5. It is a good, well-marked trail, 2.2 miles long over diverse terrain. Stay left when you meet the Chiquito Trail and go left again as the trail crosses behind the Upper San Juan Campground.

Tustin

Peters Canyon Regional Park, Jamboree Rd. and Canyon View Ave., ☎ 714/538-4400, is the county's newest park. Containing 350 acres, it offers five miles of hiking, horseback and mountain biking trails. There is also a large reservoir, but fishing is not permitted.

BIRDING

Anaheim Hills

Anaheim Hills Golf Course is a good place to spot owls in the eucalyptus groves.

Corona del Mar

Crystal Cove State Park provides good birdwatching.

Dana Point

The threatened California gnatcatcher resides in **Overview Park** at the end of Blue Lantern St.

Huntington Beach

Bolsa Chica Ecological Reserve provides year-round birding. In the spring and summer, the songbirds and marine birds are prevalent; in the fall, the shorebirds; and in the winter, waterfowl. During April and May, visitors can watch the aerial courtship displays of the Least terns and the snowy plovers. Every April, **Amigos de Bolsa Chica, ☎ 714/897-7003**, hold a day-long celebration acknowledging the return of the Least tern to its nesting islands here. A wooden walkway runs across some of the marsh, permitting visitors to see two sand islands: South Island, the summer nesting spot for California least terns and snowy plovers, and North Island (the closest of the two), which is the nesting spot for elegant terns, royal terns, Forster's terns, Caspian terns and black skimmers.

Other good birding spots around town include **Huntington Central Park**, a 350-acre city park on Golden West St. between Slater and Ellis Aves.; **Huntington Beach Wetlands**, Brookhurst and Pacific Coast Highway; **Carr Park**, Springdale and Heil; the Santa Ana riverbed along the eastern edge of the city; **Shipley Nature Center and Walking Trail**, Talbert St. and Golden West St.; **Sunset Park**; and the flood control channels.

On Horseback

Catalina Island

Catalina Stables & Kennel, ☎ 310/510-0478, conducts 1½-hour guided trail rides.

Dana Point

Doheny State Beach is the end of the five-mile San Juan Creek Bike Trail and an equestrian trail that links with another heading inland to San Juan Capistrano.

Fullerton

Lucky Copper Corals, 219 Clair Ave., ☎ 714/738-9303, and **V&H Stables**, 851 W. Bastanchury Rd., ☎ 714/441-2061, rent horses.

Huntington Beach

Huntington Central Park, Talbert Ave. and Golden West St., ☎ 714/960-8847 or 536-5281, has a 25-acre equestrian center, ☎ 714/842-7656, with riding trails, a full-time riding school and Sunday afternoon polo matches.

GTE Everything Pages Summer Classic, ☎ 714/536-5258, is a five-day equestrian show and fundraiser for the Huntington Beach Art Center that is held every August. Over 300 horses and riders from Mexico and the southwestern United States participate. The event is held at the Central Park Equestrian Center, Golden West St. and Talbert Ave.

Laguna Beach

The Irvine Co. Open Space Reserve, ☎ 714/832-7478, features docent-led bicycle and horseback tours. Reservations are a must.

Laguna Niguel

Aliso/Wood Canyons Regional Park, Alicia Pkwy. and Awma Rd., has bike and horse trails.

Newport Beach

Upper Newport Bay Ecological Reserve, ☎ 714/640-6746, four miles northeast of town, is a 752-acre coastal wetland with a 10-mile loop trail. The reserve is popular for biking, hiking, fishing and boating, as well as horseback riding.

Orange

Irvine Regional Park offers horse and pony rides. There is a four-mile equestrian trail.

Country Trails & Riding School, 1 Irvine Park Rd., Orange 92613, ☎ 714/538-5860, rents horses.

San Juan Capistrano

Gold Times Stables, 28441 San Juan Creek Rd., ☎ 714/496-9913; **Ortega Equestrian Center**, 26822 Pasea Altrevida, ☎ 714/661-3130; and **San Juan Creek Stables**, 28640 Ortega Hwy., ☎ 714/493-8141, rent horses.

Sycamore Trail, 26282 Oso Rd., ☎ 714/661-1755, rents horses and leads one-hour trail rides.

On Wheels

BICYCLES

Balboa

Balboa Pier is one of the nation's cleanest, most colorful bike paths/boardwalks. Bikes and inline skates are available for rent.

Brea

Carbon Canyon Regional Park, 4422 Carbon Canyon Rd., ☎ 714/996-5252, is reached by taking the 57 Freeway north to the Lambert Rd. exit and heading east. Follow the signs for Highway 142 and look for the entrance on the right. Park to the left of the park entrance and take the dirt path farther east that forks to the right. Follow the trail past the streambed and the orange grove. At the base of a hillside is **Telegraph Canyon Trail**, which will take you to the summit of Chino Hills State Park, 10,000 acres of wilderness. It is a 12-mile round trip.

Bicycle paths also are available in **Tri-City Park**, Kraemer and Golden, ☎ 714/993-8232, and **Ted Craig Regional Park**.

Catalina Island

Although the interior of the island has been off-limits to rental cars and bicycles since 1989, it is possible to cycle there if you obtain a permit from the visitors center. Only mountain bikes are allowed and helmets must be worn.

Brown's Bikes, 107 Pebbly Beach Rd., Avalon, ☎ 310/510-0986; **Catalina Rentals**, ☎ 310/510-1600; and **Island Rentals**, 125 Pebbly Beach Rd., Avalon, ☎ 310/510-1456, can provide you with a bicycle.

Cleveland National Forest

Spur Meadow Cycle Trail and **Kernan Cycle Trail** are two of the most popular biking trails in this area.

Huntington Beach

The city boasts over 3,000 miles of hiking and biking trails. There are designated bike routes along 75% of the city streets, and there are paved bike trails 44 miles inland along the Santa Ana River.

Santa Ana River Bikeway, one of longest uninterrupted bike paths in Orange County, stretches 29 miles from Anaheim Hills to the shoreline at Huntington Beach.

Huntington State Beach, Pacific Coast Highway at Brookhurst Ave., ☎ 714/536-1454 or 848-1566, is 8½ miles long and is paralleled by a paved bike path, the best in Orange County.

Irvine

William R. Mason Regional Park, 18712 University Dr., ☎ 714/854-2491, near the University of California Irvine campus, has bike trails that go past a lake with ducks and a playground. There's also a fitness course.

For inside pointers, contact **Bicycle Club of Irvine**, ☎ 714/553-6944.

MOTOR VEHICLES

Cleveland National Forest encompasses the **Corral Canyon Off-Road Vehicle Area**, where there are trails for a variety of off-road vehicles.

Easy motorcycle trails include **Wrangler, Corral, Greenhorn** and **Bobcat**. Trails of medium difficulty include **Bronco Flats, Sodbuster** and **Wrangler Tie**. Difficult trails include **Bronco Peak, Tombstone, Sidewinder** and **Gun Slinger**.

Easy ATV trails include **Corral** and **Bobcat**. Those of medium difficulty include **Corral, Bobcat, Wrangler** and **Greenhorn**. The most difficult ATV trails are **Bronco Peak, Sidewinder** and **Gun Slinger**.

Those with four-wheel drive will find **Bronco Peak, Bronco Flats, Sidewinder,** and **Gun Slinger** the most difficult. Other four-wheel drive trails include **Bobcat Meadow, Los Piños** and **Bear Valley**.

On & In the Water

Anaheim

Santa Ana River Lakes, 4060 E. La Palma, ☎ 714/632-7830 or 632-7851, offers freshwater fishing for a fee daily between 6 am and 4 pm and between 5 and 11 at night. Take Highway 91 (Riverside Pkwy.) to Tustin Ave., go one block north to La Palma, then turn right to the entrance. There are three lakes from which bass, catfish, crappie and trout can be taken. Boats, rods and reels are available for rent, and there is a concession stand. No swimming, sailing or camping is allowed.

Balboa

This is one of the largest small-boat harbors in world. The first Surfboard Riding Championships in the United States were held here in 1932. "Surfing the Wedge" has become a part of the surfers' vernacular. Located off **West Jetty Park** at the southernmost tip of Balboa Peninsula, The Wedge is highly prized by southern California body surfers and bodyboard enthusiasts. The park also affords lovely views of Laguna Beach, Catalina Island and the mouth of Newport Bay.

Catalina Passenger Service, Balboa Pavilion, 400 Main St., ☎ 714/673-5245, takes you to Avalon on Catalina Island in 75 minutes aboard *Catalina Flyer*, the largest passenger-carrying catamaran in the United States. The ship makes one round-trip daily from March through November. *Pavilion Queen* and *Pavilion Paddy* provide narrated 45- and 90-minute sightseeing cruises around Newport Bay.

Newport Harbor Cruises, ☎ 714/673-5245, also provides sightseeing excursions around the harbor.

Davey's Locker Sportfishing, 400 Main St., ☎ 714/673-1434, rents 14-foot motor-powered skiffs capable of seating four. Half-day and all-day fishing trips are available, and whale-watching cruises are offered in season.

Newport Landing, 309 Palm, Suite F, ☎ 714/675-0550, arranges half- and three-quarter-day sportfishing trips.

Walk On Water, Inc., ☎ 714/675-6800, rents boats and Ski-Doos.

Electric Boat Co., 510 E. Edgewater, ☎ 714/673-7200, rents 12-foot single or double kayaks, 14- and 21-foot sailboats, 16-foot motorboats or pontoon boats, and 18- to 20-foot electric boats. Harbor maps are provided.

Fun Zone Boat Co., 600 E. Edgewater Pl., ☎ 714/673-0240, fax 714/673-8413, e-mail funzoneboats@newportbeach.com, Web site www.newport-beach.com/funzoneboats, provides narrated harbor cruises hourly. The firm also operates *MS Phoenix*, a restored 109-foot sidewheeler originally built for the Wrigley family in 1930. *Phoenix*, the only motor sidewheeler still in operation, is the world's largest glass-bottom boat, and can accommodate 200 people.

Balboa Boat Rentals, 510 E. Edgewater Ave., ☎ 714/673-7200, offers island cruises. Located adjacent to the auto ferry, it also rents surrey-topped electric boats, single and double kayaks, 14-foot sailboats, 16-foot motor boats, 18- and 20-foot electric boats, wave runners, and 17- and 19-foot offshore boats.

Capistrano Beach

Capistrano Beach Park, Pacific Coast Hwy. and Beach Dr., ☎ 714/661-7013, is less crowded than Huntington Beach or Laguna Beach, and is popular for surfing and volleyball.

Catalina Island

Catalina Adventure Tours, PO Box 1314, Avalon 90704, ☎ 310/510-2888, on Pleasure Pier, arranges day or night glass-bottom boat tours. The company also provides tours of the town.

Catalina Banana Boat Riders, 107 Pebbly Beach Rd., Avalon, ☎ 310/510-1774 or 800/708-2262, arranges half- and full-day trips.

Catalina Safari Tours, PO Box 5044, Two Harbors 90704, ☎ 310/510-2800, takes water tours out of Two Harbors.

Scico Sightseeing Tours, PO Box 737, Avalon 90704, ☎ 310/510-2000 or 800/4-AVALON, has tours aboard motor- and glass-bottom boats.

Submarine Tours, ☎ 714/756-9002, explores the underwater world from an Atlantis submarine.

Santa Catalina Island Co., Box 737, Avalon, ☎ 310/510-2500, offers 40-minute glass-bottom boat tours by day or night; 55-minute coastal cruises to Seal Rocks; a 55-minute "flying fish" boat tour that departs in the evening between May and mid-October; and two-hour sunset buffet cruises from May through September aboard an old paddlewheeler.

Underwater Marine Park at Casino Point was designed for scuba divers in 1962. It contains the Lover's Cove Undersea Gardens, kelp forests, underwater caves and a sea fan grotto.

Argo Diving Service, Box 2289, Avalon 90704, ☎ 310/510-2208, fax 310/510-2337, gives lessons, conducts guided underwater tours and leads boat dives.

Avalon Boatstand/Joe's Rent-a-Boat, Pleasure Pier, Avalon, ☎ 310/510-0455 or 510-1922, rents motorboats, rowboats, pedal boats, paddle boards and fishing tackle.

Catalina Diver's Supply, Box 126, Avalon 90704, ☎ 310/510-0330 or 800/353-0330, is located on the Pleasure Pier. Its 42-foot diving boat runs daily between April and September offering snorkel tours of the marine preserve. The company rents underwater cameras, scuba gear and snorkeling gear.

Catalina Scuba Luv, 126 Catalina Ave., Avalon 90704, ☎ 310/510-2616 or 800/262-DIVE, takes half- and full-day diving trips and rents gear.

Descanso Beach Ocean Sports, Box 386, Avalon 90704, ☎ 310/510-1226, is located on the "back" side of the casino. It conducts kayak and snorkel trips, leads natural history expeditions, holds moonlight paddles and presents a special program for children.

Wet Spot Rentals, Avalon Boat Terminal, ☎ 310/510-2229, conducts kayak trips to Seal Rock and the remote "back side" of the island. It also rents pedal boats, snorkel gear and wetsuits.

Avalon Aquatics, 615 Crescent, Avalon 90704, ☎ 310/510-1225 or 800/MR. SCUBA, conducts guided tours and gives lessons, as does **Snuba Tours of Catalina**, Two Harbors, ☎ 714/556-SNUBA.

Catalina Ocean Rafting, 103 Pebbly Beach Rd., Avalon 90704, ☎ 310/510-0211 or 800/990-RAFT, offers half-day, all-day and two-day trips around the island, plus two-hour snorkeling trips.

Catalina Mako Charters, PO Box 2350, Avalon 90704, ☎ 310/510-2720 or 800/296-MAKO, takes family day charters, island exploration tours, sportfishing expeditions and shark diving excursions.

"Keeper" Charters, Catalina Island Inn, ☎ 213/510-1624, provides half-day and all-day fishing trips, as well as sightseeing excursions.

King Neptune, ☎ 213/510-2616 or 800/262-DIVE, offers instruction and guided snorkel and scuba diving excursions, as does **Two Harbors Dive Station**, PO Box 5044, Two Harbors 90704-5044, ☎ 213/510-2800.

Avalon Tuna Club, 100 St. Catherine Way, Avalon 90704, founded in 1889, is the oldest fishing club in America. Early members included Zane Grey, Cecil B. DeMille, John Wayne and Winston Churchill.

Boat Stand Charters, Box 1449, Avalon, ☎ 213/510-2274; **Catalina Island Charter Boat Co.**, Box 2350, Avalon, ☎ 213/510-2720; and **Catalina Sportfishing**, Box 5044, Two Harbors 90704, ☎ 310/510-7265, fax 310/510-0244, all charter sportfishing trips.

Corona del Mar

Corona del Mar State and City Beach Park, Ocean Blvd. and Jasmine Ave., is one of America's most scenic parks, and the grassy bluff that overlooks the beach is popular for picnicking and viewing the sunsets. Surfing, diving, fishing and volleyball are all popular diversions here, and the snorkeling provides excellent opportunities to get up close and personal with the bright orange Garibaldi, sea bass, perch and various small sea creatures, such as tiny octopuses and seahorses. There are two coves, **China Cove** and **Pirate's Cove**, ☎ 714/644-3047. China Cove is reached by taking the stairs on Ocean Blvd. at Fernleaf St. There is no lifeguard. Pirate's Cove, which is reached by taking the steps at the north end of the Corona del Mar Beach parking lot, offers good tidepooling and beachcombing. Both coves provide excellent opportunities for swimming.

For some good tidepooling, take Margarite St. to Ocean Blvd., turn left, and go to the end of the street. Park and follow the trail to the pools.

Crystal Cove State Park, 8471 Pacific Coast Hwy., ☎ 714/494-3539, is between Corona del Mar and Laguna Beach. Covering almost 2,800 acres, it is 3½ miles long, the largest park along the Orange County coast. Very popular with mountain bikers, the park also offers fishing, swimming, surfing, scuba diving and some excellent tidepooling. Offshore is an underwater park covering 1,150 acres and extending to a depth of 120 feet within a half-mile of shore. The park has two new underwater trails. There are three areas within the park where camping is permitted.

Little Corona Beach & Marine Preserve, Ocean Blvd. and Poppy Ave., is tiny and secluded. It was created to protect the area's tidepools and sea life, and is a good spot for scuba diving.

Bayside Marina, 1137 or 1353 Bayside Dr., will rent boats, arrange charters, or conduct sightseeing trips.

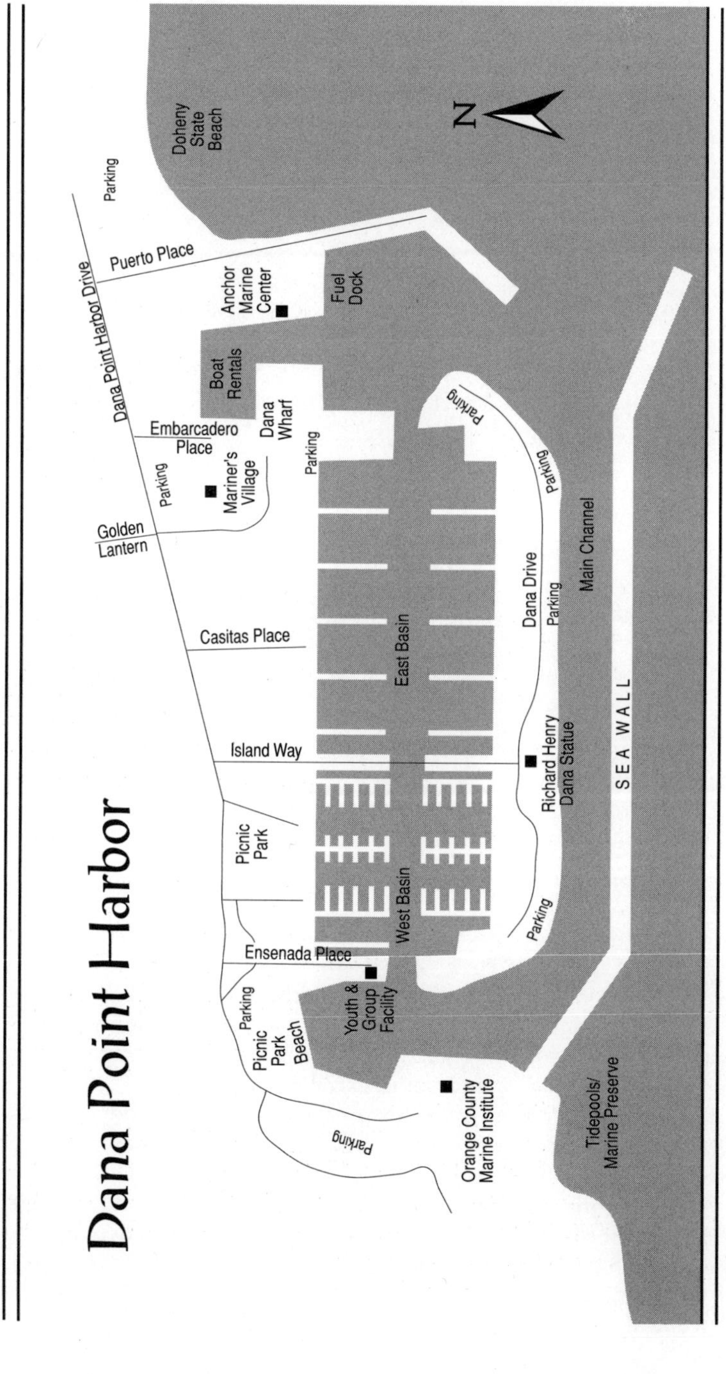

Dana Point Harbor

Doheny State Beach

N

Parking

Puerto Place

Dana Point Harbor Drive

Anchor Marine Center ■

Fuel Dock

Boat Rentals

Embarcadero Place

Dana Wharf

Parking

Parking

Parking

Golden Lantern

Parking

Mariner's Village ■

Casitas Place

East Basin

Dana Drive

Parking

Main Channel

Island Way

Richard Henry Dana Statue ■

Picnic Park

S E A   W A L L

West Basin

Parking

Ensenada Place

Parking

Youth & Group Facility ■

Picnic Park Beach

Parking

Orange County Marine Institute ■

Tidepools/ Marine Preserve

Dana Point

At the far end of Orange County, this harbor holds over 2,500 pleasure boats. Fishing and boating charters are available, and excellent tidepooling can be found at the west end of the harbor. There is a small fishing pier at the west end of Dana Point Harbor Dr. below Cove Rd.

Less than half a mile south of town is **Doheny State Beach**, 25300 Dana Point Harbor Dr., ☎ 714/496-6172 or 800/444-PARK, a 62-acre expanse that was immortalized in the Beach Boys' classic recording *Surfin' U.S.A.* The area offers excellent swimming and surfing, and there are 121 developed family campsites. Its location at the mouth of San Juan Creek makes the beach a choice area for birdwatching. Prime fishing ground is in the rocky area at the west end of the beach. Offshore, **Doheny State Marine Life Refuge** is an underwater park for snorkelers. There is a visitor center with an indoor tide pool, a 400-gallon touch tank and five aquariums.

Salt Creek Beach Park, ☎ 714/661-7013, 1½ miles northwest of town on Highway 1, sits below the posh Ritz-Carlton Hotel. A mile long, the beach is used for swimming, kite-flying and surfing (lifeguards are on duty during the summer), as well as surf fishing. Catalina Island is visible from there.

Heading north out of town from Salt Creek Beach Park, a string of small beaches appears: **1000 Steps Beach, Camel Point Beach** and **Alison Beach County Park**.

Dana Wharf Sport Fishing & Charter, 34675 Golden Lantern, ☎ 714/496-5794 or 831-1850, charters boats for the half-day, all day, twilight trips, and deep-sea fishing runs. The firm also rents equipment, takes you parasailing, operates open party boats and schedules whale-watching trips during season.

Aventura Sailing Assn., 24650 Dana Point Harbor Dr., ☎ 714/493-9493, will teach you how to sail.

Dana Point Yamaha, 24302 Del Prado, ☎ 714/661-1890, and **Pacific Water Sports**, 34291 Doheny Park Rd., ☎ 714/661-2110, rent watercraft.

Dana Harbor Yacht, ☎ 714/493-2011, and **Dana Island Yachts**, ☎ 714/248-7400, also provide cruises.

Hobie Sports Shop, 24825 Del Prado, ☎ 714/496-2366, is operated by the infamous Hobie Alter, the Dana Point resident who developed a light, foam-core surfboard. The popular Hobie Cat bears Alter's name.

Beach Cities Scuba, 34283 Pacific Coast Hwy., ☎ 714/496-5891; **Capo Beach Rentals**, ☎ 714/661-1690; **Killer Dana Surf Shop**, 24621 Del Prado, ☎ 714/489-8380; and **UP Sports**, 34105 Pacific Coast Hwy., ☎ 714/443-5161, provide lessons and rent such water-oriented gear as scuba equipment, waterskis, jetskis, surfboards, wetsuits, windsurfing gear, inline skates, skateboards and boogie boards.

Huntington Beach

Catching a wave!
*Credit: Huntington Beach
Conference & Visitors Bureau*

Host of the **U.S. Open of Surfing**, other surfing tournaments, beach volleyball tournaments and inline skating competitions throughout the summer, this community literally *immerses* itself in the waterfront lifestyle.

Recently, the city has expanded development of three miles of its beaches and renamed each one-mile segment: South Beach, Pier Plaza and Bluff Top.

Often touted as "Surf City, U.S.A.," the town holds the **Pierfest Sea & Airshow,** ☎ 714/960-3378, every September, and the **Sand Castle Festival**, 1st St. and Pacific Coast Hwy., ☎ 714/969-5621, in early October. During the Sand Castle Festival, held between the pier and the lifeguard headquarters, participants help to build an unbroken sand sculpture that measures nearly a mile long when finished.

Lifeguard Headquarters, 1st St. and Pacific Coast Hwy, ☎ 714/536-5285, will let you tour their facility.

International Surfing Museum, 411 Olive St., ☎ 714/960-3483, depicts highlights of the sport since it was introduced to the mainland from Hawaii some 80 years ago.

Surfing Walk of Fame, at the corner of Pacific Coast Hwy. and Main St., is surfing's answer to the Hollywood Walk of Fame.

Bolsa Chica State Beach, 17851 Pacific Coast Hwy., ☎ 714/846-3460 or 848-1566, 1½-miles south of Warner Ave., is across from Bolsa Chica Ecological Reserve. The lovely beach was once called Tin Can Beach because of all the hobos who lived there in makeshift tents.

Sail Catalina, 16370 Pacific Coast Hwy., ☎ 714/568-9650 or 310/592-5790, is the latest addition to the fleet linking Catalina Island with the mainland. This 49-passenger sailing catamaran is billed as the "fastest motor-sailor in the world." Passengers relax in reclining aircraft seating. There is a full bar and galley aboard.

Huntington Surf and Sport, 300 Pacific Coast Hwy., ☎ 714/841-4000, and 3801 Warner Ave., ☎ 714/846-0181, rents surfboards, boogie boards and wetsuits.

Laguna Beach

At this "Artist Colony by the Sea," the **Main Beach**, ☎ 714/497-0716, is popular for surfing, kayaking, bodyboarding, pier fishing and snorkeling. It has a white-sand beach, palm trees, pathways, playgrounds and ball courts. Other beaches include **Sleepy Hollow**, good for swimming; **Victoria**, a favorite for skim-boarding, body surfing and volleyball; **Crescent Bay**, another favorite for body surfing; **Reef Point** and **Woods Cove**, popular with divers; and **Shaws** and **Divers Coves**, where the sheltered coves are popular with scuba divers.

Divers Cove, at the foot of Cliff Dr., has an ecological preserve, making it a favorite offshore site for scuba divers.

Ruby Street Park, 1½ miles southeast of town at the west end of Diamond St., is a pocket park with a white-sand beach, intriguing tidepools and photogenic rock formations. It is popular for body surfing and skin diving.

Aliso Beach County Park, 31131 Pacific Coast Hwy., ☎ 714/567-6206, is 2.8 miles southeast of town on the Coast Highway. It has a fishing pier and a mile-long sandy beach with lifeguards. It's good for fishing, swimming and body surfing.

Crescent Bay Point Park, 1.4 miles northwest of town at the west end of Crescent Bay Dr., is a beautiful sandy beach in a sheltered cove. Seal Rock is offshore, and there are tidepools at either end of the park. This is a favorite place for skin diving, swimming, body surfing and fishing.

Crystal Cove State Park, ☎ 714/494-3539, three miles northwest on the Coast Highway, is a park sandwiched between the highway and a narrow sandy beach. Offshore is an underwater preserve for snorkelers. Good swimming and surfing here.

Heisler Park, ☎ 714/497-0706, is a photographic downtown park with meandering walkways and plenty of opportunities for fishing, swimming and skin diving.

Laguna Sea Sports, 925 N. Coast Hwy., ☎ 714/494-6965, rents diving gear, provides instruction and conducts tours. The company has its own pool on the premises.

Laguna Niguel

Laguna Niguel Regional Park, 28241 La Paz Rd., ☎ 714/831-2790, a 174-acre facilities with jogging paths, cycling paths, hiking paths and horseshoe pits, has a 40-acre lake for boating and fishing (bass, catfish and trout are stocked regularly). The north end of the park has an area for flying remote-control airplanes.

Long Beach

Alamitos Bay Beach, ☎ 310/594-0951, is 3.8 miles east along Ocean Blvd. Sheltered from the ocean by a long, narrow peninsula, it is a favorite for swimming and windsurfing.

Long Beach City Beach, between 1st and 72nd Pls., is inside the breakwater, so there is safe swimming without much surf.

Catalina Cruises, 320 Golden Shore Blvd., ☎ 800/228-2546, and **Catalina Express**, 1046 Queensway, ☎ 310/519-1212 or 800/464-4228, both offer cruises to Catalina Island.

Belmont Pier Sportfishing, Ocean Blvd. at 39th Pl., ☎ 310/434-6781, and **Long Beach Sportfishing**, 555 Pico Ave., ☎ 310/432-8993, both offer sportfishing excursions.

Shoreline Village Cruises, ☎ 310/495-5884, provides harbor cruises.

Newport Beach

The annual sailing race from
Newport Beach to Ensenada.
Credit: Newport Beach Convention & Visitors Bureau

Six miles of sandy beach includes the narrow Balboa Peninsula, which shelters Newport Bay. The harbor, home to more than 9,000 yachts and boats, is the largest small-boat harbor in the world.

Here you can tour the harbor on a paddlewheeler, a dining cruiser, a gondola or a pirate ship. You can rent electric boats, small sailboats, kayaks and canoes to explore the bay's canals, channels and passages. Bareboat and crewed charters can be arranged for overnight sails to Catalina Island, Dana Point Harbor or one of the Los Angeles marinas.

Day, evening and overnight fishing excursions can be arranged to coastal waters or to Catalina Island in search of red snapper, mackerel, barracuda, bonito, shark, yellowtail bonito, shark and halibut. Excellent fishing reports are published in the local newspapers.

Davey's Locker Sportfishing, 400 Main St., ☎ 714/673-1434; **Newport Landing Sportfishing**, 503 E. Edgewater, ☎ 714/675-0550; and **Romero's Mexico Service**, 1600 E. Coast Hwy., ☎ 714/548-8931 or 548-3481, fax 714/548-8086, charter boats for fishing.

Upper Newport Bay (Back Bay) is popular for rowing, kayaking, sculling and canoeing.

Newport Pier is a favorite among surfers.

Balboa Beach, half a mile south, runs parallel to Balboa Blvd. For a beach and surf report, ☎ 714/650-6400, ext. 905.

West Jetty Park is close to The Wedge, a legendary shore break that is a test of skill for experienced body surfers. **Newport Dunes Aquatic Park**, 1131 Backbay Dr., ☎ 714/644-0510, a lagoon in Newport Bay, is nearly surrounded by a half-mile of broad sandy beach. Sail and paddleboats can be rented. There are swimming and diving islands, and lifeguards are on duty. The park also has boat-launching ramps, game courts and various amusements.

Gondola Co. of Newport, 3404 Via Oporto, Suite 210, ☎ 714/675-1212, provides a one-hour Venetian-style cruise in a gondola. As the boat is rowed through the canals of Newport with a background of romantic music, passengers snack on a basket of fresh bread, cheese and salami. Ice and glasses are provided; wine can be purchased or you can bring your own.

Adventures at Sea, 3101 W. Coast Hwy., #209, ☎ 714/650-2412, 800/BAY-2412 or 888/4-GONDOLA, rents "neo-Venetian" gondolas with canopies that are powered with silent electric motors. The boats are available for one- or two- hour cruises (with complimentary champagne for two), or for two-hour dinner cruises.

Newport Aquatic Center, North Star County Beach, ☎ 714/646-7725, a training center for Olympic athletes, rents water equipment and conducts 1½-to 2-hour rowing, kayaking, surfskiing and canoeing clinics on Saturdays and Sundays.

Duffy Boat Rentals, 2001 W. Coast Hwy., ☎ 714/645-6427, in front of the Newport Landing restaurant, rents boats with surrey-top sunroofs in five different models and provides maps of the harbor.

Orange

Irvine Lake (Santiago Reservoir) is in **Irvine Regional Park**, ☎ 714/649-2560, reached by driving south on Santiago Canyon Rd. Watch for the entrance on your left. Fed by Santiago Creek, the 660-acre lake is stocked with catfish, bluegill, crappie, trout and bass. No fishing license is required, but there is a day-use fee. Windsurfing, waterskiing, tubing and swimming are not allowed, but boat rentals are available, ☎ 714/649-2991 (no reservations). If you have your own boat, you can launch it for a $5 fee. There is a bait and tackle shop at the lake.

San Clemente

Ole Hanson Beach Club & Pool, or Avenida Pico a half-block west of El Camino Real north of town, was used for the U.S. Olympic swimming trials before the Los Angeles Olympics in 1932. Below the club is **Norton Beach**, a good spot for fishing.

San Clemente State Beach, 225 Avenida Calafia, ☎ 714/492-3156, affords four miles of beach for swimming and surfing, plus a pier for fishing and strolling. This is a popular place to skindive for spiny lobster and abalone, and a good spot for "TOAD" surfers ("Take off and die" daredevils). The parking area is on a bluff and there are two paths leading down to the beach. There is a kiosk at the front entrance. Lifeguards are on duty. For surf and weather conditions, contact the San Clemente lifeguard, ☎ 714/492-1011.

San Onofre State Beach, just north of Camp Pendleton, is near the San Onofre Nuclear Generating Station, seven miles southeast of town on the I-5 frontage road. Nude bathing is popular at the south end of the beach.

South from town are **Califia State Beach** and **San Clemente City Beach**. North from town is **Norton Beach**. **Stewart Surfboards**, 2102 S. El Camino Real, ☎ 714/492-1085, rents surfboards, boogie boards, soft boards, wetsuits and board bags.

San Juan Capistrano

San Juan Capistrano Hot Springs, 35501 Ortega Hwy., ☎ 714/728-0400, has been a place to soak in natural hot mineral water since 1846. Sit in the large outdoor pool or rent one of 25 private, stream-side hot tubs.

San Onofre

In this area, dominated by the San Onofre Nuclear Power Plant, there are three separate beaches.

San Onofre State Beach/San Mateo Campground, ☎ 310/492-4872, is located half a mile south of the power plant and 1½ miles inland. The area provides some of California's best surfing, and the sandy 3½-mile beach offers good fishing. Wildlife is often seen along the six bluff trails.

Seal Beach

Seal Beach Pier has a bait and tackle shop and is known for good fishing. Diver Patty McCormick was born in Seal Beach.

Solana Beach

The community is blessed with two miles of beach: **Solana Beach Park**, 111 S. Sierra Ave., and **Tide Park Beach**, 302 Solana Vista Dr.

South Laguna

Camel Point Beach, ☎ 714/661-7013, can be accessed at West St., Bluff Dr., and 5th Ave. The "1000 Steps" beach access, with steep stairs anchored to the hillsides, is at 9th Ave. There is good tidepooling along this beach.

Aliso Beach County Park, 31000 block of Pacific Coast Highway, ☎ 714/661-7013, is in a large cove bisected by Aliso Creek. There is an uncrowded fishing pier here, but, unfortunately, the water is often contaminated.

In the Air

Balboa

Balboa ParaSailing, 700 E. Edgewater Ave., ☎ 714/673-1693, puts you on a swing-like seat and tows you behind a boat until you are soaring 400 feet above the water.

Catalina Island

Island Cruzers, 107 Pebbly Beach Rd., Box 2275, Avalon 90704, ☎ 310/510-1777, will take customers parasailing off land or water.

Long Beach

MegaBungee, 1119 Queens Hwy., ☎ 310/435-1880, fax 310/435-5510, next to the *Queen Mary*, offers bungee jumping with a 220-foot drop.

Newport Beach

Resort Watersports, ☎ 714/729-1150 or 800/585-0747, rents electric boats, sailboats, windsurfers, pedal boats and kayaks. It also gives lessons, arranges tours and provides free kayaking, windsurfing and sailing clinics. A guided tour departs every Sunday at 10 am and threads through the protected marshlands of the Upper Newport Bay Ecological Reserve and Regional Park.

Santa Ana

Charter Copters, 19711 Campus Dr., Suite 220, ☎ 714/222-9101, fax 714/222-9103, flies out of John Wayne Airport. The company provides fly/dine/limo packages and aerial photography, as well as pre-planned or plan-your-own tours.

Solana Beach

Sunset Balloon Flights, 162 Via de la Valle, ☎ 619/481-9122, offers hot-air ballooning.

Eco-Travel/Cultural Excursions

Brea

Curtis Theatre, Civic Center, ☎ 714/990-7722, has 199 seats and houses the Brea Civic Light Opera, Brea Youth Theatre, Prism Productions, Vanguard Theatre Ensemble and Kids Culture Club.

Catalina Island

Wrigley Memorial and Botanical Garden, Avalon Canyon Rd., Avalon, ☎ 310/510-2288, are 1.7 miles southwest of town.

Catalina Island Museum, Box 366, Avalon 90704, ☎ 310/510-2414, is on the waterfront at the base of the casino. Admission is free.

Corona del Mar

Sherman Library and Gardens, 2647 E. Coast Hwy., ☎ 714/673-2261, occupies a small city block adorned with fountains, sculptures and lush landscaping. **Discovery Garden for the Blind** favors the senses of touch and smell, and is easily navigable by people in wheelchairs. Cooking and gardening classes are provided. Tours are available. Lunch and refreshments are served in the outdoor tea garden.

Costa Mesa

Orange County Performing Arts Center, 600 Town Center Dr., ☎ 714/740-2400 or 556-2121, Web site www.ocartsnet.org/ocpac, is a $72.8 million center for the symphony, ballet, musical theater and opera. Performances of Opera Pacific and the Orange County Philharmonic Society are offered, plus guest orchestras, classical soloists and touring dance companies. Half-hour tours are conducted on Monday and Wednesday.

Pacific Amphitheater, 100 Fair Dr., ☎ 714/979-5944, located adjacent to the fairgrounds, presents summertime rock, pop and country acts.

Sculpture Garden, Avenue of the Arts and Anton Blvd., is six miles northeast of town near I-5. A lovely little park, it has a contemporary Japanese-style garden in which sandstone structures, natural rocks, running water and plants symbolize various California scenarios.

Dana Point

Then called Capistrano Point, the area was visited by Richard Henry Dana, author of *Two Years Before the Mast*, in 1835.

Orange County Marine Institute, 24200 Dana Point Harbor Dr., ☎ 714/496-2274, has a full-size replica of Dana's 120-foot brig *Pilgrim*.

Slightly more than half a mile southwest of town, the institute has a gray whale skeleton hanging from the ceiling. There is a gallery with books and gifts, and a stage for community concerts, summer theatrical performances and weddings.

Nautical Heritage Society & Museum, 24532 Del Prado, ☎ 714/661-1001, has a "lighthouse" that protrudes from the rooftop. It is the headquarters of the *Californian*, a tall ship that travels between northern and southern California throughout the year offering day-sailing programs for school children. When in port, the *Californian* anchors in the harbor next to the replica of Dana's *Pilgrim*.

Fullerton

Muckenthaler Cultural Center, 1201 W. Malvern Ave., ☎ 714/738-6595, was built in 1924 in an Italian Renaissance style. The first floor houses changing exhibits, and in 1993, a 238-seat amphitheater was added to accommodate theatrical performances. Dinner-theater is presented in the summer.

Fullerton Friends of Music, 804 E. Glenwood Ave., ☎ 714/525-9504 or 525-5836, is the oldest chamber music society in Orange County. Five concerts are performed each year at the Sunny Hills High School Performing Arts Center, 1801 Warburton Way.

Fullerton Museum Center, 301 N. Pomona Ave., ☎ 714/738-6545, focuses on Native American cultures.

Garden Grove

Shakespeare Festival, Festival Amphitheater, 12852 Main St., ☎ 714/636-7213, stages three Shakespearean plays in an outdoor amphitheater while three other plays are staged next door at the indoor Gem Theatre. Name performers, such as David Birney and Joan Van Ark, often appear in the productions.

Huntington Beach

School of Performing Arts, operated by the Huntington Beach School District, has the largest children's library in the state and the second largest in the United States.

Irvine

University of California Irvine Arboretum, Campus Dr. and Jamboree Rd., ☎ 714/856-5833, displays plants arranged according to their continent of origin.

Irvine Barclay Theatre, 4242 Campus Dr., ☎ 714/854-4646, Web site www.ocartsnet.org/ibt, presents musical and dramatic events, often showcasing name talent.

Severin Wunderman Museum, 3 Mason St., ☎ 714/472-1138, has America's largest collection of work by the French multimedia artist Jean Cocteau (1889-1963), plus a sizeable collection of Sarah Bernhardt memorabilia. The museum is located in a technology park and is rather difficult to find.

Old Courthouse Museum, 211 W. Santa Ana Blvd., was built in 1901 and has been featured in several films, including *The American President*, starring Michael Douglas.

The Bowers Museum of Cultural Art, 2002 N. Main St., is Orange County's largest museum. It displays the art of indigenous peoples in a recreation of a 1832 Spanish mission, recently renovated to add larger exhibit halls, a gourmet restaurant and a museum store.

The Irvine Museum, 18881 Von Karman Ave., 12th Floor, ☎ 714/476-2565 or 476-0294, is dedicated to California art of the Impressionist period (1890-1930). A docent-led tour is conducted every Thursday at 11:15.

Laguna Beach

Laguna Art Museum, 307 Cliff Dr., ☎ 714/494-6531, is the county's oldest cultural institution. It contains rotating exhibits of modern art and photography.

Friends of the Sea Lion Marine Mammal Center, 20612 Laguna Canyon Rd., ☎ 714/494-3050, was established in 1971 to provide medical care for the sick and injured seals and sea lions found along the coast. Volunteers make up 98% of the work force.

Laguna Playhouse, 606 Laguna Canyon Rd., ☎ 714/497-ARTS or 497-9244, was established in 1920. Supposedly, Harrison Ford was discovered here in 1965 while performing in *John Brown's Body*. **Festival of the Arts**, 650 Laguna Canyon Rd., got started in 1932 when struggling Depression-era artists hung their works from the trees by the side of the road in hope of attracting buyers. Now, 150 artists display their work in outdoor, covered booths; there is live entertainment daily; and free art workshops, demonstrations and tours are provided. Principal awards include the Roy Ropp Memorial Award in painting, the Colgate-Palmolive Award in sculpture and the Carl W. Callaway Memorial Award in theater arts.

Festival of the Arts/Pageant of the Masters, ☎ 714/494-1145, 497-6582 or 800/487-3378, Web site www.foapom.com, is one of the country's most unusual artistic offerings. Held during July and August in a canyon amphitheater just blocks from the beach, the pageant is accompanied by a full pit orchestra and narrated by a professional who has emceed the Academy Awards and the Olympics. One after another, on the main stage and elsewhere, scores of incredible recreations are unveiled in which cast members pose to look exactly like the figures in famous paintings, sculptures, porcelain pieces, posters and other artworks.

La Habra

La Habra Depot Theater, 311 S. Euclid St., ☎ 310/905-9708, 905-9625 or 694-4264, occupies a former Pacific Electric Railroad depot.

Long Beach

Long Beach Museum of Art, 2300 E. Ocean Blvd., ☎ 310/439-2119, occupies a 1912 mansion on a bluff by the sea. The old carriage house is now the museum store.

The new **Aquarium of the Pacific** is the first world-class aquarium in southern California. The $118 million waterfront structure was designed to house 12,000 marine animals.

Also new is **Latin American Art Museum**, 621 Alamitos Ave., which opened late in 1996 in the historic art deco Hippodrome Skating Rink.

San Clemente

Cabrillo Playhouse, 202 Ave. Cabrillo, ☎ 714/492-0465, Web site www.sanclemente.com/cabrilloplayhouse, celebrating 30 seasons as the San Clemente Community Theatre, is in a remodeled home and contains just 66 seats.

Santa Ana

Bowers Museum of Cultural Art & Kidseum, 2002 N. Main St., ☎ 714/567-3600, spent $12 million on a 1992 expansion that restored the original Spanish mission-style buildings and created Orange County's largest museum. A film, *California Legacies: The Story of Orange County*, runs continuously. The Kidseum is open Wednesday through Friday from 2 to 5 pm, and on weekends from 10 to 4.

Orange County Historical Society, ☎ 714/557-7074, conducts periodic tours to historic sites.

Whittier

Sheriffs Training and Regional Services (STARS) Center, 11515 S. Colima Rd., ☎ 310/946-7081, has a museum depicting the history and activities of the Los Angeles County Sheriff's office. It displays a Hughes 300 helicopter, a replica of a 19th-century sheriff's office and jail, and videos of famous cases. Guided tours are available by reservation. Admission is free.

Where To Stay

B&Bs, Hotels & Inns

Anaheim

Disneyland Hotel, ☎ 714/956-6425, is adjacent to Disneyland park and connected to it by monorail.

Literally scores of other hotels and motels in every price range can be found at or near the famous entertainment park.

Buena Park

Ramada Inn, 7555 Beach Blvd., ☎ 714/522-7360, fax 714/523-2883, provides 148 rooms within walking distance of Knott's Berry Farm, Movieland Wax Museum, Ripley's Believe It or Not! Museum, Wild Bill's Wild West Dinner Extravaganza and Medieval Times.

Catalina Island

Hotel St. Lauren, Box 2166, Avalon 90704, ☎ 310/510-2299 or 800/645-2478, is a charming Victorian with a pink-and-white exterior that is ornamented with five floors of exterior white railings. Built in 1987, but looking a century older, the hotel overlooks Avalon Bay and is a block from the beach. There are 42 rooms with ceiling fans, rosewood furniture and brass-fixtured bathrooms, plus a sixth-floor rooftop patio. A continental breakfast is served.

Zane Grey Pueblo Hotel, ☎ 310/510-0966 or 800/3-PUEBLO, is a Hopi Indian-style building with ocean and mountain views that the author built in 1926 for his home. It has an outdoor pool surrounded by gardens.

Glenmore Plaza Hotel, ☎ 310/510-0017 or 800/4-CATALI, is a 100-year-old Victorian once frequented by such celebrities as Clark Gable, Teddy Roosevelt and Amelia Earhart. A continental breakfast is provided and wine and cheese are served in the evening.

Catalina Canyon Hotel & Conference Center, 888 Country Club Dr., Avalon 90704, ☎ 310/510-0325 or 800/253-9361, is an upscale hotel with tennis, golf, a heated outdoor pool, a spa and a sauna.

➡ *NOTE: Hotel bookings on Catalina Island often include such "extras" as golf course privileges, boat rides, tour packages and the like.*

Dana Point

The Ritz-Carlton, 33533 Ritz-Carlton Dr., ☎ 714/240-2000, overlooks Salt Creek Beach Park. A touch of elegance comes when high tea is served during the week between 2:30 and 5 pm and on weekends between 2 and 6 pm in the library.

Sea Bluffs at Dana Point, 25411 Sea Bluffs Dr., ☎ 800/846-4440, caters to guests 55 or over. There are 180 condos and a clubhouse with a dining room, library, fitness center, theater and outdoor pool protected by 24-hour monitored gates and in-home security systems.

Newport Beach

Newport Beach Marriott Hotel & Tennis Club, 900 Newport Center Dr., ☎ 714/640-4000 or 800/228-9290, has 570 rooms and 15 suites with private balconies or patios. It also provides two pools, eight lighted tennis courts, a health club and a sushi bar.

San Clemente

Casa Tropicana B&B, 610 Avenida Victoria, ☎ 714/492-1234, Web site www.casatropicana.com, is located at the San Clemente Pier. The building has an art deco exterior and only nine rooms, most with whirlpools and gas fireplaces.

San Marcos

Lake San Marcos Resort, 1025 La Bonita Blvd., Lake San Marcos 92069, ☎ 800/447-6556, has 142 rooms and a host of amenities, including boat rides on the 80-acre lake, two 18-hole golf courses. seven tennis and paddle tennis courts, a fitness center, two outdoor pools and a spa. Quail's Dinnerhouse is located lakeside.

Camping

Eight coastal camping parks in Orange County, all along Highway 1 (aka Pacific Coast Highway, Coast Highway, or just PCH), require making a reservation through the state Mistix system (☎ 800-444-7275) to guarantee a spot. There is a non-refundable $3.95 fee for the campsite, plus a nightly fee. Reservations can be made from eight weeks to 24 hours prior to your time of arrival.

Anaheim

In case you flew in to California but want to "rough it" in the back country, **Club Travel Motorhome Rentals**, 16292 Harbor Blvd., ☎ 714/775-2730, rents RVs.

Featherly Regional Park, 24001 Santa Ana Canyon Rd., ☎ 714/637-0210, provides campsites. Take Highway 142 west to Valencia Ave. and turn left (south). Turn left at Highway 90 (Imperial Highway) and take another left at Yorba Linda. Proceed east to the park.

Santa Ana Canyon is an excellent overnight camping spot for families.

Catalina Island

Hermit Gulch Campground, Avalon Canyon, ☎ 310/510-TENT, has 53 sites and indoor hot showers. Just a mile from Avalon, the campground is open year-round and is near hiking trails. You can rent a teepee or a tent.

Catalina Camping Cabinets, Box 5044, Two Harbors 90704-5044, ☎ 213/510-2800, will send you a free camping guide.

Camping Catalina, Box 5044, Two Harbors 90704, ☎ 310/510-7265, fax 310/510-0244, can book you into **Black Jack Campground, Little Harbor Campground, Parson's Landing Campground** (primitive camping on the island's undeveloped west end), **Two Harbors Campground** (seaside camping a quarter-mile from the village of Two Harbors), **Conservancy Cove Camps** (primitive camping in pristine coves accessible only by boat), or **Catalina Yurt Cabins** in Goat Harbor (also in a secluded cove accessible only by boat). A yurt is a circular domed tent used by Mongols.

To acquire a camping or hiking permit, ☎ 213/510-0688 or 510-2800.

Cleveland National Forest

Within this 420,000-acre wilderness are the **Boulder Oaks, Bobcat Meadow, Four Corners Trailhead, Corral Canyon, Burnt Rancheria** and **Laguna** campgrounds.

There also are three lakes: **Little Laguna, Big Laguna** and **Water-of-the-Woods.**

Adjacent camping facilities can be found at Morena Reservoir in **Morena County Park,** Barrett Lake in the **Hauser Wilderness** and at **Pine Creek Wilderness.**

Blue Jay Campground, ☎ 800/283-CAMP, is 12 miles west of Lake Elsinore. It is open year-round. **Falcon,** a smaller campground, is in the same area.

Upper San Juan Campground, ☎ 619/673-6180, is open from April to October. There are 18 campsites for tents and motor homes.

For more information, contact **Descanso Ranger District**, 3348 Alpine Blvd., Alpine 92001-9630, ☎ 619/445-6235 or 473-8824. By car, take the

Buckman Springs exit off I-8. Other Ranger Districts are headquartered in San Diego, Corona and Ramona.

Huntington Beach

Bolsa Chica State Beach provides RV camping in the winter.

San Clemente State Beach

Located at 225 Avenida Calafia, ☎ 714/492-3156, this state-operated facility provides a general campground with 157 campsites and a separate trailer area that has 72 spaces with water.

Santa Ana Mountains

Ronald W. Caspers Wilderness Park, ☎ 714/831-2174, has a campground.

Where To Eat

Balboa

Newport Landing Restaurant, 503 E. Edgewater, ☎ 714/675-2373, offers not only waterfront dining but also one-hour dinner cruises aboard an electric boat.

Buena Park

Think you've seen everything McDonald's has to offer? At **"Big Train" McDonald's,** 7861 Beach Blvd., ☎ 714/521-2303, you can enjoy the traditional McDonald's menu or a McPizza while riding the McThriller, an action simulator ride that's the first of its kind in the country.

Catalina Island

Catalina Clambake, Box 2704, Avalon 90704, ☎ 213/510-0598, prepares a "steamed clambake in a can for carryout use." The dinner includes a 1¼-lb. lobster, three-quarters of a pound of steamers, mussels, corn on the cob, red bliss potatoes, sourdough rolls and drawn butter.

   Armstrong's, 306 Crescent Ave., Avalon 90704, ☎ 310/510-0113, broils its fish, chicken and steak over mesquite, a special Southwestern treat.

Corona del Mar

Five Crown Restaurant, 3801 E. Coast Hwy., ☎ 714/760-0331, occupies a building that has, at various times, been a residence, an inn, a gambling parlor and a house of ill repute. Now it's a reproduction of Ye Olde Bell, an inn at Hurley-on-the-Thames, England.

Costa Mesa

Scott's Seafood Grill & Bar, 3300 Bristol, ☎ 714/979-2400, serves such outstanding entrées as baked oysters Rockefeller, crab-stuffed mushrooms with lemon butter sauce, and beefsteak tomato and sweet red onion salad dressed with basil vinaigrette and crumbled blue cheese. It's also into the craze of holding "smokers" for cigar lovers. Scott's smoker is held on one Monday evening each month (on the patio!).

Other places currently holding smokers are **Antonello Ristorante**, 1611 Sunflower, Santa Ana, next to South Coast Plaza, which is likely to augment its "Cigar Night" with medallions of free-range veal tenderloin in a blackcurrant sauce over a porcini mushroom risotto; and **The Velvet Turtle**, 17555 Castleton St., Industry, ☎ 818/912-5358, fax ☎ 818/913-5257, which provides a champagne greeting, a four-course dinner, cognac tastings and a jazz duo, as well as complimentary cigars!

Fullerton

Cousin Jenny's Pasties (pronounced PAST-ease), Harbor Blvd. and Chapman Ave., serves those delicious meat pies that originated in the Cornwall mining region of England 200 years ago. When British miners migrated to Pennsylvania, Michigan and Montana, their pasties came too.

Huntington Beach

BrewBaker's, ☎ 714/374-2337, is a microbrewery where you can literally brew your own beer.

In this community, which celebrates German Heritage Day in July, holds Dachshund Races in September and October, and German Day in October, you'll automatically begin to think of such dishes as sauerkraut and strudel. When you do, head for **Old World Village**, 7561 Center Ave., ☎ 714/898-3033, just off I-405 and Beach Blvd. In this Bavarian-style village with cobbled streets, you will find five establishments simply *aching* to slake your hunger: **Old World German Restaurant**, ☎ 714/895-8020, which celebrates Oktoberfest from September to November; **Ein-becker Inn**, ☎ 714/892-9997, a sidewalk café; **Old World Bakery**, ☎ 714/891-1362; **Randy's Weinstube**, ☎ 714/894-8937, which provides live European entertainment; and **Rathskeller**, ☎ 714/894-6612, a German pub.

Irvine

Bistango Gallery Restaurant, across the street from the Irvine Museum, is both a gallery and a restaurant, as the name implies. The gallery includes contemporary art showcasing watercolors, sculpture and oil paintings. The restaurant specializes in California cuisine with an Italian flavor.

Chanteclair, 18912 MacArthur Blvd., ☎ 714/752-8001, fax 714/955-1394, is a four-star French restaurant with live entertainment nightly. Try the Cajun-charred ahi with garlic ginger sauce or the grilled salmon with julienne of fennel and pernod sauce.

Laguna Niguel

Mijouri Sushi Bune Restaurant, 30251 Golden Lantern, ☎ 714/363-8840, is in the Laguna Heights Marketplace, Marina Hills Blvd. and Golden Lantern Ave. It is an unusual "floating" sushi bar, where selections glide past you on little handmade rafts.

Long Beach

Listen up, ladies! If you're looking for an evening of romance, visit **The Gondola Getaway**, 5437 E. Ocean Blvd., ☎ 310/433-9595, where you can dine aboard a Venetian-style gondola while the oarsman plays Italian music and the sun slowly sinks into the sea.

Mission Viejo

Sooner or later, you've got to try a Mexican meal while you're in southern California. At **Tortilla Flats**, 27792 Vista Del Lago, ☎ 714/830-9980, you can dine on the edge of Lake Mission Viejo while you eat California-Mexican cuisine in an ivy-covered building with a tile fountain in front.

Newport Beach

Chart House, 2801 W. Coast Hwy., Newport Beach 92663, ☎ 714/548-5889, is always good, always reliable.

Hornblower Dining Yachts, 2431 W. Coast Hwy., Ste. 100, ☎ 714/646-0155, provides dinner cruises and brunch cruises, as well as harbor tours and private charters. Pick from a selection of more than 20 yachts. The company also operates out of Marina del Rey, ☎ 310/301-6000.

Chimayo, 327 Newport Center Dr., ☎ 714/640-2700, offers an exceptional menu with a New Mexican flair. Try their cornmeal-crusted buttermilk onion rings with spicy BBQ sauce or the mesquite-grilled salmon in a corn husk with poblano pesto. Even the selection of ice creams is out of the ordinary: tequila-raisin, chocolate chile and pumpkin among them.

Newport Landing, 503 E. Edgewater, ☎ 714/675-2373, is near the Fun Zone and the auto ferry on Balboa Island. A two-story establishment (with excellent views of the harbor from the upper deck), it provides live entertainment on the weekends. House specialties include the Big Kahuna, a tropical drink, and there is a champagne brunch every Saturday and Sunday. Try the lobster taquitos in red corn tortillas, the blackened ahi with jalapeño jelly, creamy crab and artichoke soup or calamari steaks in chardonnay, lime, capers and herb butter. The restaurant offers a nice kids' menu, and cruise-and-dine packages are available.

Riverboat Café, 151 E. Coast Hwy., ☎ 714/673-3425, is a floating restaurant.

DINNER THEATER

Buena Park

Jousting tournaments are served on the side!
Credit: Medieval Times Dinner & Tournament

Medieval Times, 7662 Beach Blvd., ☎ 714/521-4740 or 800/899-6600, stages lively 11th-century tournaments, such as jousting by costumed knights on horseback, in a 1,120-seat castle-like setting. While the knights joust, the audience enjoys a four-course dinner (but be forewarned: no silverware is provided). There are nightly performances and matinees on Sunday.

Wild Bill's Wild West Dinner Extravaganza, 7600 Beach Blvd., ☎ 714/522-6414 or 800/883-1546, offers two hours of Western-style entertainment along with your family-style meal. There are nightly shows and matinees on Saturday and Sunday.

Costa Mesa

South Coast Plaza Village restaurants, ☎ 714/675-9726, host "Play Mystery for Me," in which a theatrical group stages different murder mysteries every Saturday at 7.

Huntington Beach

Tibbie's Music Hall, 16360 Pacific Coast Hwy., ☎ 714/840-5661, offers musical dinner-theater with performing waiters at Peter's Landing.

Irvine

The Mezzanine, 19800 MacArthur Blvd., ☎ 714/955-CLUE, features "Whodunnit Dinner Theater" Friday and Saturday at 8, just south of John Wayne Airport.

Newport Beach

Tibbie's Music Hall, 4647 MacArthur Blvd., ☎ 714/252-0834, advertises the "Best dinner theater in Orange County."

COMEDY CLUBS

Irvine

Improv Comedy Club and Restaurant, 4255 Campus Dr., ☎ 714/854-5455, across from the University of California Irvine campus, stages shows at 8:30 and 10:30 daily.

In & Around San Diego

San Diego skyline.
Credit: James Blank, San Diego Convention & Visitors Bureau

Portuguese explorer Juan Rodriguez Cabrillo landed in San Diego Bay in 1542 and claimed the region for Spain.

When the early Spaniards marched out of Mexico, across what we now know as Arizona, and into California in 1769, it was for the expressed purpose of reaching the Pacific Ocean. The first phase of that expedition ended when they reached present-day San Diego.

Here, Father Junipero Serra built the first Spanish mission, Mission San Diego de Alcala, the first in a string of 21 missions that eventually would stretch all the way to the Monterey Peninsula. This, then, is the *birthplace* of California, and California has not forgotten its roots. Nowhere in the state is the Spanish influence felt more strongly than it is in and around San Diego. Nowhere is the lingering influence of Mexico felt more prominently. One needs to look no farther than the names of the towns (San Luis Obispo), the streets (avenida, calle, camino), the rivers (rios) and mountains (montañas) to recognize the legacy of those early pioneers. The Spanish-style architecture remains. The Mexican-flavored foods remain.

The telephone book proliferates with surnames like Garcia, Rodriguez, Hernandez, Ochoa and Gomez.

But while the old lingers on, San Diego is *not* an old-fashioned city. Indeed, it is a very *modern* city, a *vital* city, a *vibrant* city, a *growing* city.

Whatever your preference – the past, the present, or the future – you're bound to find it somewhere in San Diego.

Getting Around

Traffic flows in and out of San Diego on stressed-concrete arteries – the interstate highway system.

Interstate 5 provides the link with Los Angeles to the north and the Mexican border to the south. Interstate 15 helps north-south traffic avoid the center of Los Angeles in trying to reach the city's eastern suburbs and beyond. Interstate 8 carries the east-west traffic, linking San Diego with Yuma, Arizona and beyond.

San Diego International Airport is one of the nation's finest and most scenic.

Amtrak, ☎ 619/239-9021 (schedule information) or 800/872-7245 (reservations), connects San Diego with Orange and Los Angeles Counties. The train makes eight daily round trips, stopping in San Diego, Solana Beach, Oceanside, San Juan Capistrano, Santa Ana, Anaheim and Fullerton on its way to downtown Los Angeles.

Coaster Rail Transportation, ☎ 800/COASTER (262-7837), leaves the old Santa Fe Depot on Kettner Blvd. between Broadway and B Sts. and the Old Town Transit Center at San Diego and Congress Sts. It journeys north along the coast to Sorrento Valley, Solana Beach, Encinitas, Carlsbad

San Diego

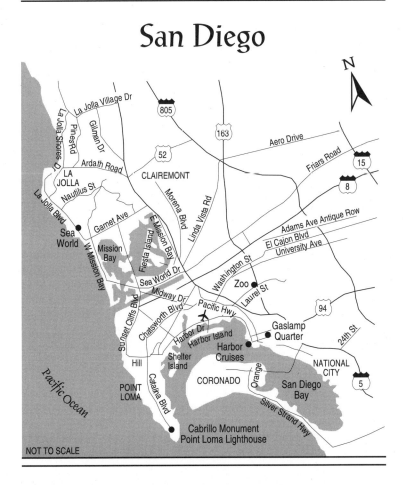

Poinsettia (Avenida Encinitas and Poinsettia Ln.), Carlsbad Village (Grand Ave. between Washington and State Sts.), and Oceanside Monday through Friday.

Touring

San Diego

California's second largest city and the sixth largest city in the United States, San Diego spreads over 320 square miles and serves a population of more than a million people.

Diver Greg Louganis, swimmer Florence Chadwick, golfers Mickey Wright and Billy Casper, baseball Hall of Famer Ted Williams, football player Marcus Allen, and actors Michael Damian, Robert Lansing and Ted Danson were all born in San Diego.

San Diego's Gaslamp Quarter.
Credit: Bob Yarbrough, San Diego Convention & Visitors Bureau

Mission San Diego de Alcala, San Diego Mission Rd., ☎ 619/281-8449 or 283-7319, now well over 200 years old, still stands and is open for viewing. Ask for a self-guided Tote-a-Tape Tour.

Gaslamp Quarter is a beautifully preserved 20-square-block area that reflects the charm of San Diego during the early 1900s. Western gunman Wyatt Earp of Tombstone fame once stayed there.

Balboa Park, ☎ 619/239-0512, was built in 1935 for the second California Pacific International Exposition. Designed to depict an old Spanish village, it is the largest cultural city park in the country. The park contains 13 museums within a distance of just a few blocks:

★ **Centro Cultural de la Raza**, Park Blvd., ☎ 619/235-6135, presents exhibits of indigenous, Mexican and Chicano artists; film and video screenings; literary programs; and workshops.

★ **Hall of Champions**, 1649 El Prado, ☎ 619/234-2544, is one of the few multi-sport museums in the country, highlighting

San Diego's contributions in 40 different sports. There is a theater inside the hall that shows continuous sports films.

★ **Japanese Friendship Garden,** ☎ 619/232-2721.

★ **Museum of Photographic Arts,** 1649 El Prado, ☎ 619/239-5262, offers changing exhibits. Lectures and docent tours are available, and there is a museum store.

★ **Museum of San Diego History,** El Prado, ☎ 619/232-6203, traces the area's history from 1850 to the present. The museum is operated by the San Diego Historical Society.

★ **Reuben H. Fleet Space & Science Center,** El Prado, ☎ 619/238-1168, 238-1233 or 232-6866, stages an OmniMax theater presentation in addition to the hands-on exhibits inside the Science Center.

★ **San Diego Aerospace Museum,** 2001 Pan American Plaza, ☎ 619/234-8291, Web site www.aerospacemuseum.org, displays over 65 U.S. and foreign aircraft and spacecraft. There is an International Aerospace Hall of Fame there, and a museum store.

★ **San Diego Automotive Museum,** south of the Prado, ☎ 619/231-AUTO, displays more than 80 vehicles, including horseless carriages, brass cars, classics, exotic cars, motorcycles and future prototypes.

★ **San Diego Model Railroad Museum,** 1649 El Prado, ☎ 619/696-0199, is located on the lower level of the Casa de Balboa Building. It depicts the history of railroads in the Southwest with 24,000 square feet of operating model train exhibits. Visitors can play engineer in the interactive Toy Train Gallery.

★ **San Diego Museum of Art,** 1450 El Prado, ☎ 619/232-7931, is the city's largest museum. Docent-guided tours are available. There is a Sculpture Garden Café, ☎ 619/696-1990, and a museum store, ☎ 619/696-1971.

★ **San Diego Museum of Man,** 1350 El Prado, San Diego, ☎ 619/239-2001, an anthropology museum that sells ethnic arts, jewelry, clothing and books.

★ **San Diego Museum of Natural History,** El Prado, ☎ 619/232-3821, offers several whale-watching trips during the winter season. These and other explorations into the area's canyons, deserts, mountains and preserves are led by volunteers called Canyoneers (ext. 203).

★ **Spanish Village Art Center,** ☎ 619/233-9050, has 35 studio/galleries that display the work of over 300 artists – painters, potters, jewelers, sculptors, glassblowers and wood-carvers.

★ **Timken Art Gallery,** 1500 El Prado, ☎ 619/239-5548, displays European and American masterworks.

★ **Mingei International Museum of World Folk Art**, 1439 El Prado, ☎ 619/239-0003, is a new addition to Balboa Park. Previously located in La Jolla, the museum exhibits the artwork – ceramics, textiles, toys, objects of daily use – of people from all cultures.

A "Passport to Balboa Park" is available. A coupon book that is valid for one week, it allows individuals to visit 10 Balboa Park museums (a $44 value) for just $18. The booklet can be purchased at any participating museum, at the Balboa Park Visitors Center, or at the Times Arts Tix Book in Horton Plaza.

Balboa Park also contains the **San Diego Zoo**, ☎ 619/234-3153, one of the world's finest. From I-5, take the Pershing Dr. exit. From Highway 163 South, take the Park Blvd. exit.

Spreckles Organ Pavilion in Balboa Park offers free outdoor concerts at 2 pm every Sunday afternoon, featuring the 4,400-pipe Spreckles organ. Summer evening concerts are held every Monday at 8 and every Tuesday through Thursday at 6:15.

Starlight Bowl, ☎ 619/544-7800, also located in Balboa Park, provides music under the stars.

Balboa Park.
Credit: Bob Yarbrough, San Diego Convention & Visitors Bureau

Old Town Trolley Tours, 4040 Twiggs St., ☎ 619/298-8687, features fully narrated tours of the city, making stops at Old Town, Embarcadero, Seaport, Marriott, Horton Plaza, Coronado, San Diego Zoo, Aerospace Museum and Balboa Park. Visitors can tour at their own pace and may get off and reboard as they wish, free of charge. The company also offers an exclusive tour to the Nuclear Submarine Base, Pt. Loma, Miramar Naval Air Station, North Island Naval Air Station and Naval Station San Diego.

San Diego Scenic Tours, ☎ 619/273-8687, takes tours to Tijuana, Mexico.

San Diego Harbor Excursion, 1080 N. Harbor Dr., ☎ 619/234-4111 or 800/442-7847, leaves Broadway Pier in downtown San Diego for Coronado Island every hour on the hour from 9 am to 9 pm (10 pm on Saturday and Sunday only). The ferry returns from the Ferry Landing Marketplace on Coronado Island every hour on the half-hour, 9:30 am to 9:30 pm (10:30 pm on Saturday and Sunday). The excursion takes 15 minutes each way.

San Diego Water Taxi, Fish Harbor Pier, Seaport Village, ☎ 619/235-8294, provides scheduled service to the Ferry Landing Marketplace, Glorietta Bay Marina across from Hotel Del Coronado, and Le Meridien Resort on Coronado Island for $5.

Sea World, 1720 South Shores Rd., ☎ 619/226-3901 or 226-3929, Web site www:\\4adventure.com, is located on Mission Bay. Covering 15 acres and holding 6.7 million gallons of water – enough to fill 220 backyard swimming pools – it is the world's largest marine mammal exhibit. "Marooned! With Clyde and Seamore" tells a story of castaways, jungle drums and mysterious islanders with river otters, a Pacific walrus and the comedic sea lion duo, Clyde and Seamore. "Wings of the World" is an exotic bird show. At Dolphin Bay, guests touch and feed bottlenose dolphins, and listen to them on hydrophones. The new "Shamu Backstage" is a 1.7-million-gallon interactive killer whale exhibit that allows guests to wade into shallow water, reach over an acrylic panel and actually touch the whales.

Shamo, the killer whale.
Credit: Bob Couey, Sea World of California

Virtual World, in Mission Valley's Hazard Center, ☎ 619/294-9200, is said to be "the world's first digital theme park." At the controls of your own inter-dimensional travel vehicle, you and seven other pilots are dropped into another dimension, where you are free to move and interact at will. Every adventure is unique. Afterward, you receive a "mission review" – an instant replay of the adventure from a bird's-eye viewpoint. You also receive a "Pilot's Log" – a printed record of your adventure.

INFORMATION SOURCES

Visitor Hotline, ☎ 619/581-5003.

Visitors Bureau, 1200 Third Ave., San Diego 92101, ☎ 619/232-3101.

San Diego Convention & Visitors Bureau, 104 B St., Suite 1400, San Diego 92101-4237, ☎ 619/232-3101, fax 619/696-9371.

Greater San Diego Chamber of Commerce, 402 W. Broadway, San Diego, ☎ 619/232-0124.

Chula Vista

ARCO Training Center, 1750 Wueste Rd., ☎ 619/482-6222, is a $65 million, 150-acre U.S. Olympic Committee Facility with venues for track and field, canoe/kayak, cycling, field hockey, soccer, archery (the largest permanent range in North America), and rowing. There is a 15,000-square-foot canoe, kayak and rowing boathouse, plus four tennis courts, a 400-meter track, six acres for field events, and a cycling criterium course. Plans call for the addition of an aquatic complex and a gymnasium. Tours are available.

INFORMATION SOURCES

Bayfront Visitor Information Center, E St. exit off I-5, ☎ 619/425-4444, Web site www.ci.chulavista.ca.us.
Visitor Information Center, E St./Bonita Rd. exit off I-805.
Chamber of Commerce and Convention & Visitors Bureau, 233 Fourth Ave., Chula Vista 91910, ☎ 619/420-6603.

Coronado

Although often referred to as an island, Coronado actually is a peninsula between San Diego Bay and the ocean. From the north, it is linked to San Diego by a ferry service and by water taxis. From the south, it is joined to the mainland by the 2.3-mile San Diego-Coronado Bay Bridge.

Until 1888, when the imposing Hotel Del Coronado was built, the "island" was little more than a sand spit. **Silver Strand State Beach** is still popular for surfing and swimming, and **Coronado Beach**, by the Hotel Del Coronado, is a favorite for beach sports like frisbee and smash ball.

All but frozen in time around the turn of the 20th century, Coronado – "The Enchanted Island" – is an almost magical place. Frank L. Baum wrote his classic *Wizard of Oz* here.

Summer band concerts are held at the bandstand in **Spreckles Park**, Orange Ave. between Sixth and Seventh, on Sunday evenings at 6 pm.

In the spring, a **Flower Show Weekend** features a Book Fair, Footlighter's Artisans Fair, a pancake breakfast and Art-in-the-Park.

On the Fourth of July there is a parade (160 entries), rough water swim, 15K run, 5K walk, Art-in-the-Park, Concert-in-the-Park and fireworks over Glorietta Bay. In August the San Diego Unified Port District presents **Cinema-on-the-Bay**, screening films from a barge that is anchored offshore. The event is free.

Winter brings a Christmas parade, the San Diego Harbor Boat Parade of Lights, Lamb's Players Theatre "Festival of Christmas," and "An American Christmas," presented at the Hotel Del Coronado.

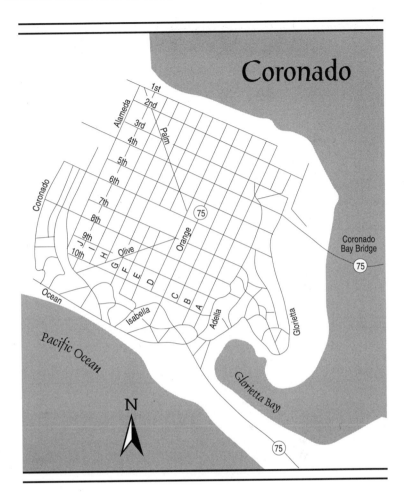

On the north end of the peninsula is a Naval Air Station and "Carrier Row" (inquire about military tours).

INFORMATION SOURCES

Visitor Information Center, 1111 Orange Ave., Suite A (second floor), Coronado 92118, ☎ 619/437-8788 or 800/622-8300.
Coronado Visitors Bureau, 1047 B Ave., Coronado 92118-3418, ☎ 800/622-8300, e-mail corcvb@aol.com.
Coronado Chamber of Commerce, 1009 C Ave., Coronado, ☎ 619/435-9260.

Imperial Beach

This area extends from the Coronado Bridge to the Mexican border. There is a pier for fishing.

For information, contact the **City of Imperial Beach Travel Information**, 825 Imperial Beach Blvd., Imperial Beach 91932, ☎ 619/423-8300, fax 619/429-9770; or the **Imperial Beach Chamber of Commerce**, ☎ 619/424-3151.

La Jolla

Artifacts found in this area indicate that there were Indian settlements near the shore over 3,000 years ago. In 1905, Scripps Institution of Oceanography started operations here. In the mid-1960s, the University of California San Diego was inaugurated. Today, La Jolla (The Jewel) lies within the boundaries of the City of San Diego.

An upscale residential community (one of the main streets is called Wall Street) along the northern coastline, La Jolla has a number of charming boutiques and unusual little cafés to explore. And some things are just for *fun*. If you visit La Jolla in March, for example, see the **Easter Hat Parade**, Girard Ave. and Prospect St., ☎ 619/454-1444. It's La Jolla's version of the Rose Bowl Parade, but keep it under your hat.

In August, see the **Off the Wall Street Dance**, Wall St. and Herschel Ave., sponsored by the UCSD Medical Center, ☎ 619/534-1503.

INFORMATION SOURCES

Golden Triangle Chamber of Commerce, ☎ 619/558-1744.
Convention & Visitors Bureau, ☎ 619/232-3101.
Visitor Information Center, ☎ 619/276-8200.

Oceanside

The earliest settlers in the San Luis Rey Valley were the Luiseño Indians. Later, eight ranches became established there. Now, each ranch has developed into a separate city.

Much of the community's daily life centers around the **Oceanside Pier**. Residents and visitors fish from the pier, watch as swimmers surf in the water below, or simply stand on the pier to see the sun going down.

The first pier was built in 1888 at the foot of Wisconsin St., but it was destroyed a year later by heavy surf. In 1894, a 400-foot pier was built at the end of Third St., about three-quarters of a mile from the previous pier. That pier was later extended to 600 feet, and was replaced entirely in 1903 by a 1,300-foot pier. In 1915, storms damaged the pier, making it necessary to remove a 400-foot section, but in 1925, the pier was again lengthened, this time to 1,340 feet. With the outbreak of World War II, a Navy observation tower was built on it, which caused a section to collapse in 1943. A new 1,544-foot pier was built in 1947, but destroyed by a storm in 1983. The present pier, 300 N. Pacific St., was completed in time for the city's centennial in 1988. It is the longest pier on the West Coast.

Stretching away from the pier in both directions are white sandy beaches, 3½ miles of them. And right on the beach near the pier is a row of 24 **Roberts' Cottages**, 704 N. The Strand. These little waterfront cottages, built in 1928, are painted a bright salmon color and have multicolored roofs. They originally were known as the A.J. Clark Beach Cottages, and later became the Surf Motor Court. Many now are available for vacation rental.

Future plans call for a $305 million development of shops, restaurants, vacation timeshares and a hotel to be built on the bluffs opposite the pier. Construction began on the **Pier Plaza Project** in 1996. When the project is completed, nearby Pacific St. may be turned into a pedestrian esplanade.

An **amphitheater** (no phone) capable of holding 3-5,000 people sits next to the pier.

Over 950 boats, ranging from 25 to 51 feet in length, are moored in the Oceanside harbor, just north of the downtown area, outside the gates of Camp Pendleton.

Frequent daily rail service is provided on Amtrak, Coaster and Metrolink from the new **Oceanside Transit Center**, 235 S. Tremont St. Tickets for the Metrolink commuter train, ☎ 213/808-5465, can be purchased from a vending machine. The fare depends on distance you wish to travel.

Camp Pendleton USMC Base

In 1942, the U.S. government bought Rancho Santa Margarita y Flores and turned it into a West Coast training base. Today, 125,000-acre Camp Pendleton, ☎ 619/725-4111, 725-5569 or 800/697-1314, located just north of town, is the world's largest military training base.

The original adobe ranch house, built about 1827, was restored in 1947 and houses the base commanding general. Also restored are the old chapel and the bunkhouse, now an amphibious vehicle museum. Portions of the facility are a haven for several endangered species.

Self-guided tours are permitted Monday through Friday between 7:30 am and 4:30 pm (get a brochure at the main gate on Vandegrift Blvd.)

San Luis Rey

Mission San Luis Rey de Francia, 4050 Mission Ave., San Luis Rey 92068, ☎ 619/757-3651, is just four miles east of town on Highway 76. The "King of the Missions" was founded in 1798 by Father Fermin de Lasuen, the 18th in California's string of 21 missions.

Named for St. Louis IX of France, patron of the Secular Franciscan Order, the mission was built between the existing missions at San Diego and San Juan Capistrano. The original decorations were done by the Indians, and the mission served the largest Indian population (over 2,000) of any mission of its day.

Until the mid-1800s, it was the largest building in California. At its peak, over 56,000 head of livestock grazed on its grounds.

In 1833 the church reluctantly turned the property over to the Mexican government. Over the next 12 years, the land was sold to private buyers. Then, in 1850, California entered the Union.

In 1865, just one month before his assassination, Abraham Lincoln returned the mission to the church.

The museum now houses the largest collection of 18th- and 19th-century Spanish vestments in the United States. The new **Junipero Serra Hall** is a 17,500-square-foot facility used for meetings.

For more information, contact the **Visitors Information Center**, 928 N. Coast Hwy., Oceanside 92054, ☎ 619/721-1101, 722-1534 or 800/350-7873, fax 619/722-8336. The center is open seven days a week. Or **KOCT**, Channel 17 community cable TV, ☎ 619/722-4433.

Carlsbad

Named for the popular 19th-century Karlsbad spa in Europe, "The Village by the Sea" has become a major commercial flower-growing center. Enough ranunculi are grown here each year to supply the American market and still send four million bulbs to the Netherlands.

The bird of paradise was first developed commercially here and is the city's official flower.

The 50-acre flower field at **Carlsbad Ranch** behind Pea Soup Andersen's east of I-5 on Palomar Airport Rd., ☎ 619/431-0352, e-mail: FlowerFlds@aol.com, is ablaze with sunflowers in March and April. As they are harvested, the hills become covered with brightly colored ranunculus in April. Beginning in November and running through December, the Poinsettia Star appears – a 166-foot display of more than 2,000 potted Ecke poinsettias arranged in the shape of a giant star.

In the late 1800s, a retired sea captain, John Frazier, drilled for and hit mineral water, which he began to sell to the passengers on trains passing through. Soon, the water was claimed to have miraculous healing powers, and Frazier sold out to a German immigrant, Gerhard Schutte, who established the California Land and Mineral Water Co. Schutte's mansion, which was built in 1887, is now Carlsbad's popular **Neimans Restaurant**.

Today, Carlsbad has become a beach town 36 miles north of San Diego, situated on several miles of beach between two lagoons.

Carlsbad State Beach, a mile south of town on Carlsbad Blvd. at Tamarack Ave., ☎ 619/729-8947, is a long sandy strand accented by patches of pebbles. There are lifeguards, restrooms and picnic areas.

A recent $55 million **Batiquitos Lagoon** restoration project moved over two million cubic yards of sand onto the beaches. The nation's largest wetlands restoration project, it also established five new nesting sites, put two new bridges over Carlsbad Blvd., and created two jetties to protect the mouth of the lagoon.

Buena Vista Lagoon, a 200-acre habitat for nearly 200 species, is located between Carlsbad and Oceanside. Hill Street runs along the north side of the lagoon. The new **Buena Vista Lagoon Audubon Society Nature Center**, ☎ 619/439-2473, has exhibits, a staff of docents and a gift shop. It will arrange field trips.

Carlsbad Village Faires, which are held on the first Sunday of May and November, are the largest single-day street fairs in California.

INFORMATION SOURCES

Tourist Information Center, housed in the Carlsbad railroad depot, built in 1887.

Carlsbad Chamber of Commerce, 5411 Avenida Encinas, Suite 100, Carlsbad 92008, ☎ 619/931-8400.

Carlsbad Convention & Visitors Bureau, PO Box 1246, San Diego 92018-1246, ☎ 619/434-6093 or 800/227-5722.

Del Mar

The early settlers of this area were the San Dieguito hunters of 9000 B.C. For a great many years, the town's only significant feature was the 40 x 198-foot Taylor natatorium, "the only bathing pool on the Pacific coast built into the surf."

Taylor and a man named Loop then began to sell 50 x 140-foot lots for $100 each ($600 with a house on them). To preserve the clean atmosphere of the town, the deeds prohibited the sale of intoxicating liquor, gambling and the operation of a livery stable on the premises.

In December 1889, torrential rains uprooted trees and washed away the railroad tracks, the roads and the bridges. By Christmas, the town was isolated. Early the following year, the hotel burned down, not to be replaced for many years.

Del Mar Beach, popular for volleyball and surfing, runs the length of the town.

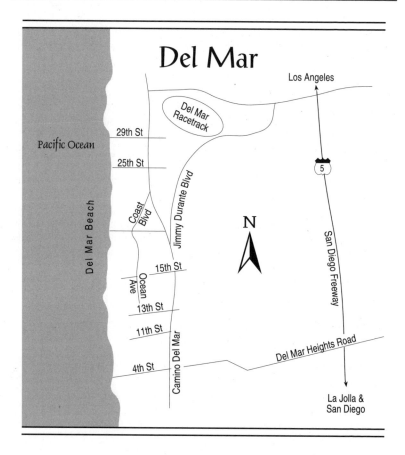

Del Mar Fairgrounds, ☎ 619/793-5555, on Jimmy Durante Blvd. one mile northeast of town, hosts the **San Diego County Fair** from mid-June through early July.

A new **Del Mar Library** opened in November 1996 in the former Saint James Church. Prior to that, a trailer had served as the town's "temporary" library for 20 years.

INFORMATION SOURCES

Greater Del Mar Chamber of Commerce, 1104 Camino del Mar, Del Mar 92014, ☎ 619/755-4844 or 793-5292, fax 619/755-0056.
City of Del Mar, 1050 Camino del Mar, Del Mar 92014, ☎ 619/755-9313, Web site www.delmar.ca.us.
San Diego County, Web site www.uniontrib.com.

Encinitas

The original town, founded in 1882, grew up around the railroad depot, but in June 1986, four small communities – Encinitas, Leucadia, Olivenhain and Cardiff-by-the-Sea – united to form the new Encinitas along six miles of coastline between two lagoons.

Quail Botanical Gardens, 230 Quail Gardens Dr., ☎ 619/436-3036, includes 30 acres of canyons and sunny hillsides, rare plants, a waterfall, self-guided trails, banana palms and America's largest collection of bamboos. It is one of the world's most diverse and botanically important plant collections. A chaparral area on the grounds serves as a natural bird refuge. Tours are available, and there is no admission charge on the first Tuesday of each month.

For more information, contact **Encinitas North Coast Chamber of Commerce**, 138 Encinitas Blvd., Encinitas 92024, ☎ 619/753-6041.

Vista

Taylors Herb Garden, 1535 Lone Oak Rd., ☎ 619/727-3485, is the West Coast's largest herb grower.

Rancho Buena Vista Adobe, 640 Alta Vista Dr., ☎ 619/945-4919 or 726-1340, originally was one of six ranchos claimed by Mission San Luis Rey. The last 1.9 acres of an original 1845 Mexican land grant were purchased by the city in 1989 and the house was furnished with turn-of-the-century antiques. Guided tours are available and docents weave tales of the walled skeleton, the lady in white and the prized stallion. Annual events include a quilting show, a treasure sale, a Victorian tea, Cinco de Mayo (the fifth of May, a cherished Mexican holiday), Family Day, Pioneer Luncheon, Ice Cream Social and the Holiday Home Tour.

For more information, contact **Vista Chamber of Commerce**, 201 Washington St., Vista 92084, ☎ 619/726-1122.

Escondido

Heritage Walk and Museum, 321 N. Broadway, ☎ 619/743-8207, is in Grape Day Park between Washington Ave. and Valley Parkway. Operated by the Escondido Historical Society, it displays buildings preserved from the city's early days. Escondido's first library is now the museum office. Other structures on display include a furnished 1890 Victorian house and a restored 1888 Santa Fe train depot.

San Diego Wild Animal Park, 15500 San Pasqual Valley Rd., ☎ 619/234-6541, 234-3153, 480-0100, 747-8702 or 231-1515, Web site www.sandiegozoo.org, is an extension of the San Diego Zoo containing more than 2,500 animals and 3,000 species of exotic plants. The animals are seen in their natural environments; there are no cages on the 700-acre grounds (1,500 acres have yet to be developed). Visitors ride the Wgasa Bushline Monorail for a 50-minute, five-mile tour. Red plastic "zookeys" operate 30 audio information stations throughout the grounds. Animal shows include a bird show at Benbough Amphitheater, an elephant show, and a rare and wild America show at the Village Amphitheater. Visitors can purchase bird food to feed the lorikeets. There is a 1¾-mile Kilimanjaro Safari Walk, and a 1¼-mile walk through protea, fuchsia, epiphyllum, conifers, succulents, and Bonsai gardens at the Kupanda Falls Botanical Center.

Widely known for its educational programs, ☎ 619/738-5057, the Animal Park offers **Summer Swamp Nights**, which include a nighttime monorail ride, dining under the stars, and an evening of fun and adventure, from Thursday through Sunday. **Kindersafari**, a program for children four to six years of age, discusses desert life with "How Dry I Am," presents a pre-Halloween program in "Creepy Crawlers," and teaches the children about monkeys in "It's a Jungle Out There." **Photo Caravan**, ☎ 619/738-5022, a 1¾-hour excursion into the animal enclosures aboard an open truck, comes in two versions: (1) East Africa/Asian Plains or (2) South Africa/Asian Waterhole. **Family Safari** is somewhat similar to the Photo Caravan except that it also gives people a chance to feed some of the animals. **Roar & Snore**, ☎ 619/738-5022 or 800/934-CAMP, is a program offered between May and September that allows visitors to tent out overnight on Friday or Saturday.

The new **Mombasa Lagoon** is called "the largest single improvement to the Animal Park since it opened in 1972." The lagoon, which occupies five acres in the heart of the $1.2 million Nairobi Village renovation project, allows visitors to:

★ Climb into a pelican's eggshell resting within the bird's very large nest and curl up in a ball.

★ Hop like a frog from lily pad to lily pad along the shores of the lagoon.

★ Venture into the lagoon on a floating walkway and visit Lemur Island Peninsula, where they can watch ring-tailed lemurs glide through the air from branch to branch, and experience life as a turtle inside a human-size turtle shell.

★ Catch insects by climbing an enormous spider web.

★ See a bat-eared fox exhibit.

★ Crawl into an aardwolf dwelling.

★ Rest in a large weaver bird nest and watch the birds build nests that are suspended from tree branches to protect their young.

★ See a newly-renovated pet kraal, a rare albino American alligator, and Harry and Violet, two warthogs.

★ Visit meerkats and pudus (small, hollow-toothed deer native to the Andes) in newly-renovated exhibits.

The **Palomar Mountains** extend 25 miles along the northern boundary of San Diego County and are one of few southern California mountain ranges not to border on the desert. Distinct fault lines run along the north and south, making both sides of the range very precipitous. Indians called the mountains Pauuw (mountains), and the Spanish, noticing a number of band-tailed pigeons in the area, called them Palomar (pigeon roost). Today, many people call them "Mystery Mountains" because few people lived there at the time plans for **Palomar Observatory** were first formulated. Going up, cars had to climb a steep, nerve-wracking grade; coming down, they tied trees to their car bumpers to slow their descent. (The local Indians used the discarded trees at the bottom of the mountains for firewood.) A new road from the south, "Highway to the Stars," was built to the observatory site, opening the mountains to visitors.

INFORMATION SOURCES

San Diego North County Convention & Visitors Bureau, 720 N. Broadway, Escondido 92025, ☎ 619/745-4741, fax 619/745-4796. **Escondido Chamber of Commerce**, 720 N. Broadway, Escondido 92025, ☎ 619/745-1183 or 800/848-3336.

El Cajon

El Cajon (The Box) hosts a **Mother Goose Parade** (☎ 619/440-6161) each November. **Gillespie Field** (☎ 619/448-3101) is the county airport.

Santee

Old **Padre Dam** at the west entrance of Santee Valley was built by the Spanish for irrigation. It was first mentioned in history books written in 1773. The aqueduct was started in 1813 and took eight years to complete.

For more information, contact **Santee Chamber of Commerce**, 10315 Mission Gorge Rd., Santee 92071, ☎ 619/449-6572.

Adventures

On Foot

Chula Vista

Extensive hiking trails that lace the area may lead to the sighting of a burrowing owl, which lives underground, comes out during the day, and makes sounds like a rattlesnake. The owls are often found on golf courses and around airports in the area.

Nature Center, 1000 Gunpowder Point Dr., ☎ 619/422-2473/81, Web site www.sdcc12.ucsd.edu/-wa12/cvnature.html, includes aquaria, terraria, and other displays describing the 215 species of birds that fly the coastal waterways. It features the world's only exhibit of the light-footed clapper rail. Visitors can hand-feed stingrays, batrays and sharks. The center, which is located on San Diego Bay in the 316-acre **Sweetwater Marsh National Wildlife Refuge**, has an observation tower and a deck. There are bilingual interpretive trails, a visitor information center and a bookstore. Group tours are offered. The center can be reached on the San Diego trolley.

Chula Vista Heritage Museum, 360 Third Ave., has observation decks, hands-on exhibits interpreting the surrounding marshland habitat, and a 1½-mile walking trail. It can be reached by shuttle bus, which departs every 20 minutes from a parking lot just west of I-5 at E St.

Coronado

Coronado Touring, ☎ 619/435-5444 or 435-5892, leaves **Glorietta Bay Inn**, 1630 Glorietta Blvd., on Tuesday, Thursday and Saturday at 11 on a 1½-hour narrated walking tour. The tour examines the 1888 Hotel Del, passes the Duchess of Windsor Cottage, and allows you to see the restored Crown Manor mansion – the *Wizard of Oz* house in which author L. Frank Baum once lived.

Hotel Del Coronado rents tapes to those who would prefer a self-guided tour.

Del Mar

Beach jogging is popular here, and there is a boardwalk along Pacific Beach and Mission Beach south of town that is a magnet for inline bladers and walkers.

Torrey Pines State Reserve, N. Torrey Pines Rd., ☎ 619/755-2063, is two miles southeast of town at the north end of the Del Mar Scenic

Parkway. It is a 1,750-acre reserve for the world's rarest pine tree, *Pinus Torreyana*, which grows only here and on Santa Rosa Island off the California coast. Flanking both sides of Los Penaquitos Lagoon, the reserve admits pedestrians and cyclists free. There are self-guided tours and docent-led nature walks that leave the museum every Saturday and Sunday at 11:30 and 1:30. The small interpretive museum sits on the south bluff, from which well-marked ½- to 1½-mile trails radiate. No dogs are allowed, and picnicking is allowed only on the beach.

Encinitas

Cardiff State Beach is good for beachcombing.

Escondido

Palomar Mountains have no extensive trail system, but there are two popular trails in the area. Ask locally for a trail map.

La Jolla

Torrey Pines State Reserve, ☎ 619/755-2063, includes six hiking trails: **Guy Fleming Trail,** a loop two-thirds of a mile long; **Parry Grove Trail,** a half-mile loop; **Razor Point Trail,** a hike to the point covering two-thirds of a mile; **Beach Trail,** three-quarters of a mile to Flat Rock and the beach; **High Point Trail,** just 100 yards long; and **Broken Hill Trail,** a 1.2-mile access to the beach north and a 1.3-mile access to the beach south.

  Biodiversity Trail is somewhat hidden in a residential area. Turn west off La Jolla Shores Dr. onto La Jolla Farms Rd. and drive one block. Get a self-guided trail pamphlet at the entrance. The trail covers half a mile through a 152-acre reserve that supports over 200 plant species, 88 bird species and a dozen mammal species. On a clear day, look offshore, where the brownish patches mark the submerged kelp forests in La Jolla Bay. Where the water takes on a deeper blue, the submarine Scripps Canyon drops abruptly to 900-foot depths.

  La Jolla Walking Tours, Colonial Inn, 910 Prospect St., ☎ 619/453-8219, conducts a two-hour guided walk filled with entertaining stories of La Jolla's history, architecture and famous people (actors Gregory Peck and Cliff Robertson, golfer Gene Littler, and actress Raquel Welch were born here).

  Torrey Pines golf course, 11480 N. Torrey Pines Rd., ☎ 619/453-0380 or 452-3226, is a legendary course among golfers.

  Trouble getting a tee time? **PGA Preferred Tee Time,** 178 13th St., Del Mar 92014, ☎ 619/793-8286, can arrange tee times at all the best courses. **M&M Tee Times,** 7445 Girard Ave., Ste. 11, La Jolla, ☎ 619/456-8366, fax 619/456-8399, provides the same service.

Oceanside

Two miles of sidewalks allow you to circle the entire harbor. Benches and picnic tables are provided.

The Nature Center, 2202 S. Coast Hwy., ☎ 619/439-2473, is on Buena Vista Lagoon on the south edge of town. It is operated by the Buena Vista Audubon Society, which helps to interpret the intriguing coastal wetlands habitat.

San Diego

There is a scenic seawall/walkway at the waterfront that is perfect for strolling.

Although southern California is usually recognized as a mecca for golf, tennis also deserves a great deal of attention, which it got in 1996 when the International Tennis Hall of Fame named San Diego the "Tennis City of the Year." A number of famous tennis players came from this area, including Maureen "Little Mo" Connolly (San Diego), Louise Brough Clapp (Vista), Pat Channing Todd (Rancho Santa Fe) and Karen Hantze Susman (Rancho Santa Fe). **Morley Field** (☎ 619/299-8647) has 25 tennis courts and is the home of Maureen Connolly Stadium. **George E. Barnes Family Junior Tennis Center** is in nearby Ocean Beach. ☎ 619/531-1527.

Solana Beach

This community has embarked on a $19 million project to widen its pedestrian walkways and to install off-street bicycle lanes along Highway 101.

BIRDWATCHING

Carlsbad

Birdwatching is excellent at **Batiquitos Lagoon**, nesting site for the California least tern and the snowy plover.

There is an Audubon Society Nature Center at **Buena Vista Lagoon**.

Del Mar

Freeflight, 2132 Jimmy Durante Blvd., trains exotic birds.

On Horseback

Chula Vista

Extensive trails can be found in this region for riding.

Del Mar

National Horse Show is held in May. Thoroughbred racing begins in late July and runs to mid-September.

San Diego

Sandi's Rental Stable, 2060 Hollister St., ☎ 619/424-3124, provides one-hour trail rides along the river, three-hour scenic beach rides, and chuckwagon meal rides. Discount coupons are available at many hotels and motels.

RODEOS

Carlsbad

Camp Pendleton Rodeo is held in June.

On Wheels

Carlsbad

Cycling is popular along the beach. **Carlsbad Cyclery**, 2796 Carlsbad Blvd., ☎ 619/434-6681, rents bikes.

Coronado

There are 15 miles of dedicated bike and inline skating paths on Coronado. **Bikes & Beyond**, 1201 First St., Suite 122, ☎ 619/435-7180, is located at The Ferry Landing Marketplace. The shop rents inline skates, kites and beach games, as well as bikes.

Mike's Bikes, 1343 Orange Ave., and **Holland's Bicycle Shop**, 977 Orange Ave., ☎ 619/435-3153, also rent bikes.

Encinitas

Cycles by the Sea, 2185 San Eligo Ave., ☎ 619/753-0737, rents mountain bikes for exploring the rolling hills of Rancho Santa Fe.

La Jolla

There are marked scenic biking routes here, plus a boardwalk along Pacific Beach. Mission Beach south of town also is great for biking.

Oceanside

Camp Pendleton has many miles of open roads that are good for biking.

San Diego

Seaport Village
Credit: James Blank, San Diego Convention & Visitors Bureau

Balboa Park, Mission Bay, the beaches, Seaport Village, the Gaslamp District, the Harbor and Shelter Islands, Old Town, Heritage Park, the waterfront bike path and Coronado are all great places to cycle. You are allowed to take a bike on the ferry to Coronado. **Rent a Bike**, 1st Ave. and Harbor Dr., ☎ 619/232-4700, rents mountain bikes, 10/12-speed road bikes, kids' bikes and tandem bikes. It provides free delivery and pickup to any location. With the rental, customers receive free helmets, maps, bike racks and locks. **Hamel's**, 704 Ventura Pl., ☎ 619/488-5050, rents bikes, skateboards, inline skates and surfboards.

RAILROADS

"Ticket to Tecate," San Diego Railroad Museum, 1050 Kettner Blvd., San Diego 92101, ☎ 619/595-3030 or 888/228-9246, provides a day-trip to Mexico, a tour of the Tecate brewery, shopping and dining, along with a ride on the Iron Horse.

On & In the Water

Carlsbad

Carlsbad State Beach provides swimming, windsurfing and skin diving as well as surf fishing from the rocks. Jetskis and waterskis are popular in **Agua Hedionda Lagoon**. Swimmers, surfers and skin divers also like **South Carlsbad State Beach**. **Cardiff State Beach** has surfing, a boardwalk and a fishing area. In July, the **Body Surfing Championships** are held here, followed by the **World Body Surfing Championships** at Oceanside in August. **Snug Harbor Marina**, 4215 Harrison St., ☎ 619/434-3089, 1.7 miles southeast of town near I-5, rents jetskis and waterskis. You can also get a driver for waterskiing here.

Chula Vista

While the sea provides opportunities for sailing and windsurfing, freshwater fishing is available in **Lake Otay**, east of town on Otay Lakes Rd. As the street name implies, there are two lakes here, an upper lake and a lower lake. Only the 1,000-acre lower lake is open to fishing and then only on Wednesdays and weekends. Fishing begins in late January and is best in mid- to late February. Since 90% of the shore is lined with tules and cattails, virtually no fishing is possible from shore, but trolling is allowed. The water is 100 feet deep in places. There is a hard bottom and a tapering underwater bar.

Coronado

There is good fishing off the pier at the Ferry Landing Marketplace and off the breakwater at the Hotel Del Coronado. Surf fishing is popular along the ocean side of the peninsula. Scuba diving is good at the kelp beds and in Shipwreck Alley. There are three pools at **Coronado Municipal Swimming Pool**, 1845 Strand Way, ☎ 619/522-7342. **Coronado Boat Rentals**, 1715 Strand Way, ☎ 619/437-1514, rents motorboats, sailboats, jetskis, paddleboats, canoes and kayaks. They also provide waterskiing instruction, arrange fishing charters and conduct sunset sail cruises in the bay or the ocean.

Cuyamaca Rancho State Park

Sweetwater River is stocked with fish near the park headquarters at Sweetwater Bridge and in the Green Valley Campground area. **Cuyamaca Lake** has trout, bass, catfish, crappie and bluegill. Boat rentals, ☎ 619/765-0515, are available.

Del Mar

Torrey Pines State Beach, 1½ miles south along Highway 101, offers beach swimming, surfing and surf fishing below massive, multicolored cliffs. Lifeguards are provided along the northern half-mile of the beach. **Black's Beach** (nude) is beyond a rocky headland two miles south of the parking lot. **Del Mar Oceansports**, ☎ 619/792-1903, offers weekend scuba diving classes in La Jolla Cove for beginners. **Always an Adventure**, ☎ 619/944-4518, ferries divers to the offshore kelp beds.

Encinitas

Cardiff State Beach, 2.4 miles south of town on Old Highway 101 is popular with surfers, swimmers and surf fishermen. **Leucadia/Beacons Beach** offers swimming and surfing, but there are no lifeguards. **Stone Step Beach** provides swimming and surfing. **San Elizo State Beach**, 1.6 miles south of town at the end of Chesterfield Dr., ☎ 800/444-7275, is a mile-long beach at the base of some sandstone cliffs. It has surfing, swimming, surf fishing and tidepooling. Tidepooling provides an opportunity to see delicate nudibranchs (sea hares that squirt ink when alarmed), sea anemones, and urchins and is best at low tide (local dive and bait shops can provide you with a tide table, and many newspapers print them daily). Wear old tennis shoes and take dry clothes and a towel.

   Moonlight Beach, at the west end of Encinitas Blvd., ☎ 619/729-8947, is popular with swimmers and boogie boarders. **Swami's** (aka Sea Cliff Roadside Park), a stretch of beach about a mile south of Moonlight Beach, is a well-known surfing area. The beach is so named for an Indian guru who founded the Self-Realization Fellowship Center atop the bluff here in the 1940s. Stairs lead down to the water. **Water Girl**, 642 1st St., ☎ 619/436-2408, is a new shop – the first surf shop especially for women, who constitute only 4% of all surfers. Owner Ilona Wood-Rerucha also runs the Surf Diva School and has formed a surf team.

Escondido

Freshwater fishing is available at **Dixon Lake**, ☎ 619/741-4680; **Henshaw Lake**, ☎ 619/782-3501; and **Lake Wohlford**, ☎ 619/738-4346. **Hodges Lake**, ☎ 619/465-FISH, 20 miles north of San Diego off I-15, allows fishing on Wednesdays, Thursdays and weekends. A 1,000-acre city reservoir, the lake has depths to 100 feet. The water is stained brown and there are lots of tules near shore. The season takes off in late February, peaks through March, and stays good until April or May.

La Jolla

A good area for tidepooling, La Jolla hosts a **Polar Bear Swim** in January; the **Longboard Invitational Tournament and Luau**, ☎ 619/543-3892, in

August; and the **La Jolla Rough Water Swim**, ☎ 619/456-2100, in September. **La Jolla Shores**, north of town, is a popular place for swimming, snorkeling and scuba diving. **La Jolla Cove** has water 10 to 35 feet deep with kelp beds, abalone, spiny lobster and a host of other underwater attractions. On the second Sunday in September, the cove is the site of the annual **Rough Water Swim**, which attacts more than 1,400 participants.

Underwater Park, just off Cove Beach, ☎ 619/576-9599, covers 6,000 underwater acres. Divers can expect to see jack mackerel, bonito, sardines, anchovy, halibut and the large orange Garibaldi, California's state fish. **Windansea**, end of Nautilus St. between the village and Bird Rock, is one of the best surfing beaches along the West Coast. The best seasons are late summer and fall. **San Diego Diver's Supply,** ☎ 619/459-2691, rents diving gear. To check on current surf conditions, ☎ 619/221-8884.

Oceanside

Oceanside Harbor.
Credit: Oceanside Chamber of Commerce

Oceanside Harbor is the largest municipal pleasure boating facility in southern California. It is estimated that the surfing industry contributes $26 million a year to the local economy. A hundred businesses in Oceanside are somehow related to surfing.

In May, the community hosts the **La Jolla YMCA Surf Contest**, ☎ 619/453-3483. In June, there is the **ASAP Pro/Am Surf Contest**, ☎ 619/479-1845; the **Bodyboard International Championships**, ☎ 619/453-3483; and **Bud's "The Body Glove" Surf Tour**. July brings the **AAU Surf Contest** and the **West Coast Pro/Am Surf Contest,** ☎ 619/433-6187. The **World Bodysurfing Championships**, ☎ 619/966-4536, come in August, along with the **Oceanside Longboard Surfing Championships**, ☎ 619/439-5334. And in September, the **NSSA Surf Contest** arrives.

Other water-related annual events include the **Bud Ocean Festival** lifeguard competition and the **Mako Fishing Tournament**, ☎ 619/758-4515, in July; the **Synchronized Swim Show**, ☎ 619/966-4141, and the **Novice Swim Meet**, ☎ 619/966-4141, in August; and the **Labor Day Pier Swim**, ☎ 619/941-0946, in September.

➡ *Surf Chairs enable the disabled to enjoy the beach. Like an overstuffed lounge chair on big yellow plastic wheels, the chairs are covered by an umbrella and can easily go through six inches of water. The chairs*

*also are available at Ocean Beach and Mission Beach in San Diego;
at La Jolla Shores in La Jolla; in Del Mar; and in Huntington Beach.*

Two jetties provide good fishing. No license is required to fish from the pier. **Helgren's Sportfishing Trips**, 315 Harbor Dr. South, ☎ 619/722-2133, organizes half- and three-quarter-day fishing excursions, plus twilight and nighttime fishing trips to local waters, the outer islands, or as far as northern Mexico. Two-hour whale-watching excursions are chartered, after which each passenger receives a certificate.

Harbor Paddle Sports, 1400 N. Harbor Dr., ☎ 619/439-3050, rents kayaks and provides instruction. **Capt. Les George**, ☎ 619/722-2963 or 740-7245 (pager), operates a 39-foot ocean-going luxury sailing yacht, *Obsession*, out of Oceanside Harbor.

Poway

Freshwater fishing is available in **Lake Poway**, ☎ 619/748-2224, northeast of town. Located three miles east of I-15, the 60-acre lake is open Wednesday through Sunday, year-round. The lake has very clear water, lots of shoreline cover, and excellent structure. It contains rainbow trout, largemouth bass and channel catfish. Launching your own boat is not allowed, but there is a marina, as well as a snack bar and a bait and tackle shop.

San Diego

Sunset on San Diego Harbor.
*Credit: James Blank, San Diego
Convention & Visitors Bureau*

The Yellow Pages is full of places that rent boats and watersports equipment.

Classic Sailing Adventures, Shelter Island Marina Inn, ☎ 619/224-0800, charters afternoon and sunset cruises that include beverages and snacks.

Discover Sailing, 955 Harbor Island Dr., Gate A-D, ☎ 619/297-7426, also charters afternoon and twilight cruises plus whale-watching trips during the season.

H&M Landing, 2803 Emerson St., ☎ 619/222-1144, schedules part- and full-day sportfishing trips; a twilight fishing trip to the Point Loma kelp beds that leaves at 6:30 pm; and fishing excursions to Baja.

Islandia Sportfishing, 1551 W. Mission Bay Dr., ☎ 619/222-1164, offers part-day , full-day, and overnight fishing trips.

San Diego Harbor Excursion, 1050 N. Harbor Dr., ☎ 619/234-4111 or 800/44-CRUISE, takes one- and two-hour harbor cruises, plus whale-watching trips from December through mid-March.

Baywatch Cruises, ☎ 800/335-2785, provides day or evening cruises in San Diego Bay aboard a 50-foot luxury yacht.

Fisherman's Landing, 2838 Garrison St., ☎ 619/221-8500, fax 619/222-0799, Web site www.fishermanslanding.com/, provides fishing, whale-watching, and ecology cruises on individually- owned 43- to 124-foot boats capable of sleeping up to 38 people.

Freshwater fishing, ☎ 619/465-3474, is available at 17 lakes throughout the county. The lakes are open from sunrise to sunset and charge a $3.50 daily permit fee. All of the lakes have given up bass weighing 13 pounds or more.

Santee

Santee Lake Regional Park & Campground, 9040 Carlton Oaks Dr., ☎ 619/448-2482 or 596-3141, incorporates seven lakes for fishing and boating. The lakes are stocked weekly. Lakes #1- #5 can be used for fishing; lakes #6 and #7 are reserved for campers. There is a campground, a general store, a bait and tackle shop, and a boat rental facility (at Lake #5).

Solana Beach

Swimming, surfing, snorkeling, scuba diving, boating, fishing, tennis, biking and inline skating are all available in this small waterfront community.

Fletcher Cove, Lomas Santa Fe Dr. and Highway 101, offers surfing, volleyball and basketball.

San Elijo Lagoon between Solana Beach and Cardiff provides good birding and the **San Elijo State Beach.**

On Snow

Adventure Ski & Snowboard School, San Diego, ☎ 619/222-6466, teaches students *on a revolving carpet* in front of a full-length mirror.

In the Air

Carlsbad

At **Carlsbad Aircraft Pilot Supply**, Carlsbad/Palomar Airport, 6743 Montia, ☎ 619/438-7680, 686-0695 (pager) or 800/759-5667, "Tailspin Tommy" and "Cash Register Kate" provide biplane or Cub flights ranging in length from 20 minutes to an hour.

Del Mar

Beautiful Morning Hot Air Balloon Co., 1342 Camino del Mar, ☎ 619/481-6225 or 800/658-8489; **A Skysurfer Balloon Co.**, 1221 Camino del Mar, ☎ 619/481-6800 or 800/660-6809; **Del Mar Balloons**, 1342 Camino del Mar, ☎ 619/259-3115 or 800/400-3115; **California Dreamin**, ☎ 619/438-9550 or 800/373-3359, fax 619/471-1394; **Dream Flights**, ☎ 619/321-5154 or 800/933-5628; **American Balloon Charters**, ☎ 619/327-8544 or 800-FLY-OVER; **Pacific Horizon**, 1342 Camino del Mar, ☎ 619/756-1790 or 800/244-1790; and **Del Mar Balloons**, ☎ 619/259-3115 or 800/400-3115, all schedule hot-air balloon flights.

La Jolla

Paragliders take off from the cliffs just north of Black's Canyon. Contact **Torrey Pines Hang Gliding Assn.**, 10020 N. Torrey Pines Rd., ☎ 619/457-9093, for tips and information.

Torrey Pines Glider Park, 2800 Torrey Pines Scenic Dr., ☎ 619/452-3202, charters glider flights.

San Diego

Parachutes Over San Diego, 10 miles east of I-805 on Telegraph Canyon Rd., ☎ 619/421-0968 or 800/707-5867, trains you and takes you skydiving *all in the same day.* **Air Adventures Sky-Diving**, Brown Field Airport, ☎ 619/661-6671, also offers sky-diving trips.

Dream Flights, Empire Polo Club, Mejohl Lake, ☎ 619/321-5154 or 800/933-5628, schedules hot-air balloon trips.

Barnstorming Adventures Ltd., ☎ 800/759-5667, provides 25- , 35- , and 60-minute flights in an open-cockpit biplane. Helmet, goggles and pilot are provided.

Corporate Helicopters of San Diego, ☎ 619/291-4356 or 800/345-6737, takes helicopter flights for photography, charters, flight instruction and sightseeing.

Solana Beach

Sunset Balloon Flights, 162 Via de la Valle, ☎ 619/481-9122, charters hot-air balloon flights.

Eco-Travel/Cultural Excursions

El Cajon

Heritage of the Americas Museum, 2952 Jamacha Rd. on the campus of Cuyamaca College, ☎ 619/670-5194, sits on a hill with a commanding view of campus. Exhibits include minerals, meteorites, fossils, seashells, tribal tools, effigiers, ornaments, baskets and jewelry. There is a small art gallery.

Escondido

San Pasqual Battlefield State Historic Park, 15808 San Pasqual Valley Rd., ☎ 619/220-5430 or 489-0076, marks the site of the only major battle of the Mexican War that was fought in California. The 50-acre park features a visitor center with a bookstore, an amphitheater and a half-mile nature trail. During the battle, which took place on Dec. 6, 1846, Brig. Gen. Stephen W. Kearny led the American forces and Maj. Andres Pico commanded the Mexicans. It was the war's bloodiest battle.

Palomar Observatory is owned and operated by California Institute of Technology and includes a museum. The observatory's principal instrument is the 200-inch Hale Telescope, the largest productive telescope in the world.

California Center for the Arts, 340 N. Escondido Blvd., is a 12-acre complex consisting of a concert hall, a theater, a museum and a conference center.

La Jolla

John Cole's Book Shop, 780 Prospect St., ☎ 619/454-4766, is housed in the former Wisteria Cottage, Ellen Browning Scripps' guest house circa 1905. Each room displays a different kind of book – cookbooks in the kitchen, fiction in the dining room, and so on.

Museum of Contemporary Art, 700 Prospect St., ☎ 619/454-3541, has reopened after a two-year, $9 million renovation that added garden paths, landscaping and more space for outdoor sculptures. The 97,000-square-foot facility, once the home of Ellen Browning Scripps, has a beautiful view of the ocean.

Stephen Birch Aquarium-Museum, 2300 Expedition Way, ☎ 619/534-FISH, Web site www.aqua.ucsd.edu/, contains more than 600 types of marine animals, including the giant Pacific octopus. There are over 1,500 fish on display, making it the largest oceanographic exhibit in America. Outdoors is a tidepool plaza. Indoors, a 70,000-gallon tank contains a giant kelp forest that is kept in constant motion by a wave-making machine.

Stuart Collection of Sculpture consists of sculptures scattered throughout the University of California, San Diego campus. Walking tour maps are available at information kiosks at the entrance to campus on Gilman Dr. and on North Torrey Pines Rd.

Oceanside

Several new cultural centers have opened recently: **Oceanside Museum of Art**, 704 Third St., ☎ 619/721-2787; **Oceanside Sea Center**, 221 N. Coast Hwy., ☎ 619/966-0111, where visitors can see and touch interactive exhibits; and **Brooks Theater**, 217 N. Coast Highway, a former movie theater, now a small performing arts center.

Pacific Coast Players, ☎ 619/757-3451, was formed by a group of retired and active professionals from the theater, motion pictures, and TV who continue to perform periodically.

Heritage Park Village and Museum, 201 Peyri Dr., ☎ 619/433-8297 or 966-4545, began as a bicentennial project. Located near Mission San Luis Rey, which occupies a hilltop to the south, this recreated village contains a Main Street with a general store, blacksmith shop, livery stable, Western saloon, doctor's office, the Libby one-room schoolhouse, a ladies' boutique, an old-fashioned ice cream shop that sells cones and sundaes, the *Blade* newspaper building, the Portola Inn and a park containing a gazebo. Adjacent to the park is the 100-year-old All Saints Episcopal Church and cemetery.

San Diego

Among the museums not located in Balboa Park and therefore not described earlier in this section (the city has some 90 museums in all) are:

★ **Cabrillo National Monument**, tip of Point Loma at the end of Catalina Blvd., ☎ 619/557-5450, commemorates Cabrillo's landing here in 1542, just 50 years after Columbus reached the New World. It has a restored lighthouse and is a great place to watch the California gray whale migration.

★ **Maritime Museum**, 1306 N. Harbor Dr., ☎ 619/234-9153, is a floating display that includes the 1863 bark *Star of India*, the oldest iron-hulled sailing ship afloat; the 1898 ferryboat *Berkeley*; and the 1904 steam yacht *Medea*.

San Diego Zoo, 2920 Zoo Dr., Balboa Park, ☎ 619/231-1515, 234-6541 or 234-3153, Web site www.sandiegozoo.org, has several new features:

- ★ **Bai Yun** and **Shi Shi**, the only two giant pandas in the United States, occupy a new $1.3 million habitat.
- ★ **Hippo Beach** is a unique underwater area for viewing river hippos.
- ★ **Polar Bear Plunge** is an Olympic-size, 130,000-gallon pool for the polar bears, chilled to a maximum 65 degrees and stocked with trout and arctic char.

Simon Edison Centre for the Performing Arts includes the **Old Globe Theatre**, California's oldest professional theater and a Tony-award winner; and **Cassius Carter Centre Stage**, Balboa Park, a 225-seat theater in the round.

Southeast Community Theatre showcases African-American directors and actors in plays written by African-Americans, and **Teatro Mascara Magica** is a common ground, multicultural theater that produces the work of ethnic artists.

Vista

Antique Gas & Steam Engine Museum, 2040 N. Santa Fe Ave., ☎ 619/941-1791 or 800/587-2286, occupies 40 acres in Guajome Regional Park. It contains over 20,000 items relating to equipment used in California's lumbering, mining, oil drilling and construction industries. Exhibits include a blacksmith and wheelwright shop, a country kitchen and parlor, a steam-operated saw mill, and a to-scale train.

Where To Stay

B&Bs, Hotels & Inns

Carlsbad

La Costa Resort & Spa, Costa del Mar Rd., ☎ 619/438-9111 or 800/854-5000, is one of the classic southern California golf resorts. In fact, this place, which hosts the first annual event on the PGA tour each January (the Mercedes Championship), has two 18-hole courses. There also are 21 tennis courts with grass, clay and composite surfaces. Every accommodation from rooms to two- and three-bedroom suites is done in salmon, peach and terra cotta with hard-carved mahogany tables and dressers, signed artworks and plush carpeting. There also are fitness experts, facialists and massage therapists. Shiatsu, body scrubs, aromatherapy, facials, pedicures, manicures, mud wraps, massages, saunas, Swiss showers, Roman pools and nutrition counseling are available.

Four Seasons Resort Hotel Aviara, located over the Batiquitos Lagoon, is the area's newest hotspot. Its Spanish Colonial-style building has 331 rooms, and there is an 18-hole golf course designed by Arnold Palmer.

Carlsbad Inn, 3075 Carlsbad Blvd., ☎ 619/434-7020 or 800/235-3939, has 198 rooms and condominiums, some with fireplaces and private spas. The complex has an old English appearance and is located on the beach.

Pea Soup Andersen's, I-5 at the Palomar Airport exit, ☎ 619/930-3812/3 or 800/266-7880, is a Best Western franchise with 144 rooms, garden and pool. The locally famous restaurants use recipes dating to 1924.

Coronado

Hotel Del Coronado.
Credit: San Diego Convention & Visitors Bureau

Hotel Del Coronado, 1500 Orange Ave., ☎ 619/522-8000 or 800/HOTEL-DEL, built in 1888, is an enormous wooden structure with turrets, spires, gazebos and lush courtyard gardens. It has an Olympic-size swimming pool and a tennis court complex. Thomas Edison personally supervised the work when electricity was first installed. The Duchess of Windsor is said to have met the Prince of Wales at the Hotel "Del." The movie classic *Some Like It Hot*, starring Jack Lemmon, Tony Curtis and Marilyn Monroe, was filmed here. Room 3502 is said to be haunted by Kate Morgan, who was found dead outside the hotel in 1892 (a 1989 investigation found that she had been murdered by her estranged husband). The hotel has 691 rooms and several top-notch restaurants. If you can't stay here, at least stop by to see it because the imposing front entry, gardens, woodwork, chandeliers, picture-lined corridors, and the gift shops are certainly worth the stop.

The Old Town Trolley picks up passengers at the Hotel Del every 30 minutes. It then goes to downtown San Diego and makes a circle through Gaslamp Quarter, the San Diego Zoo, Balboa Park and Seaport Village – a two-hour trip. Passengers can get on and off as they please.

Le Meridien San Diego, 2000 Second St., ☎ 619/435-3000 or 800/543-4300, fax 619/435-3032, has 300 rooms with great views of the San Diego skyline and Coronado Bridge. There is a main hotel and a number of private single-story villa suites, plus a spa, a tennis complex with six lighted courts, and a gourmet restaurant. There is a private boat dock and three pools scattered among the grounds, which are adorned with flamingos, black swans, babbling brooks and aviaries. Located adjacent to Tidelands Park, it is a short walk from the hotel to The Old Ferry Landing.

Loews Coronado Bay Resort, 4000 Coronado Bay Rd., ☎ 619/424-4000 or 800/23-LOEWS, fax 619/424-4400, sits on a private 15-acre peninsula. It has 440 rooms with oversized bathrooms and whirlpool tubs, and a private 80-slip boat marina. There is a tennis complex and a private health club with weight room, spas, saunas, a personal trainer and a staff of masseuses and masseurs. Along with three pools, two spas and a large sundeck, guests can engage in waterskiing or sailing. The restaurant, Azura Point, specializes in seafood.

Glorietta Bay Inn, 1630 Glorietta Blvd., ☎ 619/435-3101 or 800/283-9383, fax 619/435-6182, occupies the former mansion of sugar baron John D. Spreckles, who owned the entire island at the turn of the century. Spreckles, a former owner of the Hotel Del, built the place for his home in 1908. The house has a brass-and-marble staircase and an oval-shaped music room, which was built to house a 41-pipe organ. In 1926 the home was converted into an inn. It has 98 units, including 11 in the original mansion.

Del Mar

L'Auberge Del Mar Resort & Spa, 1540 Camino del Mar, ☎ 619/259-1515 or 800/553-1336, fax 619/755-4940, has 120 rooms and suites, some with fireplaces. There are two outdoor heated pools, two lighted tennis courts, a full European spa, a fitness center, jogging paths and 5.2 acres of gardens. Located just a block from the beach, the resort provides lovely village, garden and coastal views. Live music is featured on Wednesday, Friday and Saturday evenings.

Escondido

Welk Resort Center, 8860 Lawrence Welk Dr., ☎ 619/749-3000 or 800/932-9355, fills its 1,000 acres with three 18-hole golf courses and a hotel with 132 rooms, each with private balcony or patio overlooking a golf course. The resort features live, year-round musical dinner/luncheon theater. Here, and at a number of other southern California resorts, special golf packages are offered at very appealing rates. Check "em out.

Zosa Ranch, 9381 W. Lilac Rd., ☎ 619/723-9093, is a B&B with genuine hacienda hospitality. The nine rooms share 6½ baths, and a four-bedroom, fully furnished guesthouse also is available. The 22-acre country estate sits on a high plateau in the Monserate Mountains, surrounded by avocado and citrus trees. There also are such exotic fruits as fuyus (a smaller, firmer and crispier type of persimmon) and cherimoyas (members of the custard-apple family with a pitted rind) on the grounds. A health and fitness sports court features tennis, basketball, volleyball and billiards. There is a pool and a spa, plus numerous opportunities for bicycling, walking and jogging.

La Jolla

La Valencia Hotel, 1132 Prospect Ct., ☎ 619/454-0771 or 800/451-0772, has a convenient downtown location and once was a favorite lunch spot for mystery writer Raymond Chandler. (The La Jolla Public Library, ☎ 619/552-1657, sponsors an annual Raymond Chandler Festival each August.) Built in 1926, the historic Spanish Colonial-style hotel overlooks the ocean, has a gilded elevator, and is the home of the elegant Sky Room restaurant (see *Where To Eat,* below).

Colonial Inn, 910 Prospect, ☎ 619/454-2181, has stately white pillars in front and is patterned along the lines of a small, European-style hotel. The first-floor Whaling Bar is decorated with ivory carvings and harpoons.

The Lodge at Torrey Pines, 11480 N. Torrey Pines Rd., ☎ 619/453-4420 or 800/288-0770, has 75 rooms, all with balconies, and provides its guests with a welcome cocktail, free continental breakfast and a complimentary golf cart.

La Jolla Bed & Breakfast Inn, 7753 Drape Ave., ☎ 619/456-2066 or 800/582-2466, fax 619/456-1510, occupies a house that was once inhabited by march king John Philip Sousa in the 1920s. The house is one block from the beach and convenient to downtown. There are 10 bedrooms in the main house and six more in the annex, three with fireplaces. Built in 1913 and renovated in 1984, the house is across the street from the Museum of Contemporary Art. Complimentary wine, cheese and other refreshments are served each afternoon; and guests may take their continental breakfast in their room, in the dining room, or in the garden.

Oceanside

Oceanside Marina Inn, 2008 Harbor Dr. North, ☎ 619/722-1561, 722-1821 or 800/252-2033, fax 619/439-9758, is at the mouth of the harbor. One- and two-bedroom suites are available with fireplaces and full kitchens. There is a heated pool, a spa, a sauna and a BBQ area. A complete continental breakfast is provided. (*NOTE: This inn is not to be confused with the Best Western Oceanside Inn at 1680 Oceanside Blvd.,* ☎ *619/722-1821.*)

Poway

Poway Country Inn, 13845 Poway Rd., ☎ 619/748-6320 or 800/648- 6320, fax 619/748-0135, Web site www.poway.com/cntryinn, is a charming little spot just off the I-15 freeway.

San Diego

Hotel St. James, 830 6th Ave., ☎ 619/234-0155 or 800/338-1616, fax 619/235-9410, is a Clarion Carriage House in the historic Gaslamp Quarter. San Diego's original highrise hotel was built in 1913 and features the Joan Crawford Bar, which came out of the movie star's own home. The hotel has 99 rooms in your choice of Victorian or Southwestern decor. The lounge, Harborview Terrace, sits atop the 12-story hotel and provides some excellent views. Horse-drawn carriages tour the area.

Rancho Bernardo Inn, 17550 Bernardo Oaks Dr., ☎ 619/487-1611 or 675-8400, sits on 265 acres in the shadow of the San Pasqual Mountains. Facilities include a championship golf course, 12 tennis courts, two swimming pools with adjoining hydro-spas, a fitness center and two excellent restaurants.

San Marcos

Lake San Marcos Resort, 1025 La Bonita Dr., Lake San Marcos 92069, ☎ 619/744-0120 or 800/447-6556, fax 619/744-0748, has 142 rooms on a mile-long 80-acre lake southeast of town. There are two 18-hole golf courses, tennis, paddle tennis, four swimming pools, an outdoor hot tub and a fitness center. Canoes, aqua bikes and platform party boats are available for rent.

Camping

Carlsbad

South Carlsbad State Beach, ☎ 619/438-3143, is four miles south of town along Carlsbad Blvd. The pebbly beach, much used for surfing, is a narrow strand with lifeguards, a picnic area and restrooms. Overnight camping is allowed in the blufftop campground, ☎ 800/444-PARK for reservations, but there are no hookups.

Coronado

There is an RV campground on the north end of **Silver Strand State Beach**.

Escondido

La Jolla Indian Campground, Star Route Box 158, Valley Center 92082, ☎ 619/742-1297 or 742-3771, northeast of Escondido, sits in the foothills of Palomar Mountain next to a natural flowing stream stocked with catfish. Innertubes can be rented, and flush toilets, showers, chemical toilets and pay phones are available. There are 800 campsites and an RV section.

Oceanside

The city permits limited RV beach camping. **Guajome Regional Park and Campground**, 3000 Guajome Lakes Rd., ☎ 619/694-3049 or 565-3600, has 35 sites with water and electricity. An historic adobe house also is available. There are hiking trails and a small lake on the 569 acres. A good spot for birdwatching.

San Diego

Campland, 2211 Pacific Beach Dr., ☎ 800/4-BAY-FUN, provides beachfront camping and an RV resort with full hookups.

Santee

Santee Lake Regional Park & Campground, 9040 Carlton Oaks Dr., ☎ 619/448-2482 or 596-3141, has 152 full-hookup RV sites, including some waterfront locations. Tent sites also are available by the day, week, or month. There is a general store, a bait and tackle shop and a boat-rental facility.

Where To Eat

Carlsbad

Fidel's, 3003 Carlsbad Blvd., ☎ 619/729-0903, provides fine Mexican dining.

Coronado

Peohe's, 1201 First St. at B Ave., ☎ 619/437-4474, occupies a colorful waterfront site adjacent to the ferry landing. The menu offers seafood and steak with a slight touch of Hawaiian flavoring.

Del Mar

Cilantros, 3702 Via de la Valle, ☎ 619/259-8777 or 259-2002, is upscale, yet affordable. It serves contemporary Southwestern cuisine.

The Poseidon, 1670 Coast Blvd., ☎ 619/755-9345, provides dining "on the beach." There is a cozy fire ring for after-dinner cappuccino and dessert.

Escondido

Vintage Tea Room, 217 E. Grand Ave., occupies the rear of the Gilded Lily Antiques and Vintage Clothing Store. Servers in Victorian dress serve imported English teas in china teapots, fresh-baked scones with clotted cream, mango/pineapple chutney, imported cheese and crackers, and traditional British finger sandwiches.

La Jolla

Chart House, 1270 Prospect St., ☎ 619/459-8201, is part of a popular chain of restaurants specializing in seafood, but also providing meat and poultry entrees. Particularly outstanding is their salad bar, easily a meal in itself.

Sky Room, on the 10th floor of La Valencia Hotel, 1132 Prospect St., ☎ 619/454-0771, is one of the city's most romantic restaurants. It overlooks the colorful La Jolla Cove and has only 12 tables, so reservations are a must. The restaurant is closed on Sundays.

Elario's Restaurant & House of Jazz, 7955 La Jolla Shores Dr., ☎ 619/459-0541, is located atop the Summer House Inn. There is nightly jazz entertainment and a wine list that has been acclaimed by *The Wine Spectator* magazine.

La Jolla Gallery & Café, 7616 Girard Ave., ☎ 619/459-9597, is a fine café inside an art gallery.

Pannikin Café, 7467 Girard Ave., ☎ 619/454-5453, occupies a bungalow-style building and is known for its "Lox, Stalk and Bagel" plate and its gruyere-topped French onion soup.

Oceanside

Chart House, 314 Harbor Dr., ☎ 619/722-1345, fax 619/721-9531, a member of the same chain as the restaurant in La Jolla, juts out over the harbor and affords some magnificent views.

Rancho Santa Fe

Delicias, 6106 Paseo Delicias, ☎ 619/756-8000, serves new California cuisine in a firelit dining room or on a heated, canopied patio. Expensive, but worth it.

Mille Fleurs, 6009 Paseo Delicias, ☎ 619/756-3085, across from Delicias, serves dinner only on weekends and lunch during the week. The flower-filled fountain courtyard is used for lunch. It also serves new California cuisine. It, too, is very expensive.

San Diego

Casa Guadalajara, 4105 Taylor St., ☎ 619/295-5111, fax 619/295-5152, offers an interesting selection of *antojitos* (appetizers), *sopas* (soups), and *ensaladas* (salads) and a nice variety of *carne* (meat), *puerco* (pork), *pollo* (chicken), and *pescado* (seafood), including grilled fish tacos, plus combination plates ranging from $6 to $14. There also are some delicious desserts, such as deep-fried ice cream, kahlua gelato, buñuelo and cinnamon sprinkled ice cream, and flan. Visit on Friday or Saturday for dancing and mariachi music.

Café Sevilla, 555 Fourth Ave., ☎ 619/233-5979, fax 619/2334-8889, e-mail: sevilla@cnsii.com, located in Gaslamp Quarter, should satisfy your taste for Spain with live entertainment nightly and flamenco dancing every Friday and Saturday. Patio dining is available.

Humphrey's, 2241 Shelter Island Dr., ☎ 619/224-3577 or 224-3411, has a terrific lobster clambake, including a 1¼-lb. lobster steamed with clams and mussels. The Casablanca Lounge is great for watching sunsets, and their "Concerts by the Bay" outdoor musical series has featured such performers as Harry Belafonte, Johnny Mathis, Kenny G, Ray Charles, George Benson and Lee Ritenour. The Sunday brunch includes compli-mentary champagne, omelettes made to order, create-your-own sundaes and chocolate-dipped strawberries.

Kooky's Diner, 1425 Frazee Rd., ☎ 619/294-2926, resembles a 1950s diner and is open around the clock. Customers are served by "skatresses."

Corvette Diner Bar & Grill, 5946 Fifth Ave., ☎ 619/542-1476, is a great place to go with friends. A party of eight rides a limo to the diner; eats cheeseburgers with fries, bottomless Coca-Colas, and chocolate brownie sundaes; receives something called a "bazooka fun box"; and goes home in style... all for $199.95 (including tax and gratuity).

Seau's The Restaurant, 1640 Camino del Rio N., #1376, ☎ 619/291-7328, is operated by San Diego Charger Junior Seau. Located in the Mission Valley Center, the restaurant combines a museum-like environ-ment with the feel of a stadium. Try Mama Seau's chicken or beef teriyaki.

Hornblower Dining Yachts, 1066 N. Harbor Dr., ☎ 619/234-8687, also operates yachts for dinner cruises out of Berkeley, Long Beach, Marina del Rey, Newport Beach and San Francisco.

San Diego Harbor Excursion, 1050 N. Harbor Dr., ☎ 619/234-4111 or 800/442-7847, provides a 2½-hour dinner cruise on San Diego Bay with a three-course dinner and dancing to live music.

DINNER THEATER

Escondido

Lawrence Welk Theatre, 8860 Lawrence Welk Dr., ☎ 619/749-3448, is a 330-seat dinner theater located seven miles north of town off I-15. A museum contains memorabilia of band leader Welk's life and career.

San Diego

Mystery Café in the Imperial House Restaurant, 505 Kalmia St., ☎ 619/544-1600, is a murder mystery dinner theater located near Balboa Park.

Bahia Resort Hotel, 998 W. Mission Bay Dr., ☎ 619/488-0551 or 800/288-0770, houses the Comedy Isle comedy club. The hotel is near San Diego International Airport.

Palm Springs Area

The Land Of Fun & Sun

As the story goes, Hollywood grew and prospered – and with it, the local resorts, country clubs, and tennis facilities – until everything was so overcrowded, so expensive and so exclusive that even the members of the Hollywood movie colony found it difficult to get some peace and relaxation.

Two of those celebrities, Charlie Farrell and Ralph Bellamy, began to look for something better. They found it in a small, sun-drenched community in the desert east of Los Angeles – a place called Palm Springs.

Farrell and Bellamy built their own tennis resort there, and their friends clamored to join. Soon, Palm Springs became the favorite getaway for an ever-expanding group of actors and actresses, directors and producers. Some enjoyed the warmth of the desert during the otherwise chilly winter months. Some enjoyed escaping the harassment of the media. Others simply enjoyed a private retreat within reasonable distance of their workplace: Hollywood.

Hedy Lamarr had a house on the northeast corner of El Alameda and Hermosa Drive. Gloria Swanson had a hideaway where she could entertain Joseph Kennedy. Darryl Zanuck and Howard Hughes were notorious for their use of Palm Springs as a place to bring their paramours.

Originally, there wasn't an 18-hole golf course in all of Coachella Valley, but in 1951, the first one opened (Thunderbird). Soon, golf began to surpass even tennis as the most popular pastime in the area. The region continued to grow, spurred on by such annual events as the Bob Hope Desert Classic, the Dinah Shore LPGA Golf Tournament, the Skins Game and the Frank Sinatra Celebrity Golf Tournament.

In time, the surrounding communities benefited from this growth as well. Today, they line Highway 111 from its junction with Interstate 5 at Indio on the east to its other junction with Interstate 5 at Cabazon on the west – a veritable showcase of glittering hotels, resorts, restaurants, bistros and boutiques intersecting with streets bearing such familiar names as Bob Hope, Dinah Shore, Fred Waring, Gene Autrey, Gerald Ford and Frank Sinatra.

Lana Turner, Barbara Stanwyck and Robert Taylor, Natalie Wood and Robert Wagner, and Cary Grant and Barbara Hutton all honeymooned here.

But there is more to this region than a sense of being in Hollywood East.

To the east of Palm Springs, Indio serves as the market center for most of the nation's date crop. To the south and west, the terrain becomes mountainous and there are remnants of century-old gold mines scattered among the apple orchards near Julian and Ramona.

There also are the Indians, descendants of the original settlers of this lush and varied area, and the names of their reservations reflect the heritage of generations: Cahuilla, Manzanita, Los Coyotes, Santa Rosa, Capitan Grande and Morongo.

If you have been planning to pamper yourself, now is the time – and this is the place.

Palm Springs Area

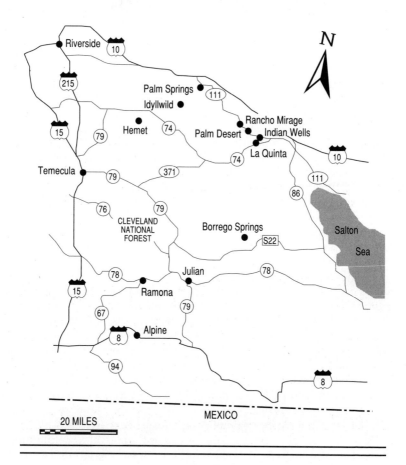

Getting Around

The region described in this section of the book is sandwiched between two east-west interstates. To the south is Interstate 8, connecting Yuma, Arizona and San Diego. To the north is Interstate 10, connecting the Colorado River city of Blythe with midtown Los Angeles.

Few north-south roads penetrate this land of mountains, state parks, national forests and Indian reservations. The primary ones are state routes 78 and 79, both extremely scenic links to such little-known but highly interesting communities as Julian, Ramona, Hemet and Borrego Springs.

Touring

Borrego Springs

Anza-Borrego Desert State Park, ☎ 619/767-5311 or 800/444-7275, covers 900 square miles. It is America's largest state park. Rainfall averages less than seven inches a year. Temperatures often exceed 100° from April through November.

The visitor center, 200 Palm Canyon Dr., ☎ 619/767-4205, fax 619/767-3427, is open only on weekends and holidays from June through September.

Borrego Days, a local festival held every October, highlights a parade featuring 101 marching dachshunds and a horseshoe tournament.

For more information, contact **Borrego Springs Chamber of Commerce**, 622 Palm Canyon Dr., Box 420, Borrego Springs 92004, ☎ 619/767-5555, 559-5524 or 800/559-5524.

Cleveland National Forest

Descanso Ranger District, Alpine 92001-9630, ☎ 619/445-6235 or 473-8824, is accessible by taking the Buckman Springs exit off I-8. Other ranger districts in the region can be found in San Diego, Corona and Ramona.

Hemet

Although relatively unknown elsewhere, Hemet is the largest city in San Jacinto Valley.

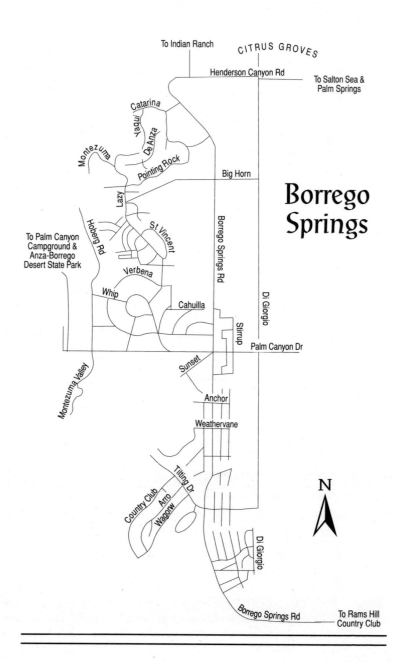

To Indian Ranch

CITRUS GROVES

Henderson Canyon Rd

To Salton Sea &
Palm Springs

Catarina

Yaqui

De Anza

Montezuma

Pointing Rock

Big Horn

Borrego
Springs

Lazy

To Palm Canyon
Campground &
Anza-Borrego
Desert State Park

Hoberg Rd

St Vincent

Borrego Springs Rd

Verbena

Whip

Di Giorgio

Cahuilla

Stirrup

Palm Canyon Dr

Sunset

Montezuma Valley

Anchor

Weathervane

Tilting Dr

Country Club

Arro

Wagon

Di Giorgio

N

Borrego Springs Rd

To Rams Hill
Country Club

Prior to the 1800s, the area was inhabited by Luiseño and Cahuilla Indians, but smallpox epidemics in 1833 and 1862 left only the Soboba Indians.

In 1888, the railroad reached the valley, and with it came civilization.

Annual events include the **Oldlympics** and a **Renaissance Fair.**

For more information, contact **Hemet Visitor & Tourism Council,**, 395 E. Latham Ave., Hemet 92543, ☎ 909/658-3211 or 800/334-9344, fax 909/766-5013, e-mail vedc@pe.net.

Julian

Gold was discovered in Julian, 57 miles northeast of San Diego, in 1869. The town is set in the Cuyamaca Mountains, which the Digueño Indians called "Ah-ha Kwe-ah-mac" (No Rain Behind). After the discovery of gold, hundreds of Yankee and Chinese prospectors poured in. In the 1870s, the town had eight saloons, five stores, two hotels, two cafés, two livery stables and two blacksmiths. Drue Bailey, a Confederate war veteran, named the place for his cousin, Mike Julian.

But Julian's gold boom lasted only 10 years, and by 1888 most of the prospectors had moved on to Tombstone, Arizona. The ranch property passed through various hands until it was acquired by the Dyar family. But during the Depression, the Dyars were forced to sell the rancho to the state for half its appraised value, thus creating Cuyamaca Rancho State Park.

In all, the mines in southern California's "high country" (4,230 feet elevation) produced $4 to $5 million in gold. You can still pan for gold at **Julian Gold Mining Co.** on Main St., ☎ 619/765-3105, a clear indication that things haven't changed a good deal in Julian over the years.

At **Julian Barber Shop**, 3411 Highway 79, ☎ 619/765-1073, two miles south of town, you can get a haircut... or buy an antique.

There's an **Antique Quilt Show** in July, and a **Weed Show** in August. The **American Legion BBQ** in July is followed by the **Lions Club Banjo/Fiddle Contest and Bluegrass Festival** at Frank Lane Park in September, ☎ 619/586-7376 or 579-5300.

But the big thing in Julian is **Apple Days**, which begin October 1. While a melodrama is being staged upstairs in the Town Hall, apple pies are being sold downstairs. You can buy a whole pie or just a slice.

Julian's apples are best in the fall, and the harvest generally runs from mid-September through mid-November. You can find retail stands at **Apple Bar Ranch**, 3.9 miles northwest of town at 3767 Wynola Rd.; **Farmer's Fruit Stand**, 3.9 miles northwest of town at 4510 Highway 78; **Manzanita Ranch**, 3.9 miles northwest of town at 4470 Highway 78; **Meyer Orchards**, 2.8 miles west of town at 3962 Highway 78; and **Julian Cider Mill**, 2103 Main St., which also sells nuts, dried fruit, honey and produce.

If you're so inclined, you can pick your own apples at **Eden Creek Orchards**, 1052 Julian Orchards, ☎ 619/765-2102.

The local paper, *The Julian News*, prints "Julian Apple Bucks" – coupons that can be used as cash.

It may be hard to believe, but historians claim the first apples were brought to the area in the early 1870s by a man named James Madison.

Julian apples won blue ribbons at the Chicago World's Fair in 1893, at the St. Louis Fair and at the San Francisco Fair in 1915.

Country Carriages, ☎ 619/765-1471, will take you through town in a horse-drawn carriage.

Mission Santa Ysabel, 23013 Highway 79, ☎ 619/765-0810, is in nearby Santa Ysabel. The are some lovely murals, a small museum and an Indian burial ground. Self-guided tours are permitted from 7 am until dusk.

INFORMATION SOURCES

Julian Chamber of Commerce, Box 413, Julian 92036,
   ☎ 619/765-1857, fax 619/765-2544.
Julian InfoCenter, ☎ 619/765-0707, operates 24 hours daily.
Julian Historical Society, ☎ 619/765-0436.

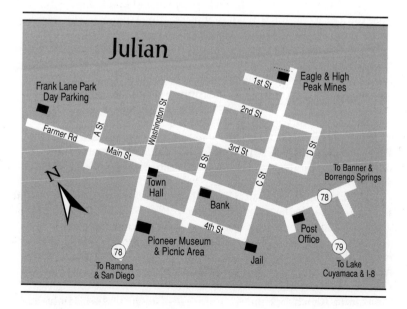

Alpine

Summers Past Farms, 15602 Old Highway 80, Flinn Springs 92021, ☎ 619/390-1523, fax 619/390-0912, operates an herb nursery, a gift shop, an espresso bar and an herbal soap shop/factory. Herbal craft workshops are scheduled, as are seasonal musical events.

Ramona

Once inhabited by Iipay Indians, who called the area Valle de Pamo, Santa Maria Valley was renamed by the Spaniards in 1778. Ramona, the area's first settlement, was originally called Nuevo (New).

East of Escondido on Highway 67, the surrounding region is largely agricultural. Crops include apples, citrus, avocados and Christmas trees.

Rancho Santa Fe, a wealthy planned community nearby, is comprised of large estates and horse ranches. Bing Crosby and Douglas Fairbanks Sr. were early residents. (If you plan to play some golf, keep an eye out for actor Victor Mature, now in his 80s, who is retired and living in Rancho Santa Fe). The community has a picturesque village center.

For more information, contact **Ramona Chamber of Commerce**, 1306 Main St., Suite 106, PO Box 368, Ramona 92065, ☎ 619/789-1311 or 789-1317.

Idyllwild

For a place with a population of only 2,500 people, Idyllwild is unexpectedly lively. **Tree Monument**, on Village Center Dr. next to the Idyllwild Inn near Strawberry Creek, is a 50-foot totem pole carved in 1989 from a dying ponderosa pine. The toem depicts an eagle (American freedom), a mountain lion (strength), a squirrel (industriousness and resourcefulness), a raccoon (entertainment), a coyote (ability to survive), a butterfly (new life in its metamorphosis from caterpillar to butterfly), Indian Chief Algoot (a tribute to the local Cahuilla Indians), and a local icon, Ernie Maxwell. The ides to include the butterfly came from a six-year-old girl.

In June, the Lions Club holds a **Timber Festival** in County Park. Activities include men's and women's lumberjack events and a greased pole climb.

Out There, ☎ 909/659-7006, fax 909/659-7007, arranges canoeing, ori-enterring, snowshoeing, rock climbing, mountain biking, natural history, kayaking, back country and cross-country skiing trips.

For more information, contact **Idyllwild Chamber of Commerce**, 54274 N. Circle Dr., Box 304, Idyllwild 92549, ☎ 909/659-3259.

Idyllwild

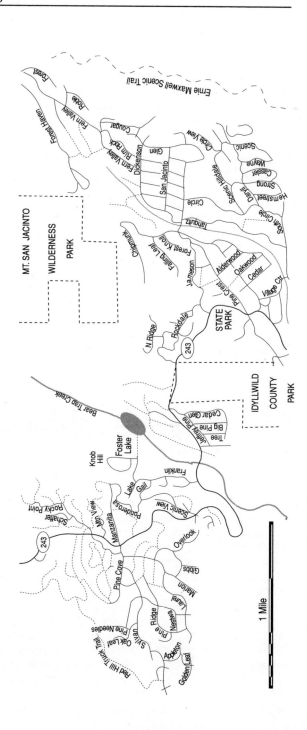

1 Mile

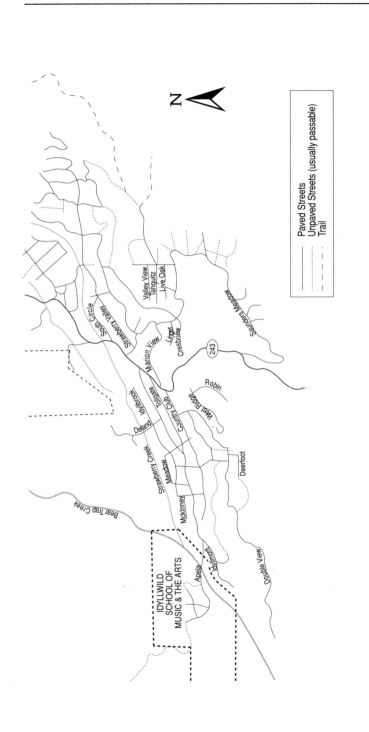

Palm Springs

Entering town from the west, one is struck by the sight of acres upon acres of wind turbines, similar to those found in the mountains around Tehachapi (see *The Central Valley*, page 113) and in Altamont Pass east of San Francisco. Operated by **Desert Wind Energy Assn.**, ☎ 619/329-1799, the display includes 3,500 of the 15,000 wind turbines currently in use throughout the state. California produces 80% of the world's wind-generated electricity. Producing nearly 600 million kilowatt-hours of electricity every year, enough to serve the needs of about 100,000 homes, this field of wind turbines supplies about 1% of California's total energy requirement.

An estimated three million visitors a year pass through Coachella Valley, attracted by the magnificent climate and the area's reputation as "the playground of the stars." There are over 14,454 rooms available in 231 hotels and motels, not including condominiums, timeshares and rental properties. There also are 600 tennis courts, 90 golf courses and 30,000 swimming pools – one swimming pool for every five people.

Palm Springs has a female private eye (Lynn Howard, ☎ 619/329-1612) and a regional airport, ☎ 619/323-8161. Actor Alan Ladd owned a hardware store here. Edie Adams, the actress wife of comedian Ernie Kovaks, is a realtor here. William Powell's wife "Mousie" (Diana Lewis) lives here. Countless other actors and actresses from Hollywood's Golden Age also live here quietly in retirement.

VillageFest is held year-round on Thursday evenings between 7 and 10 along Palm Canyon Dr., downtown between Baristo and Tahquitz Sts., ☎ 619/320-3781.

Palm Springs Air Museum, 107 S. Indian Canyon, ☎ 619/320-1389, fax 619/320-2548, although new, has one of the world's largest collections of flying WW II aircraft. Housed in a 46,000-square-foot, $30 million facility are about 30 warplanes, including a B-17 Flying Fortress, the P-38 Lightning, a P-40 Warhawk, the P-47 Thunderbolt, a P-51 Mustang, the F4U Corsair, a F6F Hellcat and the F8F Bearcat. Also on display is General MacArthur's Super Constellation, *Bataan*. There are docent-guided tours on Saturday and Sunday at noon and 2 pm, and there are movies in Buddy Rogers' "Wings" Theater.

Palm Springs Celebrity Tours, 4751 E. Palm Canyon Dr., Ste. C, ☎ 619/770-2700, and **Gray Line Tours**, 333 S. Indian Canyon Dr., ☎ 619/325-0974 or 800/635-1859, point out the haunts of the famous and infamous. **Palm Springs Carriage Co.**, Tahquitz Canyon and Palm Canyon, ☎ 619/320-8765, offers a 20-minute ride in a horse-drawn carriage or 40- and 60-minute celebrity tours featuring the homes of such personalities as Clark Gable, Greta Garbo, Elizabeth Taylor, Kirk Douglas, Goldie Hawn, Col. Parker, Trini Lopez, Pat Kennedy and Peter Lawford.

Desert Adventures Jeep Tours, 611 S. Palm Canyon Dr., Ste. 7445, ☎ 619/864-6530 or 324-JEEP, arranges excursions to such places as **Santa Rosa Mountain National Scenic Area**, ☎ 619/251-0812, located just outside of town.

A man ran for Mayor of Palm Springs a few years ago, campaigning throughout town in drag. Indeed, except for West Hollywood, no place in southern California has a greater concentration or a more vocal body of gays and lesbians than Palm Springs.

➡ NOTE: *Telephone numbers in the Palm Springs area are listed here with a 619 area code. Be advised, however, that the telephone company expects to change this to 760.*

For more information, contact the **Palm Springs Visitors Information Center**, 2781 N. Palm Canyon Dr., ☎ 619/778-8418 or 800/347-7746, Web site www.palm-springs.org.; or **Palm Springs Tourism**, 401 S. Pavilion Way, Palm Springs 92262, ☎ 619/778-8415, 800/927-PALM or 800/34-SPRINGS, fax 619/323-3021.

Cathedral City

An 18,000-square-foot., $5.1 million IMAX Theater showing 12 movies per day has recently opened. ☎ 619/324-7333.

Indian Wells

Jazz at Indian Wells, an annual four-night extravaganza, draws thousands of fans each year. ☎ 619/341-3537.

La Quinta

Named for the oldest resort in the Palm Springs area, La Quinta (secluded country retreat) has slowly grown into a full-service city. Ginger Rogers was married here. Frank Capra wrote *It Happened One Night* here and lived here in retirement.

La Quinta Historical Society Museum, 77-885 Calle Montezuma, ☎ 619/564-1283, displays artifacts of the area from Indian days to the present.

La Quinta Sculpture Park, 57325 Madison St., ☎ 619/564-6464, occupies 20 acres surrounding a three-acre lake. Positioned throughout the park are over 100 pieces of sculpture. Open daily from 9 to 5 and evenings for special events, the park is closed from mid-June to the end of August. There is a gallery and a gift shop.

Covered Wagon Tours, ☎ 619/347-2161 or 800/367-2161, fax 619/775-7570, conducts guided, narrated two-hour tours and dinner tours.

Palm Desert

Originally called Palm Village, this community is becoming known as the "new" Palm Springs.

Civic Center Park between San Pablo Ave. and San Pascual Channel and between Fred Waring Dr. and Magnesia Falls Dr., has gardens, a lake, a playground, an amphitheater and facilities for tennis, volleyball and basketball. This is where the town's civic offices are located. Within the park are 24 pieces of artwork – sculpture outdoors and paintings indoors – including some paintings of Emmet Kelly, the famous clown.

Other artworks throughout the community include 10 pieces located on the campus of the College of the Desert, four pieces on Fred Waring Dr. between Highway 111 and Cook St., six pieces at Park View/Painters Path and Highway 111, and more than a dozen other pieces throughout.

Palm Desert has the area's largest enclosed mall.

El Paseo Dr. is a two-mile-long business district chock-full of smart little boutiques – a welcome relief for those who are tired of malls. There are 14 pieces of public sculpture positioned along El Paseo, including a copper-coated giraffe by William Allen and the whimsical Deux Visages III by Pascal Giacomini. Ask for a map and descriptive brochure at the Chamber of Commerce.

For more information, contact **Palm Desert Chamber of Commerce**, 72990 Hwy. 111, Palm Desert 92260, ☎ 619/346-6111 or 800/873-2428, fax 619/346-3263.

Palm Desert also operates its own radio station, located at 1610 AM on the dial. The station presents information about the town, traffic, weather and civic events.

Rancho Mirage

In 1925, William Everett esablished the Eleven Mile Ranch midway between Indio and Palm Springs. In 1932, the Rio del Sol Ranch was developed, add a swimming pool that attracted the attention of Jean Harlow. Greta Garbo bought a small bungalow here, and Frank Morgan, the Wizard of Oz in the movie of the same name, bought a home on Sahara Rd. in Magnesia Falls Cove (the house is still standing).

In 1934, the area adopted the name of Rancho Mirage. Twelve years later, Eleven Mile Ranch became the White Sun Guest Ranch, a place where Yule Brynner often enjoyed riding horses. About that time, Thunderbird Ranch also was developed, resulting in **Thunderbird Country Club**, the desert's first 18-hole golf course.

Ambassador Leonard Firestone, Desi Arnaz and Lucille Ball, Bob Hope, Randolph Scott, Hoagie Carmichael, Bing Crosby and other celebrities built homes on the Thunderbird course. Lucy became the first honorary mayor of Rancho Mirage, to be followed by band leader/comedian Phil Harris. Harris' wife, actress Alice Faye, still lives here. Ernest Breech Jr., chairman of Ford Motor Co., had a home at Thunderbird, and he named an automobile after the club. Former President Gerald Ford bought the Breech property in 1975.

In 1952, **Tamarisk Country Club** got started and hired the legendary Ben Hogan to be the club pro. The Marx Brothers were early members. President Eisenhower, Jack Benny, Sammy Davis Jr., Danny Kaye and Dean Martin all either played or belonged here. Frank Sinatra built a home adjacent to the club.

In 1953, Bing Crosby founded the **Blue Skies Village** mobile home park and named the streets after Jack Benny, Burns and Allen, Claudette Colbert, Greer Garson, Danny Kaye, Barbara Stanwyck... and himself.

In 1961, Ambassador Walter Annenberg began construction of a 32,000-square-foot main house and guest quarters on over 400 acres of land at the intersection of Wonder Palms Rd. and Rio Del Sol (now Frank Sinatra and Bob Hope Drs.). His guests have included Queen Elizabeth, Prince Phillip, Prince Charles and Presidents Eisenhower, Nixon, Reagan and Bush.

Called "The Playground of Presidents," Rancho Mirage is now one of the wealthiest cities per capita in the United States. Residents include tennis star Rod Laver, actors Patrick McNee and George Montgomery, golfer Al Gieberger, and baseball great Johnny Bench. President Gerald Ford lived here in the 1970s and the famous Betty Ford Clinic is nearby.

INFORMATION SOURCES

Rancho Mirage Chamber of Commerce, 42-464 Rancho Mirage Lane, Rancho Mirage 92270, ☎ 619/568-9351, fax 619/779-9684, e-mail ranchmir@ix.netcom.com.

Palm Springs Desert Resorts Convention & Visitors Bureau, 69-930 Highway 111, Ste. 210, Rancho Mirage 92270, ☎ 619/770-9000, 800/41-RELAX, 800/967-3767 or 800/417-3529, Web site www.desert-resorts.com.

Temecula

Like many of the communities along the Pacific coast north of Los Angeles, this is wine country. Twelve vineyards currently operate in the valley (ask the Chamber of Commerce for a map and a guide).

Thornton Winery, 32575 Rancho California Rd., ☎ 909/699-0099, fax 909/699-5536, also operates **Café Champagne**, ☎ 909/699-0088, which offers lunch, dinner and a Sunday brunch. The café is closed on Mondays, except for holidays.

Van Roekel Vineyards & Winery, 34567 Rancho California Rd., ☎ 909/699-6961, is the area's newest winery.

Bordering the Santa Margarita River, the city hosts an annual **Great Temecula Tractor Race and Chili Cook-Off** at the Temecula Show Grounds, Diaz and Winchester Rds., ☎ 909/676-4718, in October.

Destination Temecula, 27403 Ynez Rd., Ste. 217, ☎ 909/695-1232 or 800/584-8162, fax 909/695-1232, provides a tour of the area.

For more information, contact **Temecula Valley Chamber of Commerce**, 27450 Ynez Rd., Ste. 104, Temecula 92591, ☎ 909/676-5090, fax 909/694-0201.

Adventures

On Foot

Borrego Springs

Anza-Borrego Desert State Park has several hiking and riding trails, including the **Palm Canyon Trail**, a three-mile trip from the Borrego Palm Canyon Campground. Guided programs include a 20-minute **Backroom Tour** that examines pelts, bones, mounted birds and fossils, and a 45-minute version that includes a slide show. **Desert Explorations** is a 15-minute slide show and outdoor nature walk. Dancing phantom lights similar to those reported in New Mexico and western Australia have been seen in this region. There is an underground visitor center with maps, information and exhibits. A wildflower map is available for 25¢.

For a wildflower alert, send a stamped, self-addressed postcard to **Wildflower Notification**, Visitor Center, Anza-Borrego Desert State Park, Borrego Springs 92004, ☎ 619/767-4205.

Ocotillo in bloom at Anza-Borrego.
Credit: San Diego Convention & Visitors Bureau

Cleveland National Forest

Laguna Mountain Recreation Area has many good hiking trails. **Wooded Hill Nature Trail** involves a 1½-mile trail that goes to one of the highest points in the area, 6,223 feet (a trail brochure is available). A shorter, half-mile loop does not go to the peak. It is a difficult hike and no horses or vehicles are allowed.

Big Laguna Trail is a five-mile hike. One trailhead is opposite the Laguna Campground parking lot near the amphitheater. After a mile, you enter the meadow. The trail turns west, then bends around another portion of meadow containing Big Laguna Lake. Horseback riding is allowed. Many wildflowers can be seen around the lake in April and May. The trail continues north, providing access down a ravine to a link with Pine Creek Rd. and Noble Canyon Trail. Continuing connects you with Noble Canyon Trail near Sunrise Highway and the Penny Pines parking area.

Indian Creek Trail, a four-mile hike, was the first riding/hiking trail connecting Cuyamaca Rancho State Park with the Laguna Mountain Recreation Area. It connects the Noble Canyon Recreation Trail on Laguna Mountain with the East Mesa Trail in Cuyamaca Rancho State Park. Take Sunrise Highway to the Penny Pines trailhead about five miles north of Mt. Laguna. Park and take Noble Canyon Trail two miles west to a junction with the Indian Creek Trail. From there, it is two miles to the viewpoint and four miles to Cuyamaca.

Lightning Ride Trail, 1.3 miles long, begins near the Laguna Campground amphitheater. It is a fairly strenuous climb with many switchbacks. No horses or vehicles are allowed.

Desert View Nature Trail is a 1.2-mile loop beginning in the Burnt Rancheria Campground and following the mountain rim. On a clear day you can see the Salton Sea. In places, the trail joins the Pacific Crest Trail. No horses or vehicles are allowed.

Kwaaymii Cultural Trail is a half-mile hike with signs that indicate the Indian use of native plants. It starts near the visitor information office and climbs to Pinyon Point. No horses or vehicles are allowed.

Horsethief Trail covers 1.2 miles. It is near the north end of Horsethief Rd. and is not accessible by vehicle. It is an access point to the Pine Creek Wilderness Area, but a visitor permit is required for overnight entry.

Sunset Trail, a four-mile hike, begins across the road from the Meadows Information Kiosk at the 19.1-mile marker on Sunrise Highway and goes to Water-of-the-Woods (watch for animal tracks). Kwaaymii Indian grinding holes can be found in some of the granite rocks.

Espinosa Trail covers 6.4 miles, and the western 2.9 miles, which are in the Pine Creek Wilderness Area, are open to hikers and horses only. Pick up the trail at Japatul Station and go to the eastern section of Corral Canyon Rd.

Noble Canyon Trail, a 10-mile path for hiking or horseback riders only, begins along Pine Creek Rd. north of Pine Valley and terminates at the

Pacific Rest Trail near Oasis Spring in the Laguna Mountain Recreation Area.

Lakes within the national forest include Little Laguna Lake, Big Laguna Lake and Water-of-the-Woods.

Pine Creek Wilderness covers 13,000 acres and requires a (free) visitor permit. Intended purely for hiking, not even a bicycle is allowed inside the wilderness area. There are several trails, including the **Espinosa Trail** from Japatul Station (mentioned above) and another that begins at Interstate 8. Pine Creek contains rainbow trout and bass.

Descanso

Set in **Cuyamaca Rancho State Park**, this region is interwoven with hiking trails.

Paso Nature Trail is an easy half-mile loop, a self-guided trail with 16 trail signs. The trailhead is at the north end of the picnic area at the Paso Picacho Campground.

Indian Trail is another easy trail that goes by the site of an old Indian village. Plaques describe Indian uses for various plants. The trail covers a half-mile one way, and the trailhead is by the flagpole at the Park Head-quarters/museum parking lot.

Green Valley Falls Trail is an easy three-quarter-mile hike leading to some pretty, but seasonal, waterfalls. The hike is best made in the spring or early summer.

Stonewall Peak Trail is a moderate four-mile hike that begins on the opposite side of the main road from the entrance to Paso Picacho Campground. **Stonewall Peak Loop Trail** begins the same way, but is a bit longer and descends to the north by means of a rough trail to the Los Caballos horse camp. It then turns west around the base of Stonewall Peak to the trailhead by either Cold Stream Trail or California Riding and Hiking Trail. The latter route is good for seeing wildflowers and birds, but be sure to wear hiking boots.

Azalea Glen Loop Trail makes a moderate four-mile loop with one somewhat steep section. The trail partially follows a stream and you can expect to see blooming azaleas in May, June and July, as well as lots of birds.

Juaquapin Trail makes a moderate three-mile loop from the turnoff for the museum/Park Headquarters or from Sweetwater Bridge. Part of the trail follows a stream, and there are wildflowers plus an occasional deer.

Idyllwild

Idyllwild County Park, at the west end of County Park Rd., ☎ 909/659-3850, has five miles of hiking trails among its 202 acres. The visitor center contains some exhibits, and there are Indian petroglyphs on the grounds.

Mt. San Jacinto State Park, on the northern edge of town, ☎ 909/659-2607, is crowned by 10,804-foot Mt. San Jacinto. Hiking and backpacking are allowed, and there is a 33-site campground, as well as a visitor center. Hiking trails in the area include:

★ **Ernie Maxwell Scenic Trail**, a five-mile round-trip that begins in Humber Park.

★ **Fuller Ridge Trail**, a strenuous 7½-mile hike with a gain of 3,000 feet in elevation to San Jacinto Peak.

★ **Seven Pines Trail**, a moderate four-mile day hike to Deer Springs with a gain in elevation of 2,600 feet.

★ **Marion Mountain Trail**, a strenuous one-day hike of 5.9 miles to San Jacinto Peak with an elevation gain of 4,400 feet.

★ **Deer Springs Trail**, a moderate 3.3-mile day hike to Suicide Rock with a gain of 1,700 feet in elevation. The trail begins on Highway 243 across from the Idyllwild Nature Center.

★ **Spitler Peak Trail**, a strenuous five-mile day hike to Apache Peak.

★ **South Ridge Trail** to Tahquitz Peak.

★ **Devil Slide Trail**, a strenuous 7.7-mile hike from Humber Park to Tahquitz Peak with an elevation gain of 4,400 feet. The trail is limited to 25 permits on weekends and holidays from Memorial Day through Labor Day. Permits can be obtained from the U.S. Forest Service, Box 518, Idyllwild 92549.

Julian

Cuyamaca Rancho State Park, Highway 79, ☎ 619/765-0755, is the county's best mountain park. A strenuous 11-mile hike to the peak at 6,512 feet, **Cuyamaca Peak Trail** provides views of Mexico, the Salton Sea and the Pacific Ocean. **Stonewall Peak**, at 5,730 feet, can be reached by an easy two-mile hike. In **Green Valley**, tiny Sweetwater River runs through a rocky gorge. There are deep pools and waterfalls along the way. In all, the park has more than 110 miles of hiking trails (see *Descanso*, above, for a partial listing), and the birdwatching is good, with desert, coastal and mountain species all to be found there.

Mount Laguna, County Highway S-1 off Highway 79, is nearly 6,000 feet tall and has miles of hiking trails. It is particularly popular after a snowfall (about February or March). The visitor center has trail maps, information, books and a few local exhibits.

LeeLin Wikiup, 1645 Whispering Pines Rd., ☎ 619/765-1890 or 800/6-WIKIUP, home of the LeeLin Llamas, arranges llama treks.

Julian Llama Treks, ☎ 800/LAMAPAK, conducts half-day (four- to six-hour) llama treks with lunch included.

Volcan Mountain Nature Preserve, ☎ 619/765-2311, presents hikes and educational programs.

La Quinta

Lake Cahuilla Recreation Area offers some excellent hiking and horse trails.

Palm Desert

Santa Rosa Mountains National Scenic Area Visitor Center, 51-500 Highway 74, ☎ 619/862-9984, fax 619/862-9240, is a new facility with exhibits, a short interpretive trail, access to other trails, docent-led field trips and classes, and a bookstore.

Palm Springs

Tahquitz Canyon holds the desert's most beautiful waterfall, but it is not open to the public.

Indian Canyons, ☎ 619/325-5673, can only be entered by paying an admission fee as you pass the toll gate at the end of S. Palm Canyon Dr. **Palm Canyon** is 15 miles long, provides fine hiking and horseback riding trails, and offers a trading post where maps, refreshments, books, jewelry, pottery, baskets and weavings can be purchased. **Murray Canyon** contains hiking and horseback riding trails and the opportunity to see some bighorn sheep, wild ponies or the least bells vireo, an endangered bird. **Andreas Canyon** contains Indian rock art, a perpetual creek and hiking trails. In October, the Indian tribes hold a "Dinner in the Canyons," ☎ 619/778-0225, a dinner, native dancing, an art exhibit, and a silent auction to benefit the Agua Caliente Cultural Museum.

Palm Springs Desert Museum, ☎ 619/325-0189, conducts nature hikes each Wednesday and Saturday at 9 am from October through April. Hikes visit such local sites as Morongo Preserve, Wellman's Divide, San Jacinto Peak, Black Rock Canyon, Ramona Trail, Araby Trail and Pushwalla Canyon.

Trail Discovery Hiking Service, ☎ 619/325-HIKE, is a professional hiking guide service.

Rancho Mirage

Michael J. Wolfson Park has several walking paths, including a Braille Trail, on which bronze Braille plaques and audio presentations by Frank Sinatra and Dinah Shore help the visually impaired to enjoy an educational nature walk.

ROCK CLIMBING

Idyllwild

Lily Rock (or Tahquitz Rock) in Humber Park has 140 routes to the top.

Suicide Rock has more than 250 routes along its faces, including some with such colorful names as Spring Cleaning, Knocking on Heaven's Door, Sahara Terror, Blanketty Blank, Coffin Nail and Godzilla's Return.

Nomad Ventures, 54415 N. Circle Dr., ☎ 909/659-4853, can provide equipment, books, classes and guides.

Palm Springs

Oasis Waterpark, 1500 S. Gene Autry Tr., ☎ 619/320-6630, has three covered towers, 40 feet tall and covering more than 7,000 square feet. The park provides instruction and organizes rock climbing tours.

GOLF

If golf isn't an adventure anywhere else, it certainly is here. You can tee off where Palmer teed off, putt where Nicklaus putted, escape from a sand trap that Player failed to manage...

Few places hold an equal share of golf's heritage.

Borrego Springs

Ram Hill Country Club, 1881 Rams Hill Dr., ☎ 619/767-5124, provides a real challenge – seven lakes and 54 sand traps to navigate. There's also a driving range.

La Quinta

La Quinta Hotel has two courses: the Dunes Course, 50-200 Ave. Vista Bonita, ☎ 619/345-2549, and the Mountain Course, ☎ 619/564-7610, both designed by Pete Dye.

PGA West, 56-150 PGA Blvd., ☎ 619/564-6666 or 564-7170, has two 18-hole courses: the TPC Stadium Course designed by Pete Dye, and the Jack Nicklaus Resort Course.

La Quinta Resort & Club, 49-499 Eisenhower Dr., ☎ 619/564-4111, allows guests to play the hotel's Dunes and Mountain courses, the TPC Stadium Golf Course, or the Jack Nicklaus Tournament Course at PGA West.

Rancho La Quinta Country Club, 48500 Washington St., ☎ 619/777-7755, features a course designed by Robert Trent Jones Jr.

Palm Desert

This community is the home of 27 of the valley's 90 golf courses. Apparently that's not enough. The city will soon open **Desert Willow**, a new municipally-operated public golf course. The city also hosts an annual golf cart parade.

Golf Center at Palm Desert, 74-945 Sheryl, ☎ 619/779-1877, a nine-hole par 3 course, has a covered, misted, lighted driving range and hosts an open Skins game every Thursday. They also arrange golfing vacations, ☎ 619/346-3331, fax 619/346-4473.

Bighorn Golf Club, 255 Palowet Dr., ☎ 619/341-4653, is in the Santa Rosa Mountains and is very hilly. A private course, it was the venue for the Skins game from 1992 to 1996.

Jude E. Poynter Golf Museum, Fred Waring Dr. and San Pablo Ave., ☎ 619/341-2491, is housed in the College of the Desert.

Indian Wells Golf Resort, 44-500 Indian Wells Lane, ☎ 619/346-4653, and **Marriott's Desert Springs Resort**, 74-855 County Club Dr., ☎ 619/341-1756, each have two 18-hole golf courses.

Palm Springs

Tahquitz Creek, 1885 Golf Club Dr., ☎ 619/328-1005, fax 619/324-8122, has two courses designed by Arnold Palmer, the Legend Course and the Resort Course. Also available are a practice tee, a chipping and putting green, and lessons for men, women and children.

Tommy Jacobs' Bel Air Greens, 1001 S. El Cielo Rd., ☎ 619/322-6062 or 800/95-BELAIR, has a nine-hole executive course and a night-lighted, covered and misted driving range. There's also a miniature golf course, a bar and a restaurant. Who is Tommy Jacobs? Jacobs once won the Bob Hope Chrysler Classic, tied for first in the Masters, and held both the 18-hole and the 54-hole record for the U.S. Open.

Trouble getting a tee time? **Par Tee Golf**, ☎ 619/323-8360 or 800/PAR-TEE-1, will set things up for you.

Rancho Mirage

Mission Hills Country Club is the long-time home of the Dinah Shore LPGA Classic.

Mission Hills North Golf Course, 70-705 Ramon Rd., ☎ 619/770-9496, is an 18-hole course designed by Gary Player. There also is a driving range adjacent to the course.

Westin Mission Hills Resort, 71-501 Dinah Shore Dr., ☎ 619/328-3198, has a Pete Dye-designed 18-hole course, a driving range, two practice greens, a pro shop and several restaurants.

TENNIS

Before golf, it was tennis that spurred the growth of the Palm Springs area. It continues to be a large part of the allure – and the recreation – today.

Indian Wells

Hyatt Grand Champions Tennis Stadium, 44650 Indian Wells, ☎ 800/999-1585, seats 11,500 people. It hosts three major tennis events annually: the Newsweek Champions Cup and the State Farm Evert Cup tournaments in March, and the State Farm Challenger tournament in October.

Palm Desert

Palm Desert hosts the annual **Palm Desert Senior Cup**, ☎ 619/346-1276.

Palm Springs

Hilton Plaza, 251 N. El Segundo, ☎ 619/323-8997, has six courts. Ladies' Day is Monday. Men's Day is Tuesday.

   Palm Springs Tennis Club, 701 W. Baristo Rd., ☎ 619/778-9947, 568-2180 or 800/854-2324, has hosted the likes of Don Budge, Alice Marble, Martina Navratilova, Billy Jean King, Bobby Riggs, Rod Laver and Jimmy Connors.

On Horseback

Descanso

Holidays on Horseback, 24928 Viejas Blvd., ☎ 619/445-3997, takes 1½- , 2- , 3- , and 4-hour trail rides into the Cuyamaca Mountains.

Julian

Mount Laguna Stables, 20 miles from town on Sunrise Highway, ☎ 619/473-9053, rents horses.

   Julian Donkey Treks, ☎ 619/765-1182, offers a bumpier ride.

La Quinta

Ranch of the 7th Range, ☎ 619/777-7777, organizes breakfast rides, horse-drawn hay rides and Western hoe-downs.

Horseback riding near Palm Springs.
Credit: Jack Hollingsworth, Palm Springs Desert Resorts Convention & Visitors Bureau

Palm Springs

Indian Canyons, ☎ 619/325-5673, rents horses.

Smoke Tree Stables, 2500 Toledo Ave., ☎ 619/327-1372, features guided or independent trail rides.

Ramona

This is horse-ranching country. Some train horses, but it is not uncommon to see llama and buffalo in the fields. **San Diego Country Estates**, a 3,000-acre planned community, has an International Equestrian Center.

Rancho Mirage

Equestrian Centers International, 35050 Via Josephini, ☎ 619/321-2235, fax 619/328-6402, rents horses and provides 20 miles of horse trails.

Sage

Rancho Pavoreal Guest Ranch, 43000 Stanley Rd., ☎ 909/787-3007 or 800/507-1376, is in Sage, but the mailing address is 27475 Ynez Rd., #289, Temecula 92591. The ranch has an Olympic-size swimming pool, king-size beds, private baths and over 2,000 acres to ride on. Rooms bear such names as Marie Windsor, John "Duke" Wayne, Gene Autry, Gabby Hayes and Andy Devine. Riding lessons, either Western or English, are offered.

Warner Springs

Warner Springs Ranch, Highway 79 south of Temecula, ☎ 619/782-4270 or 767-0353, has an equestrian center as well as golf, 15 tennis courts, eight swimming pools, wet and dry saunas, massages, mineral springs and glider rides.

RODEOS

Julian

Julian Gold Rush Rodeo is held every August.

Ramona

Ramona hosts an annual rodeo and is the site of the **Casey Tibbs Memorial**, a memorial to the former world champion rodeo rider.

On Wheels

BICYCLES

Cleveland National Forest

Spur Meadow Cycle Trail and **Kernan Cycle Trail** are both pleasant and stimulating bike trails.

Descanso

Cuyamaca Rancho State Park, 12551 Highway 79, ☎ 619/765-0755, provides 120 miles of trails. Volunteers man the museum, patrol the trails on mountain bikes or on horseback, lead interpretive walks, and assist in maintaining the trails. Mountain bike trails include:

- ★ **Green Valley Campground Loop**, a four-mile trip.
- ★ **Granite Springs Primitive Camp**, an 11½-mile trip with water available once you reach the camp.
- ★ **School Camp Loop**, an easy ride that covers eight miles and follows a fire road.
- ★ **Middle Park Loop**, a 7½-mile ride.
- ★ **West Mesa Trail**, a 6½-mile, tree-covered trail.
- ★ **Cuyamaca Grand Loop**, a 15-mile extension of the West Mesa Trail that makes a nice day trip if you take a lunch along.
- ★ **Cuyamaca Peak Fire Road**, a steep, 3½-mile ride on a paved surface. Control your downhill return.

Idyllwild

This region has 200 miles of dirt roads and 40 miles of trails for mountain biking, but no rentals are available.

Coyote Run is an easy two-mile ride on a dirt road. It runs from the north end of Hurkey Creek County Park to the waterfalls on Hurkey Creek.

Fobes Ranch Road is an easy-to-moderate 20-mile ride beginning three miles south of Lake Hemet on Highway 74 in Garner Valley.

South Fork Trail begins on the south side of Highway 74 four miles west of Mountain Center near the large gravel bin turnout. It covers 2½ miles, including a steep descent to the South Fork of the San Jacinto River during the last half-mile.

Thomas Mountain and Ramona Trail makes a challenging 17-mile loop. The trail begins a mile south of Lake Hemet on Highway 74 and passes through Tool Box Campground. A new two-mile section, opened in 1996, connects that campground and the Thomas Mountain Campground.

Santa Rosa Mountain Trail is a dirt road that ascends from an elevation of 4,500 feet to an elevation of over 8,700 feet in 13 miles. The dirt road begins on the right-hand side of Highway 74, six miles east of the junction with Highway 371, and goes to Toro Peak.

Saw Mill Rd. is rough and steep. Just off Highway 74 near Pinyon Flats, this old Forest Service road links up with the Cactus Springs Trail, where it continues on for six more miles.

La Quinta

Bear Creek Channel Bike Path has shaded rest stops along the way, a part of the community's Art in Public Places program.

Palm Desert

Tri-A-Bike, 44-841 San Pablo, ☎ 619/340-2840 or 340-2870, rents bicycles.

Palm Springs

Bighorn Bicycles, 302 N. Palm Canyon Dr., ☎ 619/325-3367, rents bikes hourly, by the half-day, or all day. It also arranges tours from November through May. The Great Estates Tour passes the homes of Liberace, Jack Benny, Elvis Presley and others. The Down Valley Golf Course Tour makes an 18-mile round trip through three golf courses and three cities. There also is an Indian Canyons Tour.

Dune Off-Road Rentals, on the south side of Highway 111, ☎ 619/325-0376 or 567-2105, also rents bikes.

Rancho Mirage

A Bike Rental at Mac's Desert Cyclery, 70-053 Highway 111, ☎ 619/321-9444 or 321-2453, rents bicycles.

MOTOR VEHICLES

Cleveland National Forest

Corral Canyon Off-Road Vehicle Area includes the Bobcat Meadow, Los Piños and Bear Valley four-wheel-drive routes. The most difficult trails are **Bronco Peak, Bronco Flats, Sidewinder** and **Gun Slinger** Trails.

Easy ATV trails include **Corral** and **Bobcat.** Those of medium difficulty include **Wrangler** and **Greenhorn.** The most difficult are **Bronco Peak, Sidewinder** and **Gun Slinger.**

There also are a number of motorcycle trails in the forest ranging from easy to difficult. The easier trails include **Wrangler, Corral, Greenhorn** and **Bobcat.** Those of medium difficulty include **Bronco Flats, Sodbuster** and **Wrangler Tie.** The most difficult motorcycle trails are **Bronco Peak, Tombstone, Sidewinder** and **Gun Slinger.**

Hemet

Every March, the **Jeep Cavalcade,** a weekend trek by four-wheel-drive vehicles, traces the original expedition of Spanish explorer Juan Bautista De Anza to Borrego Springs in 1774. The event is limited to 150 vehicles and all must have a metal top or a roll bar, seat belts for each passenger, a fire extinguisher, a muffler, and a tow rope, strap, cable, or safety chain. ATVs and motorcycles are not allowed.

Palm Springs

Desert Adventures, 611 S. Palm Canyon Dr., Ste. 7445, ☎ 619/324-5337 or 864-6530, e-mail info@red-jeep.com, Web site www.red-jeep.com, organizes jeep tours. **Mystery Canyon Adventure** investigates the San Andreas Fault and the Painted Hills, allows you to take the "hike of death," and shows you where *Star Trek, the Motion Picture* was filmed. The Indian Canyons Adventure travels to sparkling pools, towering waterfalls and the Indian Canyons Trading Post. There also is a Santa Rosa Mountains Adventure.

Off-Road Rentals On-Site Quads, 59511 Highway 111, ☎ 619/325-0376, rents off-road vehicles.

Desert Safari, ☎ 888/TO SAFARI, organizes four-hour group expeditions. They leave daily at 8:15 am.

Magic Carpet Rides, ☎ 619/321-8170 or 970/544-0909, rents Harley-Davidson motorcycles, including low riders, soft tails, sportsters and fat boys, by the half-day, day or week.

On & In the Water

Hemet

Construction of **Lake Hemet Dam**, four miles east of Mountain Center on Highway 74 in Garner Valley, began in 1892. At the time, it was the largest solid masonry dam in the world built specifically for land development and irrigation. Owned and operated by the Lake Hemet Municipal Water District, the lake is 1½-miles long, a half-mile wide, and 135 feet deep when full. It sits at an elevation of 4,340 feet. The Forest Service has free fishing areas along the north shore, but for day use only. Boating, camping (☎ 909/659-2680) and fishing (rainbow trout, channel catfish, largemouth bass and bluegill) are available. The lake has two public recreation areas.

Adventure Institute, 36155 Whittier Ave., ☎ 800/526-9682, schedules kayak tours to San Diego Bay (Point Loma), Mission Bay, Dana Point, Balboa Bay, Point San Pedro, Lake Hodges, Lake Perris and the Colorado River (Topock Gorge).

Domenigoni Valley Reservoir Project, a $1.9 billion effort to build three dams and flood 4,500 acres, is scheduled for completion in 1999. Lake Domenigoni is being completed on the edge of town with a one-acre swimming lagoon on the west side, a swimming pool on the east side, and two marinas, one near the east dam and one near the west dam. Crest Trail runs along the north side of the reservoir, while a trail from the east-side dam leads to Cactus Valley. Lake Skinner, farther south, will be joined to the main reservoir by a canal and will offer camping, fishing, boating and a swimming pool, ☎ 909/925-1505. The two lakes will be separated by the Dr. Roy E. Shipley Reserve in Rawson Canyon. There is a visitor center at 300 Newport Rd., ☎ 800/211-9863.

Lake Perris, ☎ 909/657-0676, provides swimming, fishing, boating and a visitor center.

Idyllwild

Lake Fulmore, 10 miles north on Highway 243, is a two-acre lake stocked with rainbow trout. The lake occasionally freezes over in winter.

Strawberry Creek and **Fuller Mill Creek**, about seven miles north of town off Highway 243, have trout.

Dark Canyon Creek, about eight miles north of town off Highway 243, also is stocked with trout.

For a recording that contains a weekly fishing report, ☎ 310/590-5020.

Julian

Lake Cuyamaca, 15027 Highway 79, ☎ 619/765-0515, is a mile-long reservoir containing trout and panfish. Free fishing lessons are offered on Saturdays. There is a bait and tackle shop, and boats are available for rent,

☎ 619/765-0515. A campground is nearby and food is available at **Lake Cuyamaca Restaurant,** ☎ 619/765-0700.

La Quinta

Lake Cahuilla Recreation Area, ☎ 619/564-4712, 909/275-4310 or 800/234-7275, is between Avenues 56 and 58 west of Jefferson St. Set in the foothills of the Santa Rosa Mountains on the west side of Coachella Valley, the 135-acre park is at the end of the Coachella Branch of the All-American Canal. Swimming is allowed and boating too, but no motors are permitted. The reservoir, which is only about 12 feet deep, is a half-mile long and half as wide at its widest point. Striped bass, largemouth bass, trout, catfish and crappie can be caught. Annual catfish and trout derbies are staged.

Ramona

Freshwater fishing is available at nearby **Sutherland Dam** and the **San Vicente Reservoir.**

Santa Ysabel

Lake Henshaw, 26439 Highway 76, ☎ 619/782-3501, allows fishing.

Temecula

Lake Elsinore, 16 miles northwest on Highway 74 via I-15, affords boating, waterskiing, fishing, camping and swimming.

Lake Skinner County Park at the end of Warren Rd., ☎ 909/926-1541, is a 1,200-acre reservoir with boat rentals, ☎ 909/926-1505, hiking, horse trails and fishing. No canoes or kayaks are allowed and boats must observe the 10 mph speed limit.

Striped bass to 39.8 lbs, catfish to 33.4 lbs, largemouth bass, crappie and bluegill are in the lake, and there is a special fishing area for the physically disabled. Camping is available, ☎ 909/926-1541 or 800/234-PARK, on 300 developed sites. No swimming is allowed in the lake, but there is a pool that remains open from Memorial Day through Labor Day. In August, there is an annual Catfish Derby, and in November, a Trout Derby.

Vail Lake is 11 miles east of town on Highway 79. The reservoir covers one square mile and contains bass, catfish, trout and panfish. There are boat rentals, but swimming and waterskiing are not allowed. An RV campground is nearby.

On Snow

Palm Springs

Cross-country skiing is available in the winter at the top of the **Palm Springs Aerial Tramway.**

In the Air

Borrego Springs

Borrego Valley Airport hosts an annual three-day akrofest (aerobatics) competition.
Air Borrego, ☎ 619/767-5328, is a new charter service.

Hemet

Hemet Ryan Airport, half-hour southeast of Riverside, provides skydiving, glider rides, hot-air ballooning and airplane rides.

Skydiving Adventures, 36155 Whittier, ☎ 909/925-8197 or 800/526-9682, offers an hour's training in ground school, then flies you to 10,000 feet where, in tandem with an instructor, you freefall for about 35 seconds and then parachute four or five minutes back to earth. Your adventure will be captured in a still picture or on videotape. Skydivers must be over 18 and weigh less than 230 pounds.

Sailplane Enterprises, 36095 Whittier Ave., ☎ 909/658-6577 or 800/586-7627, provides glider flights of 20 minutes or longer. The company also operates out of Thermal Airport, a half-hour southeast of Palm Springs.

La Quinta

A Rainbow Rider's Adventure, ☎ 619/564-7405 or 340-5545, fax 619/564-7445, features one-hour rides in a hot-air balloon.

Palm Desert

Desert Balloon Charter, ☎ 619/346-8575, provides free pickup at your hotel.

Fantasy Balloon Flights, ☎ 619/398-6322 or 800/GO-ABOVE; **American Balloon Charters,** ☎ 619/327-8544 or 800/359-6837; and **Dream Flights,** ☎ 619/321-5154 or 800/933-5628, all feature hot-air balloon excursions.

Palm Springs

Palm Springs Aerial Tramway, One Tramway Rd., ☎ 619/325-1391, operates two enclosed 80-passenger cars at least every half-hour from 10 am Monday through Friday and 8 am on weekends and holidays. The last car up leaves at 8 pm. To reach the terminal from Palm Springs, take Tramway Rd. off Highway 111 and drive up the hill for 3½ miles. The tram goes from the Valley Station at 2,643 feet to the Mountain Station at 8,516 feet and is the world's largest single-span lift. At the top, the threshold to the 13,000-acre **Mt. San Jacinto Wilderness State Park**, is a restaurant, gift shop, cocktail lounge, snack bar, observation area and a movie theater that shows a 22-minute film on the history of the tramway. In the park adjacent to the tramway, there are campsites, 54 miles of hiking trails, and facilities for horse and mule rides.

Aerial Tramway.
Credit: Arthur Coleman, Palm Springs Desert Resorts Visitors Bureau

    Parachutes Over Palm Springs, ☎ 619/345-8321 or 800/535-5867, will introduce you to parachuting.

    American Balloon Charters, ☎ 619/327-8544 or 800/FLY-OVER, schedules hot-air balloon flights lasting 30-40 minutes or 60-75 minutes, sweetheart (two-person) balloon flights, balloon races and balloon-and-jeep scavenger hunts.

Temecula

A Rainbow at Dawn, ☎ 909/676-2709 or 800/446-6222; **A Skysurfer Balloon Co.**, ☎ 800/660-6809; **D&D Ballooning**, ☎ 909/694-5351; **Grape Escape Balloon Adventure**, ☎ 909/698-9772; **DAE Flights**, ☎ 909/676-3902; **Fantasy Balloon Flights**, ☎ 800/GO-ABOVE; and **Sunrise Balloons**, ☎ 800/548-9912, all offer hot-air balloon flights.

Thermal

The Balloon Ranch, 82-550 Airport Blvd., ☎ 619/398-0682, and **Desert Ballon Charter**, 82-540 Airport Blvd., ☎ 619/398-8575, provide hot-air balloon rides.

Warner Springs

Sky Sailing, 31930 Highway 79, ☎ 619/782-0404, Web site www.globalwebs.com/skysailing, provides 20- to 40-minute glider rides for one or two passengers.

Eco-Travel/Cultural Excursions

Hemet

Ramona Bowl, 27400 Ramona Bowl Rd., ☎ 909/658-3111, 658-3114 or 800/645-4465, fax 909/658-2695, is a natural amphitheater in the foothills above the city that seats 6,500 people. (Girard Blvd. becomes Ramona Bowl Blvd.) Every year since 1923, excluding the Depression year of 1933 and the World War II years between 1942 and 1945, California's Official Outdoor Play, based on the 1884 Helen Hunt Jackson novel *Ramona,* has been presented in April and May. The story of Ramona and her hero Alessandro requires a cast of 400 and is America's oldest outdoor drama. Raquel Welch once played the title role.

When the community started a "Save Our Station" movement to preserve its historic 1914 Santa Fe railroad depot, **Hemet Area Museum,** which had been operating out of a storefront in town, contributed its entire $35,000 treasury. The campaign succeeded, the station was purchased, and the museum was invited to move into the depot's old freight house.

The **Boboba Indian Reservation** and the **Cahuilla Indian Reservation** are located in this area. Ramona's grave is supposedly located on the Cahuilla Reservation.

Orange Empire Trolley Museum, ☎ 909/657-2605, is in nearby Perris. Open weekends and holidays from 11 to 5, the museum provides rides on antique trolley cars.

Idyllwild

Indian Relic Archaeological Site, a mile north of town on Pinecrest Ave., is small (0.1 acres) and undeveloped, but historically and scientifically significant.

Pine Cove Park, three miles north of town on Rocky Point Rd., contains 19 acres with controlled access.

Julian

Julian Pioneer Museum, 2811 Washington and 4th Sts., ☎ 619/765-0227, which contains pioneer memorabilia, is housed in an old brewery.

La Quinta

La Quinta Historical Society, 77-885 Avenida Montezuma, has a video entitled *Gem of the Desert,* narrated by actor William Devane, that relates the history of the area.

Sculptureland, 57-325 Madison, ☎ 619/564-6464, fills 20 acres with over 100 sculptures. It is the largest outdoor display of sculpture in America.

Palm Desert

The Living Desert Wildlife & Botanical Park, 47-900 Portola Ave., ☎ 619/346-5694, fax 619/568-9685, contains 1,200 acres of plants and animals associated with the world's desert regions. Tours and school programs are offered, and there is a story-telling period in the Discovery Room every Wednesday at 3:30. The facility is closed during August and on Christmas Day.

Aerie Art Garden, 71225 Aerie Rd., ☎ 619/568-6366, displays desert plants and sculpture on a 20-acre hillside estate. There also is an indoor watercolor gallery. Open by appointment only.

College of the Desert, 43-500 Monterey Ave., ☎ 619/773-2506, 346-8041 or 568-9921, is a two-year college, a satellite campus of Cal-State San Bernardino. It hosts the Joana Hodges Piano Conference and Competition each year. There is a public golf driving range. An entertaining **Street Faire** is held there every Saturday and Sunday morning beginning at 7 am.

Chapman College, 41555 Cook, ☎ 619/341-8051, provides full undergraduate and graduate programs.

McCallum Theatre, Bob Hope Cultural Center, 73-000 Fred Waring Dr., ☎ 619/346-6505 or 340-2787, fax 619/341-9508, contains 1,250 seats and is located on the College of the Desert campus. Performers who have appeared there include Liza Minnelli, Mikhail Barishnikov, Willie Nelson, Tony Bennett, Frank Sinatra, Zubin Mehta, James Brown and Ella Fitzgerald.

A new 43,000-square-foot **Multi-Agency Library** is a joint venture of the City of Palm Desert, Riverside County and the College of the Desert.

Palm Springs

Village Green, 200 block of S. Palm Canyon Dr., ☎ 619/323-8297, fax 619/320-2561, preserves a number of historic buildings around a small mid-town park. **Ruddy's 1930s General Store Museum,** ☎ 619/327-2156, contains an authentic collection of 6,000 unused household items from the 1930s and '40s. **Agua Caliente Cultural Museum,** ☎ 619/323-0151, 778-1079 or 325-5673, preserves the culture of the local Cahuilla Indians. **McCallum Adobe Museum,** ☎ 619/323-8297, built in 1884, is the oldest building in town. **The Cornelia White House** was built in 1893 on railway ties from the defunct Palmdale Railway.

Palm Springs Desert Museum, 101 Museum Dr., ☎ 619/325-7186 or 325-0189, adjacent to the Desert Fashion Plaza in downtown Palm Springs is now open year-round following a recent $6.5 million expansion and renovation program. The program added 20,000 square feet to the facility, including the **Steve Chase Art Wing and Education Center**, which provides a 90-seat lecture hall, four classrooms and two art storage vaults. The first Friday of each month, admission to the museum is free (unless there is a special exhibition underway).

Annenberg Theater, 101 Museum Dr., ☎ 619/325-4490, is associated with the Palm Springs Desert Museum and contains 450 seats.

Historic Plaza Theatre, 128 S. Palm Canyon Dr., ☎ 619/327-0225, is a renovated 717-seat movie theater in which the first offering was the 1936 world premiere of *Camille*, starring Greta Garbo and Robert Taylor (rumor

Cast members of *Palm Springs Follies*.
Credit: Palm Springs Desert Resorts Convention & Visitors Bureau

has it that Garbo sneaked in and watched from the back of the theater). Jack Benny broadcast his radio show from here when he was on a working vacation. Today, the theater is the venue for *The Fabulous Palm Springs Follies*, ☎ 619/327-0225, an old-fashioned, high-energy musical review in which each member of the cast is at least 50 years old. *The Follies'* seven-month season runs from November through May.

Nortel Palm Springs International Film Festival, ☎ 619/778-8979, held each year in January at the Plaza Theatre, screens 120 films from over 25 countries. Past winners of festival awards include Lucille Ball, Leslie Caron, Cyd Cherise, Tony Curtis, Marvin Hamlisch, James Earl Jones, Ruby Keeler, Sophia Loren, Henry Mancini, Frank Sinatra and Jimmy Stewart.

Palm Springs Film & Entertainment Museum on Palm Canyon Dr., ☎ 619/324-1413, is the community's latest tribute to the entertainment industry

Moorten's Botanical Garden, 1701 S. Palm Canyon Dr., ☎ 619/327-6555, contains over 3,000 varieties of cactus. Guided tours are available.

On the edge of town sits the **Agua Caliente Indian Reservation**, ☎ 619/325-5673. Although a small tribe (320 members), the Cahuilla Indians own 42% of Coachella Valley, including the downtown Spa Resort Hotel & Casino. In April, the tribe hosts the **Agua Caliente Indian**

Heritage Festival, ☎ 619/322-4581, which features Indian music, dances, storytelling, pottery firing and foods. A new cultural museum has been built just north of the Indian Canyons toll gate, and the tribe provides day-long excursions into three nearby canyons.

Ramona

Guy B. Woodward Museum of History, 645 Main St., ☎ 619/789-7644, in the foothills of the Cuyamaca Mountains, is another complex of historic old buildings, plus exhibits including Indian artifacts, photos, and a collection of women's clothing and accessories dating from 1700-1800. The 1886 Verlaque House on display there is the only Western adobe home of French provincial design still in existence.

Rancho Mirage

Eisenhower Medical Center, 39000 Bob Hope Dr., ☎ 619/568-1234, occupies 100 acres and includes the 261-bed **Eisenhower Memorial Hospital, Annenberg Center for Health Sciences, The Betty Ford Center** for alcohol and chemical dependencies, and the **Barbara Sinatra Children's Center.**

Heartland, the California Museum of the Heart, 39-600 Bob Hope Dr., ☎ 619/32-HEART, is a 4,831-square-foot facility that includes exhibits, the 104-seat Happy Heart Cinema and the Heart Rock Café.

Where To Stay

B&Bs, Hotels & Inns

It can fairly be said that there are more top-quality hotel and motel rooms per square mile in this region than virtually anywhere else in the world. A great deal of the fun in visiting this wonderful place comes from checking out the accommodations until you find a place that is precisely to your liking. The following recommendations should set you off on the right foot.

Borrego Springs

Palm Canyon Resort, 221 Palm Canyon Dr., Borrego Springs, ☎ 619/767-5341 or 800/242-0044, is unspoiled. Although it offers a hotel, restaurant, lounge, two pools, spas, a deluxe RV park, golf, tennis, hiking and biking, the resort has a slow-down-and-take-it-easy feeling about it. What's more, it's affordable.

Indian Wells

Renaissance Esmeralda Resort, 44-440 Indian Wells Lane, ☎ 619/773-4444 or 800/468-3571, fax 619/773-9250, Web site www.desert-resorts.com, has 560 rooms and 44 suites. It was named one of California's top 10 resorts by *Golf Magazine* on the basis of its two 18-hole golf courses designed by Ted Robinson. The resort also provides seven tennis courts (two lighted), a regulation beach volleyball court, a basketball court and two swimming pools.

Hyatt Grand Champions Resort, 44-600 Indian Wells Lane, ☎ 619/341-1000 or 800/233-1234, fax 619/568-2236, also has two 18-hole Ted Robinson golf courses. Golfers also will enjoy the putting green and driving range. The resort has 336 rooms, all suites, four swimming pools and two spas. There are 12 tennis courts with a variety of three surfaces (the resort is host to the annual Newsweek Champions tennis tournament). Horseback riding, balloon rides, hayrides and jeep tours also are available.

Julian

Julian Lodge, 4th and C Sts., ☎ 619/765-1420, is a mountain B&B designed after the Washington Hotel, built in 1885. A continental breakfast is furnished.

The Julian White House, 3014 Blue Jay Dr., ☎ 619/765-1764 or 800/WHT-HOUS, occupies a Colonial mansion. **Shadow Mountain Ranch**, 2771 Frisius Rd., ☎ 619/765-0323, has rooms in the main house, plus cabins named Gnome Home and Tree House. There is a lap pool and a hot tub, and activities include archery, badminton, croquet and horseshoes.

For further information, contact **Julian Bed & Breakfast Guild**, PO Box 1711, Julian 92036, ☎ 619/765-1555.

La Quinta

La Quinta Hotel Resort & Club, 49-499 Eisenhower Dr., ☎ 619/564-4111 or 800/598-3828, Web site www.desert-resorts.com, offers 640 rooms and 27 suites. One of the area's oldest resorts, the accommodations here are primarily of the cottage variety and the original buildings were made out of material, bricks and tiles, that were hand-crafted on the grounds. This is not to say that the resort is old, run-down, and in need of repair. Far from it. La Quinta is one of the priciest resorts in the area. Greta Garbo, Bette Davis, Clark Gable and Errol Flynn all once stayed here. The resort has its own golf course or guests can play at PGA West. There also are 30 tennis courts.

Palm Desert

Marriott's Desert Springs Resort & Spa, 74-855 Country Club Dr., ☎ 619/341-2211 or 800/228-9290, overlooks the 17th hole of Palms golf course. It is the area's largest hotel, with 895 rooms and 51 suites, and has a 57-station, 3,000-square-foot gym.

Shadow Mountain Golf & Tennis Resort, 45-750 San Luis Rey, ☎ 619/346-6123 or 800/472-3713, fax 619/346-6518, features 100 condominiums. It also offers 16 all-weather tennis courts and four swimming pools, one a figure 8.

For the budget-minded, **Holiday Inn Express** and **Embassy Suites** also can be found in Palm Desert.

Palm Springs

For a touch of the Palm Springs that once was, a stay at **Ingleside Inn**, 200 W. Ramon Rd., ☎ 619/325-0046 or 800/772-6655, fax 619/325-0710, e-mail ingleside@earthlink.net, Web site www.prinet.com/ingleside, is definitely recommended. Built in 1925 as a private residence for Humphrey Birge, head of Pierce Arrow Motor Car Co., it was converted 10 years later into an exclusive inn by Ruth Hardy. (In those days, you couldn't call for a reservation; you had to be invited.) Greta Garbo, Bob Hope, John Travolta, former President Gerald Ford, Salvador Dali, Greer Garson, David Hasselhoff, Cyndi Lauper, Goldie Hawn, Madonna, J.C. Penney, Tom Selleck, Arnold Schwarzenegger and Donald Trump have slept there. Howard Hughes stayed there frequently, often using false names. Opera star Lily Pons and her husband, band leader André Kostelanetz, went there for a night and stayed 13 years! The inn is convenient to the downtown area and has 30 rooms, villas and suites. A complimentary breakfast is served with a copy of *The Los Angeles Times*. On the premises is Melvyn's Restaurant (see *Where To Eat*, below).

Givenchy Hotel & Spa, 4200 E. Palm Canyon Dr., ☎ 619/770-5000 or 800/276-5000, fax 619/324-7280, is one of the area's newest hotels. Sitting on 14 acres, the hotel provides 98 rooms, suites and villas; two swimming pools; two gyms; tennis courts; and a rose garden containing 452 varieties of roses (including the Givenchy). The King of Beauty Spa program is patterned after that offered at Givenchy's original spa in Versailles, France.

The Palms, 572 N. Indian Canyon Dr., ☎ 800/753-7256, is a California inn built around a courtyard pool. It is a health and fitness establishment. Guests begin their day with a walk, followed by water aerobics, a broth break, exercise, a veggie break, yoga and an evening juice cocktail. Their diet tapers gradually to 1,000 calories a day, consisting of low-fat food prepared without salt, sugar or preservatives.

Oasis Water Resort, 4190 E. Palm Canyon Dr., ☎ 619/328-1499 or 800/247-4664, offers 80 two-bedroom, two-bath villas, each with a fully equipped kitchen, private patios and private garages with automatic openers. There are eight swimming pools, nine hot spas and five lighted tennis courts. Villas can be rented by the day, week or month (bargain off-season rates are offered between October and January and between May and July).

Spa Hotel & Casino, 100 N. Indian Canyon Dr., ☎ 619/325-1461 or 800/854-1279, fax 619/325-3344, Web site www.desert-resorts. com, is owned and operated by the Agua Caliente Indians. Predictably, it contains a Las Vegas-style casino. Enjoying an excellent downtown location, the five-story hotel was built atop some ancient hot springs, once a favored tourist attraction. There are 230 rooms and 20 suites.

Along with these traditional types of lodgings, Palm Springs offers a potpourri of less traditional accommodations. Among them is **The Willows**, 412 W. Tahquitz Canyon Way, ☎ 610/320-0771, fax 619/320-0780, a Mediterranean-style villa that was built in 1927 for Samuel Untermeyer, a former Secretary of the Treasury. The house contains eight rooms with stone fireplaces, a private hillside garden with a waterfall and a swimming pool. It is located near Palm Springs' Desert Museum and Le Vallauris restaurant. Later, the house became the home of Marion Davies, long-time mistress of publisher William Randolph Hearst. Guests have included Albert Einstein, Clark Gable and Carole Lombard.

Estrella (star) **Inn**, 415 S. Belardo Rd., ☎ 619/320-4117 or 800/237-3687, fax 619/323-3303, was built on four acres in 1929. It has three pools and three courtyards. The Fountain Courtyard is surrounded by seven Mediterranean revival bungalows, each with two bedrooms and two baths, a fireplace and a kitchen. The Rose Garden Courtyard has eight bungalows and six studios, all with fireplaces and full kitchens. The Bougainvillea Courtyard provides oversize guest rooms, each with a wet bar and a patio or balcony, and one- or two-bedroom suites, each with a kitchen. Bing Crosby, Tyrone Power and Marilyn Monroe once stayed there, as did Orson Welles and the tempestuous Lupe Velez (once married to Johnny Weismuller).

La Mancha Private Villas and Court Club, 444 N. Avenida Caballeros, ☎ 619/323-1773, was built in 1976. The 67 private villas have been occupied by such personalities as Whoopi Goldberg, Sally Field, Richard Pryor, Billy Crystal, Penny Marshall, Mickey Rooney, Mickey Rourke, Elizabeth Taylor, Watergate figure John Dean and Hollywood madam Heidi Fleiss.

McLean Rentals, 477 S. Palm Canyon Dr., ☎ 619/322-2500 or 800/777-4606, e-mail ps4rent@aol.com, specializes in renting out-of-the-ordinary accommodations such as:

★ **Elvis Presley's Honeymoon Hideaway**, the Alexander Estate. In May 1967, this is where Presley and his bride Priscilla spent their honeymoon night. Presley continued to use the place through the late 1960s. The grounds include a large pool, private garden, tennis court and fruit orchard. Cost: $1,500 per night; three-night minimum.

★ **Elvis' home** in the foothills of the San Jacinto Mountains. Other than Graceland, this is the only home Presley ever owned. It occupies 5,000 square feet on a two-acre lot and has four bedrooms, a cathedral beamed ceiling in the living room, a full bar in the dining room and a pool. Rate: $1,200 per night; three-night minimum.

★ **Liberace's home**, recently refurbished at a cost of several hundred thousand dollars. The house contains four bedrooms (one with musical note wallpaper) and five baths. There is a sketch of Liberace done by his brother above the fireplace. The front yard contains lighted Italian sculpture and a sparkling fountain. Price: $3,000 per week.

★ **Groucho Marx's home**, hidden behind high steel gates. This four-bedroom house has a large pool and palm trees in the back yard and a guest house by the pool. Other owners have included singer/actor Mario Lanza and Western film star Hopalong Cassidy. Tariff: $4,000 per week or $10,000 per month.

★ **Bette Davis' house**, which has three bedrooms, stone fireplace, floor-to-ceiling French doors, outstanding landscaping, an Olympic-size pool, a tennis court and two guest houses, each with its own fireplace. Price: $12,000 per week.

As previously mentioned, Palm Springs has a large gay and lesbian clientelle, whose preference for lodgings includes **The "550," Alexander Resort, Aruba Resort Apartments, Atrium, Avanti Resort, Camp Palm Springs, Casa Rosa, The Columns, Desert Stars Resort, Harlow Hotel, Hot Desert Knights, Inn Exile, INNdulge Palm Springs, InnTrigue Resort, Triangle Inn** and **Vista Grande Villa.**

Desert Shadows Inn is nudist. **Terra Cotta Inn** is "clothing optional."

Rancho Mirage

Marriott's Rancho Las Palmas Resort & Country Club, 41-000 Bob Hope Dr., ☎ 619/568-2727 or 800/458-8786, fax 619/862-4569, Web site www.desert-resorts.com, has 450 rooms and 22 suites in the two-story units that are positioned comfortably on 240 acres. There's a 27-hole Ted Robinson golf course, a nine-hole putting green, two heated outdoor pools and 25 tennis courts, three with red clay and 22 with a hard surface. There is an old-world Western feeling about this place, restful and understated.

Westin Mission Hills Resort, 71-333 Dinah Shore Dr., ☎ 619/328-5955 or 800/554-0287, fax 619/770-2199, Web site www.desert-resorts.com, sits at the corner of Dinah Shore and Bob Hope Drs. Its 360 acres contain 16 two-story Moroccan-style buildings with 472 rooms and 40 suites. One golf course was designed by Gary Player; the other by Pete Dye. There are seven night-lighted tennis courts and three swimming pools, one with a 60-foot waterslide.

Camping

Cleveland National Forest

Laguna Mountain Recreation Area has campgrounds at **Burnt Rancheria** and **Laguna**, and provides camping information for **Meadows, Desert View, Camp Ole Fire Station** and **Garnet**.

Other campgrounds in the forest include **Boulder Oaks, Bobcat Meadow, Four Corners Trailhead** and **Corral Canyon**.

Adjacent facilities that provide camping opportunities include **Morena County Park** and Reservoir, **Hauser Wilderness** and Barrett Lake and **Pine Creek Wilderness**.

Descanso

Cuyamaca Rancho State Park, 12551 Highway 79, ☎ 619/765-0755 or 800/444-PARK, permits camping in the **Paso Picacho Area** (81 developed sites, two group sites, and four environmental sites) and in the **Green Valley Area** (85 developed sites).

Arroyo Seco is a trail camp at a 4,290-foot elevation. It is located 1½ miles northwest of Green Valley Campground and eight miles southwest of Paso Picacho Campground.

Granite Springs, another trail camp, sits at 4,850 feet elevation, 4½ miles northeast of Green Valley Campground and seven miles southeast of Paso Picacho Campground.

Los Caballos Horse Camp has 16 campsites and **Los Vaqueros Group Camp** has 45 corrals. The latter is closed in the winter.

Julian

William Heise County Park, ☎ 619/694-3049, has interpretive trails and allows camping. Take Pine Hills Rd. to Frisius Rd. and turn left on Frisius.

La Quinta

Lake Cahuilla has provisions for RV and tent campers at 150 sites, 65 with full hookups.

Where To Eat

Borrego Springs

If **The Coffee & Book Store**, 590 Palm Canyon Dr., Ste. 202, ☎ 619/767-5080, has that big city look, all you have to do is step outside.

Kendall's Café, 528 The Mall, ☎ 619/767-3491, serves a mouth-watering half-pound buffalo burger.

La Casa Del Zorro Desert Resort, 3845 Yaqui Pass Rd., ☎ 619/767-5323, is a Southwestern-style dining room with gorgeous desert views. The **Fox Den** lounge has a fireplace and a piano bar that overlooks the pool.

Idyllwild

River Rock Café, 26290 Highway 243, ☎ 909/659-5047, is a European-style bistro.

The Chart House, 54905 N. Circle Dr., ☎ 909/659-4645, a chain, has been recommended at other locations throughout this guide for good reason. Their food, service and ambience are always excellent. Who wouldn't love a restaurant that provides caviar on its salad bar?

Indian Wells

Le St. Germain, 74-985 Highway 111, ☎ 619/773-6511, fax 619/773-6510, is a well-known name in French cuisine around Los Angeles.

Julian

Golden Apple, 2128 4th St., ☎ 619/765-2130, is rustic, colorful and always reliable.

Mom's Pies Etc., 2119 Main St., ☎ 619/765-2472, and **Julian Pie Co.**, 2225 Main St., ☎ 619/765-2449, serve apple pies "like Grandma used to bake." They're so good, in fact, that they draw people from throughout the San Diego area, especially during the fall apple-harvesting season.

Rongbranch Café, 2722 Washington St., ☎ 619/765-2265, adds a touch of Western flavor to your buffalo burger.

La Quinta

La Quinta Cliff House, 78-259 Highway 111, ☎ 619/360-5991, has received awards for its design. The food is prepared with a Hawaiian flavor (try Kimo's hula pie for dessert).

Cunard's, 78-045 Calle Cadiz, ☎ 619/564-4443, occupies the former home of photographer Mary Mead Maddock and has seven dining areas:

the patio, the Quarry Room, the Saloon, Michele's Room, Barbara's Room (which has a private fireplace), Living Room (which has a fireplace, a beamed ceiling and bookcases) and the Garden Room.

Palm Desert

Cuistot (chef, in French), 73-111 El Paseo, ☎ 619/340-1000, serves lunch Tuesday through Saturday and dinner Tuesday through Sunday. Chef Bernard Dervieux formerly was with Le Francais, an outstanding French restaurant in Wheeling, Illinois.

Palm Springs

Bono's Restaurant, 1700 N. Indian Canyon Dr., ☎ 619/322-6200, is owned by entertainer/Congressman Sonny Bono. (If the food wasn't good, would the residents have made him their mayor?)

Le Vallauris, 385 W. Tahquitz Canyon Way, ☎ 619/325-5059, fax 619/325-7602, is located near the Desert Museum and Fashion Plaza. Lunch and dinner are served daily and there is a Sunday brunch between 11:30 and 2:30. Owned by the same people who operate Le St. Germain in Indian Wells, the restaurant has served such dignitaries as Gen. George Patton, Ambassador Walter Annenberg, President Gerald Ford, actors Robert Redford and Kirk Douglas, and actresses Elizabeth Taylor and Suzanne Sommers. Pricey!

Melvyn's at the Ingleside Inn, ☎ 619/325-2323, is one of the authors' personal favorites. The lounge is open from 10 am to 2 am, and there is a piano bar with dancing. Special events, such as fashion shows, are scheduled regularly.

Lyons English Grille, 233 E. Palm Canyon Dr., ☎ 619/327-1551, serves a mean steak-and-kidney pie.

Rancho Mirage

The Chart House, 69-934 Highway 111, ☎ 619/324-5613. Need we say more?

Lord Fletcher Inn, 70-385 Highway 111, ☎ 619/328-1161, looks like an old English inn. Try the chicken and dumplings, the potato pancakes, and the English rice pudding served with raspberries or cinnamon and whipped cream.

Santa Ysabel

Julian Pie Co., 21976 Highway 79, ☎ 619/765-2400, is a branch of the store in Julian, which is just seven miles down the road.

Dudley's Bakery, Highway 78/79, ☎ 619/765-0488 or 800/225-3348, is famous for its Mesa Grande Mission Bread and 17 other bread varieties that are fresh-baked daily. Equally famous are their sweet rolls, cakes, pies, cookies and jams. Phone ahead and your order will be ready when you arrive.

DINNER THEATER

Julian

Pine Hills Lodge and Dinner Theatre, ☎ 619/765-1100, presents plays, dramas and musicals on most Friday and Saturday nights. A BBQ dinner is served at 8 before the curtain. Lodging is also available. Take Pine Hills Rd. to Blue Jay Rd. and follow the signs.

The Mexican Border

Mexico's relationships with the United States have not always been friendly. During the Mexican War (1846-48), the Baja Peninsula was occupied by U.S. troops and the commander of the American fleet proclaimed that the peninsula was annexed to the United States, but the land was returned to Mexico when a peace treaty was eventually negotiated.

The only time American soil has been invaded was when Pancho Villa attacked the little village of Columbus, New Mexico in 1916. The attack brought a massive retaliation from the United States under the leadership of Gen. John J. "Black Jack" Pershing.

Still, the Baja Peninsula was a difficult region for the Mexican central government to administer – remote and isolated. In 1853, William Walker, an American soldier of fortune, invaded Baja and proclaimed himself president of a new republic. Mexico ejected Walker and his followers the next year.

In 1911, socialist revolutionaries from Mexico and members of the International Workers of the World (Wobblies) in America, stormed Tiajuana and tried to establish a socialist revolution in Mexico. It lasted one month before the Mexican Army pushed them back across the border.

Many still believe that southern New Mexico, southern Arizona and California were forceably *taken* from the Mexicans by a larger, stronger, more affluent neighbor to the north.

Even today, questions of illegal immigration, drug smuggling and the exploitation of cheap Mexican labor as a result of the NAFTA accords are very sore subjects to many Mexicans and Americans alike.

Regardless, it is undeniable that a great deal of southern California's charm stems from its relationships with Mexico, both past and present. The Mexican influence is everywhere: In the vocabulary, in the red tile roofs seen on so many buildings, in the food, the dress, in the widespread use of patios (not only in homes but in office buildings) and in the customs of generations of Californians, Hispanic and Anglo alike.

It is unfortunate that so many people speed along the busy highway between Yuma, Arizona, and San Diego and never take the time to explore Mexico, even though the border is never more than 10 miles south of the interstate.

The Mexican Border

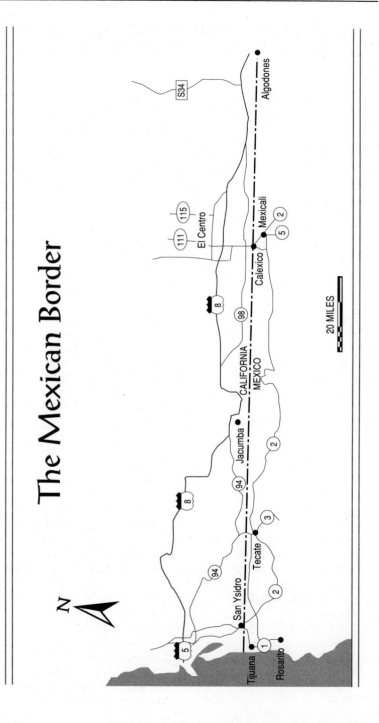

Getting Around

If you cross the border, remember at all times that Mexico is a foreign country and you are a guest. Be courteous, not demanding. Do your best to use some Spanish; it's a pleasant, romantic tongue and you can make yourself understood rather easily. Mexicans feel flattered when you try to speak their language, even if you handle it poorly. Most Mexicans speak English quite well. Your biggest problem probably will come from trying to interpret the signage. This abbreviated vocabulary may be helpful. As far as pronunciation goes, remember that two Ls (*camillia*) and ñ (the symbol over the N is called a tilde) are both pronounced *ya*; a J is pronounced liked an H; and an H isn't pronounced at all.

English-Spanish

Stop	*Alto*	Help	*Ayudar*
Highway	*Carretera*	Street	*Calle*
Number	*Numero*	Money	*Dinero*
Left	*Izquierda*	Right	*Derecho*
Water	*Agua*	Check	*Cuenta*
Room	*Sala*	Bed	*Cama*
Day	*Día*	Night	*Noche*
Today	*Hoy*	Tomorrow	*Mañana*
Yesterday	*Ayer*	Now	*Ahora*
Sunday	*Domingo*	Who?	*¿Quien?*
Monday	*Lunes*	What?	*¿Qué?*
Tuesday	*Martes*	When?	*¿Quando?*
Wednesday	*Miércoles*	Where?	*¿Dónde?*
Thursday	*Jueves*	How?	*¿Como?*
Friday	*Viernes*	Where is —?	*¿Dónde esta —?*
Saturday	*Sabado*	Menu	*Carta*
Restaurant	*Restaurante*	Post office	*Correo*
Bank	*Banco*	Change	*Cambio*
Breakfast	*Desayuno*	Please	*Por favor*
Lunch	*Almuerzo*	Thank you	*Gracias*
Dinner	*Cena or Comida*	You're welcome	*De nada*

Do you speak English?	*¿Habla inglés?*
How are you?	*¿Como esta?*
What time is it?	*¿Qué hora es?*
How much?	*¿Quanto dinero?*
Woman	*Dama*
Man	*Hombre.* In restaurant bathrooms, you might see *Caballero* (cowboy)
Child	*Niña* (girl), *niño* (boy)

Numbers are relatively easy, too.

1	*Uno*
2	*Dos*
3	*Tres*
4	*Cuatro*
5	*Cinco*
6	*Seis*
7	*Siete*
8	*Ocho*
9	*Nueve*
10	*Diez*

If you visit Mexico (and we certainly hope you do), take some proof of citizenship. A driver's license or Social Security card will do. A tourist card is not needed in border cities for stays up to 72 hours. If you plan to stay longer than that, they are available at the border, free of charge.

You will want to bring back some souvenirs and gifts (doesn't everyone?). Until you get pretty far inland, your American currency will see you through nicely, and so will travelers' checks and credit cards, but not personal checks. Generally, your duty-free exemption will be $400. For more specific information, get a copy of *U.S. Customs Pocket Hints* (Customs Publication 506) and *U.S. Customs GPS and the Traveler* (Customs Publication 515) from the **Department of the Treasury**, U.S. Customs Service, Washington, DC 20229.

If you are driving, remember that the Mexicans drive on the same side of the road that we do. They use the metric system of kilometers, rather than miles, and the metric system of litres instead of gallons for measuring gasoline. You do not need a copy of your auto registration *if* you stay in Baja. For more information, contact your nearest **Mexican Consulate** or phone ☎ 800/446-8277. Do get a copy of *Driving in Mexico*, which is provided free by the Mexican Ministry of Finance.

Distance Conversion

Kilometers	Miles
1	.6
2	1.2
5	3.0
10	6.0
20	12.0
50	31.0
100	62.0
200	124.0

Gasoline Conversion

Gallons	Liters
5	18.9
6	22.7
7	26.5
8	30.3
9	34.1
10	37.9

Your U.S. auto insurance is not valid in Mexico. Buy some Mexican auto insurance at the border.

Mexican law is not like American law. It is based on the Napoleonic Code, which means that a person who becomes involved in a crime is presumed guilty. If you should have a serious accident in Mexico, you and your car may be detained until the guilty party is determined, and damages must be paid on demand. Your American insurance carrier cannot send an adjuster to help you, and Mexican authorities will not accept your American insurance policy as proof of financial responsibility.

Once again: Be sure to purchase some Mexican auto insurance when you cross the border. It is not expensive and it could save you a great deal of grief.

Gasoline is abundant in Mexico. The dominant vendor is PEMEX, American currency is always accepted, and the staff will understand English.

If you have trouble on the road in Mexico, highway assistance is available. There are emergency telephones every two miles along the highway with which to contact the "Green Angels," Mexico's version of the AAA.

Also, be careful when you park your car. Auto theft is common along the border... and a terrible way to end your vacation. Leave your car in a fenced and lighted area, if at all possible, and someplace where there is a good deal of foot traffic. ALWAYS lock, and use an anti-theft device, such as the inexpensive Club or one of the more sophisticated systems like the Ravelco (6920 Oak Knoll, Richmond, TX 77469, ☎ 713/341-6222).

Many people prefer to park on the American side of the border and walk or taxi to the other side. Even then, be careful where you park or your car might get across the border faster than you do.

If you take a cab (*ruta*) in Mexico, always ask the driver to tell you the amount of the fare *before* you get into his vehicle. If the amount sounds like more than you're willing to pay, check with another cab driver.

Although tipping is a standard practice elsewhere in Mexico, *do not tip a cab driver* here.

If you intend to do some extensive touring – too much to do on foot or in a cab – and you are hesitant to drive your own car into Mexico, there's one other possibility: Renting a car. Hertz, Avis, Dollar and Budget all maintain offices in Tijuana.

None of this is intended to frighten you or to discourage you from visiting Mexico. Most Mexicans are warm, friendly, law-abiding people, and you should encounter no problems if you simply exercise good judgment and are careful of your car, your belongings and your person.

Touring

Algodones, Mexico

Directly opposite the unincorporated and insignificant little town of Andrade, California, Algodones is easternmost among the cities that abut the Mexican/American border. Santa Rosa, a larger and much lovelier Mexican community, is 25 miles farther south. Yuma, Arizona, is just 8½ miles to the east, on the other side of the Colorado River.

In the late 1800s this was a station on the old stagecoach route from Yuma to San Diego. Today, its features are heralded on billboards along Interstate 8, just a few miles north of the border: "Doctors, pharmacies, dentists."

Americans by the thousands go across the border to buy medicines or to acquire medical services that they can't get at home. Cancer cures, AIDS cures, herbal cures from China and Thailand, cures based on superstition. All of these and more are available in Mexico.

Actor Steve McQueen, star of the movie *Papillon* and the TV series *Wanted Dead or Alive*, went to Mexico when he discovered that he was dying of cancer, only to learn that the "miracle cures" they were advertising there couldn't help.

Buses connect Algodones with Mexicali, Mexico to the west.

Algodones Dunes

Early settlers called them the "walking hills." These enormous sand dunes are 27 miles of west of Yuma, Arizona, and 20 miles east of Brawley. Some crests reach heights of more than 300 feet.

Actually divided into two areas– the **Imperial Sand Hills National Natural Landmark**, ☎ 619/337-4400, and the **Algodones Dunes Off-Highway Vehicular Area** – the dunes harbor a rare flower, the silver-leafed dune sunflower and a rare lizard, the silvery zebra-tailed lizard (*Callisaurus draconoides*).

Until 1914, automobiles could not cross this sandy desert, so the State of California built a plank road consisting of two 2 x 12-inch planks laid parallel to each other and bound with cross-ties. Later, a sturdier replacement was built of four-inch-thick planks attached to cross-ties and bound with steel straps. Double sections were provided in some places to permit passing. For 10 years, before the first true highway was built, this was the only means of passage across this stretch of southern California by car. A rest stop on Interstate 8 preserves a portion of the old plank road for tourists to see.

Hugh Osborne Scenic Overlook, beside Highway 78, provides a marvelous panoramic view of the dunes.

Calexico/Mexicali, Mexico

The two largest cities directly opposing each other across the border between Mexico and the United States have adopted interesting names: **Calexico**, for **Cal**(*ifornia*) and (*M*)**exico**, and **Mexicali**, for **Mexi**(*co*) and **Cali**(*fornia*).

CALEXICO

Calexico, which has about 25,000 residents, is called the "Gateway to Mexico." It sits astride Highway 111 just a few miles south of the interstate.

Originally, this was a tent city, erected to shelter the crews working on the valley's first irrigation project for Imperial Land Co. The first adobe to replace the tents later became the post office.

There are two airports here, **Imperial County Airport** and **International Airport**, ☎ 619/768-2175, and the Imperial Valley campus of **San Diego State University**, 720 Heber Ave., ☎ 619/357-5520.

In mid-1996, a new $42 million international port of entry was completed seven miles east of town, almost two years behind schedule. Known as the **Calexico East Port of Entry**, it will henceforth serve all of the trucks crossing the border in this region.

De Anza Hotel, 233 4th St, ☎ 619/357-1112, built in 1930, is a colorful three-story building with a red tile roof and tile floors. It is located just three blocks from the border. In earlier times, movie stars stayed here while they gambled across the border in Mexicali. Recently, the old hotel was converted to a retirement home for low-income seniors.

Enrique S. Camarena Memorial Library was named for a federal officer who was killed while investigating a drug operation in Mexico. The officer had gone to school in Calexico.

For more information, contact **Calexico Chamber of Commerce**, PO Box 948, 1100 Imperial Ave., Calexico 92231, ☎ 619/357-1166, fax 619/

357-9043; or the **Mexican Consulate**, 331 Second St., PO Box 2478, Calexico 92231, ☎ 619/357-6284.

MEXICALI, MEXICO

Now numbering over 800,000 inhabitants, Mexicali was first known as La Laguna del Alamo (*the cottonwood lagoon*). Rio Nuevo (*new river*) runs through the town, separating Mexicali proper on the east side from Pueblo Nuevo on the west side. South of town are the Sierra de los Cucapas mountains.

El Centro, California, is just 13 miles away; Yuma, Arizona, 80 miles; San Diego, California, 108 miles; Tecate, Mexico, 88 miles; and Tijuana, Mexico, 108 miles. This makes Mexicali the most centrally-located border city in Baja California.

In 1887, Mexico divided Baja California into two federal districts. Their capitals were in La Paz and Enseñada. The Enseñada capital was later moved to Mexicali.

In 1952, the Northern Territory was made into a state, Estado de Baja California. (It should be noted that it is a mild insult to tell a Mexican that you are from "The United States." They too are from the united states: the united states of Mexico.)

The Valley of Mexicali is an extension of the California Imperial Valley, which benefited tremendously when the Imperial Valley was opened to irrigation in 1902. It shouldn't be surprising, then, to learn that the Mexicali area is rich in agriculture, primarily wheat and cotton. In fact, this is Mexico's largest cotton-growing region and the world's largest cotton gin, **Compania Industrial Jabonera del Pacifico**, is located at the south end of town.

Once, Mexicali was known for gambling, prostitution and opium refining. It also was a popular destination for Americans until Prohibition ended in 1933 and the Mexicans outlawed gambling in 1935.

On a per-capita basis, Mexicali has one of the highest concentrations of Chinese residents in Mexico. Lured by the promise of high wages, the Chinese came to seek work as laborers. A peak near town is named **El Chinero** in memory of 160 Chinese who died while trying to cross the pitiless San Felipe Desert. For a time, the desert itself was known as **El Desierto de los Chinos** (*Desert of the Chinese*), made notorious by the unscrupulous boatmen who would unload their human cargo near the mouth of the Colorado River and tell them that Mexicali was just a short distance away.

At one time, there was a substantial *Chinesca* (Chinatown) in Mexicali, with underground tunnels that linked bordellos, opium dens and Calexico on the other side of the border. During Prohibition, the tunnels also were used by bootleggers.

Mexicali once served as the Mexican headquarters for Sun Yatsen's nationalist Chinese party.

Mexicali

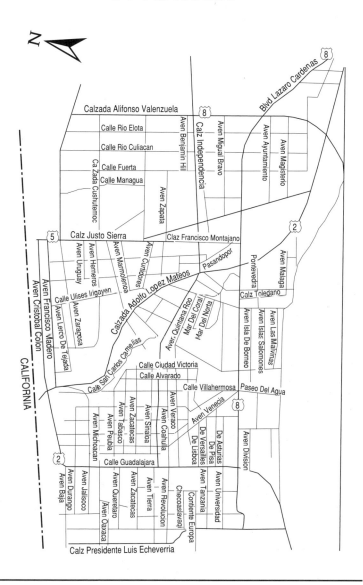

In recent years, the introduction of *maquiladoras*, Mexican assembly plants associated with foreign (predominantly American) manufacturing companies, has introduced a new source of revenue to the region. At the present time, there are over 150 *maquiladoras* operating at 11 different industrial parks near Mexicali. One of the most recent newcomers is the South Korean electronics giant Daewoo, which has announced plans to build a $300,000 picture tube plant in Mexicali.

A relatively new "sulphur fragrance" has been coming from a geothermal plant in the area... and has been causing complaints.

Nearby, there are thermal springs in Cañon de Guadalupe and salt flats at Laguna Salada.

A $400 million natural gas pipeline was completed between the United States and Mexicali in 1996.

As to climate, Mexicali is at sea level, which means that it enjoys (or endures, depending on your point of view) something of a desert climate. The area receives a little over three inches of rain a year. The coldest months are from December to February, and the hottest, June to September. At times, it can be 120° during the day and 60° at night.

Long-time residents of Mexicali are known as Cachañillas (pronounced *catch-a-KNEE-yahs*).

Fiestas del Sol, a 17-day festival that runs from October 9-26, celebrates the founding of the city.

Mexicali has an airport, four institutions of higher learning and a regional museum.

Street signage here is notoriously poor.

For more information, contact **Mexical Tourism and Convention Bureau** information booth, Blvd. Adolfo Lopez Mateos and Calle Compresora, ☎ 0115265-52-58-77 or the **State Secretary of Tourism**, Calle Calafia and Calz. Independencia, ☎ 56-10-72 or 56-11-72, fax 56-12-82.

Jacumba

From an Indian word meaning "hut by the water," this tiny town is noted for its mineral springs and baths.

In 1852, James McCoy founded this town and built a small fort for protection against the Indians. He is said to have held off 500 Indians during one raid.

East of town, where Highway 98 intersects with I-8, **Jacumba Outstanding Natural Area** lies between the interstate and the Mexican border.

Tecate, Mexico

Set in a bowl-shaped valley in the lower Sierra Juarez mountains, Tecate (translated as "where the sun passes") is the oldest border town in Baja.

The Yuma Indians called the valley Zacate and revered the nearby 5,000-foot Monte Cuchuma (aka Pico Tecate), the valley's most outstanding geographic feature. The Kumyais, a subtribe of the Yumas, still revere the mountain.

In 1892, a national rail system connected Tecate with Tijuana and Mexicali. The railroad now carries only freight, meaning that the nearest passenger service is in Mexicali, but there is frequent bus service to Mexicali, Tijuana, Enseñada and Puerto Peñasco.

A new toll road links Tijuana and Mexicali by way of Tecate.

The countryside surrounding Tecate produces grapes, olives and grains.

There is an annual celebration of the grape harvest, usually held on the first Sunday in July, and the Tecate-Enseñada bicycle race is said to be the largest in the world.

Parque Hidalgo, the municipal park, hosts Saturday evening summer band concerts when government funds are available.

Museo Municipal, Ave. Benito Juarez between Calle Santana and Calle Esteban, is a museum of regional art and archaeology a mile west of Parque Hidalgo.

Cerveceria Cuahutemoc, Ave. Hidalgo between Calle Lazaro Cadenas and Calle Alvaro Obregon, produces Tecate and Carta Blanca beer, two of Mexico's biggest sellers. Tecate is the only beer in Mexico named for a town, and it was first brewed in 1943, but after 10 years, the brewery went broke. In 1954, it was purchased by Cerveceria Cuahutemoc, the highly-successful brewers of Carta Blanca and Bohemia beer. Today, the company also produces Chihuahua, Indio and High Life beer and has two subsidiaries, Dos Equis and Sol. It also has breweries in six other Mexican cities.

West of town is the village of Francisco Zarco and the **Museo Comunitario del Valle de Guadalupe**, which has an interesting collection of Russian and Kumiai Indian artifacts. The village is also the home of **Monte Xanic Winery**.

For more information, contact the **Tourist information booth**, border crossing at Calle Lazaro Cardenas and Calle Madero; or the **State Tourist Office**, south side of Parque Hadalgo, ☎ 665-4-10-95.

Border Field State Park

Located just north of the Mexican border (see *Palm Springs Area*, page 245), the park is often closed because of contamination from Tijuana.

This was a Navy landing field during World War II.

San Ysidro/Tijuana, Mexico

SAN YSIDRO

Once named Tia Juana, this border community changed its name to honor the patron saint of Madrid after realizing that its original name was causing too much confusion among those headed for Tijuana across the border.

The area near the pedestrian footbridge linking these two neighboring cities has been closed occasionally due to recent fights, assaults, robberies and rowdy behavior. A genuine pity.

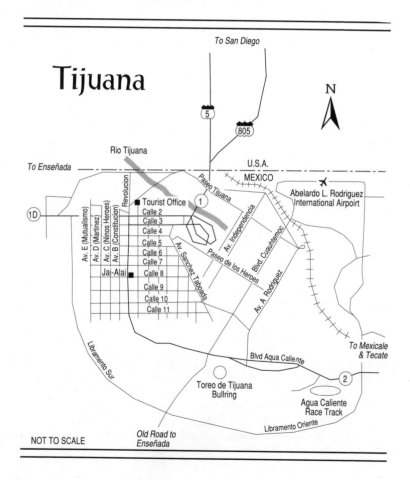

Tijuana

To San Diego

N

To Ensenada

Rio Tijuana

U.S.A.
MEXICO

Abelardo L. Rodriguez
International Airpoirt

Tourist Office

Calle 2
Calle 3
Calle 4
Calle 5
Calle 6
Calle 7
Calle 8
Calle 9
Calle 10
Calle 11

Jai-Alai

Av. E (Mutualismo)
Av. D (Martinez)
Av. C (Ninos Heroes)
Av. B (Constitucion)
Revolucion

Paseo Tijuana
Av. Independencia
Av. Sanchez Taboada
Paseo de los Heroes
Blvd. Cuauhtemoc
Av. A. Rodriguez

Libramento Sur

To Mexicale
& Tecate

Blvd Aqua Caliente

Toreo de Tijuana
Bullring

Agua Caliente
Race Track

Libramento Oriente

NOT TO SCALE

Old Road to
Ensenada

TIJUANA, MEXICO

The border never closes at the "Window of Mexico."

If you are driving a passenger car to downtown Tijuana, take the Centro Comercial off-ramp, which cloverleafs, and exit on Third St. Follow Third St. to Avenida Revolucion and turn right into the Woolworth parking lot at Third and Revolucion.

If you are driving a trailer, however, take the Ensenada Freeway.

When you return to the United States, be prepared for long delays at the border, especially on Monday mornings. Two-hour waits are not uncommon. If you can, wait until 7 or so in the evening, after the rush hour has passed, to cross the border. (Turn your car radio to 690 AM. Border crossing times at San Ysidro and at Otay Mesa are broadcast every 15 minutes.)

Using the telephone to call into Mexico can be somewhat confusing. When dialing a Tijuana number from somewhere else in Mexico, dial 91-66 and then the six-digit telephone number. When dialing from the United States, dial 011-52-66 before dialing the six-digit telephone number.

This region was called Ti-uan ("near the water") by the early Indians. In 1829, it was the site of the 25,000-acre Tia Juana Ranch. A town wasn't settled until 70 years later.

Not until 1929 did Tijuana became popular with its North American neighbors, who came to enjoy the Agua Caliente race track, the Grand Casino and freedom from the restrictions of Prohibition. It now receives 45 million tourists each year.

With nearly two million population, Tijuana is now the fourth largest city in all of Mexico.

The city has an average rainfall of just 12.4 inches a year, almost all of it coming between December and April. A constant breeze blows off the Pacific, five miles away. During the summer, fogs often set in at night but lift in the early morning.

Visitors can take a trolley from San Diego to Tijuana since the two are just 16 miles apart. Greyhound buses also connect the two cities. In town, a **Mexicoche** bus goes through the downtown area, to the jai alai fronton, to Agua Caliente and to Ensenada and Rosarito.

Abelardo L. Rodriguez Airport, ☎ 83-21-02 or 83-24-18, is just south of the border and two miles northeast of Tijuana.

A visit to Mexico provides you with an opportunity to see some sports that are unfamiliar to most Americans: dog racing, bullfighting and jai alai. Each affords an interesting experience.

Greyhound racing is held in **Hipodrómo Caliente**, Blvd. Agua Caliente and Tapachula 12027, ☎ 81-78-11. There are races on weekday afternoons and there are nightly races except on Tuesdays.

Tijuana has two bullrings: **El Toreo de Tijuana**, Agua Caliente Blvd. 100, ☎ 80-18-08, and **Plaza Monumental**, the second largest bullring in the world, located west of the city beside the Pacific Ocean. The four-month season runs from May until September. All fights begin at 4 pm.

Fronton Palacio Jai Alai de Tijuana, Av. Revolución and Calle 8, ☎ 85-25-12/24/33, is in the Zona Centro. Similar to a high-speed game of handball in which the players wear a curved mitt or sling for handling the hard-rubber ball, jai alai is one of the fastest sports in the world. Matches are played every evening (except Thursday) at 8, and betting is permitted. (You place a bet according to the color of the armband your chosen team is wearing.)

INFORMATION SOURCES

Tijuana Information Center, Ave. Revolucion between 3rd and 4th Sts., downtown, ☎ 88-05-30; just past Customs as you enter Mexico; Ave. Revolucion at 1st St.; Ave. Revolucion #77 between 1st and 2nd Sts., Zona Centro; or Paseo de los Heroes at Ave. Independencia, opposite the Cultural Center.

Tijuana Convention & Visitors Bureau, ☎ 84-05-37/38.

Chamber of Commerce Information Center, ☎ 88-16-85 or 85-84-72, fax 85-84-72.

State Tourism Assistance Office, ☎ 88-05-55, fax 81-95-79.

U.S. Consulate, Tapachula #96, Col. Hipodromo, Tijuana, ☎ 81-74-00, fax 81-80-16, near Agua Caliente Race Track.

Mexican Consulate in San Diego, ☎ 619/231-5843 or 231-0337, fax 619/231-9046.

Baja Norte Information, ☎ 619/298-4105 or 800/522-1516.

Secretaria de Turismo de Baja California, PO Box 2448, Chula Vista, CA 91912.

Rosarito, Mexico

Eighteen miles south of the U.S. border, Rosarito is an endless stretch of beaches and desert hills. A popular resort area for American tourists, the town has 500 stores and 100 restaurants.

At an elevation of 2,500 feet, it has a landing strip, *maquiladores* and a cattle ranch.

San Borja Mission is 22 miles up a nearby arroyo.

For a free fun guide, contact ☎ 619/234-5652 or 800/962-2252.

Ensenada, Mexico

➡ *NOTE: The prefixes on local telephone numbers are undergoing revision. The numbers listed here may no longer be valid, so it might be wise to check with Information or a local telephone book before trying to reach a local attraction.*

The "Cinderella of the Pacific" is located just 70 miles south of the border and is linked to Tijuana by a toll road.

Before the capital of Baja California moved to Mexicali, Ensenada ("bay") held that distinction. Now its economy is based largely on tourism and fish canneries. Many American retirees live here, particularly in **Chapultepec**, the residential section atop the hill north of town.

If you drive into town, park at the **Plaza Marina** on the waterfront and explore the town on foot.

The mountainous **Punta Banda** peninsula lies southwest of **Todos Santos Bay**, on which the city is situated. At the end of the peninsula, 23 miles south of town, is **La Bufadora**, a blowhole that shoots streams of water up to 100 feet in the air. Lying in the ocean off the peninsula are the Todos Santos ("all saints") Islands. At Christmas, there is a parade of boats and a fiesta on Todos Santos Bay.

The weather is usually cold and raw in the winter, and there is generally fog in the early morning, especially during the summer.

Cruise ships anchor offshore and ferry their passengers to the pier for a few hours of sightseeing and shopping.

The airport is in El Cipres, five miles south of town.

Viajes Guaycura, Lopez Mateos 1089, ☎ 617/8-3718, charters half-day bus tours of the city and the surrounding area.

For more information, contact the **Tourist Office**, on Lopez Mateo Blvd. and Ave. Espinoza, across the dry Arroyo Ensenada and south of Fonda Santa Maria, ☎ 91-617-8-24-11, fax 91-617-8-36-75; or **Ensenada Tourism & Convention Bureau**, Blvd. Costero and Calle Las Rocas, ☎ 78-2411 or 78-3675, fax 78-8588.

Puerto Nuevo, Mexico

Puerto Nuevo ("Newport") is known throughout the region for its lobster.

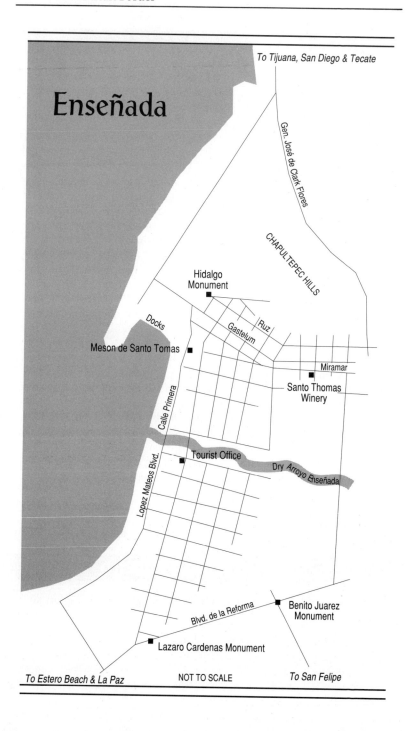

Enseñada

Adventures

On Foot

Border Field State Park

This area is a favorite of hikers. **Border Field Trail** begins in the southwesternmost corner of the United States, where a monument marks the border between Mexico and California. Follow the bluff trail to the beach and turn north along the shoreline. On the other side of the dunes is the **Tijuana River Estuary**, a breeding ground and nesting spot for more than 170 species of native and migratory birds. After 1½ miles, you will reach the mouth of the Tijuana River. Most of the time, the river is fordable at low tide, but use caution. After crossing the river you will be on Imperial Beach, which offers good swimming and surfing. The trail ends at the Imperial Pier, the oldest in the county, built in 1912.

Enseñada, Mexico

Jogging is superb along the wide sandy beaches here and in nearby Puerto Nuevo, and there is some fine hiking in the nearby hills.

Mexicali, Mexico

The **Rio Hardy** area is excellent for hunting doves and waterfowl.

Rosarito, Mexico

There is good hunting for deer and small game in this region.

TREASURE HUNTING

South of the border from Mt. Signal, cone-shaped **Signal Mountain** looms against the skyline. Old mines pock-mark the sides of the mountain.

According to legend, the Cocopah and Yuma Indian tribes engaged in a battle long ago. The Cocopahs escaped to Signal Mountain with their injured chief and a fortune in gold that they had stolen from the Yumas. The gold supposedly was buried near the mountain.

Another tale of treasure involves a cave full of stolen loot. As the story goes, a gang was being chased by a posse after it had committed a robbery. The posse killed one of the outlaws, but the gang escaped in two buckboards and headed toward Signal Mountain. Along the way, the gang abandoned the dead outlaw and a store of rifles in one of the buckboards, while they loaded their loot – jewelry, gold coins, bullion – into the other buckboard. The treasure, buckboard and all, was hidden in a huge cave, and the gang then used dynamite to conceal the cave's entrance. Eventually, all of the outlaws were caught and killed before any of them could return for the loot. Over the years, fortune-hunters claim to have located a wagon wheel, a man's bones, a fuse and some black powder... but no one has been able to find the hidden cave.

Even in a four-wheel-drive vehicle, the region is formidable. Following a storm, the washes are impassible, and between storms the deep sand can be a substantial hazard.

On Horseback

Border Field State Park

This park has numerous fine riding trails.

Enseñada, Mexico

The wide sandy beach is excellent for horseback riding. The same is true at nearby Puerto Nuevo.

Rosarito, Mexico

Rosarito has miles of riding trails.

CHARREADA (MEXICAN RODEO)

In Mexico, the *charro* (cowboy) is judged more on his style than on his time in a given event. *Charreadas* are more festive than American rodeos, and given to the wearing of elaborate costumes and playing of music.

In Tijuana, *charreadas* are held throughout the city on Saturdays and Sundays from May through September. Some of the largest sites are **Lienzo Charro La Misión**, Ave. Braulio Maldonado, ☎ 66-80-41-85, in the Zona Misión; **Cortijo San José**, in the Playas Tijuana district; and **Lienzo Charro Misión del Sol** near the Plaza Monumental bullring.

For more information, contact **Charro Association**, ☎ 81-34-01 or 81-26-11.

On Wheels

Algodones Dunes

Algodones Dunes Off-Highway Vehicle Area just off I-8 is a specially designated area for driving OHVs through the sand dunes.

Rosarito, Mexico

In this hilly country beside the ocean, mountain biking is excellent.

Calexico

There is excellent off-road motoring in the **Colorado Desert** beside the highway.

San Felipe, Mexico

The nearby sand dunes provide for top-notch off-road driving.

On & In the Water

Border Field State Park

Fishing is good for perch, corbina and halibut, both in the surf and in the estuary.

Ensenada, Mexico

South of town, **Estero Beach** is long and clean for swimming, and it has mild waves.

Surfers prefer such beaches as **California, La Joya, San Miguel** and **Tres Marías.**

Scuba divers like **Punta Banda** beach.

A map of the best surfing and diving area can be obtained at the Tourist Office.

➡ *CAUTION: There are few lifeguards on these beaches.*

Whale-watching excursions to **Scammon's Lagoon** are offered from January through March.

Marlin and swordfish are caught offshore. The town also has a fishing pier. Bottom fishing is good in the winter, but the best fishing takes place between April and November.

Gordo's Sportfishing, Sportsfishing Pier, ☎ 617/8-2190, charters fishing trips and whale-watching excursions.

Rosarito, Mexico

One of Baja's widest and longest sandy beaches makes for ideal swimming.

Surfing is good at **Popotla** (Km 33), **Calafia** (Km 35.5) and **Costa Baja** (Km 36) off the Old Enseñada Highway.

There is a small fishing pier at Km 33 on the Old Enseñada Highway and surf casting is allowed from the beach.

San Felipe, Mexico

Some 800 species of saltwater fish, including sea bass, corvina, halibut and cabrilla, haunt these waters, making this one of the best saltwater fishing spots in Baja.

In the spring (March through May), yellowtail, grouper, snapper, whitefish, squid and pinto bass predominate.

In the summer (June through August), sailfish, dolphin, marlin, roosterfish, yellowfin tuna, bonita, sierra and wahoo move in.

In the fall (September through November), sailfish, dolphin, marlin, roosterfish, skipjack, bonita, tuna and sierra get most of the attention.

In the winter (December through February), yellowtail, grouper, pinto bass, snapper and whitefish prevail.

Tijuana, Mexico

Freshwater fishing is available in the lake behind **Rodriguez Dam**.

Eco-Travel/Cultural Excursions

Campo

San Diego Railroad Museum, Forest Gate Rd. off Highway 94, ☎ 619/595-3030 (Monday through Friday) or 478-9937 (Saturday and Sunday), houses vintage locomotives, freight and passenger cars in a 1915 depot. Tours of equipment shops and restoration areas are conducted at noon and 2:30, as are 16-mile, 1½-hour train rides. The tour of the museum is free; the train ride costs $10.

Enseñada, Mexico

Monuments to former presidents **Hidalgo**, **Benito Juarez** and **Lazaro Cardenas** embellish the streets.

At **Plaza Civica**, you can pick up a horse-drawn carriage in which to tour the town.

Riviera del Pacifico, Blvd. Costero and Ave. Riviera, ☎ 617/6-4310, is a former gambling hall, built in the 1920s. The white adobe, hacienda-style mansion once was very popular with the Hollywood stars. Now officially known as **El Centro Social, Civico y Cultural de Ensenada**, the building occasionally hosts art shows and civic events. Tours are available.

Our Lady of Guadalupe, Ave. Floresta and Juarez, is the city's largest cathedral.

Bodegas de Santo Tomas winery, Av. Miramar #666, ☎ 78-3333 or 78-2509, is Baja's oldest winery. Three 45-minute tours are given daily, permitting visitors to sample 14 different wines as they nibble on bread and cheese. **La Embotelladora Vieja Restaurant** occupies a section of the winery that once was used to store wines in huge wooden vats for aging.

Cavas Valmar, Calle Ambar #810, ☎ 78-6405 or 74-2469, is a small "boutique" winery.

Husson's Cantina, Av. Ruiz #113, ☎ 78-3210, is the oldest bar in the Californias. In 1882, Johan Husson and two of his brothers traveled from Germany to New York City, then on to here. Ricardo Husson, the current owner/manager, represents the third generation to operate the bar, which has been frequented through the years by such celebrities as Marilyn Monroe, Bing Crosby, Steve McQueen and Phil Harris. Husson's *negra* (dark) and *clara* (pilsner-like) beers are now being sold in southern California.

Aduana Maritima, Av. Ryerson #1, is the oldest public building in Baja. Built in 1887, it is a former customs house, but now serves at the **National Institute of Anthropology & History**.

Museo de Ciencias, Av. Obregon between Calles 14 and 15, ☎ 8-7192, is dedicated to the "accurate and natural sciences."

Estero Beach Museum, six miles south of town, ☎ 76-6235, contains Mexican folk art.

Laguna Hanson National Park is located nearby in the Sierra de Juarez mountains.

Mision San Miguel Arcangel de la Frontera, the ruins of a 1787 Dominican mission, is at Km 65.5 along the Tijuana-Ensenada free road.

Mision de Santo Tomas, the ruin of a 1791 Dominican mission, is in El Palomar, 29 miles south of town on Highway 1.

Mexicali, Mexico

Parque Chapultepec, Ave. Madero at Calle Altamirano, is the classic center of old Mexicali.

Casa de la Cultura, the cultural center, is located on Parque Chapultepec.

El Teatro del Estado, Blvd. Lopez Mateos, hosts theater, dance and music.

Lago Xochimilco has a small zoo.

Plaza de Toros Califia, Ave. Califia two blocks from Blvd. Lopez Mateos, hosts bullfights every other Sunday from October to May. Get a seat on the *sombra* (shady) side of the arena, even through they cost a little more.

Tijuana, Mexico

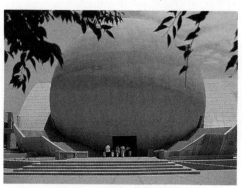

Tijuana Cultural Center.
Credit: Bob Yarbrough, San Diego Convention & Visitors Bureau

There is a monument to **Abraham Lincoln** here.

Tijuana Cultural Center, Paseo de los Héroes y Mina, ☎ 011-52-668-41111, features an Omnimax Space Theater in a sphere 85 feet tall, held upon a stylized hand to symbolize the earth housing a world of culture. The complex also houses four exhibit halls and a multilevel cultural and historical museum.

Mexitlan, Ave. Benito Juarez No. 8901, Zona Centro, ☎ 38-41-44 or 38-41-01, contains 200 miniature scale-model (1:25) replicas of Mexico's most famous historical monuments.

State Park Jose Maria Morelos y Pavon, Blvd. Insurgentes 16000, ☎ 25-24-69/70, has an aquarium, a theater and a Children's Creative Center.

Hipodrómo Caliente, Blvd. Agua Caliente and Tapachula 12027, ☎ 81-78-11, was a world-famous race track in its day. Such well-known horses as Phar Lap, Seabiscuit and Round Table once ran at Agua Caliente. The grounds also feature a zoo.

Palacio de Gobierno ("Governor's Palace"), Avenida Obregon, is surrounded by parks. Two blocks southwest of the palace is **Mexicali Brewery**.

Where To Stay

B&Bs, Hotels & Inns

Calafia, Mexico

According to a 15th-century Spanish romance novel, Calafia was the queen of a mythical island named California. This **Calafia**, located six miles south of Rosarito, (from the U.S.) PO Box 433857, San Diego 92143-3857, ☎ 800/CALAFIA or 011-52-661-2-15-80, fax 011-52-661-2-15-81, is not a city but a stand-alone "historic, cultural and touristic polycenter" perched on a bluff beside El Descanso Bay. The facility includes a hotel, restaurant, night club, conference center, tourist center, Mesoamerican anthropological art gallery and an extension of the university campus. Nearby are the **Cristo del Mar** ("Christ of the Sea") **Chapel**, a part of the old **El Descanso Forte**, and the *Corona Aurea* galleon.

Calexico

Hollie's Fiesta Hotel, 801 Imperial Ave., ☎ 619/357-3271, has 60 rooms, a pool, a restaurant and a bar.

Enseñada, Mexico

Hotel Paraiso las Palmas, Blvd. Sanginez 206, is the area's newest ocean-view hotel. From the United States, write 482 W. San Ysidro Blvd., Suite 2507, San Ysidro 92173.

Mexicali, Mexico

Hotel Crowne Plaza, Blvd. Lopez Mateos and Ave. de los Heroes, C.P. 21000, ☎ 57-36-00, fax 57-05-55, is a five-star hotel with 158 rooms and suites, a gym, a coffee shop, a restaurant, a bar and a day nursery.

> ➡ *NOTE: Under Mexico's system of evaluating accommodations, it's usually a good idea to knock at least one star off the rating; i.e., reduce a five-star hotel to four stars.*

Hotel Colonial, Blvd. Lopez Mateos and Calle Calafia No. 1024, ☎ 56-13-40 (to -52), fax 66-47-06, is a four-star hotel with 145 rooms, a laundromat, a travel agency, a car rental agency and two pools.

Hotel Lucerna, Blvd. Benito Juarez No. 2151, ☎ 66-10-00, a four-star establishment, has 190 rooms, a coffeeshop, two restaurants, three bars, a night club, a car rental agency, a day nursery, a beauty parlor, a gym, a gift shop and a travel agency.

Puerto Nuevo, Mexico

The Grand Baja Resort, Km 44.5 Carretera Libre, offers a veriety of ocean-front condominiums, including 60 one- and two-bedroom villas and 40 junior suites. Each villa has a fully equipped kitchenette and satellite TV. There is a swimming pool, a spa, two lighted tennis courts, a playground and a basketball court. It is just a short walk to **Puerto Nuevo Lobster Village**, site of more than 30 restaurants, almost all of them specializing in the famous Puerto Nuevo lobster. From the United States, contact 2630 E. Beyer Blvd., #44, San Ysidro 92143, ☎ 011-52-661-4-1493.

Hotel New Port Beach, Km 45 Carretera Libre, ☎ 800/582-1018, provides 147 ocean-view rooms, a heated outdoor pool, a spa, a workout room, tennis courts and a restaurant and bar.

Rosarito, Mexico

This waterfront resort community has numerous luxury resorts, oceanfront condos, hotels and RV parks.

Rosarito Beach Hotel & Spa, ☎ 011-52-661-20144, fax 011-52-661-21176, has been in service since 1926. During that time, it has entertained author Damon Runyon, race car driver Barney Oldfield, and movie personalities like Vincent Price, Mickey Rooney, Lana Turner, Orson Welles, Burgess Meredith and Rita Hayworth. Just 45 minutes from downtown San Diego, the hotel has 280 rooms, swimming pools and a spa. Kids under 12 stay free, and seniors get a 20% discount. On Friday and Saturday there is a Fiesta Mexican Dinner Buffet. In the United States, write PO Box 430145, San Diego, CA 92143-0145, ☎ 619/498-8230 or 800/343-8582.

Brisas Del Mar Hotel, Blvd. Benito Juarez #22, ☎ 01152 661/2-25-47 or PO Box 1867, Chula Vista, CA 91912-1867, ☎ 800/697-5223, is located in downtown Rosarito. A small hotel with only 71 rooms, it is air-conditioned and has satellite TV, a heated pool, a spa, a restaurant and a bar. There's also a volleyball court.

Las Rocas Hotel & Suites, Km 38.5 Tijuana-Ensenada "Libre" Road, ☎ 011-52-661-2-21-40, or PO Box 189003-HLR, Coronado, CA 92178-9003, ☎ 888/527-7622, is a multistory hilltop hotel overlooking the ocean. It has 26 luxury suites with a fireplace, coffeemaker, refrigerator and microwave; eight deluxe rooms; and 40 regular rooms. All rooms have an oceanfront view and a private terrace. There are two restaurants, two bars, two pools, three spas, tennis courts and live music on the weekends.

Quinta Pacifica, 25500 Benito Juarez Blvd., ☎ 011-52-661-2-12-15, features beachfront *cabanas* (cabins) – the only ones in Rosarito. Each has two bedrooms, two baths, a living room, a dining room, a fully equipped kitchen, a patio with BBQ grill and daily maid service.

Oasis Hotel & RV Resort, Km 25 Tijuana-Enseñada Highway 1-D, ☎ 011-52-661-3-3250/53/55 in Mexico and PO Box 158, Imperial Beach, CA 91933, ☎ 619/291-6292, 800/522-1516 or 888/709-9985 in the U.S., is 15 miles south of Tijuana on the toll road to Enseñada. The beachfront property has 100 all-suite rooms, 22 fully equipped RV units, 55 full hookup RV sites, two pools, two spas, a children's pool, gym, sauna, tennis court, putting green, game room, convention center and the Camello Beach restaurant & bar with live music on weekends.

Tecate, Mexico

Rancho Tecate Resort County Club, ☎ 665-4-00-11, fax 4-02-11 in Mexico or ☎ 619/234-7951 in the U.S., is six miles southeast of town off Highway 3. It is a sprawling, hacienda-style resort with a nine-hole golf course, pool, tennis courts and a lake stocked with fish. Some suites are available.

Hacienda Santa Veronica, 74818 Vellie Dr., Suite 4, Palm Desert, CA 92260, ☎ 66-85-97-93 in Mexico or ☎ 619/341-9811 or 298-4105 in the U.S., is a newer ranch than Rancho Tecate and is located near Km 98 on Highway 2, 20 miles east of Tecate. Originally a breeding ranch for fighting bulls, elementary bullfighting lessons are still offered to guests. Mission-style condos have fireplaces and patios, while the resort provides six tennis courts, offroad racetracks for motorcycles and four-wheelers, equestrian trails, a pool, a volleyball court and a basketball court. There also is a restaurant, a bar and an RV park.

Rancho La Puerta, PO Box 2548, Escondido, CA, ☎ 800/443-7565, fax 619/744-5007, is located near sacred Monte Cuchuma. A pricey health resort frequented by CEOs and Hollywood stars, the rancho was founded in a remodeled stable by Hungarian Edmond Szekeley and his wife Deborah as the "Essence School of Life" in 1940. Today, the 125-acre resort and the **Golden Door** spa in Escondido, California are run by their son Alex. The resort is not open on a day-by-day basis. A week-long regimen includes mountain hiking, low-impact aerobics, yoga, t'ai chi, swimming and weight-training. Accommodations include cottages and suites, most with fireplaces and each with a garden. The dining hall serves organic fruits and vegetables grown in the rancho's subsidiary, Rancho Tres Estrella. Massages and herbal wraps are available, and there are four swimming pools, six aerobic gyms, five whirlpools and three saunas on the grounds.

Tijuana, Mexico

Grand Hotel Tijuana, Blvd. Agua Caliente No. 4500, ☎ 81-70-00, is a five-star hotel located near the Agua Caliente Race Track and Tijuana Country Club.

Holiday Inn Tijuana, Pueblo Amigo, Via Oriente #9211, Zona Rio, ☎ 83-50-30/31/32, which also has a five-star rating, is the closest hotel to the border crossing.

Country Club Hotel, Blvd. Agua Caliente and Tapachula St., ☎ 01152-66-817733 or 800/303-2684, has rooms overlooking the Tijuana Campestre golf course. It is just one block from the U.S. Consulate.

Howard Johnson Hotel El Conquistador, Blvd. Agua Caliente #1777, ☎ 81-79-55, near Agua Caliente Race Track and the Tijuana Country Club, has a four-star rating.

Hotel Plaza Las Glorias, Blvd. Agua Caliente #11553, Col. Aviacion, ☎ 81-72-00, is located between the country club and the greyhound race track. It has 200 rooms and suites, an outdoor pool, a spa, tennis courts and golf facilities.

Hotel Real del Rio, Jose Maria Velasco #1409, Zona Rio, ☎ (66) 34-31-00, bears a four-star rating and is Tijuana's newest hotel. It has 103 rooms and two junior suites.

Hotel Otay Bugambilias, Ave. Tijuana #1600, Col. Industrial Nva., ☎ 23-84-11/12/13/14/15/16, a four-star hotel, is nearest the airport.

Camping

Enseñada, Mexico

Cortez Trailer Park and **Playita Trailer Park** are on Highway 1 north of town.

Playa Enseñada RV Park is south of town.

Call ☎ 011-52-671-23022 for information on all of these.

Where To Eat

Calexico

A typical American small town. The best dining in Calexico can be found either in Carrow's or at Denny's.

Both **Sam's Club** and the **Sizzler Restaurant** have recently gone out of business, leaving only **McDonald's**, **Subway**, **Wendy's**, **Burger King**, **KFC**, **Domino's Pizza**, and **Jack in the Box**. Suggestion: Go across the border to eat.

Enseñada, Mexico

La Cueva De Los Tigres ("the tiger's cave") is two miles south of town at Playa Hermosa, ☎ 011-52-617-66450. Try the breaded abalone steak sauteed in butter and topped with crabmeat and white wine.

Restaurant Haliotis ("abalone" in Greek), Av. Delante #179, ☎ 76-3720, serves lobster and abalone year-round.

Restaurant Sorrento, Cortez Hotel, Av. Lopez Mateos #1089, ☎ 78-3563, has an Italian menu.

Restaurant Sofia y Alma serves seafood. While you're here, try the fish tacos. Delicious!

If you insist on eating "American" food, there's a **KFC** at Lopez Mateos Blvd. and Blvd. de la Reforma.

Mexicali, Mexico

There are numerous Oriental restaurants in town, due to the heavy Chinese population. You can even get shark's fin tacos!

Asadero Los Brasa, Islas Bahamas No. 801, Montealban; **La Lena**, Calz. Cuauhtemoc No. 354, Cuauhtemoc; **Los Buffalos Cachanilla**, Centro Comercial; and **Villa del Seri**, Ave. Reforma and Calle "D," are steak houses.

Mariscos el Trailero, Carretera a San Felipe Km. 18, and **Nuevo Hunan**, Blvd. Benito Juarez No. 3810, serve seafood.

Las Campañas, Blvd. Justo Sierra No. 375, specializes in French cuisine.

Mandolino, Ave. Reforma No. 1070, caters to Italian tastes. American fast food chains are represented at **Burger King**, Centro Comercial Gigante, Blvd. Benito Juarez; **El Pollo Loco**, Blvd. Lazaro Cardenas No. 1087; and **Round Table Pizza**, Centro Civico, Av. Romulo O'Farril No. 971-A.

Rosarito, Mexico

La Casa de La Langosta, Quinta Plaza Shopping Center south of town, ☎ 011-52-661-2-09-24, serves ocean-fresh seafood, including Puerto Nuevo-style lobster.

Restaurant Bar La Escondida, Ave. Anzuelo #12, ☎ 011-52-662-02225, also serves lobster Puerto Nuevo-style. Almost every seat has an ocean view.

La Masia Restaurant, Quinta Del Mar at Blvd. Benito Juarez 25.5, ☎ 011-52-661-30290, offers a nice Sunday brunch and has a piano bar with live music and dancing. Dishes include Shrimp tequila, flamed at your table; fish served Vera Cruz-style; broiled quail; and crêpes suzette.

Tecate, Mexico

The town's better restaurants include **La Escondida**, Calle Ortiz Rubio facing the east side of the plaza; **El Asadero No. 2**, Av. Juarez facing the north side of the plaza; **El Tucan**, attached to Motel El Dorado; and **La Carreta**, Av. Juarez 270 at Calle Santana.

Tijuana, Mexico

For steak, try **El Rodeo**, Av. de los Charros #8, Col. Sandoval, ☎ 011-52-21-65-47, or **Restaurante La Escondida de Tijuana**, Sta. Monica #1, ☎ 01152-66-814458. The latter also serves seafood and features dancing to live music.

La Costa, 8131 7th St., ☎ 011-52-66-858494, has a menu listing 67 seafood entrées. Proprietors Adrian Pedrin and sons call their cuisine "the freshest seafood in Baja."

La Leña, Blvd. Agua Caliente 11191, ☎ 011-52-668-62920, has an extensive – and excellent – menu.

Mariscos Don Pepe, Blvd. Fundadores 688, ☎ 01152-66-849086, is a seafood restaurant open daily for lunch and dinner. Try the seven seas soup.

Coronet Restaurant & Piano Bar, 1939 Seventh St., ☎ 01152-66-855551, is an intimate little restaurant that has served former presidents Richard Nixon and Ronald Reagan, plus a number of movie personalities.

Bocaccio's Nueva Marianna, Blvd. Agua Caliente and Blvd. General Salinas #2500, ☎ 011-52-66-86-22-66 or 86-18-45, and **Viviana's**, Blvd. Agua Caliente #1092, Col. Revolucion, ☎ 81-70-86, serve international cuisine.

Tour de France, Gobernador Ibarra #252, Col. America, ☎ 81-75-42, has a French menu, and **La Specia**, Blvd. Paseo de los Heroes #10051, Suite 6, ☎ 34-29-41 or 34-36-33, serves Italian.

La Casa de Alfonso, Esteban Canto #2007, Col. Davila, ☎ 81-89-55/56/57, provides Spanish (as opposed to Mexican) food, and the menu at **Restaurant Argentino de Tony**, Local 19-A, Centro Comercial Pueblo Amigo, Oriente #60 and Paseo de Tijuana, ☎ 82-81-11, is Argentine.

There's a **Hard Rock Café** at Ave. Revolucion No. 520, Zona Centro, ☎ 85-02-06 or 85-25-13.

Also check out **Yuppies Sports Café**, a bar/disco at Paseo de los Heroes and Diego Rivera No. 10501, Zona Rio, ☎ 34-23-24 or 34-21-41, and **Señor Frog's**, Via Oriente 60 in the Pueblo Amigo Shopping Center, Zona Rio, ☎ 011-5266-82-49-62, arguably Tijuana's most popular restaurant.

Colorado River Valley

Desert to the east of you, desert to the west of you. It's easy to appreciate the profound impact that water can have on such a place, and on the people who choose to live there.

This is barren, desolate country. There are few towns... and few people to inhabit them. The hardy individuals who do live here are sun-browned, leather-faced, hard-scrabble people who are used to getting by without many of life's modern-day conveniences. They are hard-working people, many of them field hands and ranchers.

Until the introduction of air conditioning, there wasn't much to attract people to this country. The climate was severe. Few tourists ventured by, particularly during the hottest part of summer. It was difficult to eke out a meager existence.

The singular exception was the lure of gold and silver.

Almost from the beginning, prospectors chipped and chiseled their way through the mountains in every direction, seeking those elusive metals. A very, very few were lucky. Most were not. Some simply disappeared, never to be heard from again.

The Colorado River was discovered in 1540 by Hernando de Alarcón, who named it Rio Grande de Buena Esperanza ("Great River of Good Hope"). A later explorer named it Rio del Tizón ("River of the Firebrand"), and when Father Kino passed through in 1701, he called it the Rio de los Martires ("River of the Martyrs").

Today, all of that has changed. Air conditioning has made life in our homes, cars and RVs bearable. Water from the Colorado River, now controlled by a series of dams, is channeled into the surrounding fields for crop irrigation. Tourists pour in to enjoy every variety of watersports – boating, jetskiing, windsurfing, waterskiing, rafting, innertubing, fishing.

Less than 30 minutes north of Needles, Las Vegas-style gambling has invaded the little riverside community of Laughlin, Nevada, which now has a score of top-notch, high-rise hotel/casinos that feature gambling and name entertainment.

Getting Around

With a single exception, the east-west routes through this region are all interstate highways – I-8 through Yuma, Arizona, on the south; I-10 through Blythe in the mid-section; and I-40 through Needles to the north, just below the Nevada state line. The exception is a rather heavily-traveled State Route 82 that heads west from Parker, Arizona, through the Granite

Colorado River Valley

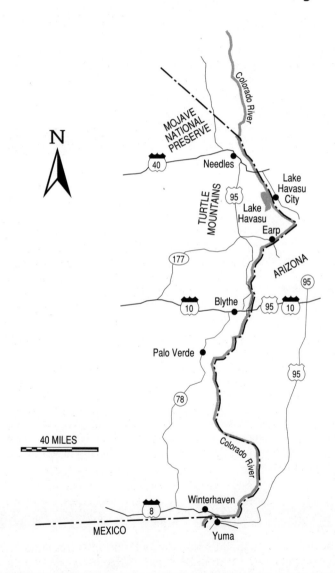

Mountains, the Iron Mountains and the Sheep Hole Mountains to Twentynine Palms.

North and south, a state route leads past the ghost town of Tumco to Highway 78 and Interstate 10 just west of Blythe. Highway 95 provides a direct, albeit desolate, route to Needles and Interstate 40 or, 100 miles beyond, Las Vegas, Nevada.

If you happen to be a member of the AAA, ask for a copy of their Colorado River map.

Touring

Yuma, Arizona

With a population only slightly over 60,000, Yuma is the largest city on the Colorado River between Lake Mead and the Mexican border. Indeed, it is the third fastest-growing metropolitan area in the United States, having expanded by 30% since 1980.

Just across a bridge from California, Yuma was discovered by the Spaniards as they searched for the legendary Seven Cities of Cibola. It sits at the confluence of the Colorado and Gila Rivers, and is in the heart of a vast agricultural region producing citrus, cotton, dates and nuts.

From 1854 to 1858, the town was known as Colorado City. Later, it was called Arizona City, and finally, Yuma in honor of the local Indians.

By mutual agreement, Arizona and California set the Colorado River as the legal boundary between the two, but in the days before dams kept the nation's rivers on a predictable course, flooding was an all-too-common occurrence. It flooded so often and with such force that it eventually changed course, leaving those who lived on about 150 square miles of land in Yuma in a quandary. Land that once been on the *east* side of the river was now on the *west* side of the river. Both Arizona and California laid claim to it; both states tried to collect taxes on it; some residents voted in one state, some voted in the other, and some voted in both. To help clear up the confusion, both states agreed to keep their hands off the area until the dispute could be legally resolved. While they waited, the residents of the disputed land did not have to pay taxes, they were not required to have license plates on their automobiles, and they were allowed to do pretty much as they pleased because no laws could be enforced. A federal court ultimately decided that the disputed land belonged to Arizona.

Yuma has sunshine 93% of the time. Only three inches of rain falls each year. Humidity seldom exceeds 30%. The temperature averages 75.2° F, but the August average is 105.4° and the January average just 36.8°.

North of I-8 on Highway 34 en route to Blythe, there is an interesting **Pre-Columbian Indian Trail Exhibit** just before you reach the junction with Highway 78. Near there is **Picacho State Recreation Area**, a 26,000-acre, 31-mile-long preserve containing 260 species of birds, fox, bobcat, coyote and mule deer. Across the Colorado on the Arizona side of the river is the **Imperial National Wildlife Refuge**, PO Box 72217, Martinez Lake, AZ 85365, ☎ 520/783-3371.

Continuing northward, driving parallel to the river, you encounter **Draper Lake, Walker Lake, Three Fingers Lake** and **Davis Lake Park**.

For more information, contact **Yuma Convention & Visitors Bureau**, 377 S. Main St., Yuma, AZ 85364, ☎ 520/783-0071; or the **Cultural Council of Yuma**, ☎ 520/783-2423.

Winterhaven

There is evidence that gold was discovered in the nearby Cargo Muchachos mountains 75 years before the gold strike that launched the '49ers gold rush. Gold was known along the Colorado River in the 1770s, and mining in the Cargo Muchachos is said to have been carried on in 1780 with the founding of Spanish settlements along the river. Yuma (Quechan) Indians tell stories of tribal ancestors who were forced to dig gold for the early Spaniards.

In the 1700s, two missions were established on the California side of the Colorado River – only 12 miles apart – by four Franciscan padres from Mexico: Fathers Diaz, Morena, Garces and Barrenecha. The missions were called Mision La Purisima Concepcion and Mision San Pedro y San Pablo de Bicuner.

The Yuma Indians resented the intrusion, and when Captain Don Fernando Rivera arrived with a large group of colonists and 1,000 head of cattle en route to Los Angeles in 1781, the Indians revolted, killing all of the men, capturing all of the women and children, and destroying both missions. No ruins remain of the small wooden buildings, each barely large enough to hold 20 worshippers. E Clampus Vitus, an organization dedicated to preserving California history, has placed a memorial plaque below an old cemetery about a mile south of Laguna Dam near the All-American Canal, believed to have been the site of the Mision San Pedro y San Pablo de Bicuner. Some Yuma Indians believe the foundation for the La Purisima Mission lies below the present St. Thomas Church near the tribal museum on Indian Hill.

Later, Winterhaven was the project headquarters during construction of the All-American Canal.

On the northern edge of town, where the river makes an eastward bend, the remnants of a route cut by teams of mules can still be seen. The mules hauled supplies from Yuma and gold out of Picacho until 1908, when the construction of Laguna Dam put a halt to water transportation on the Colorado.

ALL-AMERICAN CANAL

Five miles west of Yuma, Interstate 8 crosses the All-American Canal, one of the world's largest irrigation canals. The canal extends 80 miles across the desert and serves 675,000 acres of land in California, plus acreage across the border in Mexico.

The canal was built during the 1930s and the first water was delivered in the 1940s. Beginning at Imperial Dam, 20 miles northeast of Yuma, the gravity-flow canal drops a total of 175 feet and provides 2.6 million acre-feet of water per year to nine cities and 500,000 acres of farmland in Imperial Valley.

OLD PLANK ROAD

Midway between Yuma, Arizona and the California community of Brawley, the **Algodones Dunes** create an American Sahara.

In the early 1900s, when auto traffic was drawing increasing numbers of tourists from their homes, this natural barrier was a serious handicap to the City of San Diego. Los Angeles had already won the railroads and, without a way to traverse the sand dunes, San Diego stood to lose the automobile traffic as well.

San Diego businessman "Colonel" Ed Fletcher sponsored a race to determine which would be the better route to the West Coast, Los Angeles or San Diego. The race was set for October 1912.

Fletcher chose a route through the Imperial Sand Hills and, with a team of six horses to pull his automobile through the deep sand, he won the race to the Colorado River in a time of 19½ hours.

Arizona agreed to build a bridge across the Colorado. San Diego announced plans for a big celebration to honor the opening of the Panama Canal in 1915. San Diego's future looked bright, except for the dunes. Escorting cars across the dunes with a six-horse team was not particularly practical.

Fletcher raised the money to buy materials for a plank road through the dunes, and the first planks were laid in February 1915. The "auto railroad" was completed in two months, but it had problems. Drivers were required to keep their tires on a row of planks barely two feet wide. Broken planks often interrupted traffic. Strong winds blew sand across the road an average of two or three days per week, rendering the road impassable about one-third of the time. In 1916, a stronger, wider plank road was laid.

From 1915 until 1926, the Old Plank Road was the only means of travel through these dunes by wagons and cars.

For the best view of the sections of the road still remaining, take I-8 west from Yuma to the Gray's Well exit, then continue westward along the frontage road on the south side of the interstate.

FELICITY

Less a town than a roadside attraction, Felicity, ☎ 619/572-0100, is a 2,700-acre townsite north of I-8 at the Sidewinder Rd. exit. It has a restaurant, a gift shop, a few apartment houses and a train station (where no train ever stops).

Jacques-André Istel, a one-time parachutist and investment banker, and his Chinese wife Felicia declared the place "the Center of the World" in 1985 and buried a time capsule under a 19-foot pyramid there. (In 1961, Istel broke the world parachute record and left the Marine Corps to found some parachuting schools. He is considered the "father" of parachuting as a sport.)

Felicity is open from Thanksgiving to Easter.

Palo Verde

Twenty miles south of Blythe on Highway 78 is this little community of fewer than 1,000 full-time residents, home of three bars, three gas stations, a convenience store, a post office, a small museum and one church.

A lagoon splits the town, and there are small fishing cabins and homes dotting both banks.

Just across the river on the Arizona side is **Cibolo National Wildlife Refuge**, PO Box AP, Blythe 92225, ☎ 602/857-3253, a 16,627-acre sanctuary reachable only by boat.

Blythe

Although the year-round population of Blythe is just 10,000, the winter population expands as the "snow birds" from the north and east are drawn to the warm southern California climate.

Here, the primary industry is agriculture – nearly $100 million worth per year.

The **Rice Valley** sand dunes border the northeast side of town and the **Palen Dunes** border the southwest side.

To the north is the **Colorado River Indian Reservation**, ☎ 520/669-9285.

Blythe's closest neighbors are the communities in Arizona, just across the river. **Quartzsite**, an excellent rockhounding region, is just 21 miles from Blythe (contact the **Quartzsite Chamber of Commerce**, ☎ 602/927-5600). **Parker** is only 35 miles away (contact **Parker Chamber of Commerce**, ☎ 602/669-2174).

Parker Dam, just north of Quartzsite, is the deepest dam in the world. Self-guided tours are available daily.

Blythe also has a small airport.

For more information, contact **Blythe Chamber of Commerce**, 201 S. Broadway, Blythe 92227, ☎ 619/922-8166 or 800/445-0541.

Earp

Originally called Brennan, this little town had a post office, a service station and an old shack once occupied by the famous gunfighter Wyatt Earp, who arrived in 1864 to drive stagecoaches between San Bernardino and Prescott, Arizona. Earp was appointed a peace officer along the route during the railway development period.

In 1901, Wyatt staked a claim on the Happy Day gold mine in nearby Whipples, but he continued living in Brennan. The house that once hosted his friends, Bat Masterson and Doc Holliday, burned down a few years ago.

Earp died in 1929 and the Santa Fe Railroad changed the name of Brennan to Earp in his honor.

Lake Havasu

A popular resort area for those who enjoy watersports (and gambling in the upriver town of Laughlin, Nevada), Lake Havasu is popular for boating, waterskiing, jetskiing and fishing. House-boat rentals are available, as well as waterfront hotels, motels and condos.

The endangered Yuma clapper rail breeds in the marshes all along the Colorado River from the Nevada state line south to the Sea of Cortez.

For more information, contact **Lake Havasu State Park**, ☎ 602/855-2784.

LAKE HAVASU CITY

This rapidly growing town on the banks of Lake Havasu sits on the Arizona side of the river. It was founded in 1964 by Robert McCulloch, owner of the firm that manufactures chain saws. In 1971, McCulloch bought the London Bridge, doomed to destruction, and transported it to America, stone by stone. He had it reconstructed in Lake Havasu City as a means of publicizing his still-new community.

An **English Village** has grown up around the mainland end of the bridge.

For more information, contact **Lake Havasu City Convention & Visitors Bureau**, 1930 Mesquite Ave., Suite 3, Lake Havasu City, AZ 86403, ☎ 602/453-3444 or 800/242-8278.

Needles

As Blythe sits astride Interstate 10 where it crosses the Colorado River, Needles sits astride Interstate 40 where the highway crosses the river farther north. In years past, this was the old Route 66, perhaps the nation's most famous highway. Linking Chicago and Los Angeles, Route 66 was one of the nation's first major interstate highways.

Once a steamboat landing and an old supply station, the town became a stop on the Santa Fe Railroad in 1883. The train station and Harvey House hotel have been preserved.

In October, the city celebrates **Fort Mojave Indian Days,** ☎ 619/326-4591, fitting, since the town sits between two Indian reservations, **Fort Mojave** to the south and **Chemehuevi** ("egg-eaters"), an offshoot of the Paiutes, to the north.

Adventures

On Foot

Blythe

Hiking is popular throughout the riverside hills both north and south of town.

Havasu National Wildlife Refuge

The refuge contains over 300 miles of river shoreline for hiking and birdwatching.

For more information, contact **Havasu National Wildlife Refuge**, PO Box A, 1406 Bailey Ave., Needles 92363, ☎ 619/326-3853.

Imperial National Wildlife Refuge

Painted Desert Trail is a mile-long self-guided interpretive trail that is best enjoyed from November through April. Pick up a leaflet at the trailhead, which is 2.8 miles north of the refuge headquarters on Red Cloud Mine Road. The area provides some excellent birdwatching opportunities.

Palo Verde

Cibola National Wildlife Refuge, ☎ 520/857-3253, provides many excellent opportunities for hiking along the Colorado River.

Parker Dam

Buckskin Mountain State Park, ☎ 602/667-3231, on the Arizona side of the river has numerous hiking trails.

Yuma, Arizona

Betty's Kitchen, ☎ 520/627-2773, is a 10-acre wildlife interpretive area on Mittry Lake. Guided and self-guided half-mile tours are available.

GHOST TOWNS

Buckskin Mountain State Park, ☎ 520/667-3231, on the Arizona side of the Colorado River, is near the ghost town of **Swansea**.

Picacho is an 1897 ghost town about 18 miles north of Winterhaven on Picacho Road along the Colorado River. Bullfights and fiestas once enlivened this rough-and-ready mining town. All that remains today is the ruin of an old mill, an abandoned rock house and an historic marker along Picacho Road. In some places, the roadbed of a five-mile railroad spur that once ran from Picacho to a stamp mill can still be seen.

Ogilby Station was once a prosperous town on the Southern Pacific Railroad in the Cargo Muchaco ("loaded boy") Mountains. What remains (primarily a colorful little cemetery) can be found four miles from I-8 along County Road S-34.

Tumco created its name from the initials of **The United Mines Co.** Originally known as Hedges, the town once had 3,000 residents, seven saloons (four along Stingaree Gulch alone), a store, a hospital, several bordellos and a casino. The area, which is just off S-34 between I-8 and Highway 78, peaked in 1896. There is a marker a mile east of County Road S-34 and nine miles north of I-8. **Tumco Cemetery**, very well preserved, is 22 miles northwest of Yuma near **Gold Rock Ranch**, PO Box 728, Winterhaven 92283, but it can be reached only with a four-wheel-drive vehicle (beware of open mine shafts).

Goffs was located just west of Needles and had previously been known as Blake. It had a cemetery named Desert Lawn, but not much else is known about it.

Vanderbilt, also located near Needles, was northwest of town in the New York Mountains southeast of Mountain Pass. Gold and silver were discovered there in the 1870s, and the town peaked in the 1890s, reaching a population of 500 in 1893. But by 1897, the town was dead and the arrival of the California Eastern Railroad in 1902 failed to revive it.

ROCKHOUNDING

Needles

This area contains a lot of agate, moonstone and turquoise.

Yuma, Arizona

Within 80 miles of town, rockhounds can locate kaynite, garnet, tourmaline, talc, alusite, pyrite, magnetite, agate, jasper, rhyolite, chalcedony roses, cat's eye quartz and petrified wood.

TREASURE HUNTING

Earp

A number of lost mines are reputed to be in the Turtle Mountains, west of town.

Cargo Muchachos Mountains

A **ledge of gold** was reportedly discovered near Pebble Mountain in the Cargo Muchachos range in the mid-1890s. The gold was reported to be of two types, one yellowish-red with limonite and one chocolate brown with hematite. It is said to have assayed at more than $1,000 a ton.

The **Lost Mule Shoe** treasure is said to have been found by a traveler en route from Picacho to San Bernardino. The traveler, exhausted, collapsed on a bed of nuggets in the Cargo Muchachos range. Too weak to pursue his find, he marked the spot by placing his vest on the ledge and anchoring it with a mule shoe. As far as anyone knows, the rich lode is still waiting to be found.

Winterhaven

There are numerous tales of lost treasure associated with this region. Most of them mention Yuma, Arizona as a starting point because Yuma was the only city between Tucson and San Diego in those frontier mining days.

The ill-fated **La Purisima Mission** near Winterhaven is said to have had some precious chalices that were buried by the padres just prior to the Indian revolt that led to the mission's ruin. The site of the treasure is thought to be at the end of a dirt road that leads up a steep incline to the bank of the All-American Canal.

The lost **Algodones** gold is said to have belonged to a lone prospector who was caught in a violent sandstorm in the desert near Ogilby in 1917.

The prospector's burro, Assault, was buried in the sandstorm, and all of the prospector's water and supplies were buried nearby.

On Horseback

Opportunities for horseback riding in this region are too numerous to list... if you have your own horse trailer. If you must rent a horse, however, you are fairly well restricted to one of the areas near the towns of Yuma, Winterhaven, Blythe or Needles.

Inquire locally or simply check the Yellow Pages to locate a place that rents horses.

On Wheels

Algodones

Algodones Dunes Off-Highway Vehicle Area is California's largest dune system and has been called "the dune buggy capital of the world." Housing, restaurants and other niceties are not readily available, however.

Blythe

The largest and most luxurient desert ironwood forest in the world can be found in the valley between the **Palen** and **McCoy** mountains. Take the Lovekin Blvd. exit north off I-10 in Blythe and go about six miles to Midland Rd. Then continue northwest for 13 miles to the Inca turnoff. A four-wheel-drive is recommended. Look for rabbits, mice, kangaroo rats, coyotes, kit foxes and a variety of birds.

Giant Indian *intaglios* (ground figures also known as geoglyphs or rock alignments) can be found in this area. Take Highway 95 north 15½ miles to a well-signed road that will lead you west for half a mile to the figures, which include a human figure over 160 feet long, a spiral design and a four-legged animal. A second site is half a mile northwest of the first one. (For more information about *intaglios*, contact the **Bureau of Land Management**, 641 Front St., Suite B, Needles 92363, ☎ 619/326-3896.)

Imperial Sand Dunes

Just west of the Fort Yuma Indian Reservation off I-8, a long dirt road (A207) heads northwest toward the Imperial Sand Dunes and the **Glamis Open Area**.

If you choose to stay on I-8 a little farther, look for Ogilby Road on your right. From this intersection on, the Imperial Sand Dunes will be on your right and the **Buttercup Valley Open Area** will be on your left. All three of these areas are open to off-highway vehicles.

Vidal

Rice Valley Off-Highway Vehicle Area is southwest of town. Take Route 95 north to the junction with Highway 62 and turn west (left). At dirt road PO51, turn left and go five miles to the site.

➡ *NOTE: PO51 can be extremely sandy and most drivers do their staging just south of Route 62.*

Winterhaven

A scenic and exciting trip through the Colorado Desert, not recommended for passenger cars, takes a loop through Picacho from the entrance at Indian Pass Rd. to Winterhaven.

➡ *BE ALERT: Summer storms sometimes wreak havoc in sections of Indian Pass.*

Where Indian Pass Rd. reaches Gavilan Wash, a dangerous downhill track leads to the Colorado River. You may wish to return to Ogilby Rd. and approach the Picachos from the Winterhaven entrance. When hiking in Indian Pass, look for a 100-foot-long alignment of boulders. Also watch for a number of rock circles alongside the road, sometimes called "sleeping circles" because early Indians are said to have huddled together inside them for warmth at night.

To follow the old mule track to Picacho from Winterhaven, cross the All-American Canal and proceed through a number of lush washes into the Chocolate Mountains. The road is rough, but navigable in a passenger car.

Picacho Recreation Area has private camps, boat landings and fishing resorts. The town once had a bullring and a substantial Mexican population. After Americans began to arrive, the population increased to 2,500... and the average monthly payroll to $40,000. The region attracted a number of celebrities, including Zane Grey, who found the inspiration for his *Wanderer of the Wasteland* there. Ore from the mines was hauled to the mill by narrow-gauge railway, milled, and then loaded onto a steamer for transportation to Yuma. The town of Picacho now lies underwater behind Imperial Dam.

While exploring the area, be sure to visit **Gold Rock Trading Post** near Tumco Mine and the old ghost town. Gold Rock, originally built in the 1930s, not only is a trading post, but a meeting place for rockhounds. There is a small museum of Indian stone tools, rocks with petroglyphs, old mining equipment, crystal spheres, desert driftwood and all kinds of rocks. From Tumco, cross Highway 34 and continue west on Gold Rock Ranch Rd. for about 1.6 miles.

Yuma, Arizona

Yuma Valley Railroad, 8th Ave. west to Levee Rd., ☎ 520/783-3456, travels along the banks of the Colorado River within sight of Old Mexico. Passengers ride in a 1922 Pullman coach pulled by a 1941 diesel locomotive.

INFORMATION SOURCES

California Off Highway Vehicle Handbook, California Department of Parks & Recreation, 1991.
The Tread Lightly! Guide to Responsible Four-Wheeling, Tread Lightly! Inc., 298 24th St., Suite 325-C, Ogden, UT 84401, ☎ 801/627-0077 or 800/966-9900, fax 801/621-8633.

On & In the Water

The southeastern border of California includes a 233-mile stretch of the **Colorado River**, which is one of the state's most crowded waterways. Along this stretch, eight major dams have created the following lakes: **Havasu, Squaw, Moovalya, Martinez** and **Ferguson**.

Jet skiing on the lower Colorado River.
Credit: Yuma Convention & Visitors Bureau

Boating Tips

★ The larger lakes often get rough on windy days.
★ Boaters seeking shelter from a storm in one of the coves along the shore should beware of getting trapped in the path of flash flood waters that can sweep down the washes and into the coves during rare but sudden thunderstorms.
★ Boaters also should beware of underwater or partially submerged hazards – sandbars, rocks and snags. Where fast currents empty into lakes, such as in the north basin of Lake

Havasu, partially submerged tree stumps – often 10 feet long
or more – are often found. Sandbars constantly change
position. Shoals and sandbars usually are NOT marked.

★ Currents vary from two to eight miles per hour according to
the area, the season, and the amount of water being released
through the upstream dams.

★ Rafters, common on the river, are difficult to see.

★ Ten-mile-long, 400-foot-wide **Lake Moovalya**, best known
as "The Parker Strip," accounts for numerous boating acci-
dents along the California side of the river.

★ Be particularly careful around dams. Stay away from spill-
ways, outlets and siphons. Boats approaching dams from
the upstream side have been swept over, while turbulence
on the downstream side can easily cause the boater to lose
control.

Since the river forms the border between California and the neighboring state of Arizona, visitors should acquaint themselves with the boating
and fishing laws of *both* states.

Under California law, boaters must slow to five miles per hour when
they pass within 100 feet of any bather or within 200 feet of any bathing
beach, swimming or diving platform, or landing float that is in use.

In addition to the operator of the boat, there must be an observer no
less than 12 years of age in any boat that is towing a skier. The waterski
flag must be displayed when (a) there is a downed skier, (b) a ski line
extends from the vessel, (c) a skier is in the water preparing to ski, or (d)
a ski is in the water in the vicinity of the vessel. Skiing before sunrise or
after sunset is illegal.

In the **Cibola National Wildlife Refuge**, skiing is permitted in the main
channel but not on the Old River Channel or backwater areas near
Walter's or Mitchell's Camps.

In the **Imperial National Wildlife Refuge**, waterskiing is prohibited in
all areas with the exception of an eight-mile strip through the **Picacho
State Recreation Area** and a four-mile area at the southern end of the
refuge near **Martinez Lake**.

For more information, write or call for *Safe Boating Hints for the Colorado
River* and *ABCs of the California Boating Law*, State of California Department
of Boating and Waterways, 1629 S St., Sacramento 95814-7291, ☎ 916/445-
2616. The same office also provides two Colorado River Boating Trail
Guides: *From Blythe to Imperial Dam* and *From Davis Dam to Parker Dam*.

Blythe

This area is popular for waterskiing, swimming, canoeing and boating.
Fishermen catch bass and flathead catfish here – and many people enjoy
the frogging along the marshy banks.

Imperial Wildlife Refuge

This preserve can *only* be explored by water.

Lake Havasu

Lake Havasu State Park, ☎ 520/855-7851, provides 17 miles of shoreline and over 10,000 acres of wilderness.

Lake Havasu Landing Resort & Casino, ☎ 619/858-4593, has a marina with courtesy boat slips and a bait shop. It also operates a tour boat to Lake Havasu City across the river in Arizona.

Palo Verde

Fishing is good in this area for crappie, bass and catfish to 65 pounds. The largest catfish caught in southern California was taken here.

Parker, Arizona

This riverfront city between Blythe and Needles holds an annual seven-mile **Colorado River Innertube Race** that is very popular.

For more information, contact **Parker Area Chamber of Commerce,** ☎ 602/669-2174.

Parker Dam

Buckskin Mountain State Park on the Arizona side of the river is popular with tube floaters, boaters and waterskiers.

Picacho State Recreation Area

Located on the Colorado River between Blythe and Yuma, Arizona, this region offers good fishing for bass, bluegill, crappie and catfish.

Yuma, Arizona

Martinez Lake, ☎ 520/783-9589, provides good fishing.

Mittry Lake features 400 acres of open water and 3,575 acres of wetlands. Bass and catfish fishing are good. In addition to marsh hawk, osprey, great blue heron and egret, there is a large population of the endangered Yuma clapper rail, which is larger than the black rail and likes to eat the crayfish that are abundant in these waters. Indeed, 20% of the 800 Yuma clapper rails estimated to be alive can be found here, as well as half the world's remaining population of the threatened California black rail, a bird that mostly hunts insects in the shallows and builds its nests in the reeds. Some 10,000 waterfowl converge on this oasis each year between November and February.

Watch for the ubiquitous salt cedar (tamarisk), a plant that was introduced to prevent soil erosion and quickly gained supremacy in many regions of the Southwest. Salt cedar grows by sprouting from the root. It thrives on saline soil that would kill other plants, and it drives out competition by "sweating" salt from its pores, virtually sterilizing the surrounding soil.

Three-hour river cruises are available on *Colorado King I*, a double-deck sternwheeler from Fisher's Landing at Martinez Lake, ☎ 520/782-2412. Tickets and directions to the landing are provided at Fantastic Sam's Hair Care, 1640 S. 4th Ave., Yuma.

Yuma River Tours, 1920 Arizona Ave., Yuma, AZ, ☎ 520/783-4400, charters jetboat tours through **Imperial Wildlife Refuge,** with stops at an old miner's cabin, Indian petroglyphs, Picacho and Lonesome's Knoll. A three-hour tour includes lunch. A three-hour sunset dinner cruise also is offered through the back channels and lakes to Imperial Dam.

Eco-Travel/Cultural Excursions

Bard

A market on County Road S-24 four miles northeast of town commemorates the Indian attack in 1781 that destroyed Mission San Pedro y San Pablo de Bicuner.

Blythe

For excitement, locals have to rely on the annual **Rock & Gem Show** held on the Colorado River, the annual **Christmas parade**, and whatever happens to be going on at the **County Fair Grounds**, ☎ 520/317-2965 or 800/621-8938.

Palo Verde Historical Museum, 150 N. Broadway, ☎ 520/922-8202, is open only in the winter.

Needles

At the Colorado River bridge on K St. stands an historical marker (#781) that identifies a portion of the old Indian trail, still visible in spots, that was used by Garces and his Indian guides in 1776 and by Jedediah Smith in 1826.

Winterhaven

Quechen Tribal Museum is located on the Ft. Yuma Quechan Indian Reservation, 350 Picacho Rd., ☎ 619/572-0661. It contains artifacts of early life along the Colorado River.

A historical marker at 350 Picacho Rd. (State Route S-24) indicates the spot where the Indians attacked the Spaniards at Fort Yuma in 1781 and destroyed Mission La Purisima Concepción a mile farther south.

Yuma, Arizona

St. Thomas Mission, ☎ 619/572-0283, stands on the grounds of the original Concepción Mission where Father Garces was massacred by the Yuma Indians in 1781. Guided tours are available by arrangement.

Fort Yuma (1849-85) and the **Quechan Indian Museum,** ☎ 619/572-0661, share a site by the river on the **Fort Yuma Indian Reservation,** ☎ 619/572-0544. The structure that houses the museum was built to be the fort's officers' mess in 1851.

Yuma Territorial Prison State Historic Park, 1 Prison Hill Rd. on Giss Parkway, ☎ 602/783-4771 or 800/829-YUMA, immortalizes one of the Territorial days' worst hell-holes. The prison was built on a hilltop by the prisoners themselves, and was first occupied in July 1876. It operated for 33 years, until 1909 when a new prison was built in mid-state Florence, Arizona. During that time, 3,069 prisoners, including 29 women, were incarcerated there, including such colorful desperados as Buckskin Frank Leslie and Pearl Heart. Not surprisingly, 111 of the prisoners died, primarily from tuberculosis, and although 26 convicts successfully escaped, eight others died from gunshot wounds received during the attempt. Between 1910 and 1914, Yuma Union High School occupied the buildings.

Century House Museum, 240 Madison Ave., ☎ 602/782-1841; **Quartermaster Depot State Historic Park,** 2nd Ave. behind City Hall, ☎ 602/343-2500; and **Yuma Crossing Living History Museum,** ☎ 520/329-0404, are of historic interest.

Saihati (pronounced *say-HAH-tee*) **Camel Farm,** 15672 S. Ave. 1 E, ☎ 520/627-2553, has one of the largest camel herds in North America. Two tours are conducted Monday through Saturday, with one tour on Sunday. The farm is closed between June 1 and September 30, on Thanksgiving, and on Christmas.

On the outskirts of town is a **Marine Air Station,** the place former President George Bush went in 1997 to reenact his World War II experience of parachuting from an airplane.

Just south of town is the **Cocopah Indian Reservation. Cocopah Bingo & Casino,** 15136 S. Ave. B, ☎ 520/726-8066, is located on the reservation.

Where To Stay

B&Bs, Hotels & Inns

Blythe

Hampton Inn, 900 W. Hobsonway, ☎ 619/922-9000, fax 619/922-9011, has 59 rooms and four suites, but no restaurant.

Laughlin, Nevada

Avi Hotel & Casino, 10000 Aha Macav Pkwy., PO Box 77011, Laughlin, NV 89029-7011, ☎ 800/284-2946, has the largest sandy beach on the river. The property is owned by the Fort Mojave tribe and has a lavish Las Vegas-style gambling casino. It also offers 301 rooms (including 29 spa suites), a golf course, an RV resort, shopping, a residential area and a marina with a boat launch.

Needles

Best Western Colorado River Inn, 2371 W. Broadway, ☎ 619/326-4552, fax 619/326-4562, has 63 rooms.

Yuma, Arizona

Best Western Chilton Inn, 300 E. 32nd St., ☎ 520/344-1050, fax 520/344-4877, has 119 rooms, a 24-hour restaurant, a fitness center and a coin laundry. Guests get a free continental breakfast.

If this two-story motel is booked, there are two other good Best Westerns in town, plus a nice Shilo Inn.

Camping

Long-term camping permits can be obtained from **Yuma Resource Area Office**, Bureau of Land Management, 2555 Gila Ridge Rd., Yuma, AZ 85365, ☎ 520/317-3200; and **El Centro Resource Area Office**, Bureau of Land Management, 1661 South 4th St., El Centro 92243, ☎ 619/337-4400.

Blythe

Wiley Well Campground can be found by taking I-10 west from Blythe for 14 miles, then turning south on Wiley Well Rd. for nine miles. **Coon**

Hollow Campground is three miles south of Wiley Well. Neither campground has any water.

Peter McIntyre County Park, six miles south of town, can be located by taking Intake Blvd. off I-10, following Intake to the end, and then turning east on 26th St. There is water and a small store here.

Havasu Lake

Lake Havasu Landing Resort & Casino, ☎ 619/858-4593 or 800/307-3610, has an RV park and a campground. Go south from I-40 on US 95 for 20 miles to Havasu Lake Rd. Head southeast for 16 miles to the town of Havasu Lake. The resort is east of the road near the river.

Lake Havasu State Park has 45 miles of shoreline and two camping units. The **Windsor Beach** unit is in the upper part of the lake and has boat ramps, campsites and 50 primitive camping areas that are accessible only by boat. The **Cattail Cove** unit has campsites with RV hookups plus 150 campsites that can be reached only by boat. Nearby is a marina that has a restaurant, a store and boat rentals.

Moabi Regional Park

Located 11 miles southeast of Needles on Park Moabi Rd., this park, ☎ 619/326-3831, has riverfront campsites with picnic tables and BBQ grills. A five-lane boat ramp, a general store, laundry facilities and hot showers are available, and canoes and houseboats can be rented here. Swimming, boating and waterskiing are popular, and the exciting Topock Gorge is just south of the park on the Colorado River. Off-highway driving also is permitted on designated trails.

Palo Verde

Palo Verde County Park is three miles south of Palo Verde off Highway 78.

Palo Verde Oxbow, a BLM facility, is 1.2 miles south of Palo Verde County Park on Highway 78 and half a mile east off the highway.

Pichaco State Recreation Area

There is an 18-mile dirt entrance to this area that is not recommended for large trailers. The facility is located 25 miles north of Yuma and provides fishing, desert exploring and river boating in addition to camping.

Winterhaven

Squaw Lake Recreation Site, a BLM facility, is about 20 miles from town. Take Route S-24 about 15.6 miles to Senator Wash Rd., then take Senator

Wash Rd. north to the end (about 3½ miles). Water and restrooms are available.

Yuma, Arizona

Martinez Lake has two camping sites: **Martinez Lake Marina**, ☎ 520/783-9589, which accommodates RVs and trailers, but not tents, and **Fisher's Landing**, which will take all three.

Where To Eat

Yuma, Arizona

There are no gourmet restaurants here, just solid, appetite-pleasin', stomach-fillin' food.

Field hands, GIs from the local Marine Corps base, transients and tourists fill the usual fast food emporiums in town: **Arby's, Burger King** (Yuma has three), **Carl's Jr.** (two), **Carrow's, Churches Fried Chicken, Denny's, Domino's Pizza** (three), **Famous Sam's, Furr's, Golden Corral, Hardee's, Jack in the Box** (five) and **JB's.**

Of the "better" restaurants in town, we think you'll be most pleased with **Hungry Hunter**, 2355 S. 4th St., ☎ 520/782-3637, dependable food served in a comfortable homey atmosphere, and **Basque Etchea**, 8575 S. Ave. 40 East, Tacna, AZ, ☎ 520/785-4027, a Basque restaurant in the small town of Tacna, east of Yuma along Interstate 8. (For a description of Basque dining, see the section about dining in *Bakersfield*, page 150.)

Imperial Valley

The Salton Sink has more dry land *below* sea level than anywhere else in this hemisphere.

More than once, the ancient sea called **Lake Cahuilla** filled the basin. Fossils have been found as high as 1,000 feet above the desert floor. Conch shells were once so numerous that Coachella Valley was named Conchilla Valley. The last Lake Cahuilla covered much of the Imperial, Coachella and Mexicali Valleys as late as 1450.

In 1539, three Spanish vessels under the command of Francisco de Ulloa sailed up the coast of Mexico from Acapulco to discover the Gulf of California (aka the Sea of Cortez). But not until May 1540 did Pedro de Alarcon, hoping to aid Coronado in his search for the Seven Cities of Cibola, discover the Colorado River.

Since there is no record of how far Alarcon traveled up the Colorado, it is Melchior Diaz who is credited with being the first European to reach the Colorado Desert.

Today, this is almost exclusively an agricultural region.

Getting Around

If possible, this is an even more desolate region than the Colorado River Corridor. Attempts to turn it into a retirement or a resort region have failed thus far.

Much of the area is dedicated to the Algodones Dunes, the Chocolate Mountains, the Salton Sea... and gunnery ranges. The entire northeastern portion along Interstate 10 is given over to a combination of the Mule Mountains, the Palo Verde Mountains, the Chuckwalla Mountains and the Little Chuckwalla Mountains.

Interstate 10 carries the bulk of the east-west traffic along the northern portion of the valley. Interstate 8 does the same along the southern portion. Only Highway 78, running eastward through Brawley and the Algodones Dunes, penetrates the huge region in between.

Of the north-south corridors, Highway 88 is the major link. It runs all the way from Calexico on the Mexican border, through El Centro and Brawley, along the western shore of the Salton Sea, to a junction with Interstate 10 near Indio. An alternate route, Highway 111, travels the eastern shore of the Salton Sea, passing through Thermal, Mecca, Niland and Calipatria before it too goes through Brawley on its way to Calexico and the Mexican border.

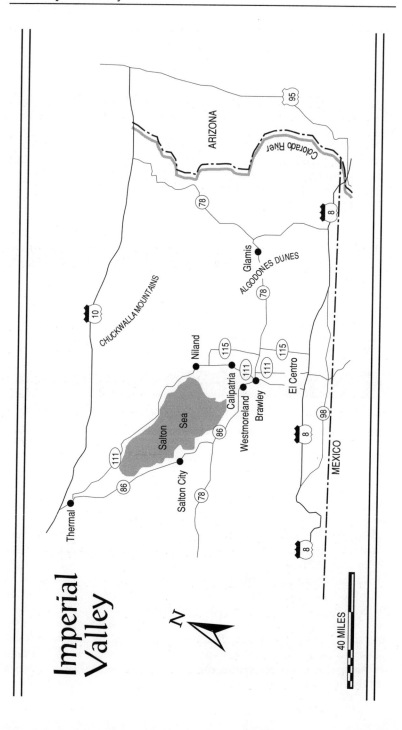

Touring

Algodones Dunes

Also known as the Glamis Dunes and the Imperial Sand Dunes, these gigantic piles of wind-blown sand extend for 45 miles – from three miles below the Mexican border to Mammoth Wash in the north.

Algodones ("cotton") Dunes constitute California's largest system of sand dunes. Novelist Zane Grey gave them a prominent role in his novel *Stairs of Sand*.

El Centro

El Centro, the birthplace of singer/actress Cher, is the largest community in the Imperial Valley. It has a population just slightly over 31,000.

The town sits 45 feet below sea level and is in the center of one of the richest farming areas in the world.

Holtville, nine miles east of town, sponsors an annual **Carrot Festival** every January.

Imperial, just north of town, harbors the **Imperial County Airport**.

The **U.S. Navy Blue Angels** aerobatic team, which maintains its winter training ground here, does an annual show for the local residents in mid-March.

Jack and Pauline McConnell, 2341 McConnell Rd., ☎ 619/352-3688, tour directors for the **Imperial Valley Farm Bureau**, arrange tours of Mexicali, Ojos Negros, San Felipe, Enseñada, Trinidad and Guadalupe.

INFORMATION SOURCES

El Centro Chamber of Commerce & Visitors Bureau, 1100 Main St., PO Box 3006, El Centro 92244-3006, ☎ 619/352-3681, fax 619/352-3246.

Holtville Chamber of Commerce, 101 W. Fifth, Holtville 92250, ☎ 619/356-2923.

Imperial Chamber of Commerce, 101 E. Fourth, Imperial 92251, ☎ 619/355-1609.

Bureau of Land Management, 333 S. Waterman Ave., El Centro 92243, ☎ 619/352-5842.

Brawley

After El Centro, the largest city in the region (population 25,000), Brawley is already gearing up for a Centennial Celebration in the year 2008.

At 113 feet below sea level, the town is even lower than El Centro, but there is an extensive canal system for irrigation and the streets of Brawley are lined with large trees. Fourteen parks contain more than 120 acres of land – six acres of parkland for every 1,000 people.

At certain times of the year, 90% of all the vegetables eaten in America come from this region. It was here that America's largest beet (45½ pounds) was grown, and it is here that the **Annual Sweet Onion Festival** is held every April. Tomatoes, cotton, melons, lettuce and other vegetables are also produced here.

The city is equally well known for its cattle breeding. Brawley produces more beef-pounds than any other place in the world.

Were it not for the vagaries of the marketplace, however, ostriches might have been more dominant in Brawley than cattle. In 1915, a local resident, Lord Mosely, stocked his farm with 2,200 ostriches and sold the plumes, which were used primarily to ornament women's hats, for $350 a pound. With the arrival of World War I, however, the demand for ostrich plumes disappeared and their price dropped to $3.30 a pound. Mosely died not long after that, and his ostriches were slaughtered.

The Southern Pacific Railroad runs through town. Boley Airport, which has direct flights to San Diego, Los Angeles, Ontario and Yuma, is just 12 miles south of town.

For more information, contact **Greater Brawley Chamber of Commerce**, 204 S. Imperial Ave., Brawley 92227, ☎ 619/344-3160, fax 619/344-7611.

Westmorland

To this community of 1,700, the addition of a 24-hour gas station/convenience store, two small restaurants (**Meno's** and **Ma & Pa's Kitchen**), and 28 homes in a span of one year has constituted a genuine building boom.

Calipatria

"The lowest-down city in the Western Hemisphere" (184 feet below sea level), Calipatria has a standard that flies the flag at exactly the same level as the Pacific Ocean.

Ramer Lake, **Finney Lake** and **Wiest Lake** are nearby. Nearby too is the **Salton Sea National Wildlife Refuge**.

For additional information, contact **Salton Sea National Wildlife Refuge**, PO Box 120, Calipatria 92233, ☎ 619/348-5278.

Salton Sea

With its surface 228 feet below sea level, the Salton Sea is a sea below a sea. It covers 230,000 acres (380 square miles) and is one of the world's largest inland bodies of salt water. It is California's largest inland body of water – 35 miles long, 15 miles wide, and an average of 20 feet deep.

The water in the Salton Sea is about 25% saltier than the Pacific Ocean. Rocks (volcanic pumice found along the lake's southern shore) float in it. Wood (ironwood) sinks in it. Some of the fish (mullet) have gizzards like birds. Vapors of dry ice at below-zero temperatures bubble up through the warm water near Niland on the southeast corner of the sea where carbon dioxide rises from a natural spring under the water.

A shallow arm of the Gulf of California once penetrated the Salton Trough as far north as Indio and possibly as far as San Gorgonio Pass above modern-day Palm Springs. Then, during post-glacial times, the Colorado River carved out the Grand Canyon and deposited the silt along what is now the boundary between Alta and Baja California. As the river emptied into the Gulf of California, the silt built up additional land masses, and eventually a delta-dike arose to separate the waters of the Gulf from those in the Salton Trough. Slowly, this inland sea disappeared through evaporation and dilution with fresh water.

There are tales of ancient ships swept into these seas by storms or tidal bores. Relics from vessels including Viking ships and Spanish galleons have been seen or found – some in the Fish Creek area of Anza-Borrego Desert State Park, some in the foothills of the Santa Rosa Mountains west of the Salton Sea, and others in the sand dunes throughout this area.

In 1900, the California Development Co. urged 12,000 people to invest in the region by the Salton Sea with the promise that Colorado River water would be diverted through an old river channel and "make the desert bloom like a rose." But in 1905, the careless construction of a head-gate caused the old Alamo River channel to silt up, thereby causing the Colorado River to create a new entry into the valley from below the Mexican border. A mile-wide breach reformed the New and the Alamo Rivers, and Mexicali and Calexico on the Mexican border were almost washed away.

In the Salton Sink, the town of Salton was flooded by a rising inland sea and nearly 50 miles of Southern Pacific Ralroad track were carried away. The floods destroyed the town of Silsby and a group of adobes near a former stage stop known as Indian Wells. The railroad spent over $4 million on an attempt to control the flood, but another breach occurred a year later.

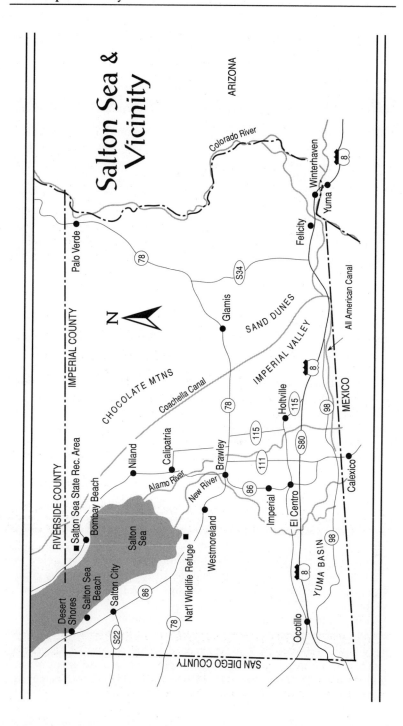

The latter breach was followed by the San Francisco earthquake, and subsequent efforts to end the formation of the Salton Sea ended.

The San Andreas fault line is clearly visible in a number of areas between Desert Hot Springs and the mud hills beyond the eastern shore of the Salton Sea.

In the washes west of the sea, palo verde trees are loaded with bursts of yellow in the spring and the smoke trees are filled with purple blooms in June.

Obsidian Butte rises from the shore of the sea, a mound of black glass. A row of power poles protrudes above the water, marking a submerged road that once connected what is now an island to the mainland.

A number of living ghost towns are scattered along both shores of the Salton Sea, sad reminders of those who once envisioned this place as an inland Riviera. The declining streets are lined with former motels forlornly peering out through shattered glass windows, empty gas stations and one-time grocery stores yearning for a customer, playgrounds that have turned to waist-high patches of weeds without knowing the sound of children's laughter, and residential areas that are lined with empty, deteriorating houses, once the embodiment of somebody's hopes and dreams. A declining number of residents continues to hold on, but one wonders if it wouldn't be wiser to bulldoze the past and begin anew.

INFORMATION SOURCES

Salton Sea State Recreation Area, PO Box 3166, North Shore 92254, ☎ 619/393-3052.

California Park Service, Salton Sea Sector, 100-225 State Park Rd., North Shore 92254, ☎ 619/393-3059.

Sea & Desert Interpretive Assn., PO Box 3166, North Shore 92254.

Salton City

This tragic wannabe has some of the essentials of a viable community – a restaurant, a police station, a library, a gas station and a small airport.

West Shores Golf Course, N. Marina Dr. to Atlantic Blvd., provides nine holes of outdoor recreation.

Niland

This small community off the southeastern end of the Salton Sea celebrates an annual **Tomato and Sportsmen's Festival**. It is not clear whether the object is to shoot at a tomato... or to throw a tomato at the nearest fisherman.

Imperial Wildlife Area, Wister Unit, is 3½ miles north of town off Highway 111.

Chocolate Mountains east of Niland are rich with old mines, historic trails and potential archeological sites. Unfortunately, they have been closed to the public since World War II and are now used as an aerial gunnery range. These and other desert mountain ranges in this region contain bighorn sheep, a protected species of which there are three varieties: the Nelson bighorn, the California bighorn and the Peninsula bighorn. The last two species are now listed as rare animals.

For more information, contact **Niland Chamber of Commerce**, PO Box 112, Niland 92257, ☎ 619/348-0552; or **California Department of Fish & Game**, 8700 Davis Rd., Niland 92257, ☎ 619/359-0577.

Chuckwalla Mountains

Within these mountains, 45 miles east of Indio, is the Munz cholla, an unusual tree-like form of cholla that grows to a height of 15 feet.

Glamis

Osborne County Park is west of town off Highway 78.

Thermal

Valeries Jean Date Gardens, 66th Ave. and Highway 86, is the nation's oldest date oasis (1928). Date shakes were invented here. And while you're at it, try their cactus shake, which is made of prickly pear syrup.

Oasis Date Gardens, 59-111 Highway 111, ☎ 619/399-5665 or 800/827-8017, is a 250-acre working date garden started in 1912. A video describing the history and cultivation of dates, man's oldest cultivated fruit, is presented. Tours are available, and there is a farm animal petting zoo. A country store provides free samples of the locally grown dates.

Adventures

On Foot

When hiking in the desert, always carry two quarts of water per person. Use sunscreen and wear sturdy shoes (not thongs or open sandals), a long-sleeved shirt and a hat. Long trousers are recommended. If you expect to be out after dark, take along some warm clothing.

At night, always carry a flashlight and watch where you walk. Snakes become active at night during the summer.

If you become disoriented, remember that a wash, when followed downhill, will eventually lead to a road, a river or a town.

THE DESERT TORTOISE

The desert tortoise is California's state reptile and can only be found in three other states: Arizona, Utah and Nevada. Avoid handling them. When frightened, they generally empty their bladders, which causes some people to drop them and possibly injure them. Emptying their bladders also can dehydrate the creatures and lead to their death. Check under your car when you are parked in the desert to be sure a tortoise isn't lying in the shade beneath it.

If it is still in print, try to get a copy of *California Off-Highway Vehicle Guidebook*, published by the **California Department of Parks & Recreation**, PO Box 942896, Sacramento 94296-0001. If it's not, see if you can locate one in a used book store. It contains many useful maps and a great deal of information about off-highway driving in California.

Algodones Outstanding Natural Area

This region, 20 miles east of Brawley on the north side of State Highway 78, was set aside by the Bureau of Land Management (BLM) to preserve the native flora and fauna. Although cyclists and off-road drivers are barred from this area, hikers are permitted.

If you visit here, be sensitive to the reason for its existence and avoid damaging anything you find.

Plants that are found in this area include creosote bush, sandpaper plant, desert buckwheat, desert witchgrass, Pierson's locoweed, silver-leaved dune sunflower, three-forked ephedra, plicate coldenia, ironwood, palo verde, honey mesquite, screwbean mesquite and desert willow.

Also sometimes encountered are the rare Pierson's milkvetch and the equally rare giant Spanish needle.

Sandfood, a parasitic plant which obtains its food by tapping the roots of nearby desert shrubs, is an unusual dune resident which appears on the surface of the ground each spring. Although it has a long, thick, succulent root, all that shows is a round, thick, sand-colored head that produces a small purple flower. The Indians considered this plant a delicacy.

Animals that can often be found include rabbits, ground squirrels, birds and lizards.

On a quiet spring evening, you might hear a gecko, one of the few lizards that has a voice. They use their voice primarily to call a mate.

For more information, contact the **BLM El Centro Resource Area**, 1661 S. 4th St., El Centro 92243-4561, ☎ 619/353-1060; or the **BLM California Desert District**, 6221 Box Springs Blvd., Riverside 92507-0714, ☎ 909/697-5200.

Chuckwalla Mountains

Although a four-wheel-drive vehicle is required to get in, there are several nice hikes in these mountains, including **Ship Creek**, **Black Butte** and **Viewpoint**. **Corn Springs Wash** makes a nice hiking or backpacking trip.

Mecca

Painted Canyon is northeast of town, about 15 miles north of the Salton Sea. Take Highway 111 north to Mecca and then turn off on Highway 195.

Ocotillo

To locate **Rockhouse Canyon Trail**, begin at I-8 in Ocotillo and take County Road S-2 16 miles to the turnoff for Bow Willow Canyon and Campground. Follow the good hard-packed sand road 1½ miles to the campground. Walk up Bow Willow Canyon on the signed jeep trail a short distance, then turn left (south) across a few hundred yards of wash to pick up the foot trail. Climb steadily through granite boulders, agave and cholla until the trail begins to descend toward Rockhouse Canyon, where it intersects with the Rockhouse Canyon Jeep Trail. Follow the jeep trail west (right) for one mile to Swartz's abandoned rock house. A foot trail then takes you down into Bow Willow Canyon. Keep to the right again and follow the canyon. You will encounter the bitter-tasting coyote melon along the way. Soon there will be a barrier designed to keep off-road vehicles from entering the upper reaches of the canyon. Past the barrier, the canyon widens, leaving an easy two-mile hike over soft sand back to the Bow Willow Campground.

Ocotillo Wells

Six miles south of Ocotillo Wells on Split Mountain Rd., a marked turnoff leads to **Elephant Tree Discovery Trail**. Botanists disputed the existence of elephant trees until a 1937 expedition established their existence once and for all. Elephant trees flourish with barrel cacti, cholla, ocotillo and smoke trees along this 1½-mile trail.

Truckhaven Trail, on County Road S-22 north of Ocotillo Wells, is a good place to find petrified palm wood.

Salton City

To reach **Calcite Canyon Trail**, take County Road S-22 west from Highway 86 north of town to Calcite Jeep Road, which is located just west of a microwave tower. Follow the jeep road as it drops into the south fork of Palm Wash and then starts to climb northwest. The road dips and then climbs the last half-mile toward an old calcite mine. Two miles from the trailhead, the road ends at the mining area. At one point along the Middle Fork of the trail, the passage is so narrow it has been dubbed "Fat Man's Misery."

Salton Sea

Salton Sea National Wildlife Refuge, 906 W.Sinclair Rd., Calipatria 92233-0120, ☎ 619/348-5278, is the office. To get to the refuge itself, take Sinclair Rd. off Highway 111 six miles south of Niland and keep driving until you reach the gate. The refuge encompasses 35,484 acres of salt marsh and open water, plus 2,000 acres of adjacent pasture and freshwater marsh. Camping and picnicking are not allowed, but tours through the main waterfowl concentration areas can be arranged with the refuge manager. The **Sea and Desert Interpretive Center**, located here, is open daily, October through May, and presents a 20-minute video covering the history of the sea.

Ironwood Nature Trail in the Salton Sea National Wildlife Refuge is particularly interesting and informative. Pick up a brochure at the office and look for the numbered posts that will identify areas of special interest. Watch for these, in particular:

- ★ **Post 3** - Salt Grass. This plant excretes salt through its leaves. Touch the blades of grass and then taste the salt on your fingers.
- ★ **Post 4** - Whitefield Stream. In this fresh, spring-fed water, look for young tilapia and polywogs. The area also contains muskrats, raccoons, kit fox, bobcats and coyotes.
- ★ **Post 6** - Alkali Goldenbush. A cold tonic is made from the leaves of this plant.

★ **Post 7** - Dyebush. Gently pinch the stems and see the color on your fingers.

★ **Post 10** - Cheesebush. Gently rub the stems with your fingers and smell the cheese. Do not break off the stems; it could kill the plant.

Hiking also is available in **Salton Sea State Recreational Area**. For further information, write to 100-225 State Park Rd., North Shore 92254, ☎ 619/393-3052 or 393-3059, fax 619/393-1338, e-mail shorvitz@ix.net-com.com.

Bureau of Land Management, ☎ 619/337-4456 or 337-4400, arranges desert hikes to **Hag's Tooth Arch**, **Imperial Sand Dunes**, **Tumco** and **Sacatone**. The hikes are limited to 25 people and begin at 8 am. The trailheads are reachable by passenger car, but require a 1½- to 2-hour drive each way, so carpooling is encouraged.

HUNTING

Duck hunting is permitted in Brawley. **Finney Lake** in Calipatria provides good hunting. In Niland, Fish & Game permits hunting at its **Wister Unit** on the Salton Sea, and the Salton Sea State Recreation Area allows hunting, too.

ROCKHOUNDING

There is gold in the **Cargo Muchacho Mountains** south of Tumco. Just west of **Coral Reef** is a good place to look for fossils. **Davies Valley** offers nice agates in the mountains east of town. West of Draper Lake you can find geodes and agate.

Thw mountains west of **Imperial Dam** offer agate, as do the hills west of **Martinez Lake**. Agate may also be found in the mountains east of **Ogilby**.

There is petrified wood east of Painted Gorge.

The **Palo Verde Mountains** offer fire agate, and chalcedony roses are in the **Coon Hollow** area. Farther west, just below the Riverside County line, geodes can be found. West of **Picacho State Park** there is agate and petrified palm. In the mountains south of **Picacho Mine**, there is gold.

Northeast of **Superstition Mountain**, fossils can be found. Walker Lake is the place to look for geodes and agate west of the lake. The mountains southwest of Westmorland contain fossils.

BIRDWATCHING

Calipatria

Ramer and **Finney Lakes** form a migratory bird refuge.

Niland

The **Hasard Unit** of the Fish & Game Refuge on the Salton Sea near here provides good birdwatching.

Salton Sea

Some 380 species have been noted around the Salton Sea, including the blue-footed booby, the brown booby and the frigate bird. You can see species here that cannot be seen anywhere else in California. Winter is the most productive season, since the sea is a major stop on the Pacific Flyway. Along the northern end of the sea, the best areas to concentrate on are **Whitewater River Delta, Johnson Ave.**, the **State Park headquarters, Salt Creek** and **81st and 84th Sts.** Along the southeastern shore of the sea, try **Wister** fish hatchery and wildlife area, **Red Hill Marina** and the mouth of **New River.**

Salton Sea National Wildlife Refuge is a wintering area for waterfowl. Peak populations are present in December and January.

TREASURE HUNTING

Ocotillo

There is a tale of treasure associated with the **Rockhouse Canyon Trail.** As the story goes, Nicolas Swartz removed $18,000 in gold from a remote mine before building a rock house in this canyon in 1906. Swartz died without telling anyone the location of his mine, but some believe there is a clue to its whereabouts somewhere in or around his old stone house. Unfortunately, there are *two* rock houses in the area, and either one could have been Swartz's original house.

Salton Sea

A dirt side road from the All-American Canal at the end of Parkside Dr. running east from the Salton Sea Recreation Area headquarters leads to **Dos Palmas Spring.** (Pioneer Herman Ehrenberg, who founded a town in Arizona bearing his name, was murdered here on Oct. 9, 1866.) A stagecoach driver was murdered and robbed of his cargo of gold in this region. When the robber went into a bar and paid for his liquor in gold, it aroused suspicion and the sheriff was notified. Before the robber could escape, he was shot and killed, but his stash of gold was never found.

Juan de Iturbe's lost pearl ship must be somewhere in the Salton Sea or buried under the sands of Algodones Dunes. In March 1615, Iturbe and Pedro Alverez de Rosales sailed up the Gulf of California. Along the way, their divers were very successful in gathering pearls, and the adventurers also traded biscuits for pearls among the friendly Indians. At 27 degrees latitude, however, the party was attacked by savages and Iturbe continued northward alone through a narrow waterway that opened into a vast sea. Believing that he had found the fabled Straits of Anian, a legendary passage between the two oceans, he ventured as far as 34 degrees latitude (right around present-day Palm Springs). Realizing that he had not found the Straits of Anian, Iturbe tried to return south, only to find that his ship was land-locked. Abandoning the ship and its cargo of pearls, Iturbe and his crew worked their way overland to the Gulf, where they were subsequently rescued. There are occasional reports from people who claim to have seen a ship intermittently exposed in the wind-blown sand dunes.

Superstition Mountain

Hank Brandt, a French-Canadian who had already discovered a rich mine in Baja, found an even richer one near Superstition Mountain. Brandt said the mine is in a place where jade, several petrified palms, the imprint of a petrified ship in sandstone and some whale bones or mastodon tusks are found. He said there are two dry lakes marked with two ironwood trees, a canyon with reddish-brown sandstone walls, a wall of purple talc, a double-decked cave, and another cave filled with *ollas* (clay pots made by the Indians) in the area. He said there is a seepage around which a large swarm of bees continually buzzed, and a canyon filled with mesquite near a high bank out of which cropped a boulder with a huge ocotillo on top. Brandt said that the mine is in a hidden valley above that spot. Some who have searched for the spot have placed the mine within five miles of Fish Creek Mountains.

On Horseback

Although there are few horse-rental establishments in this region, inquiring among local shopkeepers or checking the local Yellow Pages might turn up a horse when you decide to go riding. Certainly, there is plenty of lovely country in which to ride once you get away from the mile-after-mile of cultivated farm fields and the fenced cattle compounds.

RODEO

Brawley

The annual **Cattle Call Celebration** is held every November and lasts an entire week. It comes complete with parade, chili cook-off, mariachi festival and rodeo. The rodeo is one of the largest professional rodeos in California and attracts some 50,000 spectators.

On Wheels

When out in the wild throughout this region, beware of suspicious objects. Since World War II, much of this area has been used as a gunnery range. If you see any unexploded ordnance, *don't touch it!*

Bikers should be prepared to walk their bikes through washes. Wide, knobby tires are better than thin, touring tires.

OHV RULES

All off-highway vehicle riders must wear an approved safety helmet. OHVs must be equipped with a whip that extends at least eight feet above the ground and bears either a red or an orange flag that is at least 6 x 12 inches in size.

Within 50 feet of any camp or any group of people and within 500 feet of Highway 78, Gecko Rd., Grays Wells Rd., and the roads within Gecko and Roadrunner Campgrounds, the speed limit is 15 miles per hour.

Algodones Sand Dunes

Cyclists and off-road drivers flock to these dunes, just 20 miles east of Brawley off SR 78, ☎ 619/337-4400. Off-highway vehicle activity is permitted on more than two-thirds of the dunes – more than 118,000 acres. The most popular areas for off-road driving are:

★ Mammoth Wash at the north end of the dunes.
★ Glamis/Gecko just south of State Highway 78.
★ Buttercup Valley just south of I-8 near the Mexican border.

Organized competition or commercial off-highway events, such as sand drags, closed-course racing and hill climbs, are sometimes conducted. A Special Recreation Use Permit from the BLM is needed.

Immediately north of State Highway 78, BLM established the **Algodones Outstanding Natural Area** to protect sensitive plant and animal species. The use of off-road vehicles in that area is prohibited.

Chuckwalla Mountains

There are dirt roads that run into several canyons along the northeast of this range. One leads to a petroglyph site in an oasis of dense palm trees.

Bradshaw Trail is an east-west road for four-wheel-drive vehicles. Take I-10 east from Indio about 45 miles to the Red Cloud Mine exit. On the south side of the interstate, get on the dirt Red Cloud Mine Rd. heading south. (The Chocolate Mountains Aerial Gunnery Range is just south of this trail, so it's a good idea not to wander south of the road.)

Another nice vehicular route involves taking I-10 about three miles west from Desert Center to the Eagle Mountain exit. Get on the frontage road paralleling the south side of the interstate and continue going west. Although the road usually is manageable in an ordinary car, there are several sandy stretches. There are beautiful stands of cactus around here, best seen from February through mid-June.

Glamis

This is an important staging area for off-roaders along State Highway 78.

Salton Sea

Bradshaw Trail runs from the Salton Sea to the Colorado River and is very popular with off-roaders. Just be careful: the trail goes through a number of hazardous areas.

On & In the Water

Calipatria

Wiest and **Romer Lakes** are popular for swimming, boating, jetskiing and fishing. **Finney Lake** south of town is good for fishing.

The **Colorado River** is less than an hour away.

Niland

Jetty fishing is available at the **Niland Marina**.

Fishing in the Salton Sea also is good at **Bombay Beach**, at the Fish & Game **Wister Unit**, from the rocks at **Red Hill Marina**, at the Fish & Game **Hasard Unit**, and from the rocks at **Black Rock**, 12 miles southwest of town. Locals catch bass and catfish from **Highland Canal**, southeast of town.

Small boat launching is allowed at **Red Hill Marina** and **Black Rock**.

Bashford's Aquaculture, 10590 Hot Mineral Spa Rd., ☎ 619/354-1315, permits catfishing on Saturdays and Sundays. No license required.

Salton Sea

Fishing for orange-mouth corvina (or corbina) is good from April to August with live bait or lures. Croaker (bairdiella) also like live or cut bait and lures, and usually can be caught between April and October.

Use canned corn to catch sargo between November and April, and nightcrawlers to catch tilapia year-round, especially when the water is warm. Tilapia are an East African perch introduced into many Southwestern canals as a means of controlling algae. They are a good eating fish with a rather nutty flavor. Boating and waterskiing also are popular on the sea. Due to the high density of the water, boats move faster.

Salton Sea State Recreation Area

Swimming, boating and fishing are available here.

Seeley

Sunbeam Lake, located south of town between Highway S-80 and I-8, provides fishing.

In the Air

Thermal

Sailplane Enterprises, Thermal Airport, ☎ 800/586-7627, offers a 20-minute introductory flight in a glider (sailplane). The aircraft can carry one or two passengers. The company also flies out of Hemet-Ryan Airport, half an hour southeast of Riverside.

Fantasy Balloon Flights, 83701 Ave. 54, ☎ 619/398-6322 or 800/GO ABOVE, arranges flights in two- to six-passenger hot-air balloons.

Eco-Travel/Cultural Excursions

Brawley

To the west is **Superstition Mountain**, feared by the early Indians because of strange noises that came from its interior. Prison convicts who once operated a rock-crushing mill adjacent to the mountain told stories of moans and rumblings in the night as well.

A California geologist theorized in 1965 that the mountain was Aztlan, fabled homeland of the Aztec nation. In the first year of the Aztec calendar, a highly civilized tribe called the Crane People began wandering from their homeland far to the north of Mexico: the Vale of Aztlan ("place of reeds and herons"), an island with seven caves in a lake surrounded by mountains and much swampy land.

It is interesting to note that Pueblo Indian legends closely match those of the Aztecs in describing their origins. According to the Pueblo, Mother Earth gave birth to their early ancestors in a dark underground world (or cave) surrounded by landlocked waters. A tremendous stone, "solid and resting upon the earth like an inverted bowl," covered the cavern. There were blue mountains to the west, red mountains to the north, white mountains to the south and yellow mountains to the east. Could the blue mountains have been the Laguna Mountains; the red mountains, Redrock Canyon in the Fish Creek Mountains or perhaps the sandstone cliffs of Mecca Hills; the white mountains, the snow-capped Sierra San Pedro Martir; and the yellow mountains, the Algodones sand dunes?

El Centro

Mesquite Lake Resource Recovery Project burns 500 tons of cow patties a day at a cost of $1 per ton and then sells the power to Southern California Edison. In the future, it plans to burn Imperial Valley crop wastes as well.

Alford's Antique Car Museum, 599 E. Main, is open on weekdays 8 to 5. Admission is free.

Holtville

Imperial Valley Swiss Museum, 1585 E. Worthington Rd., ☎ 619/356-1183, arranges tours by appointment only.

Imperial

Pioneers' Museum, 373 E. Aten Rd., ☎ 619/352-1165, is operated by the Imperial County Historical Society. Across the street from Imperial Valley College, it is open daily 10 to 4. Guided group tours can be arranged by appointment.

Niland

Fountain of Youth Spa, 10249 Coachella Canal Rd., ☎ 619/354-1340, fax 619/354-1558, and **Bashford's Hot Mineral Spa**, both east of Bombay Beach, are therapeutic natural mineral waters bubbling from the ground at 170°. They are the only springs in America with the same rock and mineral properties as the springs at Yellowstone National Park.

Scientists say the Imperial Valley has one of the largest geothermal potentials in the world.

Where To Stay

B&Bs, Hotels & Inns

Calipatria

Calipatria Inn, 700 N. Sorensen (Highway 111) at Young Rd., ☎ 619/348-7348, is done up in Southwestern decor and has a heated pool and spa. There are 40 rooms, including one two-bedroom unit. The family lobby has a fireplace, games and a library. A continental breakfast is served.

El Centro

Ramada Inn of El Centro, 1455 W. Ocotillo Dr., ☎ 619/352-5152 or 800/805-4000, offers the kind of accommodations you would expect from a part of the Ramada chain. Given a three-diamond rating by AAA, it has 148 rooms, a restaurant and bar, a heated pool and an exercise room.

Brunner's, 215 N. Imperial Ave., ☎ 619/352-6431, is just a mile north of I-8. There are 88 rooms, including 20 one-bedroom apartments, plus a restaurant and an exercise room.

Holtville

Barbara Worth Golf Resort & Convention Center, 2050 Country Club Dr., ☎ 619/356-2806 or 800/356-3806, is near El Centro. Although the rooms are reminiscent of the old-fashioned row motels from the outside, they do overlook the golf course, and the restaurant may be the best place to eat in the region.

Imperial

Best Western Imperial Valley Inn, 1093 Airport Blvd., ☎ 619/355-4500, fax 619/355-8645, features 90 rooms and 10 suites. Located next to Imperial Valley County Airport, it also has a restaurant and bar, coin laundry and an exercise room.

Camping

Algodones Dunes

Gecko Campground is a BLM facility. To get there, go east of Brawley to the point where Highway 78 intersects with Highway 115. Go east on Highway 78 11.8 miles to Gecko Rd. and turn south. The campground is 3.3 miles off Highway 78.

    Roadrunner Campground also is a BLM facility, ☎ 619/337-4400. It is just 2.3 miles farther off Highway 78 on Gecko Rd. than the Gecko Campground.

Calipatria

There are camping facilities at nearby **Finnery Lake** (no phone).

Chuckwalla Mountains

Corn Springs has a BLM campground (no phone).

El Centro

Desert Trails RV Park, 225 Wake Ave., ☎ 619/352-7275, provides 364 full-hookup sites plus a nine-hole executive golf course (**Broken Spoke Country Club**), a 200-yard driving range, five shuffleboard courts, a heated pool and a spa.

Niland

Fountain of Youth Spa, 10249 Coachella Canal Rd., ☎ 619/354-1340, fax 619/354-1558, has an RV park.

    Bombay Beach has a trailer park and permits camping. The **Wister Unit**, Fish & Game Department, allows camping. **Red Hill Marina** has a trailer park. ☎ 619/393-3052 or 393-3059 for information on these three sites.

Salton Sea

California Department of Parks & Recreation, ☎ 916/653-6995, has five separate campgrounds on Highway 111:

- ★ **Headquarters** has 15 full hookup sites and 25 campsites.
- ★ **Mecca Beach** has 109 developed campsites.
- ★ **Corvina Beach** provides primitive camping.
- ★ **Salt Creek** also offers primitive camping, but there is no water.
- ★ **Bombay Beach** permits primitive camping.

Where To Eat

El Centro

E. T.'s Glo Room Restaurant and Lounge, 1075 Adams St., is the best place to try the Imperial Valley's famous beef.

Holtville

Barbara Worth Golf Resort, 2050 Country Club Rd., has a seafood buffet on Fridays and a prime rib buffet on Saturdays. (See *Where to Stay,* above.)

California's Outback

This enormous region is noted for its rugged terrain and its hostile climate.

Strangely fertile when aided by a little rain, it provides a home for a variety of creatures that could live in no other environment. Similarly, most of the flora and fauna found elsewhere in America would die within days if it were transplanted here.

Only the hardiest of adventurers have ventured through this part of the country. Miners, mountain men, explorers. Some remain buried here, often in unmarked graves.

So desolate is the region that hundreds of square miles have been set aside by the government for use as military training centers (bombing ranges). If not here, then where?

Here, the northern portion of the Sonoran Desert abuts the southern end of the Mojave Desert. Here, there are no major metropolitan areas. Indeed Las Vegas, Nevada is closer than either Los Angeles or San Diego.

Here, truly, is California's outback.

Getting Around

Once again, east-west traffic prevails throughout this section of southern California.

Along the southern perimeter, Interstate 10 makes a beeline from Blythe near the Colorado River toward downtown Los Angeles. Interstate 40 bisects the midsection, carrying traffic from Needles, and points east to Barstow. Northeast of I-40, Interstate 15 heads northeast, linking the population centers of southern California, Los Angeles and San Diego with the pleasure palaces of Las Vegas.

If time is no factor, the more adventuresome traveler might prefer to foresake the interstates in favor of Highway 62, which skirts the northern edge of Joshua Tree National Park. US 95 connects Needles with Las Vegas, and Highway 127 heads due north out of Baker, striking out across the bleak western portion of Nevada.

California's Outback

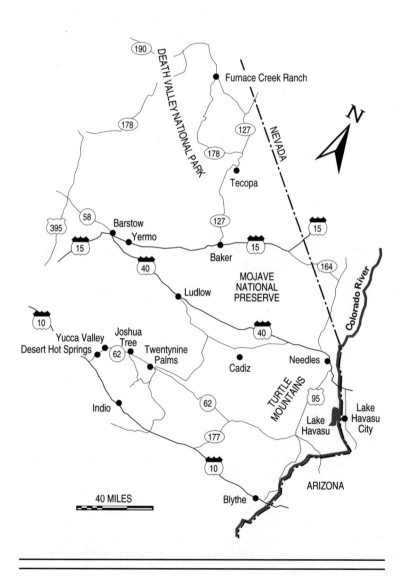

Touring

North of Desert Center

Cadiz

Cadiz Dunes can be reached from Barstow by taking I-40 east for 80 miles to the Kelbaker Rd. exit, or by taking I-40 west from Needles for 66 miles to the same exit. Go south on Kelbaker Rd. for 11 miles to the National Trails Highway and turn east. Go five more miles to Cadiz Rd., then drive southwest on the dirt road for about 2½ miles. The dunes are off-limits to off-road vehicles.

From the east side of **Old Woman Mountains**, you can see the "Old Woman Statue," a stone peak that looks like a woman with a shawl over her head. Old mining roads provide good hiking on the east and west sides of the range.

East Mojave Natural Scenic Area

Chiriaco Summit is the site of the **General Patton Memorial**, ☎ 619/227-3483, which marks the area in which Maj. Gen. George S. Patton Jr. trained American troops for the campaign against Germany's General Rommel in North Africa during the early stages of World War II. Rock-lined walkways, parts of stone walls, outdoor chapels and tank tracks are still visible. In the northeastern part of the camp is a topographical map of the entire desert training area that was used during Patton's maneuvers.

The training facility was founded here, 30 miles east of Indio, in March 1942. The headquarters were at Camp Young near Shavers Summit, as Chiriaco Summit was then known. The training base was 350 miles wide and 250 miles long, stretching from Pomona, California to Phoenix, Arizona, and from Yuma, Arizona to Boulder City, Nevada.

Ten other camps were included in the facility: Camp Coxcomb, Camp Iron Mountain, Camp Granite, Camp Essex, Camp Ibis, Camp Hyder, Camp Horn, Camp Laguna, Camp Pilot Knob and Camp Bouse. Massive tent cities housed tanks, repair shops, hospitals, aviation facilities, anti-aircraft guns and field artillery.

The world's largest training facility, both in size and in population, the camps trained nearly a million men and women for combat.

Patton left the facility in August 1942 to head Operation Torch, the strike against Rommel, and the facility was closed on April 30, 1944.

To get there, take Highway 62 east from Twentynine Palms for 52 miles to the intersection with Highway 177, then continue on Highway 62 for another 1.1 miles. Near Granite Pass, look for a gravel poleline road on the north side of the road and turn northeast. Go about 2½ miles to a sign and some fencing that mark the camp area. Continue east for 0.3 miles along the road indicated by the sign to a turnstile in the fenced area.

Kelso

Site of a neo-Spanish railroad depot on the Union Pacific line, the town is best known for the **Kelso Dunes** on the southwest side of town. The sand cascading down the steep slopes emits a frightening booming sound.

Mojave National Preserve

Designated a national preserve in 1994, this area encompasses 1.4 million acres between Interstate 15 and Interstate 40. Within its confines are mountains, mesas, red volcanic spires, cinder cones and sand dunes. Some of the petroglyphs found here are more than 10,000 years old. The average annual rainfall is just five to 10 inches, yet summer storms sometimes result in flash floods.

Three hundred species of animals live here, including bighorn sheep, mule deer, porcupines, mountain lions, coyotes, kit foxes and desert tortoises. Plants include the yucca, sage, rabbitbush and Joshua tree. Wildflower displays can be vivid in April and May.

For additional information, contact **Mojave National Preserve**, 222 E. Main St., Barstow 92311, ☎ 619/255-8801.

Turtle Mountains

The **Mopah Range** is where to find the native California fan palm (the rare *Washingtonia filifera*), the crucifixion thorn and the smoke tree.

North Of Indio

Indio

A typical "working man's town," Indio owes much of its prosperity to dates. No less than 95% of the nation's dates are grown here.

The **National Date Festival** is held every February at the Riverside County Fairgrounds, ☎ 800/811-FAIR, fax 619/863-8973, Web site www.co.riverside.ca.us/activity/datefest. Sporting an Arabian Nights theme (dress in an Arabian costume and get in free), the event features the Blessing of the Dates, as well as camel and ostrich races.

Covalda's Indio Date Shop, 83-636 Indio Blvd., ☎ 619/347-3056, fax 619/398-3551; **Indio Orchards**, 80-521 Highway 111, ☎ 619/347-7534; **Jensen's Dates & Citrus Gardens**, 80-653 Highway 111, ☎ 619/347-3897, fax 714/832-3529; or **Shields Date Gardens**, 80-225 Highway 111, ☎ 619/347-0996, fax 619/342-3288, will sell you all of the dates and date-related products you can carry. **Haldey Fruit Orchards**, Apache Trail exit off I-10, ☎ 909/849-5255, advertises itself as the "Originator of Trail Mix." For more information, contact **Indio Chamber of Commerce**, 82-503 Hwy 111, PO Drawer TTT, Indio 92202, ☎ 619/347-0676 or 800/444-6346.

Desert Hot Springs

Sitting on the "wrong" (north) side of I-10 from Palm Springs, Rancho Mirage, and the other jewels of the desert, has missed the glamor and growth of its neighbors. The town (pop.15,000) has been plagued with teenage crime problems, but it continues to serve as a gateway to Joshua Tree. **Old Indian Pueblo**, 67-616 E. Desert View, is the fruition of a World War I veteran who built the castle patterned after the Pueblo cliff dwellings in New Mexico. Using second-hand lumber, railway ties and hand-made adobe bricks, Cabot Yerxa's dream became a four-story mansion with 24 rooms – all with a different roof level. Yerxa died in 1965 at age 83. For details, contact **Desert Hot Springs Chamber of Commerce**, 11711 West Dr., Desert Hot Springs 92240, ☎ 800/346-3347.

Joshua Tree

Sixteen miles north of this little town is **Giant Rock**, a seven-story monster sitting alone in the desert. Franz Critzer, an American of German descent, moved here from Santa Monica in 1929. With chisel and dynamite, he hollowed out a home inside the rock that would be cool in the summer and warm in the winter. He erected a windsock, thereby converting the dry lakebed adjacent to Giant Rock into an airport. From that time on, Critzer made his living servicing and repairing airplanes. In 1949, Giant Rock Airport was leased by George Van Tassel, who moved into the rock with his wife and children. Van Tassel added electricity and opened a café.

One of the earliest advocates of Unidentified Flying Objects (UFOs), Van Tassel sponsored an annual UFO convention that attracted up to 15,000 people. He also wrote a book about them entitled *The Council of Seven Lights*, and constructed a dome-shaped Time Machine that would provide perpetual youth by "recharging" living cells, thereby retarding the aging process.

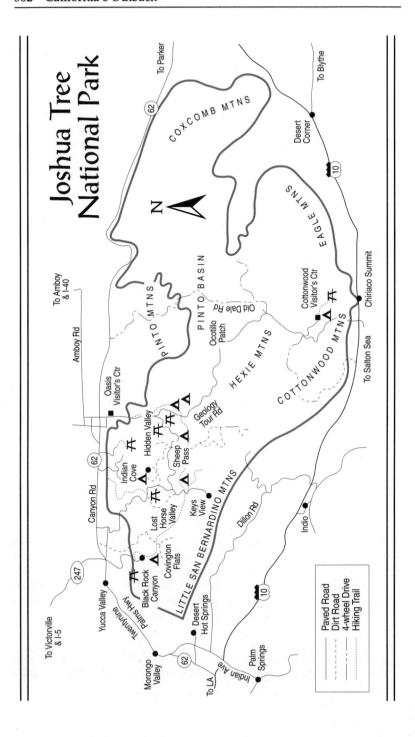

Joshua Tree
National Park

COXCOMB MTNS

To Parker
To Blythe

62

Desert
Corner

10

N

EAGLE MTNS

PINTO MTNS

PINTO BASIN

Old Dale Rd

To Amboy
& I-40

Ocotillo
Patch

Cottonwood
Visitor's Ctr

Amboy Rd

Oasis
Visitor's Ctr

HEXIE MTNS

Chiriaco Summit

Geology
Tour Rd

COTTONWOOD MTNS

To Salton Sea

Canyon Rd

62

Hidden Valley

Sheep
Pass

Indian
Cove

Indio

Lost
Horse
Valley

Keys
View

LITTLE SAN BERNARDINO MTNS

Dillon Rd

Covington
Flats

247

Black Rock
Canyon

10

Yucca Valley

Twentynine Palms Hwy

To Victorville
& I-5

Desert
Hot Springs

Palm
Springs

Morongo
Valley

62

To LA

Indian Ave

Paved Road
Dirt Road
4-wheel Drive
Hiking Trail

JOSHUA TREE NATIONAL PARK

Recently upgraded from a national monument to a national park, this area covers more than 850 square miles, about the size of Rhode Island.

The tallest known Joshua tree is 41½ feet tall; the oldest is close to 1,000 years old.

INFORMATION SOURCES

Cottonwood Visitor Center just north of I-10.
Oasis Visitor Center outside Twentynine Palms.
Joshua Tree Chamber of Commerce, ☎ 619/366-3723.
Joshua Tree National Park, 74485 National Park Dr., Twentynine Palms 92277, ☎ 619/367-7511 or 367-1488.

Ludlow

Sagging southeastward from Ludlow and reemerging at Interstate 40 between Fenner and Needles is a 75-mile stretch of old **Route 66**, "Old National Trail Highway." Also located along this stretch of American highway history are the towns of Amboy, Chambless and Essex.

Located east of Barstow on the Santa Fe Railroad line, the area around Ludlow produced over $6 million in gold, more than half the county's total, in its heyday. The Bagdad-Chase mine alone produced $4.5 million worth of gold in just seven years.

Copper and silver also are found here.

Twentynine Palms

Also known as Palm City, this small community is surprisingly old. It was founded in 1873. The first city hall was a 20-foot-high water tower supported by slanted wooden walls. They could not only handle city business there, but also could stand under the tank and take a shower.

For more information, contact **Twentynine Palms Chamber of Commerce**, 6136 Adobe Rd., Twentynine Palms 92277, ☎ 619/367-3445 or 800/533-7104.

Yermo

Calico Early Man Archaeological Site, 150 Coolwater Ln., ☎ 619/256-5102 or 256-8313, is near I-15 at the Minneola Rd. exit.

The excavation was begun by Dr. Louis Leakey in 1964, and more than 12,000 stone tools dating as far back as 200,000 years have been found, making this one of the earliest tool sites ever discovered in the Western Hemisphere.

Yucca Valley

The gateway to Joshua Tree National Park, this little community has two attractions worth visiting.

Desert Christ Park contains Antone Martin's *World Peace Shrine* sculpture. Also known as the Antone Martin Memorial, the site displays more than 50 statues, each three times life size, that were hand-carved by Martin over a period of 20 years.

Hi-Desert Nature Museum, 57116 Twentynine Palms Hwy., ☎ 619/369-7212, fax 619/369-1605, exhibits rocks, minerals, Indian artifacts and desert creatures in the Yucca Valley Community Center complex off Highway 62.

For more information, contact **Yucca Valley Chamber of Commerce,** 56300 Twentynine Palms Hwy. (Highway 62), Suite D, Yucca Valley 92284, ☎ 619/365-6323, fax 619/365-0763.

North of Baker

Baker

A 19th-century military outpost named **Soda Springs** was once situated here. Later, there was a health resort by the unlikely name of **Zzyzx.**

Now the town is the home of the **California Desert Studies Center.** For more information, ☎ 619/256-8617.

Tecopa

Tecopa Hot Springs Park, Tecopa Hot Springs Rd., ☎ 619/852-4264, is off Highway 127. The park has two free public bathhouses, famous for their mineral content, that are open 24 hours a day and are segregated by sex. There also is a nature preserve.

North of Barstow

Barstow

A mining center in the late 19th century, Barstow (pop. 21,500) provides access to the expansive **Mojave Desert.**

Barstow Station, ☎ 619/256-3839 or 800/255-6729, is a turn-of-the-century railroad station turned shopping complex.

Mojave River Valley Museum, ☎ 619/256-5452, contains exhibits related to the Indian, mining, railroad, Old Spanish Trail and Mormon Road eras.

Nearby is **Rainbow Basin National Natural Landmark,** ☎ 619/255-8760, formed by millions of years of sedimentary deposits leaving layers of red, brown, green and white on the hillsides. The area is rich in fossils and minerals. Take Highway 58 to Irwin Rd., then turn north to Fossil Bed Rd. The last three miles of the eight-mile trip are unpaved. There is a four-mile driving loop off of Fossil Bed Rd.

INFORMATION SOURCES

Barstow Chamber of Commerce, 222 E. Main St., Suite 216, Mercado Mall, PO Box 698, Barstow 92311, ☎ 619/256-8617.

California Desert Information Center, 831 Barstow Rd., Barstow 92311, ☎ 619/255-8760 or 256-8617, fax 619/255-8766, which has exhibits, films, maps and books. The center conducts special programs, has a cactus garden and trail, and displays the second largest meteorite ever found in the United States.

BLM Barstow Resource Area Office, 150 Coolwater Ln., Barstow 92311, ☎ 619/256-3591.

Death Valley National Park

This desolate region gained its name after a band of gold seekers started across the valley in the winter of 1849. Many of them died. But the discovery of borax, not gold, is what initiated the commercial exploitation of the valley. Twenty-mule teams used to haul up to 36 tons of borax per trip for a distance of 165 miles on its way to the market.

Unquestionably, the weather in this 3,367,628-acre region is severe. For generations, it was known to the Indians as To-me-sha ("ground on fire"). In 1917, the temperature ran above 120° for 43 straight days (July 6 to August 17). In 1974, there were 134 consecutive days over 100°, and in 1994, 97 days over 110° and 31 days over 120°.

In 1913, the valley experienced 4.54 inches of rain, a maximum temperature of 134°, and a minimum temperature of 15° – all records to this day.

As severe as the climate are the changes in elevation. The area ranges from 282 feet *below* sea level (at Badwater) to 11,049 feet *above* sea level at Telescope Peak.

Of 900 species of plants found here, 21 are unique to this valley.

Death Valley National Park

Legend:
- **i** Visitor Center
- ★ Point Of Interest
- □ Ghost Town
- ▲ Campground
- ····· Unpaved Road
- ▬▬ Park Boundary

INFORMATION SOURCES

Furnace Creek Visitors Center, Highway 190, ☎ 619/786-2331, has exhibits, literature and an 18-minute film. Evening nature walks and programs are availabe between November and April. Other visitor centers are located in Bishop, Independence, Lone Pine, Ridgecrest, Shoshone, Beatty, Stovepipe Wells, Baker and Scotty's Castle.

Death Valley National Park, PO Box 579, Death Valley 92328, ☎ 619/786-2331.

Death Valley Chamber of Commerce, 118 Highway 127, Shoshone 92384, ☎ 619/852-4524.

Death Valley Natural History Assn., PO Box 188, Death Valley 92328, ☎ 619/786-3285, which has guidebooks, maps, posters and videotapes available.

Furnace Creek Ranch

Sightseeing tours are available, ☎ 619/786-2345. An interesting **Borax Museum** is open 9 to 4:30.

Adventures

On Foot

Barstow

Rainbow Basin National Natural Landmark has a number of hiking trails.

A hike to **Owl Canyon** begins at the Owl Canyon Campground. From Barstow, take Highway 58 to Fort Irwin Rd. and follow it for five miles. Turn west onto Fossil Rd., a dirt road, and go three miles to the campground, where there is a marked trail into Owl Canyon. After half a mile, look for a small cave on your right. For awhile, the canyon narrows, but then it opens up to reveal a multicolored basin.

Death Valley National Park

Golden Canyon, five miles north of the entrance to Artist's Dr., has an easy two-mile trail through carved rock formations. Parking and trail guides are available.

Desert Hot Springs

Desert Dunes Country Club, 18550 Palm Dr., ☎ 619/251-5366 or 325-4653, offers an adventure of a slightly different sort. Located two miles north of I-10, it is the only desert course that is designed in the Scottish links style. There's also a lighted driving range.

Paul Edge, ☎ 619/329-8927, is a trail guide who conducts hikes.

East Mojave Natural Scenic Area

Caruthers Canyon can be found by taking Mt. Springs Rd. off I-40 28 miles west of Needles. Pass Goffs, the last place to acquire provisions, and go 27½ miles north on the main road (Ivanpah Rd. or Ivanpah-Goffs Rd.) to New York Mountains Rd. Before you reach New York Mountains Rd., the roadbed turns to dirt, but it is passable in a passenger car with good clearance. Turn left (west) on New York Mountains Rd. and go 5½ miles to an unmarked junction with a dirt road. Turn north and go two miles to a woodland area that has a series of make-shift campsites. Leave your car there (if you get to a difficult, virtually impassable wash, you have gone too far). On foot, follow the road into the canyon. Half a mile along, the road forks. The right-hand fork climbs a quarter-mile to an old mining shack. Take the left-hand fork for great views of the steep-walled canyon.

➡ *CAUTION: It is extremely dangerous to explore any of the old mine shafts that punctuate this area.*

Furnace Creek Ranch

There is good hiking here, plus a golf course, ☎ 619/786-2345, and a swimming pool that is open from 6 to midnight.

Joshua Tree

Wonderland of Rocks is a 12-square-mile assemblage of huge granite boulders. From I-10, take Highway 62 northeast to the little community of Joshua Tree and continue four miles south to the entrance of Joshua Tree National Park entrance. Go another 10 miles to Hidden Valley Campground. From there, a dirt road leads two miles to the Barker Dam parking lot. From the north end of the parking lot, there is a signed trail to the Wonderland of Rocks.

Joshua Tree National Park

Use extreme caution when hiking in this area. There are a number of abandoned mines to be avoided.

Fortynine Palms Oasis awaits at the end of a 1½-mile trail. The trailhead is at the end of Canyon Rd., south of Highway 62.

Hidden Valley, once a cattle rustlers' hideout, sits on a mile-long loop trail. Nearby is Barker Dam, built at the turn of century and frequently used by wildlife. There also are examples of Indian rock art in the area.

Lost Horse Mine, site of the ruins of a 10-stamp mill, is at the end of a two-mile, moderately strenuous trail. The gold mine was discovered while some prospectors were searching for a lost horse, hence the name. At Lost Horse Well are eight old graves, including that of Johnny Lang, the prospector who discovered the mine. Take the road south from Hidden Valley to an unpaved road leading to the trailhead.

Southeast of Hidden Valley is the trailhead for a moderately strenuous 1½-mile trail to **Ryan Mountain**.

Between the Cottonwood Visitor Center and the Oasis Visitor Center, along a self-guided quarter-mile loop nature trail, is the **Cholla Cactus Garden**. Watch your fingers!

Just south of the Cottonwood Visitor Center is **Cottonwood Spring**, a man-made palm oasis noted for its bird life. There is a mile-long trail to the spring.

At the end of the road running south and east from the Cottonwood Visitor Center is the trailhead for a moderate four-mile hike to **Lost Palms Oasis**, the largest stand of palms in the park. More strenuous sidetrips can be taken to **Victory Palms** and **Munsen Canyon**.

Throughout the park, watch for bighorn sheep, coyotes, bobcats, jackrabbits, kangaroo rats, kit foxes, golden eagles, road-runners, burrowing owls, quail, sidewinder rattlesnakes and yucca night lizards.

Kelso

Kelso Dunes are in the Mojave Desert and constitute one of the tallest dune systems in the country. From Baker, take Kelbaker Rd. about 42 miles south through the tiny town of Kelso to a signed dirt road and go right (west). Travel three miles to a BLM parking area and look for the dunes trail just up the dirt road from there. The mountains to the north are the Kelso Mountains; to the south, the Granite Mountains; to the southeast, the Bristol Mountains; and to the east, the Providence Mountains.

Mojave National Preserve

➡ *CAUTION: Abandoned mines abound in this region.*

Providence Mountains State Recreational Area, ☎ 805/942-0662, has a self-guiding nature trail that begins near the visitor center. **Mitchell Caverns** also are of interest. Hiking, camping, photography and star tracking are popular pursuits.

Pinnacles National Natural Landmark

Strictly a hiking park, visitors will find trails here that range from easy one-mile treks to strenuous hikes of more than seven miles. Be prepared to see birds, deer and a myriad of wildflowers along the trails.

Bear Gulch Caves and **Balconies Caves** require the use of a flashlight.

Twentynine Palms

Fortynine Palms Oasis provides California fan palms clustered around sparkling, boulder-lined pools full of cattails and ferns. Heading south from Twentynine Palms on Highway 62, turn left on Canyon Road (there is an animal hospital on the corner). Follow Canyon Road to the end, where you will find a parking area. The trail begins here and covers three miles, round trip.

GHOST TOWNS

Barnwell

From Goffs, a dirt road goes north for 37 miles to this tiny agricultural ghost town.

Bismarck

Located near Calico, this town once had a dog named Dorsey that carried the mail between the two communities.

Calico

Calico Ghost Town, PO Box 638, Yermo 92398, ☎ 619/254-2122 or 800-TO-CALICO, is 11 miles northeast of Barstow via I-15 (take the Ghost Town Rd. exit). Now a San Bernardino County Regional Park, this was a booming silver-mining town of over 4,000 people between 1881 and 1896. The mines produced more than $13 million in ore.

Saved from decay by Walter Knott of Knott's Berry Farm fame, the restored facility has such attractions as wooden sidewalks along Main St., a mine tour, the Playhouse Theater that presents melodrama, a museum, a "mystery shack," a shooting gallery and a train ride. A tram runs from the parking area to the town.

Calico Hullabaloo, held on Palm Sunday weekend, features horseshoe pitchin', stew cookin' and tobacco spittin' contests.

Spring Festival is held on Mothers' Day in May.

Calico Days, the year's biggest event, is held on Columbus Day in October. In addition to a Wild West parade, there are gunfights, a prospector's burro race and dances.

Western Fine Arts Show, held the first weekend in November, offers art, sculpture and Indian dances.

In the olden days, Calico's "fun houses" were located in the middle of the business district, rather than on the outskirts of town as they were in most other pioneer communities. There were 20 saloons, a large Chinatown, a dancing school, a literary society and a temperance league. The Hyena House Hotel served a breakfast of chile beans and whiskey, and the boot-and-shoe shop also sported a bar. In 1996, the town celebrated 115 years of existence.

Daggett

Located east of Barstow, this is an old silver camp. It was named for John Daggett who built the first house in town and also was the Lieutenant Governor of California from 1883 to 1887.

Death Valley National Park

Skidoo is now a ghost town. **Rhyolite** once was a prosperous frontier community.

Goffs

Located west of Needles, this old ghost town has an interesting cemetery.

Hart

From Barnwell, itself a ghost town 37 miles north of Goffs, a dirt road runs east for nine miles to the Castle Mountains and this ghost town, less than five miles from the Nevada state line. Gold was discovered here in 1907. Only a few ruins remain today.

Ivanpah

Once a rich silver-mining community, this town suffered two deaths. One occurred when the mines ran dry in 1885, and the other when a branch line of the California Eastern Railroad shut down in 1913. What remains are the ruins of two mills, a smelter and several rock and adobe homes.

Ludlow

Once known as Stagg, Ludlow is on the Santa Fe Railroad line. In its heyday, the local mines produced over $6 million in copper and silver.

Stedman, a ghost town originally called Rochester, is immediately north of the Twentynine Palms Marine Corps base near here. The town has been badly vandalized over the years, however.

Mescal

Near I-15 west of Mountain Pass, this silver camp, once called Nantan, was founded in 1887.

Providence

Originally called Hicorum, this was a company town for the Bonanza King mine. Today, all that remains are the ruins of an old stamp mill and several other buildings.

ROCKHOUNDING

Essex

Mitchell Caverns, ☎ 805/942-0662, are 15 miles north of I-40 off Essex Rd. Known for the limestone caves, this area is dotted with old mines and is a favorite of rockhounds. Guided tours of the caverns are available Monday through Friday at 1:30; Saturday, Sunday and holidays at 10, 1:30 and 3.

Turtle Mountains

Agates, jasper, creamy chalcedony roses, feldspar, quartz and fire agate can be found in these hills. The best field of chalcedony roses is around **Mopah Peak,** at the east end of the range.

ROCK CLIMBING

Joshua Tree National Park offers some excellent rock climbing. Check with the visitor center.

Yosemite Mountain Guides, ☎ 800/231-4575, leads rock climbing excursions into Joshua Tree National Park.

TREASURE HUNTING

Danby

In 1894, Thomas Scofield was working for the Santa Fe Railroad as a civil engineer. While drilling for water near here, he came across an old trail leading from a spring. Following the trail for about three hours, he came across an abandoned camp. Scofield examined some ore he found there and discovered that it was rich in gold. Taking some samples, he returned to San Francisco, located a partner, and then headed back to Danby. Although less than two months had passed, he was unable to relocate the spring, much less the trail. Scofield's partner quit in disgust, but Scofield returned off-and-on over the next 20 years, trying – in vain – to relocate his find.

Death Valley

Two Paiute Indians were searching along a dry lakebed for horses that had strayed from their camp when they noticed the mouth of a large cave. Exploring the interior, they found a bubbling lake that disgorged large amounts of black sand around its edges. Examining the sand in the sunlight, the Indians could see that it contained small nuggets and flakes of gold. Returning inside, they were surprised to see that the lake had receded, leaving tons of the black sand behind. The following day, the lake filled again – and waned again. The Indians also found a large room in the cavern that sparkled with beautiful crystals in the light of their torches. No one has been able to locate the mysterious cave since then.

In 1902, Alkali Jones left Skidoo, headed for Searchlight, Nevada. Two days later, he was caught in a sudden sandstorm and was forced to seek shelter among some boulders. When the storm had passed, Jones found pieces of milky white quartz scattered along the hillside. Searching farther, he found a vein of the quartz about three feet wide in a fissure of pink granite that ran for a distance of about 1,000 feet. Noticing a bird overhead, Jones called his find **The Golden Eagle Mine** and scribbled his claim on a piece of paper, which he put into a tobacco can and placed under a pile of rocks. Jones noted that he was just a mile south of Coffin Mountain in the Funeral range. In Searchlight, the ore Jones had carried out with him assayed $20-40,000 per ton and Jones equipped himself for a return trip to his mine. Nobody ever saw him again.

Turtle Mountains

There are three stories concerning the **Lost Arch Mine**.

Story #1 places the mine somewhere near the east end of the range. It was a placer mine originally worked by a small party of Mexicans, who built two separate adobe rooms joined by an extended roof in the shape of an arch. When the summer drought dried up their tiny stream, curtailing their sluicing operation, they hid their equipment and left, intending to return in the fall. For whatever reason, they didn't.

Story #2 claims that an old miner was found murdered in the area during the early 1900s. The man was holding a sketch of an eroded arch formation, drawn on a vague waybill that he had supposedly written while dying in order to direct his friends to a rich strike that he was developing. Pursuing this version of the story, mystery novelist Erle Stanley Gardner (*Perry Mason*) once rented a helicopter in order to look for the tell-tale arch.

Story #3 deals with Charlie Brown, a well-known individual in the Turtle Mountains in the 1930s. Brown called his mine "The Lost Arch" to fool other miners into believing that the storied lost mine had been found and claimed when, in fact, it was a new mine that he had discovered. Some say remains of Brown's cabin still exist. Relics of an old mine once operated by Brown do remain.

On Horseback

Death Valley National Park

Furnace Peak Ranch rents horses, provides trailer hook-ups, and features two restaurants, **Tino's Italian Restaurant** and **The Steak House**.

Furnace Creek

Horseback and carriage rides are available here, ☎ 619/786-2345.

Indio

Between January and March, the town hosts the **Indio Desert Circuit Horse Show** at Empire Equestrian Park. There are six shows per week, and 2,000 horses participate, making this America's largest horse show and the largest hunter-jumper event in the world.

Arena polo is played from September through October at **El Dorado Polo Club**, 50-950 Madison St., ☎ 619/342-2223 or 347-0907, fax 619/775-5938, the largest polo club west of the Mississippi. League matches are played from November through April on the club's nine playing fields.

Joshua Tree National Park

As you enter the park, request a site bulletin on horse use within the park. There are horse camps at Black Rock and at Ryan.

Mojave National Preserve

Horseback riding is permitted here.

RODEO

Barstow hosts the **Rodeo Stampede**, ☎ 619/256-8617, every September.

On Wheels

Death Valley National Park

Artist's Drive is a scenic nine-mile route through the foothills of the Black Mountains. The most scenic areas are noted here:

Aguereberry Point provides a panoramic view of the Black Mountains and the Sierra Nevada.

Charcoal kilns are 10 stone-sided silver smelters that resemble 25-foot beehives.

Dante's View overlooks both the highest and the lowest points in the contiguous 48 states.

Devil's Golf Course is an area full of salt pinnacles. It is on Badwater Rd., between Badwater and Artist's Dr.

Other scenic areas include **Bad Water, Greenwater Valley, Ibex Hills, Immigrant Pass,** picturesque **Mosaic Canyon, Pinto Peak** and **Stovepipe Wells.**

Dunes at Stovepipe Wells.
Credit: Robert Holmes, CA Div. of Tourism

Interesting trails include the **Jayhawkers Trail** of 1849 and the trail used by the **Darwin-French Party** in 1860. The story of these trails makes interesting reading.

For the best views of the sunrise, go to **Sand Dunes, Dante's View, Zabriskie Point, Badwater, Panamint Springs** or **Mesquite Springs Campground.** Zabriskie Point is on Highway 190 east of Furnace Creek.

For the best views of the sunset, try **Sand Dunes, Artist's Drive, Badwater, Ubehebe Crater, Furnace Creek Area Campgrounds, Panamint Springs** or **Father Crowley Point.**

Look for such plants as the Panamint daisy, the Death Valley sage, and the Death Valley sandpaper plant (and keep an eye out for the mysterious "moving rocks" that some people swear can move from place to place).

In case of an emergency, ☎ 619/786-2330.

Furnace Creek

This area is good for biking.

John Valley

Located southeast of Barstow, this is a state-run off-road vehicle recreation area.

Joshua Tree National Park

Although ATVs are not allowed, mountain bikes and four-wheel-drive vehicles will enjoy:

★ **Pinkham Canyon Rd.**, a 20-mile trail that begins at the Cottonwood Visitor Center and travels along Smoke Tree Wash, then cuts down Pinkam Canyon.

★ **Black Eagle Mine Rd.** begins 6½ miles north of the Cottonwood Visitor Center. The dead-end dirt road runs along the edge of Pinto Basin, crosses several dry washes and winds through some canyons in the Eagle Mountains. There are a number of side roads and many old mines.

★ **Old Dale Rd.** is 23 miles long and starts at the same point as Black Eagle Mine Rd. The first 11 miles cross Pinto Basin, a flat, dry lakebed. The road then climbs a steep hill and crosses the park boundary. Once past the boundary, there are a number of side roads that lead to old mines and private residences. Stay on the main road, and 15 miles east of Twentynine Palms you will reach Highway 62.

★ **Geology Tour Rd.** turns south from a paved road two miles west of Jumbo Rocks Campground. It is 5.4 miles to Squaw Tank, mostly downhill but a bumpy, sandy ride. From Squaw Tank, there is a six-mile circular tour through Pleasant Valley and an 18-mile dirt road that passes through interesting landscape (best undertaken in a four-wheel-drive vehicle).

★ Starting at Hidden Valley Campground or at the dirt road opposite the Geology Tour Rd. is a 13.4-mile network of roads called the **Queen Valley Roads**. Bicycle racks are provided for those who want to lock up and go hiking.

★ The road from **Covington Flats** picnic area to Eureka Peak covers 3.8 miles. It is steep toward the end, but the wonderful views from there make the effort worthwhile.

Mojave National Preserve

There are no off-road vehicle areas in this preserve and a prudent visitor will enter with a *full tank* of gas. Guidebooks are available on loan at the BLM offices in Barstow, Needles and Riverside.

- ★ **Cedar Canyon Rd.** runs east and west between Kelso-Cima Rd. and Lanfair Rd. past remnants of old ranches and homesteads. Most of **Mojave Rd.** is accessible only with four-wheel-drive.
- ★ **Cima Rd.** heads south from I-15 at Valley Wells and passes east of Cima Dome, which has one of California's densest Joshua tree forests.
- ★ **Ivanpah-Lanfair Rd.** begins 6.5 miles west of Nipton near I-15 and extends south to Goffs near I-40. The stretch through Ivanpah Valley is one of the best places to see desert tortoise in the spring. Much wildlife and 288 species of plants can be seen in this region, along with both working and abandoned mines. The road crosses the New York Mountains.
- ★ **Kelbaker Rd.** provides north-south access between I-15 at Baker and I-40. The road passes the historic town of Kelso, and farther south, passes between the Providence Mountains on the east and the Granite Mountains on the west.

Stoddard Valley

Located south of Barstow, this valley provides an off-road vehicle recreation area, ☎ 619/256-3592.

In the Air

Indio

A **Balloon & Polo Festival,** ☎ 619/775-1715, is held each October.

Eco-Travel/Cultural Excursions

Death Valley National Park

Scotty's Castle, ☎ 619/786-2331, is at the north boundary of the park. The $2 million Moorish-style mansion was built in the 1920s as a vacation retreat for a wealthy Chicagoan. Rangers conduct tours on the hour between 9 and 5. There is a visitor center.

Desert Hot Springs

Cabot's Old Indian Pueblo Museum, 67-616 E. Desert View, occupies a Hopi-style structure. It is a combination museum/trading post/gallery with a native plants garden, a desert tortoise enclosure and a petting zoo for children.

Indio

The "City of Festivals" hosts the **Southwest Arts Festival** at the Riverside County Fairgrounds, ☎ 619/347-0676, in February.

Indian Pow-Wows are held between November and December and in March at the Fantasy Springs Casino, 84-245 Indio Springs Dr., ☎ 619/342-5000 or 800/827-2946, with music, dances, Indian arts and crafts, and authentic Native American foods.

In December, the city celebrates the **International Tamale Festival** in Old Town Indio, ☎ 619/347-0676, with a kid's petting zoo, a parade, mariachi music, folkloric dancing, and 10K, 5K and 2K runs. The celebration has just been expanded to last two days.

Coachella Valley Wild Bird Center, 46-500 Van Buren St., ☎ 619/347-2647, fax 619/775-2299, offers school programs and workshops. It has a useful reference library and offers a tour and bird walk on the first Saturday of each month, October through May at 8 am.

Coachella Valley Museum & Cultural Center, 82-616 Miles Ave., ☎ 619/342-6651, occupies a 1926 home. It contains historical and cultural exhibits, a Japanese Garden and artwork. One room is devoted to dates, the principal local crop, via a 13-minute video.

Where To Stay

B&Bs, Hotels & Inns

Death Valley

Stovepipe Wells Village, ☎ 619/786-2387 or 786-2345, has 83 rooms. There also is a restaurant, a general store, a gift shop, a gas station and a landing strip on the property.

Furnace Creek Inn & Ranch Resort, PO Box 1, Death Valley 92328, ☎ 619/786-2345, fax 619/786-2307, a Fred Harvey property, has nine restaurants, dancing, an 18-hole golf course, six lighted tennis courts, swimming pools, horseback riding, hiking, biking, volleyball, carriage rides, horseshoes, life-size checkers and a landing strip with a lighted runway. Jackets are still required in the main dining room. The ranch is open year-round; the inn, from October through mid-May.

Desert Hot Springs

Two Bunch Palms Resort & Spa, 67-425 Two Bunch Palms Tr., ☎ 619/329-8791 or 800/472-4334, is rumored to have been either an illegal casino or the winter hideout of Al Capone. Whatever, it's a favorite for people like Robin Williams, Mel Gibson and Jeff Bridges.

Desert Hot Springs Spa Hotel, 10805 Palm Dr., ☎ 619/329-6000 or 329-6495, fax 619/329-6915, offers massages of every description – Swedish, Shiatsu, aromatherapy, deep muscle, sports or Reiki – *plus* hand or foot reflexology. Facials including seaweed and "teen," available only to those 16 years old and under. The beauty shop gives manicures and pedicures. There is a hair salon. You can either drink the natural mineral waters or soak in them. You can engage in aquarobics and acupressure. You can get a face lift, sea salt skin glow, glycolic body scrub or waxing. And get this: Thursday is men's day!

Camping

Barstow

Rainbow Basin National Natural Landmark permits camping at Owl Canyon Campground (☎ 619/256-8313) for a fee.

Calico

Calico Ghost Town (☎ 619/254-2122) has 100 campsites available.

Death Valley

Stovepipe Wells Village, ☎ 619/786-2387 or 786-2345, has 364 RV spaces. **Furnace Creek** and **Mesquite Springs** have fee campgrounds.

Emigrant, Wildrose, Thorndike and **Mahogany Flats** are free campgrounds, but the latter two require four-wheel-drive and Wildrose is for vehicles under 25 feet in length. Call ☎ 619/786-2331.

Spaces with hookups are available at Furnace Creek Ranch, Stovepipe Wells resort and Panamint Springs resort.

Joshua Tree National Park

Eight campgrounds are provided in the park (☎ 619/367-7511):

- ★ **Belle** has 17 sites and there is no fee.
- ★ **Black Rock** has 100 sites, but there is a fee.
- ★ **Cottonwood** has 62 sites and charges a fee.
- ★ **Hidden Valley** has 39 sites. No fee.

★ **Indian Cove**, with 101 sites. Fee.
★ **Jumbo Rocks**, with 125 sites. No fee.
★ **Ryan** has 29 sites. No fee.
★ **White Tank** has 15 sites. No fee.

Groups sites are available for a fee at Cottonwood, Indian Cove and Sheep Pass. There is water at Black Rock and Cottonwood. All camps have chemical toilets (except Black Rock and Cottonwood, which have flush toilets). Showers are not available, and there are no hookups for RVs.

Mojave National Preserve

There are year-round campgrounds at **Mid Hills** and **Hole-in-the-Wall**. Essex-Black Canyon Rd. leads north to Hole-in-the-Wall Campground.

Providence Mountains State Recreation Area

The mesas and buttes near here are pocked with holes that produce eerie sounds when the wind blows. The area is 17 miles north of I-40 on Essex Rd.

Where To Eat

Chiriaco Summit

Chiriaco Summit Coffee Shop has delicacies like fries topped with brown gravy, the DTC burger (made with Spam instead of ground beef) and Desert Rat (a green salad and bowl of soup).

Death Valley Junction

Marta Becket's Amargosa Opera House, near the junction of State Routes 127 and 190, ☎ 619/852-4441, presents dining alongside dance/mime performances at 8:15 on Mondays and Saturdays from February through April and during November; and on Saturdays only during May, October and December. No shows are given in January or from June-September.

Indio

Devane's, 80-755 Hwy 111, ☎ 619/342-5009, fax 619/342-5399, a New York-style Italian restaurant owned by actor William Devane. Lunch and dinner are served Tuesday through Friday; dinner only on Saturday and Sunday.

There are a number of fast food restaurants along Highway 111, the main link, excluding the interstate, between Indio and Palm Springs.

Index